Red Against Blue

Red Against Blue
The Liberal Party in Colombian Politics
1863–1899

Helen Delpar

The University of Alabama Press
Tuscaloosa, Alabama

Library of Congress Cataloging in Publication Data

Delpar, Helen.
  Red against blue.

  Bibliography: p.
  Includes index.
  1. Partido Liberal (Colombia)—History. 2. Colombia—Politics and government—1863-1885. 3. Colombia—Politics and government—1886-1903. 4. Partido Conservador (Colombia)—History. I. Title.
  JL2898.L5D44   329.9'861   79-19081
  ISBN 978-0-8173-5615-6 (pbk. : alk. paper)
  ISBN 978-0-8173-8388-6 (electronic)

Copyright © 1981 by
The University of Alabama Press
All rights reserved
Manufactured in the United States of America

This book was keyboarded for scanner typesetting by Ruth Kibbey and Debbie Davis.

To My Parents

Contents

List of Tables	viii
Preface	ix
1. The Origins of Colombian Liberalism: A Backward Glance	1
2. Party Alignment in Nineteenth-Century Colombia: A Regional Survey	14
3. A Liberal Profile	43
4. The Evolution of Liberal Thought	60
5. The Political Process in a Federal Setting	84
6. The Crisis of Liberalism	110
7. In the Role of the Vanquished	133
8. Road to Revolution	158
Conclusion	185
Notes	192
Bibliography	237
Index	258

Tables

1. Customs Returns for Three Caribbean Ports to the Nearest Peso in Selected Years for the Second Half of the Nineteenth Century — 17

2A. Presidential Voting, 1848 and 1856: The Coast — 19

2B. Presidential Voting, 1848 and 1856: Four Coastal Cities — 20

3A. Presidential Voting, 1848 and 1856: Cauca — 24

3B. Presidential Voting, 1848 and 1856: Selected Areas in Cauca — 25

4A. Presidential Voting, 1848 and 1856: Cundinamarca and Tolima — 30

4B. Presidential Voting, 1848 and 1856: Provinces of Bogotá, Neiva, and Mariquita — 31

4C. Presidential Voting, 1848 and 1856: Selected Areas in Cundinamarca — 32

5. Presidential Voting, 1848 and 1856: Boyacá — 34

6. Presidential Voting, 1848 and 1856: Santander — 35

7A. Presidential Voting, 1848 and 1856: Antioquia — 39

7B. Presidential Voting, 1848 and 1856: Selected Areas in Antioquia — 40

8. Rate of Exchange, Colombian Pesos per 100 U.S. Dollars — 136

9. Food Prices in Bogotá, 1878–1888 — 138

Preface

In 1979 Colombia was the only Latin American country whose political system was dominated by two political parties—the Liberal and the Conservative, associated with the colors red and blue, respectively—that could trace their origin to the mid-nineteenth century. Elsewhere the political parties born in that era had either disappeared, as in Brazil, or had been reduced to insignificance, as appeared to be the case in Uruguay. Despite, and indeed perhaps because of, their longevity, the Colombian parties were generally viewed negatively by political scientists.

> Contemporary students of the Colombian parties tend to view them as instruments of a narrow social elite which possesses most of the power and material resources available to Colombian society. This situation is either interpreted apocalyptically or fatalistically. In the former case the parties are seen as blindly suppressing the forces of change in Colombian society in order to retain for their masters the inordinate privileges which they have held for generations. The implicit or explicit expectation is that eventually the explosion will come and the traditional parties will be consumed like the sinners of Sodom and Gomorrah.
>
> Other observers, while also seeing the parties as elitist, tend to evaluate this as one of those inevitable, unpleasant facts of political life which is likely to go on indefinitely, a culturally determined shackle on the possibilities of economic, social, and political development. Thus the fatalistic observers share with the apocalyptically oriented the conviction that the traditional Colombian party system is on balance pernicious, while they differ in their expectations as to its fate.[1]

Regardless of their overall merit, such value-laden assessments at times hamper understanding of the functions performed by Colombia's parties and of the workings of the party system, about which in reality little is known. Furthermore, existing studies are often weakened by the practice of submitting Colombian parties and politicians to typologies more applicable to other political systems. Another source of weakness is the shallowness of academic knowledge of the Colombian party system. While the work of scholars such as Robert H. Dix, James L. Payne, and Mario Latorre Rueda has provided valuable insights into contemporary politics, analysis of the era before 1930 has barely begun.

The Colombian works which deal with nineteenth-century politics are mainly memoirs and biographies, genres which do not lend themselves to the analysis of entire systems. Moreover, much of the Colombian historical writing is marred by inadequate research or by partisan passion. Numerous historians in the United States have also explored topics in nineteenth-century Colombian history, but only a handful have dealt with primarily political themes.

Regardless of nationality or specialty, most historians have evaluated the Liberal generation that reached maturity in the 1850s unfavorably. This generation has been criticized above all for a doctrinaire commitment to laissez faire and an anti-statist bias that resulted in the emasculation of governmental authority, especially while the federalist Rionegro constitution was in force from 1863 to 1885. Because of its weakness, the critics say, the federal government was unable to check the political turbulence of the period or to provide the direction needed to stimulate the economic development of the nation. Conclusions similar to these are evident, for example, in Indalecio Liévano Aguirre's biography of Rafael Núñez and in William Paul McGreevey's *Economic History of Colombia*.[2] Despite the pervasiveness of this interpretation, however, it has never been adequately documented or assessed. The present study does not pretend to make such an assessment, but one of its goals is to show that the historiographical indictment of the Liberal regime is in need of qualification.

The general purpose of this work is to assist in the task of filling the lacunae in the early political history of Colombia by examining the evolution of the Liberal party from 1863 to 1899 and its role in the Colombian political system during that period. The era selected for study shows the Liberal party first as the ruling party in control of the national government (1863–85) and later as the opposition (1886–99) to the Conservative-dominated regime known as the Regeneration. In 1899 Liberals embittered by their long exclusion from public office unleashed a revolutionary upheaval of such dimensions that it marked a watershed in the political history of Colombia. The period derives continuity from the fact that many of the leading party chiefs of the 1860s and 1870s remained active in politics until the last decade of the century, though their hegemony was challenged by younger men after 1886.

Although the study focuses on the Liberal party, the emphasis could just as easily have been placed on the Conservatives. In any event, it proved impossible to analyze the Liberals in isolation from their adversaries, for Liberal positions and strategies can be fully comprehended only by comparing them or otherwise relating them to those of the Conservatives.

Throughout the study the term *Liberal party* is used as it was by nineteenth-century Colombians, for whom it embraced all who considered themselves Liberals. As this concept indicates, during the years under consideration party organization remained embryonic, and to the extent that a modern political party is distinguished by the nature of its organization,[3] the Liberals did not constitute a modern party until the twentieth century. By 1863 the term *Liberal party* had been in use for over a decade and was associated with a set of ideas and leaders presumed to have some hold on a body of more or less loyal followers. When elections were held, candidates identified as Liberals regularly competed, and electoral committees were formed to advance their cause. There were, however, no permanent structures on the national or regional levels to provide organizational continuity. Decisions were made by informal groups of Liberal notables, mainly members of Congress and other office-holders. It was not until the 1890s that self-renewing party directories came into existence and that party conventions began to be held.

Despite the flimsiness of the party's structure throughout the nineteenth century, it must be stressed that the Liberal party, along with its Conservative counterpart, was the only institution besides the Catholic Church that crossed regional and class lines. Moreover, because party identification was normally intense and permanent, other institutions like the armed forces or new parties proved unable to mount serious and sustained competition for the loyalties of politically active Colombians. Similarly, individuals who sought to bypass or drastically alter the party system found it impossible to achieve their goals, no matter how gifted or charismatic they were. The careers of Tomás Cipriano de Mosquera and Rafael Núñez, it will be seen, illustrate this point.

It is probable, therefore, that the persistence of a form of liberal democracy in twentieth-century Colombia can be attributed at least in part to the evolution of the party system in the nineteenth century. Indeed, the Colombian case may bear out the hypothesis of Eric A. Nordlinger that the likelihood of stable, nonauthoritarian government is greater when protoparties have preceded mass parties and mass suffrage. In the absence of protoparties, mass parties faced by the "participation crisis" created by the expansion of the suffrage will not have enough time to establish coherent and autonomous organizations.

> They will have neither the experienced leaders nor the firm linkages between the center and local areas required for the effective articulation and aggregation of popular demands, thereby leaving the electorate "available" for mobilization in either extremist mass movements or government-controlled organizations. Further, the national parties' lack of organizational strength and the absence of effective ties with local power centers significantly reduce their role in governmental decision-making and make the parties themselves vulnerable to "incorporation" into the (noncompetitive) governmental structure.[4]

By 1863 the Colombian Liberal party was well on its way toward developing the leadership, linkages, and organizational structure that would permit its relatively smooth evolution into a mass party in the twentieth century.

Because of the complexity of the subject under investigation, no claim to completeness can be made; in fact, several areas have been entirely ignored. The attitudes of Liberal leaders toward international affairs, both the issues in which Colombia was directly involved and those in which it was merely an interested spectator, have not been examined. Since liberalism had political manifestations in many parts of the Old and New Worlds during the nineteenth century, a comparison of the Colombian variety with its counterparts elsewhere would have been instructive, but such an undertaking was deemed beyond the scope of this study. Nor has any effort been made to relate the behavior of Colombia's Liberal party to that of contemporary political parties in other countries.

Instead, the focus is almost entirely on what came to be perceived as Liberalism within the Colombian milieu. An introductory chapter provides a brief history of the party before 1863 and discusses the Liberal constitution of that year, which governed the country for two decades. In the second chapter an effort is made to reach some conclusions about the regional and socioeconomic bases of party strength at midcentury. Election returns were among the sources consulted for this chapter, but elsewhere the emphasis is largely, though not exclusively, on political elites—i.e., those recognized as Liberal leaders by virtue of their membership in governmental bodies or party organizations. In accordance with this emphasis, chapters 3 and 4 are devoted to the personal histories of party leaders and to their intellectual orientation. The emphasis on elites was adopted for two reasons. First, it was they who generally identified problems, made decisions, and articulated policy. Second, the dearth of published materials on nineteenth-century Colombia meant that a work which concentrated on the Liberal rank and file, especially in rural areas, would have had to be narrower in scope—both with respect to chronology and geographical coverage—than the one envisioned. I hope that the present study will encourage others to explore such topics as the political relations between rural patrons and clients in the nineteenth century and the functions and composition of the "democratic societies."

The party system as it developed while the Liberals were in power is addressed in chapter 5. Much of the chapter is devoted to the electoral process, for it was the axis around which the political life of the nation revolved. In the last three chapters a narrative approach is used to discuss the party's most critical years, which saw a period of intense disunity in the 1870s, the party's exclusion from power after 1885, and its controversial appeal to arms in 1899. At the same time, however, these years also saw the beginning of efforts to create ongoing party organizations and regularized links between national and local leaders. In the last three chapters, as in the five preceding chapters, can be discerned the principal themes of the study: the regionalism that permeated Colombian politics in the nineteenth century and contributed to endemic factionalism within the party; the difficulty experienced by party leaders in imposing discipline on their followers and the resulting tendency (not always in evidence, however) to seek consensus through the conciliation of conflicting positions; and the similarities in the political problems faced by both Liberals and Conservatives, regardless of whether they were in or out of power, and in the strategies and tactics adopted by both groups.

Finally, I hope to demonstrate another theme: the impossibility of explaining the behavior of Liberal leaders in the period in question by means of a single formula or hypothesis. Although there was considerable uniformity in the background of these leaders, they did not pursue identical personal or political goals. Nor did they all hold the same beliefs, though Liberalism did exhibit what might be called an ideological core. Moreover, as practicing politicians Liberals sometimes violated or ignored their doctrinal principles because of the exigencies of the moment, and they were often ready to modify their ideas when these no longer seemed serviceable.

Such conduct invariably aroused the wrath of contemporaries—both dissident Liberals and Conservatives, who nonetheless acted in similar fashion when the occasion arose—as does comparable behavior by their twentieth-century descendants. In his book *Elecciones y partidos políticos en Colombia* (1974), Mario Latorre Rueda comments on the contradiction between doctrine and practice so frequently condemned by critics of Colombian parties:

> This contradiction is intrinsic to even the most unified party since every party contains currents that do not fuse into a single one, that disappear and recur in [a state of] constant ebullition. A party, like every social phenomenon, is changing and contradictory, [and displays] diverse and sometimes unforeseeable reactions. . . . It preserves a profound, unalterable nucleus, but around it—and that is what the critics emphasize the most—is this vast zone of changing and contradictory attitudes. A party submitted to an inexorable logic is the work of theoreticians, not of reality.[5]

The research for this study was begun in the mid-1960s in Bogotá, Colombia, where I was able to spend a year with the help of a grant from the Henry L. and Grace Doherty Foundation. Many Colombians aided me in my research, notably the historian Horacio Rodríguez Plata, who not only gave me many valuable suggestions but also put at my disposal three volumes of letters to Aquileo Parra, president of Colombia from 1876 to 1878 and an important Liberal party leader. My thanks are also due to the staffs of the National Library, the Luis-Angel Arango Library, and the Colombian Academy of History, all in Bogotá, and to the Duke University Press, which granted permission to reprint in chapter 6 material that first appeared in Helen Delpar, "Aspects of Liberal Factionalism in Colombia, 1875–1885," *Hispanic American Historical Review* 51 (May 1971): 250-74. Finally, I gratefully acknowledge the assistance of Lt. Col. Dick DeWayne Grube, U.S.A., who allowed me to consult the portions of the archive of Buenaventura Correoso which he purchased in the city of Panama, and of Ruth Kibbey, who typed the manuscript and assisted in the typesetting process.

Publication of this book was made possible, in part, by financial assistance from the Andrew W. Mellon Foundation and the American Council of Learned Societies.

Red Against Blue

1
The Origins of Colombian Liberalism
A Backward Glance

On 4 February 1863 Liberal dignitaries from all over the United States of Colombia[1] assembled in the town of Rionegro, a Liberal enclave in the staunchly Conservative state of Antioquia, for the opening session of the constitutional convention that had been convoked to draw up a new fundamental charter for the nation. The Liberal party, as victor in the destructive civil war which had ended only a few months before, had won the right to reform the republic's political institutions in accordance with its principles, an undertaking from which the defeated Conservatives were necessarily to be excluded. The drafting of a new constitution, it was hoped, would have the additional effect of restoring order and civilian government to a war-torn land.

The gathering at Rionegro should have been an occasion for satisfaction and self-congratulation on the part of the delegates in attendance. For many, however, the occasion was marred by their suspicion and mistrust of Tomás Cipriano de Mosquera, supreme war director and provisional president of the republic. A member of one of the leading families of the southern city of Popayán, Mosquera had first seen military service in the revolution for independence, during which he had become an associate and fervent admirer of Simón Bolívar. Later, like other Bolivarians, he had become affiliated with the fledgling Conservative party and had served a term (1845–49) as a progressive and energetic president, but his volatile and impetuous temperament, as well as his basic nonconformity with Conservative principles, had brought him into conflict with other party heads. In 1860, while serving as governor of his native state of Cauca, he had clashed with President Mariano Ospina Rodríguez, a Conservative, who was simultaneously at odds with Liberals throughout the country, and had withdrawn Cauca from the Colombian federation, thereby triggering a nationwide revolt against Ospina.[2] The Liberals had acknowledged Mosquera as chief of their forces, but they had done so with serious misgivings because of Mosquera's Conservative antecedents and his reputation for arbitrary and headstrong behavior.

In the ensuing years Mosquera had led the Liberals to military victory over the Conservatives, but Liberal misgivings had been confirmed by his execution without trial of three Conservative civilian officials in Bogotá and by his threatened execution of ex-President Ospina, from which he was deterred only by the intervention of various foreign diplomats and Liberal leaders. Even more serious was the campaign he had launched against the Catholic Church after capturing Bogotá in July 1861, as a result of which ecclesiastical property had been nationalized, religious communities suppressed, the Jesuits expelled, and clergymen compelled to seek governmental permission to carry out their duties. Most Liberals were anticlerical to some degree, but many felt that Mosquera's measures were unnecessarily harsh. There was also concern among some delegates at Rionegro that Mosquera would prove unwilling to surrender the extraordinary powers he had wielded during the revolution and to content himself with at best service as a civilian president bound by constitutional limitations on his authority.

The anti-Mosquera delegates at the convention were representatives of the "Radical" wing of the party, which was most powerful in the northeastern state of Santander and whose members prided themselves on their devotion to civilian and constitutional government.[3] On the other hand, a sizable number of delegates was disposed to accede to Mosquera's wishes on most issues. These included the representatives from Cauca and several delegates from Panama who had been elected in the wake of a Mosquerista revolution which had overthrown the government of that state in August 1862. A third and smaller group of delegates was made up of men who steered a middle course between the two dominant factions. Thus, at the moment of its greatest triumph, the Liberal party was weakened by a division that would not only affect the labors of the Rionegro convention but would also shape the course of the party in future years.

Factionalism had characterized the Liberal party almost from its emergence as a permanent political force in the 1840s. Many factors contributed to the centrifugal tendencies of the party: the irresponsibility of the leadership, an ideology which extolled individualism, and above all the social and economic differences among the various regions of the country, the effects of which were aggravated by inadequate systems of transportation and communication. As a result, the Liberal party was in reality an aggregation of local and regional groupings whose coalescence at critical moments could be relied upon more often than not but was not invariable or automatic.

Although the nineteenth century was well advanced before the political collectivity that became known as the Liberal party took form, several of the major themes of Colombian Liberalism appeared in the mid-1820s during the administration of Vice President Francisco de Paula Santander, who governed the tripartite nation of Gran Colombia (New Granada, Venezuela, and Ecuador) in the absence of the titular president, Simón Bolívar. Santander is generally considered the father of Colombian Liberalism, though it is just as accurate to regard him as an important forebear of the Conservative party as well. "His disciples included Lino de Pombo and Rufino Cuervo, spiritual chiefs of Granadine Conservatism, as well as Francisco Soto and Vicente Azuero, precursors of the Liberal party."[4]

While Santander headed the administration in the 1820s, various tendencies that can be described as "liberal" or "conservative" within the context of Colombian politics appeared. The vice president and his supporters in the administration and Congress favored policies aimed at reducing the influence and privileges of the Catholic clergy and at encouraging private enterprise by reforming the colonial economic structure which had survived the war for independence with relatively little modification.[5] In practice, however, the protests of "conservatives," the financial needs of the government, and Santander's cautious temperament prevented the enactment of many of the reforms supported by early "liberals." Nevertheless, anticlericalism and the encouragement of individual initiative would remain major themes of Colombian Liberalism, being modified over the years in accordance with changing circumstances. Another important Liberal theme—federalism—was still in abeyance in the 1820s, though federalist sympathies had manifested themselves in New Granada as early as 1810. Santander himself oscillated between federalism and centralism, halfheartedly espousing the former in 1828 as a means of checking Bolívar's dictatorial tendencies.[6]

The division of Colombian political leaders into two clearly defined groups has often been dated from 1826 when Bolívar returned from Peru amid disquieting reports that he intended to impose on the nation the authoritarian constitution he had penned for Bolivia and that some of his supporters were harboring monarchical projects. Subsequent events—Bolívar's cordiality to the rebellious José Antonio Páez of Venezuela; his followers' disruption of the Ocaña convention, which was to have provided a new constitution for the floundering republic; and his assumption of dictatorial powers in June 1828—led to a crystallization of two factions.[7] On the one hand were the Bolivarians, themselves divided between those who were distinguished by their often fanatical devotion to the Liberator and a more moderate group which respected Bolívar but was also committed to preservation of the Cúcuta constitution of 1821. On the other were the followers of Santander, who were opposed to the authoritarianism and militarism associated with Bolívar's personal rule. At the ill-fated Ocaña convention of 1828 the Santanderistas, unlike the Bolivarians, exhibited some party cohesion, living and eating together and trying to act as a unit.[8]

With the death of Bolívar in 1830, the Santanderistas were able to gain the upper hand, and the convention that drew up a constitution for New Granada in 1832 elected Santander president of the new state by a large majority. The solidarity of this dominant "liberal" group was soon broken, however, and two new alignments took shape. Santander became the leader of those who were considered proponents of reform, while José Ignacio Márquez, who was elected to the presidency in 1836, emerged as head of a more moderate group, which was augmented by the adherence of the surviving Bolivarians. "Aside from the military, these one-time supporters of the Liberator's autocratic authority constituted a goodly portion of the element of society which was most respected for birth, possessions, education, and ability."[9] By 1838 the Santanderistas regularly referred to themselves as *progresistas* or *progresistas liberales,* and to supporters of the Márquez administration as *ministeriales.*

These two groups were the progenitors of the Liberal and Conservative parties, but as yet they were still amorphous despite some continuity of leadership and ideology. During the 1840s several new developments would establish the composition of both parties on a more or less permanent basis. The first of these was the revolution of 1839–42, which stemmed initially from a popular uprising to protest a congressional decree (5 June 1839) closing four minor convents in the southwestern province of Pasto which contained fewer than the minimum of eight members required by Colombian law and which were under the jurisdiction of the Ecuadorian clergy. When news of the uprising reached Bogotá, it was condemned by the *progresistas,* though the *ministeriales* suspected that it had been planned by them in order to overthrow the Márquez government.[10] The Pasto revolt turned out to be but the first act in a nationwide series of uprisings to which *progresista* leaders in Bogotá eventually gave their support.

A major reason for the continuation of disorder in the south was an ill-considered revival of charges by the Márquez government against José María Obando for complicity in the assassination of Marshal Sucre in 1830.[11] Obando, a veteran of the independence movement and Santander's choice for the presidency in 1836, responded to the government's action by rising in revolt on 18 January 1840 near Pasto, thereby furnishing some *progresistas* with an excuse of withdrawing their support of the Márquez administration. Elsewhere, however, purely local grievances and ambitions seem to have acted as spurs to insurrection. Although there was evidently some attempt at direction from Bogotá, the various revolutionary movements were generally uncoordinated, their only common objective being provincial autonomy.

Under Pedro Alcántara Herrán, who succeeded Márquez in 1841, the government was able to stamp out the revolution. The war, however, had served to make complete and permanent the rift between *progresistas* and *ministeriales.* To the personal, political, and ideological bonds linking the *progresistas* was now added the shared memory of the past struggle and particularly of the severity displayed by some government leaders in crushing it. The war also affixed the motif of sectional autonomy to the political banner upheld by the *progresistas* and those who considered themselves their heirs.

The second development of the 1840s that helped to shape the Liberal party was the emergence of a new generation of political leaders, many of them gifted provincials. A number of these young men, ironically enough, received their higher education at the Central University in Bogotá after it had undergone a thorough reform in 1842–43 by Herrán's secretary of the interior, Mariano Ospina Rodríguez, designed to improve the quality and content of instruction and to inculcate "conservative" ideas through the removal of dangerous courses and texts. The reform, beneficial though it may have been in some respects, failed in its attempt to curb liberalism and may have even had a contrary effect. According to José María Samper, who was a law student in the 1840s, "the young people realized that there was an attempt to *make* them conservatives or mold them in a certain way, and out of a spirit of contradiction they all became liberals and freethinkers."[12]

In the late 1840s these young Liberals were strongly influenced by the French Revolution of 1848 and by contemporary French writers like Lamartine, Proudhon, and Eugène Sue.[13] While it is clear that they did not all imbibe the same ideas and did not as a rule develop a coherent political philosophy, as a group they became ardent exponents of reform aimed specifically at eradicating colonial practices and institutions which they felt had survived in Colombia despite the achievement of independence. Their goals to a large extent echoed those advocated by Santander and his associates earlier in the century, but the young Liberals of the 1840s and 1850s pressed them with a new urgency and a conviction that Colombia would be quickly transformed once artificial barriers to progress were lifted.

The success of these young men in shaping the content of Liberal policy at midcentury may have been due in part to the absence of the older leaders of the *progresista* movement. Santander died in 1840 at the age of forty-eight, and Francisco Soto and Vicente Azuero followed him to the grave in 1846 and 1848, respectively. José María Obando, after suffering a decisive military defeat during the revolution of 1839–42, was forced into exile from which he did not return until 1849.

The third important development of the 1840s was the broadening of the *progresista* movement into a political party capable of making a sustained appeal to nonelite segments of the Colombian population, notably the artisans of Bogotá, who numbered about 2,000 in the 1840s.[14] In October 1847 an artisans' society was founded in Bogotá with the ostensible purpose of promoting "the advancement of the arts and other branches of industry that can contribute to our welfare."[15] Its main purpose, however, was to protect the interests of the capital's artisans, who found themselves increasingly threatened by the competition of foreign products, the importation of which was encouraged by recent legislation lowering tariffs and by declining transportation costs. Despite the fact that the bylaws of the society forbade the discussion of political and religious questions, it soon became deeply involved in contemporary politics, and on 10 June 1848, at a meeting attended by over four hundred persons, the society unanimously endorsed the candidacy of José Hilario López, "citizen, general, and Catholic democrat," for the presidential term beginning in 1849.[16]

General López, a native of Popayán who had fought in the war for independence, won the support not only of the artisans but of the old *progresistas* and of the young reformers. The incumbent president, Tomás Cipriano de Mosquera, felt that López lacked the ability to be chief executive and described the latter's supporters as "anarchists" and "rebels" (*facciosos*) who constituted a "bloody and ignorant party."[17] However, the failure of Mosquera and the erstwhile *ministeriales,* who were becoming known as Conservatives, to unite behind a single candidate permitted López to win a plurality of the electoral votes cast in the presidential contest.[18] Since neither López nor the two leading Conservative candidates, Rufino Cuervo and Joaquín José Gori, won a majority, the election had to be decided by Congress. Meeting in the Church of Santo Domingo on 7 March 1849, Congress selected López on the fourth ballot by a narrow margin in a stormy seven-hour session that became one of the most controversial episodes in Colombian history.[19] The Conservatives claimed that the members of Congress had been intimidated into voting for López by the presence of armed and menacing artisans in the church. The supporters of López contended on the other hand that since the spectators had been removed from the church before the fourth ballot, the legislators had been able to vote in complete freedom.

Regardless of the truth of these assertions, the artisans' society did contribute significantly to the outcome of the election. Later becoming known as the *Sociedad Democrática,* it acted openly as an auxiliary of the López administration and apparently was able to dictate at least a few of the president's appointments.[20] Many similar societies were founded throughout the country in the following years; these *democráticas,* perhaps two hundred in number, functioned primarily as political clubs allied with the administration, and their activities were reported in Colombia's official newspaper.[21]

To nineteenth-century Liberals, the López administration was a watershed in the nation's history, marking its emancipation from the fanaticism, monopoly, and privilege of the colonial regime which had persisted even after the end of Spanish rule. Conservatives, however, were to remember the López era as one of disorder, crime, and atheism during which the elemental rights of property and liberty were flagrantly violated. It was during this period that the name *Liberal* became permanently affixed to the coalition of Santanderistas, youthful reformers, and artisans who had backed López, as well as to their supporters in the provinces. Similarly, those who had been identified with the administrations of the 1840s and opposed most of the reforms of the López administration definitively adopted the Conservative label. The existence of a Colombian political party with this name was acknowledged in the first issue (21 May 1848) of *El Nacional,* a newspaper founded in Bogotá by Mariano Ospina Rodríguez and José Eusebio Caro. According to the editors, the nucleus of the Conservative party was made up of men who loved liberty, peace, and security, and who were devoted to their families and to their work. The nucleus of the Liberal party was composed of malcontents who turned to politics in the hope of improving their lot.

In the case of both parties, factional tags appeared from time to time, and the members of one party would frequently coin what were considered unflattering designations for their adversaries. During the turbulent days of the López administration Liberals were frequently referred to as *rojos,* or "reds," by Conservatives indignant over one or another of the government's policies.

In actuality, the Liberal reforms of 1849–53 had been foreshadowed by the Mosquera administration, which "was the first consistently to attempt to bring New Granada into the economic and cultural currents prevailing in the Western world of its day." Through the influence of Florentino González, Mosquera's secretary of finance from 1846 to 1848, a tariff law was passed in June 1847 that lowered duties on most foreign goods by over 25 percent and "was the closest approximation to free trade taken by New Granada in a quarter century of independence."[22] The Mosquera administration also encouraged the establishment of steam navigation on the Magdalena River, the nation's chief artery of transportation.[23] Finally, gradual steps were taken toward the abolition of the state tobacco monopoly, which came to an end on 1 January 1850.[24]

It should also be noted that many of the reforms effected by the López administration represented the realization of aspirations and goals articulated earlier. "It may be said that a precedent petition for every measure tagged with the 7th of March label can be found between 1809 and 1840. Even such an unlikely thing as the popular election of parish priests had been previously petitioned in 1832 by the *cabildo* [municipal council] of Chiriguaná."[25]

The election of parish priests by municipal councils was but one of several anticlerical measures enacted by Liberals who deplored the temporal and spiritual influence of the clergy, especially on the unlettered masses. On 21 May 1850 a decree was promulgated ordering the immediate expulsion of all Jesuits, a step which had been urged by the Democratic Society and by a majority of the members of Congress, though President López himself hesitated before taking final action.[26] Anticlerical legislation passed by Congress the following May provided for abolition of the ecclesiastical *fuero* (body of corporate privileges) and forbade public authorities to compel the fulfillment of religious vows.

One of the most important items on the Liberal agenda was the abolition of slavery, which was effected by a law of 21 May 1851. This action was the culmination of a process begun in 1821 at the Congress of Cúcuta, convoked to draw up a constitution for Gran Colombia, which had decreed that the children of slaves were henceforth to be born free. Another process initiated at Cúcuta was completed in 1850 when a law was enacted that authorized provincial legislatures to divide the communal lands, or *resguardos,* of the Indians and allowed the latter to dispose of their property like other citizens.[27] Although it was hoped that the measure would increase agricultural production and simultaneously benefit the Indian, the law proved a boon mainly to landowners and local politicians who bought the Indian plots for a pittance and often converted them to pasture.[28]

Two of the Spanish legacies most vehemently denounced by the Liberal reformers were the prevailing tax system and centralization of power. To deal with these problems, Congress passed legislation providing for the decentralization of taxes: by a law of 20 April 1850 certain sources of revenue such as customs duties were to be reserved for the national government while all others were ceded to the provinces. In his 1851 report to Congress Secretary of Finance Manuel Murillo, who was a leader of the reform-minded Liberals, expressed the hope that the provinces would come to rely on a single direct tax on income as their sole source of revenue.[29] Another vestige of Spanish rule, privilege, was combatted by a law (15 May 1850) which permitted the practice of law and medicine without a university degree and downgraded the status of the nation's three universities, Bogotá, Popayán, and Cartagena.[30]

It is generally conceded that Colombia experienced significant social and economic change in the mid-nineteenth century, though the precise nature and causes of that change have never been systematically analyzed.[31] The regularization of steam navigation on the Magdalena River and the freeing of tobacco cultivation, both of which can be dated from the Mosquera years, were followed by an expansion of foreign trade based on the export of tobacco, which became Colombia's largest exchange earner.[32] Commerce received additional stimulus from the lowering of the tariff, another measure of the Mosquera administration. The consequences of the López reforms are even less clear, though the division of the *resguardos* may have created a more mobile rural proletariat in some regions and the abolition of slavery presumably hurt some traditional landowners. The latter, along with Colombia's artisans, are usually considered the principal victims of the midcentury changes while importers and those engaged in commercial agriculture are seen as the chief beneficiaries. Moreover, the young Liberal reformers are regarded as the representatives of the mercantile interests. None of these generalizations, however, has ever been subject to rigorous scrutiny.

Contemporaries, of course, had no doubts about the course of events. While Murillo and other Liberals hailed the achievements of the López administration, many Colombians concluded that the government's policies had ushered in an era of anarchy, socialism, and demagoguery. The echoes of their alarm reached as far as Paris, where an article in the 1850 edition of the *Annuaire de Deux Mondes* reported that Colombian demagogues had outstripped their European counterparts and that the López administration was "the most unlimited democracy with all its entourage."[33]

There were several reasons for concern over democratic excess and the threat of socialism in Colombia. In Bogotá young Liberals founded a society called the *Escuela Republicana* where they not only extolled the record of the López administration but pressed for further reforms, such as the abolition of capital punishment and absolute freedom of thought and expression.[34] While the Conservatives were sufficiently aroused by the *Escuela Republicana* to launch their own *Sociedad Filotémica*, the declamations of the middle- and upper-class youths who took part in the sessions of the Liberal club did not provoke nearly so much censure as did the activities of the many democratic societies founded throughout the country.

Although an analysis of the measures advocated by sixty-three *democráticas* established in 1851–52 "reveals a firm belief in the principles of nineteenth century liberalism and none in authoritarian or anarchistic socialism,"[35] the societies became the special target of those who deplored the excesses to which the López administration had supposedly given rise. This was partly the result of the language in which the *democráticas'* programs were couched. Another reason for the unfavorable image of the societies was the fact that they were responsible for serious disturbances in some areas, particularly in the provinces of Buenaventura and Cauca, where wealthy Conservatives were attacked and their property damaged by members of local societies.[36] Conservatives were all the more indignant because they were convinced that the local Liberal authorities did nothing to halt the depredations, and indeed the governor of Cauca, Carlos Gómez, dismissed the disorders as the natural reaction of a "people that had escaped from oppression to liberty."[37]

Conservative outrage over contemporary conditions led to a series of revolts against the government, beginning in May 1851, which were crushed with comparative ease. But many Liberals also had serious reservations about the government's course, and the result was a division within Liberal ranks which had become evident by mid-1852. One faction was composed of the doctrinaire young reformers who were eager for the continuation of change that would rapidly transform Colombia into a model republic. Led by Murillo, they became known as *Gólgotas* after a rhetorical invocation to the Martyr of Golgotha at the *Escuela Republicana*.[38] Opposing the *Gólgotas* were Liberals who supported many of the recent reforms, such as the abolition of slavery, but disapproved of some of the more extravagant proposals advanced by the *Gólgotas*. Dubbed *Draconianos* partly because of their opposition to the abolition of capital punishment, they numbered in their ranks many older Liberals, veterans of the wars of independence and the revolution of 1839–42, who considered themselves the heirs of Santander.[39] They looked for leadership to José María Obando, who had returned to Colombia in 1849. Obando's claim to the mantle of Santander was symbolized by the latter's sword, which Santander had bequeathed to Obando and had been formally presented to him shortly after his return to Bogotá.[40] Obando was more than a factional chieftain, however; he was without question the leading Liberal hero among the party's rank-and-file, and was elected to the presidency in 1852 with only little opposition from the *Gólgotas*.[41]

During Obando's presidency (1853–54) differences between *Gólgotas* and *Draconianos* became more acute. In Congress, where the *Gólgotas* had a majority, the two factions quarreled over the provisions of a new constitution which, as promulgated on 21 May 1853, provided for separation of church and state and for universal suffrage, and lessened presidential powers by permitting the popular election of provincial governors. A campaign by the *Gólgotas* to abolish or at least drastically curtail Colombia's armed forces was opposed not only by the *Draconianos*, many of whom had military backgrounds, but also by currently active army officers.[42] Meanwhile, the *Draconianos* had found another ally in the Bogotá *democrática* by promising tariff protection for Colombian products. By this time the members of the Democratic Society had become estranged from the *Gólgotas*, whose low-tariff ideas they considered harmful to their interests. In addition, the artisans were embittered by the social and economic gulf that separated them from the *Gólgotas*, who by virtue of their wealth, birth, or education were members of the elite. So great was the friction between artisans and *Gólgotas* that several violent brawls between them broke out in the streets of Bogotá in May and June 1853.[43]

The differences between the two Liberal factions culminated in a coup d'état on 17 April 1854, led by the *Draconiano* army officer General José María Melo, who established a short-lived dictatorship. By the end of the year the *Gólgotas*, having formed an alliance with the Conservatives, had succeeded in ousting Melo and restoring constitutional government. Obando, who was accused of having been a party to Melo's plot, was removed from office, though he was absolved of the crimes of treason and rebellion, and several artisans were exiled to Panama.[44]

The following years saw the Conservatives regain control of the executive branch of the national government while the Liberals took steps to mend their differences. The mid-1850s also saw the realization of the federalist idea in Colombia with the creation of eight self-governing states—Panama, Antioquia, Santander, Cauca, Cundinamarca, Boyacá, Bolívar, and Magdalena—between 1855 and 1857. This development was adumbrated during the López administration by such measures as the decentralization of taxes and the creation of fourteen new provinces, raising the total to thirty-six by 1853.[45] As it became evident that the smaller and poorer provinces were incapable of supporting themselves, there arose a movement to reintegrate the provinces as autonomous states. By this time, moreover, federalism had also been espoused by many Conservatives, who began to see advantages in the possibility of controlling one or more states.[46]

Despite the Liberal-Conservative consensus on federalism, the closing years of the decade brought a resurgence of partisan animosity, partly as a result of events in Santander, where the one-time *Gólgotas*, who were now known as Radicals, won control of the state government in 1857.[47] Under the leadership of Manuel Murillo, who was elected president of the state, the Radicals introduced a number of innovations, including a property tax which was to be the state's sole source of income, that aroused Conservative ire and produced a Conservative revolt early in 1859. Meanwhile, Liberals throughout the country suspected that Conservative President

Mariano Ospina Rodríguez was secretly abetting his coreligionists in Santander and in other ways was seeking to insure permanent Conservative control of the national government. It was in the midst of this potentially explosive situation that the rupture between Ospina and ex-President Mosquera took place. In 1856 Mosquera had indicated his displeasure at Ospina's nomination by running himself as the candidate of a third party composed of dissident Conservatives and Liberals.[48] Now, as president of Cauca, he was convinced that Ospina was conniving with his enemies within the state, and on 8 May 1860 he issued a decree announcing that Cauca was severing relations with the national government and reassuming its sovereignty.[49] It has already been stated that this act, coupled with the situation in Santander, served to ignite a major civil war that ended in Liberal victory under the leadership of Mosquera. It was to put the final touch to that victory that the Liberals gathered in Rionegro in February 1863.

While the Rionegro convention was in session from February to June 1863, the underlying animosity between Mosquera and his opponents frequently rose to the surface. On one occasion after Mosquera had addressed menacing words to the delegates, an anti-Mosquera general read aloud a letter from several army officers warning that they would hold him responsible for any attack on the dignity of the convention or its members. According to anti-Mosquera delegate Salvador Camacho Roldán, Mosquera was so mortified by the reprimand and by the applause it elicited from the delegates and spectators that he disappeared from the convention hall for a week.[50]

Equally dramatic moments occurred during debate on ecclesiastical policy, still the most burning issue of the day since clergymen and devout Catholics remained opposed to the anticlerical decrees issued by Mosquera in 1861–62 while the government was determined to force compliance. Archbishop Antonio Herrán of Bogotá had been exiled from his see in 1861 for protesting the nationalization of Church property, and other clerics who had refused to obey the government's edicts had suffered a like fate or remained in hiding. Even while the convention was in session, nuns in Bogotá were being forcibly expelled from their convents amid so great a public outcry that a Liberal there was moved to observe in his journal: "Let it be said, for the sake of truth, that this measure has been unanimously censured . . . as being impolitic, despotic, and brutal."[51]

The ecclesiastical measures adopted at Rionegro after considerable discussion represented a compromise between the Mosqueristas, who favored the imposition of stringent curbs on the Church, and their opponents, who agreed that the clergy constituted a pernicious and subversive element in Colombian society but simultaneously doubted that their influence could or should be eradicated by force.[52] Article 23 of the new constitution empowered the federal and state governments to exercise the right of supreme inspection over religious cults in order to sustain national sovereignty and preserve public tranquility and security, while Article 15 recognized the right of the individual to profess any religion publicly provided he did not endanger national sovereignty or perform any action with the intent of disturbing the peace. In order to put Article 23 into effect, a law was passed on 23 April which provided that no minister of any sect could carry on his functions without swearing obedience to the constitutions, laws, and authorities of the states and nation. Those who refused to take this oath were to be exiled from Colombia, while those presently in exile or confinement would be allowed to resume their duties provided they submitted to the terms of the new law. Another law, enacted on 19 May, ratified Mosquera's decree of 9 September 1861 nationalizing Church property.

The constitution as promulgated on 8 May 1863 accurately expressed Liberal political aims as they had evolved during the first half of the century, though some provisions, such as the two-year presidential term, were adopted partly as a means of restraining Mosquera's ambitions.[53] Unlike previous Colombian constitutions, it lacked an invocation to God and was decreed by the convention "in the name of and by the authority of the people and of the United States of Colombia." The nine sovereign states—the eight established in 1855-57, plus a ninth, Tolima, created in 1861—united and federated themselves in perpetuity, reserving for themselves all powers not explicitly delegated to the federal, or general, government, which was to have jurisdiction over foreign affairs and commerce, national defense, the monetary system, and the regulation of interoceanic routes as well as of the navigation of rivers that touched more than one state or flowed into a neighboring nation. In addition, the federal government was to share with the states control over the postal system and the development of public education.

The executive power of the federal government was to be exercised by a president who was to serve for two years and was ineligible for immediate reelection. He was to be elected by the states, each of which would cast its ballot for the individual who had won a plurality of the votes of its electors in accordance with its own electoral legislation. Legislative power was vested in a congress composed of a senate and a chamber of representatives whose members were to serve for two years. In case of the temporary or permanent absence of the president, his place was to be taken by one of three presidential alternates (*designados*) chosen each year by Congress.

Article 15 listed the rights which the federal government and the states pledged themselves to recognize and to guarantee to all inhabitants of Colombia. Among these was the freedom of the individual, which was defined as the right to commit, or to fail to commit, any act provided no injury to another individual or to the community resulted. Other guarantees included unrestricted freedom of expression and of the press; the right to property and personal security; and the right to possess arms and munitions and to traffic in them in peacetime. In addition, the death penalty was abolished, and corporal punishment for longer than ten years was forbidden.

Although the Rionegro constitution was to remain in force longer than any of its predecessors, it was the target of criticism from Liberals as well as Conservatives almost from the day of its promulgation. Some Liberals, for example, deplored the failure to create a federal district as the seat of the national government while others felt that the two-year presidential term was too short.[54] A more important issue raised by critics of the constitution was the fact that the federal government was virtually powerless to intervene on behalf of state governments threatened by rebellion, the president merely being authorized "to watch over the preservation of general order." This was, however, a delicate political matter for which no completely satisfactory solution could be found.[55]

An equally serious flaw in the constitution, in the opinion of many Liberals, was the fact that amendment was extremely difficult. According to Article 92, an amendment had to be requested by a majority of the nine state legislatures, whereupon it had to be approved by both houses of Congress and ratified by the unanimous vote of the Senate, with each of the states being allotted one vote. Amendments could also be made by a special convention convoked upon the petition of all the state assemblies. By 1874 the legislatures of five states had formally requested a change in Article 92 so that the vote of only two-thirds of the states in the Senate would be needed for ratification.[56] The proposed amendment, having been passed by the Chamber of Representatives, was still being discussed in the Senate three years later, at which time it was turned over for study to Manuel Murillo, then a member of that body. After Murillo had expressed his opinion that the amendment would violate the sovereignty of the states and that the constitution should undergo no serious modification until a generation had elapsed, the senators voted to suspend the proposal indefinitely.[57] During the twenty-three years of the constitution's existence, only one amendment succeeded in overcoming the requisite hurdles. Ratified in 1876, it provided that presidential elections be held on the same day throughout the country.[58]

Four days after the constitution was promulgated, the delegates elected Mosquera president of Colombia for a term ending 1 April 1864, when the first regularly elected chief executive would take office. The fact that Mosquera received only thirty-seven of the sixty-one votes cast suggests the division among the delegates and within the Liberal party. Even so, while dissension seemed endemic among Liberals, neither in 1863 nor later would it prove severe enough to rend the party permanently. By 1863 the concept of Liberalism had sunk sufficient roots—nourished by the ideological, political, and personal bonds among its leaders in both the capital and the hinterland—to assure the party's survival indefinitely.

2
Party Alignment in Nineteenth-Century Colombia
A Regional Survey

The purpose of this chapter is twofold: first, to provide an introduction to the nine Colombian states and to their respective societies and economies and, second, to identify areas of Liberal strength among the various regions and socioeconomic groups in the country. The second of these goals must be approached with caution because of the paucity of relevant and accurate quantitative data. Moreover, party alignment in nineteenth-century Colombia was a complex phenomenon which cannot be explained by a single scheme based on the conflict of competing socioeconomic or regional interests. Such schemes have some validity in that one party tended to have greater strength than the other among certain socioeconomic groups and in certain regions, but such patterns were not of universal applicability.[1]

The difficulty of accounting for party alignment also stems in part from the regional diversity that characterized nineteenth-century Colombia. Of the various causes of this diversity, the geography of the country was the most obvious in the eyes of contemporaries. Colombia's dominant topographical feature is the three chains of the Andes—the Western, Central, and Eastern Cordilleras—which traverse the country from south to north. Climatic changes occur as altitude increases, and the tropical conditions of lowland areas (called the *tierra caliente,* or "hot country") are transformed into temperate and cool climates at higher elevations. In the nineteenth century communications of all kinds among the various sections of the country were hindered by the rugged, irregular terrain. Communications between the interior and the Pacific and Caribbean coasts were equally difficult and were possible mainly by way of the Magdalena River and its tributaries. The introduction of steam navigation to the Magdalena, the beginning of railroad construction in the last third of the century, and the growth of the telegraphic network from 20 kilometers of line in 1865 to 9,689 kilometers in 1892 improved the situation to some extent, but the movement of human beings, freight, and ideas remained costly and arduous throughout the century.[2]

These problems were aggravated by the fact that the population, which totaled close to three million in 1870 and was estimated at between four and five million by 1900,[3] was concentrated on the slopes and basins of the Cordilleras, precisely those areas to which access was most difficult. Bogotá, the national capital and most populous city, is located nearly 1,000 kilometers from the Caribbean at an altitude of almost 3,000 meters. To reach Bogotá from the Caribbean in the second half of the nineteenth century, it was necessary to spend from one to two weeks aboard a steamer plying the Magdalena. Upon arriving at Honda, the principal river port of the interior, the traveler still had to undergo another lengthy journey by mule and coach before he or she reached the capital. It was not until the 1880s that rail service was available for part of the distance between the Magdalena and Bogotá.

Colombia's poor communications in the nineteenth century were both a cause and effect of its sluggish economic performance, especially in the decades before 1850. Modest gains based on agricultural production for overseas export were registered in the second half of the century, but these were periodically checked by falling world prices for Colombian exports and by the ravages of civil war.

In such a setting the political parties were virtually the only institutions, with the exception of the Catholic Church, that were national in scope, cutting across class and regional lines. Both parties had adherents in all regions and among all sectors of the population. Each party was associated with a cluster of ideas to which all supporters—regardless of class or regional origins—theoretically owed allegiance. Even in the period before the formation of nationwide party organizations, leaders in Bogotá corresponded regularly with their counterparts in the provinces in order to communicate and receive political news and opinions. Party newspapers kept their readers apprised of events in other parts of the country by printing excerpts from newspapers published elsewhere as well as reports from correspondents in the various regions. In short, without minimizing the destructive aspects of political conflict in the nineteenth century, it can also be maintained that the parties served as forces for national integration.

Despite the national composition of the Liberal party there were many areas of the country in which it was clearly the weaker of the two parties, while in others it was the stronger. It is difficult to identify the areas of Liberal dominance because election returns, normally the most convenient tool for determining party preferences according to region, rarely yield usable evidence, especially after 1863 when elections were often characterized by the use of fraud on the part of the incumbents and by abstention on the part of the opposition. The results of two presidential elections before 1863—those of 1848 and 1856—can be of some value in determining the geographical basis of party affiliation and will be used in the regional survey that follows. By the time these elections took place partisan alignments had crystallized, and the presidency was vigorously contested on both occasions. Moreover, the balloting was apparently conducted with a degree of electoral purity that would be absent in later campaigns. The value of the returns for 1848 and 1856 is diminished, however, by the fact that the electoral districts of 1856 differed from those of 1848 and the regulations governing the suffrage also differed. In 1848 voting was restricted to those who could meet a property qualification while in 1856 universal male suffrage was in effect.[4] In addition, in 1856 citizens voted directly for the president; in 1848 they chose electors who in turn selected the president.

The Caribbean Coast

The name *Costa*, or Coast, was applied to the three states bordering the Caribbean: Bolívar, Magdalena, and Panama. The three states shared several characteristics with respect to population, economy, and culture. The population of the three was very much mixed racially, with a preponderance of blacks, mulattoes, and mestizos, and a minority of whites. Bolívar was the most populous of the three, with a population calculated at 241,704 in 1870. The census of that year gave a population of 224,032 for Panama and 88,928 for Magdalena. The economy of all three was based on commerce, but much of the interior of each state was devoted to cattle raising and agriculture.

The chief cities of Bolívar and Magdalena—Cartagena, the capital of Bolívar; Barranquilla, also in Bolívar; and Santa Marta, the capital of Magdalena—were all located on or near the Caribbean, but they did not fare equally well as a result of the expansion of trade after 1850. In each case the crucial factor was the city's connection with the Magdalena River.[5] Both Cartagena and Santa Marta had good harbors, but their only links with the river were "merely half-choked channels and swamps" which could not be kept permanently navigable. Barranquilla, on the other hand, was located directly on the west bank of the Magdalena about nineteen kilometers from its mouth. At first, however, Barranquilla's development was impeded by a sandbar at the Bocas de Ceniza, which constitute the mouth of the river, that from time to time prevented the passage of any but small craft. This obstacle was removed by the construction in 1869-70 of a railroad between Barranquilla and Sabanilla on the Caribbean coast that bypassed the Bocas de Ceniza. The effect of the railroad was aptly summed up in 1884 by Thomas M. Dawson, United States consul in Barranquilla: "Imperfect as it is, the working of this [the Sabanilla] railroad has revolutionized the carrying trade, and made Barranquilla a port of chief commercial importance."[6] Indeed, by the end of the century Barranquilla had far outstripped its two rivals in customs receipts (see Table 1). Cartagena's decline was all the more marked because of its preeminence as Colombia's leading port during the colonial period.

To an even greater extent than Bolívar and Magdalena, Panama was primarily a commercial state whose economic life revolved around the transisthmian trade, which consisted mainly of goods destined for areas other than Colombia. Goods were transported across the Isthmus by way of the Panama Railroad, the first to be built on Colombian territory, which was constructed by a group of New York capitalists and went into operation in 1855.[7]

TABLE 1

Customs Returns for Three Caribbean Ports to the Nearest Peso in Selected Years Of the Second Half of the Nineteenth Century

Year or part of the year	Santa Marta	Cartagena	Sabanilla/ Barranquilla
1855–56	$714,032	$ 64,210	$ 153,481
1872–73	547,168	207,366	1,560,878
1882–1883 (11 mos.)	89,084	245,905	2,731,476
1892 (6 mos.)	102,111	669,424	2,751,595
1893 (6 mos.)	72,588	1,006,368	3,120,182

Source: Theodore E. Nichols, "The Caribbean Gateway to Colombia: Cartagena, Santa Marta, and Barranquilla and Their Connections with the Interior, 1820–1940" (Ph.D. dissertation, University of California, Berkeley, 1951), p.400.

Because of the peculiar economic and geographic conditions of Panama and the difficulty of communications with Bogotá, separatist sentiments were always latent and erupted periodically. In 1855 Justo Arosemena, a native of the Isthmus, urged the conversion of Panama into a self-governing state on the grounds that it was the only means of preserving Colombian sovereignty there.[8] Even after Panama had become a state, however, the feeling was expressed on occasion that the Isthmus was exploited politically and economically by the central government, which received a $250,000 annuity paid by the Panama Railroad and returned only a subvention of $25,000 to the state.[9] Such sentiments were shared to some extent by inhabitants of Bolívar and Magdalena. As early as 1835 Juan José Nieto, a future chief executive of Bolívar, complained to President Santander that the resources of Cartagena were being drained by Congress and that Colombians of the interior ridiculed and insulted the Costeños, as inhabitants of the coastal states were called.[10] These grievances reappeared in later years, most dramatically in 1875, when Costeños supported a native son, Rafael Núñez, in his unsuccessful bid for the presidency.

Undoubtedly because of its accessibility, the Coast was the only region of Colombia that attracted foreigners in significant numbers. This was especially true of Panama, where the foreign population was estimated at 4,533 in 1871.[11] By way of contrast, Santander, whose population was nearly twice as large as that of Panama, counted only 2,023 foreigners in 1870, of whom 1,946 were Venezuelans.[12] The cosmopolitan nature of coastal society is also suggested by the fact that in 1888 a large proportion of Barranquilla's business community was made up of foreigners, including individuals who hailed from Germany, the United States, England, Italy, France, the Netherlands, Cuba, Spain, and Switzerland.[13]

One consequence of the Costeño's relatively high degree of exposure to alien influences was that he was considered to be far less devout than the Colombian of the interior. As a correspondent in Bogotá lamented to the newly appointed bishop of Panama in 1876: "In general the people of the coast are lost, both because of the apparent decline in religious education and practice and because of the infernal leprosy of Masonry, which is so common there as a result of the close contact with foreigners."[14] What seems to have been most marked, especially in contrast with the interior, was the absence of external manifestations of piety. "Outward demonstrations of faith," a Barranquilla newspaper was quoted as saying in 1872, "which are so obligatory for the believer and are necessary to stimulate the religious fervor of the indifferent or the ignorant by example do not exist here; . . . and they do not exist because there is no inner piety either."[15] A writer in the *Estrella de Panamá* was similarly disturbed by the Panamanian's lack of respect for "the prescriptions of religion and decorum." On religious holidays, for example, so many public establishments remained open that "a person can hardly believe that he is living in a Christian country."[16]

An examination of returns in the presidential elections of 1848 and 1856 suggests that Magdalena constituted the most strongly Liberal area of the three coastal states in that Liberal candidates won a majority there in both contests (see Table 2A).[17] On the other hand, the Liberals fared less well in Bolívar and Panama, where they lost both elections. It should be noted, however, that they made a better showing in the cities of Cartagena, Barranquilla, and Panama in 1856 than they did in the two states as a whole (see Table 2B). In fact, the Liberals won a majority in the city of Panama, a plurality in Cartagena, and were defeated by only five votes in Barranquilla. Also striking is the relative weakness of the two major parties in Bolívar and Panama. In 1848 the plurality of Panama's votes went to Joaquín María Barriga, who was not strongly identified with either party but was backed by the incumbent president, Tomás Cipriano de Mosquera. In 1856 both states gave a plurality to Mosquera, who was running as a third-party candidate. This may have been a reflection of the notoriously personalistic, nonideological character of Costeño politics.

The Liberal strength in the coastal cities in 1856 was probably a result of the party's egalitarian rhetoric and its identification with the abolition of slavery. In 1851 the American consul in Cartagena expressed doubt that the Conservative revolution against the López government which had recently broken out in the interior would spread to the Coast:

> The Provinces of the Coast, and especially that of Cartagena, are chiefly inhabited by people of Color, all [of] whom are now free in virtue of a recent law. Nearly all, are decidedly in favor of the present Administration, and will doubtless support it, and no power that can be brought forward by the Conservative party, can stand long against the overwhelming majority of the Ministerial or democratic party.[18]

TABLE 2A

Presidential Voting, 1848 and 1856: The Coast

Bolívar, 1848[a]

Province	Liberal	Conservative	Other
Cartagena	40	87	5
Mompós (except Ocaña)	17	11	2
Total	57	98	7

Bolívar, 1856[b]

Province	Liberal	Conservative	National
Cartagena	4,403	3,710	5,277
Mompós	367	508	2,523
Sabanilla	1,439	2	2,532
Total	6,209	4,220	10,332

Magdalena, 1848[a]

Province	Liberal	Conservative	Other
Riohacha	4	12	0
Santa Marta	33	21	0
Total	37	33	0

Magdalena, 1856[b]

Province	Liberal	Conservative	National
Riohacha	1,025	414	210
Santa Marta	4,269	258	1,362
Valledupar	311	40	1,054
Ocaña (6 districts)	295	84	108
Total	5,900	796	2,734

Panama, 1848[a]

Province	Liberal	Conservative	Other
Panama	5	17	41
Veraguas	18	20	3
Total	23	37	44

Panama, 1856[b]

Province	Liberal	Conservative	National
Panama (state)	899	2,163	2,533

[a]Electoral votes.
[b]Popular votes.

TABLE 2B

Presidential Voting, 1848 and 1856: Four Coastal Cities

City	1848ª	1856ᵇ
Barranquilla	4 Liberal 0 Conservative 5 Other	321 Liberal 0 Conservative 326 National
Cartagena	0 Liberal 22 Conservative	522 Liberal 117 Conservative 474 National
Panama	0 Liberal 3 Conservative 7 Other	205 Liberal 4 Conservative 47 National
Santa Marta	7 Liberal 1 Conservative	451 Liberal 74 Conservative 123 National

ªElectoral votes by canton.
ᵇPopular votes by district.

Other statements by contemporaries indicate that blacks and mulattoes in Bolívar continued to be attracted to leaders of a Liberal orientation. When a Conservative government was overthrown in Bolívar in 1859, the Liberal provisional governor felt compelled to deny rumors that the upheaval had had racial overtones and that local blacks had been induced to participate by the prospect of loot.[19] Similarly, during the nationwide revolution of 1885, the American consul in Cartagena reported that "the majority of the Radicals [i.e., Liberals] in this city are composed of its worst element, the idle, vicious, and vindictive negroes."[20]

In the city of Panama the blacks and mulattoes who resided in the district known as the *arrabal* of Santa Ana also considered themselves Liberals.[21] So great was the identification of Liberalism with the *arrabal,* according to one contemporary, that Liberals from elite families like Justo and Pablo Arosemena were automatically taken to be Conservatives by the uninformed.[22] The remarks of the British vice-consul in Panama in the mid-1860s, when the Liberals controlled the state, are also instructive in this regard: "The public offices are almost all filled by coloured or black men, who, as a rule, are of the 'Liberal' party in politics, while those who would seem best calculated to hold such offices by their intellect and education are resting on their oars and occasionally paying forced loans."[23] From time to time tensions appeared between Panama City Liberals from elite groups such as the Arosemenas, and more popular leaders identified with the *arrabal* such as Buenaventura Correoso, who was president of the state from 1868 to 1872 and from 1876 to 1878.

The factionalism and relatively low level of party identification that characterized Panamanian politics can be seen in the activities of the Obaldía family, wealthy landowners and stockraisers in the Chiriquí region. During the revolution of 1859–62 José de Obaldía, a Liberal who had been vice president of Colombia in the mid-1850s and chief executive of Panama from 1858 to 1860, supported Santiago de la Guardia, the Conservative who succeeded him in the latter post, and in 1862 Obaldía and others described as constituting "the leading and most influential men of the Isthmus" sought unsuccessfully to crush a Liberal movement against de la Guardia headed by Correoso and "about one hundred individuals of unfamiliar names and doubtful position in the country."[24] The aftermath of the Liberal victory saw charges by Obaldía and members of his family that they were being victimized by rapacious Liberal officials in Chiriquí; at issue were lands which the local authorities claimed had been improperly appropriated by Obaldía.[25] This dispute led in 1868 to the death of one of the Liberal officials involved, allegedly at the hands of Obaldía's son Aristides, who himself was killed soon afterward while leading an unsuccessful Conservative revolt against the Correoso government.[26]

In the opinion of Joaquín F. Vélez, a Cartagena merchant and Conservative political leader, the more affluent classes in Bolívar were generally Conservative.[27] On the other hand, at least some of the principal businessmen and entrepreneurs from Santa Marta—Manuel and Tomás E. Abello and Vicente Lafaurie, for example—were Liberals.[28] This divergence may have been partly an outgrowth of the long-standing commercial rivalry between Cartagena and Santa Marta. Another factor in the Liberalism of Santa Marta and of Magdalena in general was undoubtedly the state's propinquity to the Liberal stronghold of Santander, the western part of which shared many of the geographic and economic characteristics of Magdalena.

Cauca

Cauca, which was the largest state in area in the Colombian Union, had a population of 435,078 in 1870. So heterogeneous in geography and population was the state that it was described in 1872 as a small-scale replica of the Austrian Empire where "the governor, no matter how intelligent and patriotic he may be, can do no more than to keep the peace, reconciling conflicting interests and calming ardent passions."[29]

The vast, hatchet-shaped state had four distinct regions. On the east lay an uninhabited plains area called Cáqueta. To the south was a rugged highland region populated chiefly by Indian and mestizo craftsmen and farmers. The inhabitants of southern Cauca, especially those of the Pasto district, were proverbial among nineteenth-century Colombians for their Conservatism and fanatical devotion to the Church.[30] The northern part of Cauca was made up of the humid, thickly forested Chocó. Isolated even by Colombian standards from the rest of the country, its importance stemmed from its placer gold deposits, exploited during the colonial period with the use of Negroes, who were still predominant in the sparse population.[31]

The heart of the state was the fertile valley of the Cauca River, which flows between the Western and Central Cordilleras to empty into the Magdalena. During the colonial period the Cauca Valley had been divided into large landholdings devoted mainly to sugar cultivation and cattle raising and worked by black slaves after the local Indian population had disappeared. After Independence the Valley remained an agricultural and pastoral area, the principal crops being sugar, cacao, and tobacco; the last of these was grown chiefly at Palmira, which had become Colombia's largest producer by 1875.[32]

Popayán, the major administrative center during the Spanish regime, became the capital of the state, but it was gradually eclipsed by Cali, which had a population estimated at 16,000 in 1881.[33] Even so, Cali's development was inhibited by the difficulty of communication with the Pacific Ocean, which until the mid-nineteenth century could be reached only by way of a poor road and the treacherous Daguas River. Between 1854 and 1873 an improved road was completed as far as Córdoba, twenty kilometers from the Pacific port of Buenaventura.[34] Later the emphasis shifted to railroad construction, with the completion of a railway linking Cali and Córdoba in 1882.

During the colonial period the gold of the Chocó and the products of the Cauca Valley had created a local aristocracy whose members usually resided in Popayán and intermarried among themselves, establishing "golden dynasties" that dominated the political, social, and economic life of the region.[35] They had suffered economically with the abolition of slavery in 1850, but they retained considerable political influence throughout the century. As a rule these great families—the Arboledas and the Caicedos, for example—were Conservative in their politics. Tomás Cipriano de Mosquera was a scion of one of these families.

The continued dominance of traditional elites, coupled with the economic stagnation of the Cauca Valley, generated among the region's Negroid population a smoldering resentment toward the white upper class that periodically burst into violence. One such episode, occurring during the López administration, grew out of an old dispute in Cali over the municipal commons, or *ejidos,* where the townspeople had traditionally pastured their livestock and gathered wood.[36] As far back as the eighteenth century local landowners had begun to appropriate these lands, enclosing them with fences and ditches. In 1848, during the governorship of Vicente Borrero, a Conservative and a landowner himself, several haciendas had been invaded, and the fences had been destroyed and the ditches filled up.

The culprits could not be prosecuted because no one could be found to identify them. The issue of the *ejidos* was revived in 1850 when the "plebeian" Ramón Mercado was appointed governor of the province of Buenaventura, where Cali was located. Although most of the landowners now agreed to give up part of the disputed lands, the refusal of Borrero to do so without compensation apparently delayed the proceedings and resulted in renewed attacks on the haciendas, especially those belonging to Conservatives. Meanwhile, a Conservative broadside printed in Bogotá urging that the lash (*el zurriago*) be applied to the "reds" was circulated in Cali and led to the formation of bands of Liberal *zurriagueros* who assaulted Conservatives on the streets of the city.[37] *Zurriagueros* were also active in Palmira and Cartago, where two prominent Conservatives were murdered.[38]

Mercado attempted to halt the violence in his province, but Conservatives were convinced that he was its chief instigator. To Conservative cries of outrage, he replied that the root of the disorder lay in the feudal social structure of the Cauca Valley, which was based on the unequal distribution of land and the exploitation of all who had African blood.[39] No other section of Colombia, he maintained, was more resistant to change, and the achievement of independence had not noticeably altered the situation. He believed, however, that the Liberal victory of 1849 had signified the destruction of the old regime based on privilege and the foundation of a new society based on equality. While many Liberals deplored the excesses of their coreligionists in the Cauca Valley, others agreed with Mercado's assessment. In 1864 another writer found that race still divided the Cauca Valley into two distinct societies which hated each other. The reason, he said, lay in the general poverty of the region.[40]

As might be expected in view of the Conservative preponderance among Cauca's elite, the state's blacks and mulattoes, insofar as they were politically active, were likely to be enrolled in the ranks of the Liberals. Indeed, a German visitor to the Cauca Valley in 1880 equated the Liberal party there with what he called the Negro rabble.[41] At the same time the Liberal party in Cauca also included landowners, merchants, and professional men, though few besides Mosquera and others who were at one time affiliated with Conservatism appear to have sprung from the highest reaches of society. The variety of the party's makeup in Cauca can be seen in a list of the occupations of 165 Liberals resident in downtown Buga about 1903.[42] Their occupations, which total 167 because two men had two, were as follows: well-to-do artisans, 75; landowners, 38; poor artisans, 21; merchants, 13; farmers, 8; physicians, 5; lawyers, 5; and engineers, 2.

Overall, however, the Conservative party was apparently dominant in the state as Conservatives carried Cauca in both 1848 and 1856 (see Table 3A). In 1856 Mosquera made a respectable showing in his home state, and his defection to the Liberals a few years later swelled the party's ranks with Caucanos loyal to the veteran *caudillo*. The election returns do indicate

TABLE 3A

Presidential Voting, 1848 and 1856: Cauca

Province	1848[a] Liberal	Conservative	Other
Barbacoas	10	9	0
Buenaventura	4	19	0
Cauca	30	20	0
Chocó	14	10	0
Pasto	0	20	1
Popayán	32	22	0
Túquerres	0	30	0
Total	90	130	1

Province	1856[b] Liberal	Conservative	National
Buenaventura	1,817	1,861	437
Cauca	4,433	5,215	283
Chocó	489	722	255
Pasto	2,587	4,451	3,919
Popayán	2,424	273	5,107
Neiva (3 districts)	895	155	0
Total	12,645	12,677	10,001

[a]Electoral votes.
[b]Popular votes.

that a few places in Cauca were staunchly Liberal. Results in the cantons which supported the Liberal candidate in 1848 were compared with the results in the districts of the same names in 1856. In only four cases—Almaguer, Buga, Palmira, and Quibdó—was a Liberal victory recorded in 1856 as well. Buga and Palmira, both of which are in the Cauca Valley, and Quibdó, in the Chocó, were areas of predominantly Negroid population. Conversely, when results in the cantons in which Conservatives won at least a plurality in 1848 were compared with the 1856 results in districts of the same name, seven places were found to have been predominantly Conservative in 1848 and to have supported either the Conservative or the National candidate in 1856 (see Table 3B). These seven places, which might be called the least Liberal in Cauca, were scattered throughout the state: three were in the south (Pasto, Barbacoas, and Túquerres), two were in the province of Cauca (Cartago, Roldanillo), and there was one each in the Chocó (San Juan or Nóvita) and in Buenaventura province (Roldanillo).

TABLE 3B

Presidential Voting, 1848 and 1856: Selected Areas in Cauca

Area	1848[a]	1856[b]
Almaguer	10 Liberal 6 Conservative	233 Liberal 0 Conservative 23 National
Barbacoas	1 Liberal 7 Conservative	222 Liberal 2 Conservative 490 National
Buga	11 Liberal 2 Conservative	518 Liberal 216 Conservative 10 National
Cartago	3 Liberal 8 Conservative	168 Liberal 616 Conservative 51 National
Palmira	9 Liberal 3 Conservative	1,079 Liberal 281 Conservative 33 National
Pasto	0 Liberal 21 Conservative	471 Liberal 492 Conservative 462 National
Quibdó	11 Liberal 0 Conservative	168 Liberal 139 Conservative 1 National
Roldanillo	2 Liberal 5 Conservative	132 Liberal 412 Conservative 84 National
San Juan (Nóvita)	3 Liberal 9 Conservative	1 Liberal 48 Conservative 127 National
Toro	0 Liberal 5 Conservative	0 Liberal 283 Conservative 0 National
Túquerres	0 Liberal 13 Conservative	75 Liberal 70 Conservative 355 National

---

[a]Electoral votes by canton.
[b]Popular votes by district.

Tolima and Cundinamarca

To the east of the Cauca Valley lay the state of Tolima, which had a population of 230,891 in 1870, most of whom were mestizos and other mixed-bloods. The last of the states to be created, it was carved out of territory formerly belonging to Cundinamarca and remained in many respects an appendage of it. The most important part of Tolima was the valley of the upper Magdalena, which flowed through the state from south to north, and most of the principal towns were located on or near the river. The Magdalena, however, failed to be a source of unity for the inhabitants of Tolima, partly because navigation of the river was extremely difficult and partly because commercial ties with Cundinamarca outweighed the links between the northern and southern parts of the state.[43]

The economy of southern Tolima, whose inhabitants included many Caucanos, was based mainly on extensive cattle raising and the manufacture of hats, *ruanas* (Colombian ponchos), and similar products; some tobacco was also grown. The northern part of the state, as well as that portion of western Cundinamarca bordering the Magdalena, was devoted primarily to commercial agriculture. Here was located the Ambalema district, which was Colombia's leading tobacco producer in the 1840s and 1850s. In the 1860s this region also became the center of a brief boom in indigo production launched by upper-class youths from Bogotá who had heeded the exhortations of Liberal writers to exploit the hot country of the upper Magdalena Valley. By 1870 there were 350 indigo plantations in northern Tolima and western Cundinamarca, and the value of exports rose to over $500,000 in 1870–71.[44] With the resumption of Bengalese indigo production, which had declined temporarily in the 1870s, Colombian exports fell and were negligible by 1877. Meanwhile, tobacco production also declined, both in Ambalema and the country as a whole. After 1880 the place of tobacco began to be taken by coffee, which soon became the principal export crop of Cundinamarca and Tolima as well as Colombia's principal exchange earner. In 1874 the two states together produced less than 10 percent of Colombia's coffee; by 1913 the figure had risen to nearly 24 percent.[45]

The largest portion of Cundinamarca, which had a population of 413,658 in 1870, was taken up by the sparsely inhabited plains lying to the east of the Eastern Cordillera. The Cordillera dominated the central part of the state, which was populated mainly by mestizos and Indians. Bogotá, the capital of the state as well as of the nation, was situated on the eastern edge of a fertile intermontane basin in the Cordillera, known as the savannah (*sabana*), which had been the seat of the Chibcha states conquered by Gonzalo Jiménez de Quesada in the 1530s. By 1539 Jiménez de Quesada had founded the city of Santa Fe de Bogotá, which became the center of Spanish administration in the area and later the capital of the Viceroyalty of New Granada established in 1739. Upon the separation of New Granada from the mother country, Bogotá had remained the capital of the young republic, but to many Colombian Liberals the city was a symbol of the authoritarianism and religious fanaticism they associated with Spanish rule. Certainly there could be no doubt that the clergy exerted an extremely strong influence on the city's inhabitants. It was the opinion of William L. Scruggs, who was United States minister to Colombia in the 1870s and 1880s, that "there is probably no city on the continent where the external forms of religion are more rigidly observed."[46] As he wrote these words, he perhaps had in mind the occasion in 1873 when the American legation, which was temporarily without its diplomatic insignia, was stoned by a "rabble" accompanying a religious procession because a Protestant missionary was staying there.[47]

According to a guide to Bogotá published in 1867, the city had 40,000 inhabitants at that time.[48] The same guide listed 11 printing establishments, 2 owned by the state and national governments and 9 belonging to private individuals, which published 15 periodicals. There were 6 hospitals and charitable institutions; 8 public and 17 private elementary schools; and 31 secondary schools, or *colegios,* including the Conciliar Seminary and the government-run Colegio de San Bartolomé and Colegio del Rosario, where most of the country's leaders were educated. Only 4 factories were listed—for the making of earthenware, fabrics, noodles, and chocolate—but the roster of those engaged in "manufactures, arts, and crafts," was much longer, including 16 cabinetmakers and carpenters, 7 shoemakers, and 4 turners, as well as a French shirtmaker and the Vissonni Quartet.

Despite the fact that the guide also mentioned five hotels and inns in Bogotá, the Comte de Gabriac, who visited the capital in the year of its publication, was not impressed by the city's offerings in this or any other respect. "To tell the truth," he wrote, "for weary travelers, a comfortable hotel is far more desirable than a magnificent monument, but in Bogotá there is neither one nor the other."[49] While it may not be surprising that the titled Frenchman found the city deficient in amenities, Colombian Miguel Samper called Bogotá the most backward capital in South America in a series of articles also written in 1867.[50] The streets were filthy, the water supply was poor, and nocturnal illumination came almost entirely from the moon. Public places were infested with thieves, drunkards, lepers, idlers, and even lunatics. Equally numerous were the beggars who insolently demanded alms and hurled abuse at those who refused. In fact, in 1876 Scruggs reported that when the archbishop of Bogotá had recently turned down a request for alms, the offended beggars had grabbed his robes and would have torn them off but for the timely intervention of bystanders. The incident, the minister observed, reflected the "insubordination" of the lower classes of the capital. "It is a very common thing here," he said, "when any of the peon class become offended with property owners or respectable citizens, to stone their residences; avenging themselves by breaking windows, furniture, stabbing horses, etc."[51] Such depredations, he added, normally went unpunished.

In a "Retrospect" written in 1896, when the population had probably reached 80,000, Samper reported that conditions had changed for the better: the sewage system had been improved, an aqueduct had been built, and electric lighting had been installed on many of the principal thoroughfares.[52] Charitable institutions had been founded to care for lepers, beggars, and lunatics. Samper was distressed, however, by the avarice, luxury, and dissipation which were also in evidence.

The increased affluence to which Samper and other writers referred in the late nineteenth century was made possible mainly by the traditional activities of commerce and agriculture, but the city also made a few gains in industry. According to a guide to Colombia published in 1907, by that date Bogotá boasted twelve breweries and five chocolate factories, as well as establishments for the manufacture of glass, earthenware, textiles, candles, soap, and cigarettes.[53] In addition, there were numerous mills, most of them powered by steam, which reportedly produced flour superior to that of the United States.

The savannah constituted the agricultural and pastoral hinterland of Bogotá. According to Colombian geographer Francisco Vergara y Velasco, at the end of the nineteenth century the savannah was controlled by only thirty landowners, one of whom owned 5,000 hectares of the best land.[54] The land, moreover, was not exploited to its full potential because of owner absenteeism, reliance on inept managers, and the use of outdated and inefficient methods. As a result, land on the savannah yielded an annual return of only 3 percent despite its high price.[55]

Native Bogotanos of the upper classes—landowners of the savannah who resided in the city, merchants, members of the professions, high government officials—were likely to be proud of their Castilian ancestry and of their literary talents, though such conceit as they possessed was sure to be tempered by their sardonic wit. Edouard André, a French traveler of the 1870s, found the Bogotanos to be extremely affable and gifted with a singular vivacity; their principal concern was to enrich themselves rapidly, as a result of which the only aristocracy was that of wealth.[56] According to Miguel Cané, who was the Argentine minister to Colombia in the 1880s, Bogotá was "a city of refined literary taste, of exquisite social civility, and [a place] where the most recent advances in learning are discussed as if in the bosom of a European academy."[57] Three of the French visitors in the second half of the nineteenth century, however, made a point of noting that Bogotá's pretensions to be considered the "New Athens" were somewhat exaggerated.[58]

Besides the elite, another visible segment of Bogotá society was made up of the artisans, whose political activities in the 1840s and 1850s were described in Chapter 1. Little is known about the artisans of Bogotá or other parts of Colombia in the second half of the century. It is generally believed that the low tariff policy introduced in 1846 had a deleterious effect on Colombian handicrafts, but we do not know what happened to the individuals displaced by foreign competition or whether the fate of artisans throughout the country was identical.

In Bogotá some manual workers continued to be perceived as artisans throughout the century, though the term was obviously used loosely. For example, an 1868 article in a newspaper founded to promote artisan interests claimed that they constituted two-thirds of the nation, while another article in the same organ held that at least 10 percent of Bogotá's inhabitants were artisans.[59] Still another article complained that anyone in Bogotá who wore a *ruana* or a frayed jacket was called an artisan, no distinction being made between working men and loafers.[60]

Ernst Röthlisberger, a Swiss professor who lived in Bogotá in the 1880s, believed that the city's artisans were predominantly Liberal, and it is true that they often figured prominently in Liberal politics, but there were Conservative artisans as well.[61] Both parties included among the individuals designated as electors in the presidential election of 1897 several men who could be classified as artisans, such as tailors, masons, and carpenters.[62]

It is also clear that leaders of both parties considered the Bogotá artisans to be of political value and often sought their endorsement of measures favored by party chiefs. Thus during a controversy in 1866 over the advisability of contracting a $7.5 million loan in England, both opponents and proponents of the transaction issued broadsides aimed at winning artisan support for their point of view. An opponent, for example, asked the artisans to imagine that Colombia was a poor tailor who wanted a sewing machine, a larger shop, and other improvements and was offered a loan of $7,500 at 6 percent; the tailor's enthusiasm for the loan, according to the author of the broadside, would soon be dampened by its many disadvantages, such as the fact that he would receive only $5,095 and that he would have to mortgage his rights to an expected inheritance from an uncle.[63]

Political leaders also courted the artisans by supporting the goals they espoused, such as protection of Colombian products from foreign competition and the establishment of schools for instruction in the manual arts, though cultivation of the artisans was not necessarily the only consideration prompting such support. Tomás Cipriano de Mosquera sought to curry the favor of Bogotá's artisans during his troubled presidency in 1866–67 by promising tariff reform, and in 1880 Rafael Núñez requested and obtained from Congress a bill providing for tariff protection. There does not appear to have been a mass defection of artisans from the Liberal party when Núñez cast his lot with the Conservatives in 1885. *El Taller,* a newspaper founded in 1887 in Bogotá and oriented toward artisan concerns, was a staunch defender of the new regime, but its editor, José L. Camacho, had been associated with the Conservative party for years. During their years in power in the second half of the century both parties established schools of arts and crafts in Bogotá and other cities which offered vocational training as well as basic education.

On occasion some artisans would complain of being manipulated by politicians who were interested primarily in achieving their own selfish

TABLE 4A

Presidential Voting, 1848 and 1856: Cundinamarca and Tolima

Cundinamarca, 1848[a]

Province	Liberal	Conservative	Other
Bogotá	108	130	4
Mariquita (La Palma canton)	13	0	0
Total	121	130	4

Cundinamarca, 1856[b]

Province	Liberal	Conservative	National
Bogotá	6,543	16,353	2,094
Mariquita (10 districts including La Palma)	1,279	443	22
Total	7,822	16,796	2,116

Tolima, 1848[a]

Province	Liberal	Conservative	Other
Mariquita (except La Palma)	45	21	1
Neiva	65	8	0
Total	110	29	1

Tolima, 1856[b]

Province	Liberal	Conservative	National
Mariquita (except districts attached to Cundinamarca and Antioquia)	3,200	4,687	64
Neiva (except districts attached to Cauca)	3,665	4,238	57
Total	6,865	8,925	121

[a]Electoral votes.
[b]Popular votes.

ends. This was one of the motives behind the foundation in 1866 of a society which sought the unification of all artisans regardless of party affiliation.[64] The difficulty of breaking party ties is shown by the fact that the president of the society, José L. Camacho, was a Conservative candidate for a seat in a Cundinamarca constituent assembly two years later.

In Cundinamarca and Tolima, as elsewhere, there was considerable occupational diversity among Liberals. A list of 91 Liberal officers (nearly all from these two states) taken prisoner in a Tolima town in 1900 during the War of the Thousand Days shows that 30 were merchants, 13 were farmers (*agricultores*), and 10 were artisans. The occupations of the remainder ranged from landowner (2) to lawyer (6) to photographer (1).[65] Of 205 Liberal soldiers captured at the same time, about half were farmers, and the rest day laborers, artisans, and cowboys.

The results of the presidential elections of 1848 and 1856 indicate that the Conservatives were in the majority in Cundinamarca, but that the two parties were evenly divided in Tolima (see Table 4A). The Conservative candidates were victorious in Cundinamarca on both occasions, but Tolima split its vote, preferring the Liberal in 1848 and the Conservative 8 years later. The areas of Liberal strength in both states emerge somewhat more clearly if the returns are examined on a provincial basis (see Table 4B). The state of Tolima was formed of the old province of Neiva and part of the province of Mariquita. The rest of Mariquita province, consisting of a lowland area bordering the Magdalena, was joined to the province of Bogotá to create the state of Cundinamarca. The Liberals did much better

TABLE 4B

Presidential Voting, 1848 and 1856
Provinces of Bogotá, Neiva, and Mariquita

Province	**1848**[a]	**1856**[b]
Bogotá	108 Liberal	6,543 Liberal
	130 Conservative	16,353 Conservative
	4 Other	2,094 National
Mariquita	58 Liberal	4,533 Liberal
	21 Conservative	5,086 Conservative
	1 Other	97 National
Neiva	65 Liberal	4,560 Liberal
	8 Conservative	4,393 Conservative
		57 National

[a]Electoral votes.
[b]Popular votes.

in the provinces of Mariquita and Neiva than they did in the province of Bogotá, for they were successful in both Mariquita and Neiva in 1848 and carried Neiva in 1856 while winning 46.6 percent of the vote in Mariquita. In the province of Bogotá, however, the Liberals were badly defeated in both elections.

TABLE 4C

Presidential Voting, 1848 and 1856: Selected Areas in Cundinamarca

Area	1848[a]	1856[b]
Bogotá	12 Liberal	671 Liberal
	35 Conservative	846 Conservative
		380 National
Cáqueza	8 Liberal	82 Liberal
	16 Conservative	144 Conservative
		0 National
Chocontá	2 Liberal	80 Liberal
	17 Conservative	589 Conservative
		9 National
Fusagasugá	6 Liberal	192 Liberal
	1 Conservative	45 Conservative
		101 National
Guaduas	13 Liberal	186 Liberal
	8 Conservative	73 Conservative
		123 National
Guatavita	2 Liberal	18 Liberal
	19 Conservative	402 Conservative
		4 National
La Mesa	9 Liberal	166 Liberal
	6 Conservative	162 Conservative
	1 Other	11 National
La Palma	13 Liberal	376 Liberal
	0 Conservative	43 Conservative
		0 National

[a]Electoral votes by canton.
[b]Popular votes by district.

It might also be noted that the same holds true for the capital city and its environs. In the canton of Bogotá the Liberals won 12 of the 47 electoral votes cast in 1848; eight years later they fared only slightly better in the district of Bogotá, capturing 671, or approximately 35 percent, of the 1,900 votes cast. On the other hand, the cantons of Fusagasugá, Guaduas, and La Mesa in the province of Bogotá had a Liberal majority or plurality in 1848, and the same was true of the districts of the same name in 1856. These were the only cantons and districts in the province about which this can be said. The canton of La Palma, part of Mariquita province in 1848 but transferred to Bogotá province by 1856, also returned a Liberal majority in both elections. Fusagasugá, Guaduas, La Mesa, and La Palma are all located on the western slopes of the Eastern Cordillera. Besides the national capital, there were three places in Bogotá province where the Conservatives won at least a plurality in both elections: Cáqueza, Chocontá, and Guatavita (see Table 4C). All three are highland towns not far from Bogotá.

Boyacá

The most populous state in the Colombian Union in the second half of the nineteenth century was Boyacá, which had 498,541 inhabitants in 1870. Most Boyacenses dwelled on the Andean plateaus of the western part of the state while the plains of Casanare to the east had but a small population. Boyacá was usually described as the state which contained the largest number of Indians, but it is not clear how Indians were identified in Boyacá or in any other part of Colombia. The criterion of language could not be used in central Colombia since indigenous languages had virtually disappeared by the end of the eighteenth century. No distinctive cultural traits were attributed to those regarded as Indians except that those of Boyacá and Cundinamarca were sometimes described as being taciturn and submissive, though suspicious of the whites who kept them in a serflike condition.[66]

Boyacá also had the dubious distinction of being considered the poorest state in the Union with respect to both government revenue and private wealth.[67] Two potential sources of income for the state—the salt works at Chita and the emerald mines at Muzo—were controlled by the federal government. Agriculture was confined primarily to the production of grains and other crops for local consumption while such manufactures as were made—woolen textiles and coverlets and the sisal sandals known as *alpargatas*—were also sold in local markets or in Bogotá.[68] A major reason for the poverty of Boyacá was the lack of outlets for its products. Felipe Pérez, later to be president of the state, pointed out in 1861 that the roads were wholly inadequate, especially during wet weather, and that the state lacked a port on the Magdalena as well as rivers in the populated areas.[69]

Evidence derived from the elections of 1848 and 1856 indicates that the Conservatives were preponderant among voters in the state as a whole, for Conservative candidates won majorities in both contests (see Table 5). However, Conservative strength appears to have lain primarily in the central highland regions of the state. Casanare gave a large majority to the Conservative candidates in 1848, but the results were reversed in 1856. The region of Chiquinquirá and Moniquirá in the western corner of the state, which had been detached from the province of Vélez, yielded Liberal majorities in both elections.

TABLE 5

Presidential Voting, 1848 and 1856: Boyacá

Province	1848[a] Liberal	Conservative	Other
Casanare	7	20	2
Tunja	66	153	11
Vélez (cantons of Moniquirá and Chiquinquirá)	28	11	0
Total	101	184	13

Province	1856[b] Liberal	Conservative	National
Casanare	2,410	173	263
Tundama	5,380	8,844	354
Tunja	3,221	17,726	1,078
Vélez (14 districts, including Moniquirá and Chiquinquirá)	1,802	1,123	126
Total	12,813	27,866	1,821

[a]Electoral votes.
[b]Popular votes.

Santander

The region which can be considered the bastion of Colombian Liberalism in the nineteenth century lay in northeastern Colombia, most of it being included in the state of Santander when it was founded in 1857. This region was the birthplace of several of the party's early leaders, among them Francisco de Paula Santander and Vicente Azuero, and, as will be seen in chapter 3, many Liberal chiefs of the second half of the century had close personal or political ties with the state. Not only did the Liberal candidates win by large majorities in Santander in the elections of 1848 and 1856, but Liberal strength was evident in all sections of the state (see Table 6). In 1848 the Liberal candidate won handily in the provinces of Pamplona and Socorro and in the cantons of Ocaña and Vélez, all of which became part of the state of Santander. Similarly, in 1856 the Liberal candidate was victorious in the provinces of Pamplona and Socorro and in the districts of Vélez that became part of Santander; only in the districts of Ocaña attached to Santander did the Liberal trail behind the Conservative candidate by a small margin.

The population of Santander, which totaled 433,178 in 1870, was composed primarily of whites and mestizos. During the colonial period the region that became the state of Santander developed two characteristics which distinguished it from most of the rest of New Granada. First, land was more equitably distributed, and large haciendas were rare.[70] Second, by the end of the eighteenth century southern Santander had become the center of a moderately complex cottage industry for the manufacture of coarse cotton textiles, an activity which had been carried on by the Guane Indians of the area before the Spanish conquest.[71] In fact, during the wars for independence, a Spanish officer dubbed Socorro, then the principal town of the region, the "Manchester of the Viceroyalty."[72] The textile

TABLE 6

Presidential Voting, 1848 and 1856: Santander

Province	1848[a] Liberal	Conservative	Other
Pamplona	65	25	3
Socorro	108	14	1
Ocaña (canton)	18	5	0
Vélez (canton)	49	1	0
Total	240	45	4

Province	1856[b] Liberal	Conservative	National
Pamplona	7,809	3,616	593
Socorro	6,511	5,909	267
Ocaña (14 districts)	548	596	157
Vélez (10 districts)	4,706	1,229	8
Total	19,574	11,350	1,025

[a]Electoral votes.
[b]Popular votes.

industry continued to flourish until at least the mid-nineteenth century, its products being converted into inexpensive clothing for the poor of Colombia and Venezuela.⁷³ It suffered a decline in the second half of the century as a result of the competition of foreign goods, but it was still of significance in the 1890s when an "industrial census" of Santander reported 5,800 spinning establishments (*hilanderías*) and 1,640 factories (*fábricas*) for the production of woolen and cotton textiles.⁷⁴

Another local industry of importance, introduced in the first quarter of the nineteenth century, was the weaving of hats from the nacuma palm.⁷⁵ The hats were sold internally and abroad, especially in Venezuela and the Antilles; in 1857–58 over 1.2 million were exported by way of Cúcuta, a Santander town near the Venezuelan border.⁷⁶ By the end of the century this industry had also suffered a decline, particularly with respect to exports, but according to the industrial census cited above, there were in existence in the 1890s 1,300 establishments for the production of hats.⁷⁷ Meanwhile, there had been expansion in the cottage manufacture of products of *fique* (*Agave americana L.*), such as sacks used as containers for coffee.⁷⁸

It has been suggested that some displaced textile workers in Santander turned to hatmaking in the mid-nineteenth century,⁷⁹ but in reality very little is known about the effects on the artisans of the decline in their industries. The matter is further complicated by the fact that the overwhelming majority of Santander's artisans were women who presumably worked to supplement the incomes of their husbands and fathers and were not wholly dependent on their earnings.⁸⁰ Female predominance among Santander's artisans may also explain why they were apparently more quiescent and of less political significance than the artisans of Bogotá.

After 1850 two new products—cinchona bark (*quina*) and coffee—emerged as major exports of Santander. The exploitation of cinchona bark, cut from trees on public lands near Socorro and Bucaramanga, first became of importance during the 1850s, with the value of exports reaching a peak of $860,000 in 1855–56.⁸¹ However, because Colombian bark was inferior in quality to that of Ecuador and Bolivia, it could command acceptable prices only when the latter was in short supply. Exports of bark from the Bucaramanga area experienced a short-lived resurgence in the 1870s during another period of scarcity, but the appearance of *quina* grown on Asian plantations destroyed the Colombian industry in the early 1880s.⁸²

Coffee proved to be a more durable export, both for Colombia and to a lesser extent for Santander. Before 1850 coffee was cultivated in Santander for local consumption only, but in the second half of the century rising prices and the encouragement and advice of coffee enthusiasts led to expanded production for export in various places in the state, especially in Cúcuta and Ocaña.⁸³ By the mid-1890s coffee had become Colombia's principal export and Santander was the principal growing area in the country.

The economic changes of the second half of the nineteenth century were accompanied by the decline of Socorro (which was supplanted as regional capital by Bucaramanga in 1886) and of southern Santander in general. The decadence of the south contrasted with the prosperity of the northern part of the state, which accounted for 79 percent of Colombia's coffee production in 1874. "By 1873 the differences between the north and south were notable. In Cúcuta and Ocaña, progress was revealed by the improvement of towns, the general aspect of the countryside, the movement of cargoes on the roads, the increase in public revenues, and the general satisfaction manifested by everyone."[84] Meanwhile, the growing gap between the two sections was deepened by the movement of capital from southern Santander to the north and by the exodus of laborers from the south attracted by the high wages paid in the coffee industry.

Colombian observers, as well as the few foreign travelers who visited Santander in the nineteenth century, invariably commented on the industry and frugality of the population. These traits, coupled with the pattern of land distribution, the existence of the cottage industries, and the racial homogeneity of the population, fostered the development of a society in which the sharp distinctions of class and race existing elsewhere in Colombia were blurred, though by no means obliterated. In such a society theories extolling individualism, political liberty, and economic progress, all of which were basic to nineteenth-century Colombian Liberalism, might receive a more favorable hearing than in other parts of the country, for here their acceptance would not involve so great a threat to the status quo. The Santandereano's desire for economic advancement through private initiative and resentment over government interference with this end can be seen as early as 1781 when anger over government controls on tobacco cultivation contributed to the Comunero uprising of that year in Socorro. These sentiments can also be detected in the instructions addressed to New Granada's delegate to the Central Junta of Spain and the Indies by the *cabildo* of Socorro in 1809.[85] Among the goals sought by the *cabildo* were the following: (1) distribution of the *resguardos* among the Indians, who would thereby become property owners exempt from tribute but subject to the same taxes as other inhabitants; (2) prohibition of the African slave trade and the eventual emancipation of the slaves, with some form of compensation to owners; (3) the encouragement of agriculture, commerce, and industry by the removal of political, physical, and moral obstacles to individual enterprise; (4) the opening of trade with friendly and neutral nations through all the ports of Spain and America; (5) a reduction in the number of religious holidays; (6) elimination of ecclesiastical levies, except for the tithe and first-fruits (*primicias*); and (7) the education of the young, not in those studies which "increase the sterile and burdensome classes of society but in the exact sciences and those which dispose men to the useful practice of all the arts." These goals clearly anticipate many of the policies advocated by Colombian Liberals later in the century and especially during the López administration.

Antioquia

Antioquia had perhaps the most uneven terrain in all of Colombia, being crossed from south to north by the Western and Central Cordilleras. As in Santander, the population, which totaled 365,974 in 1870, was composed mainly of whites and mixed-bloods. Antioquia also resembled Santander in that large landholdings were relatively rare.[86]

Descriptions of the Antioqueño's character often contained adjectives reminiscent of those applied to the Santandereano, and usually mentioned his business acumen, frugality, and "yankee"-style energy. Friedrich von Schenck, the German geographer who visited the state in 1878 and 1880, declared that "the Antioqueños are a strong, hard-working, and serious people; the future of Colombia belongs to them."[87] He was also struck by their large families, in which fifteen or twenty children were not uncommon, and by the "almost Puritanical" austerity of their customs. Von Schenck was not wide of the mark when he predicted the importance of Antioqueños in Colombia's future, for it was men from this region who spearheaded the industrialization of the nation in the twentieth century and dominated its economic life. Indeed, the economic supremacy of Antioquia, based on mining and domestic and foreign trade, had been established by the mid-nineteenth century.

The enterprise and industry of the Antioqueños have been traced to a number of sources: the Basque origins of many of the original settlers, the fact that they were forced to perform manual labor during the colonial period, and the inferiority allegedly attributed to the Antioqueños by other Colombians, which encouraged them to rebel against the traditional economic order. Perhaps the most convincing explanation for the economic leadership of Antioquia has been offered by Frank Safford, who argues that what enabled Antioqueños to emerge as Colombia's leading entrepreneurs was not their distinctive cultural or ethnic traits but their access to gold while the rest of the country was chronically starved for capital. Antioquia was Colombia's most important gold-producing region and is estimated to have accounted for over 46 percent of the gold mined in the country up to 1890.[88]

Another trait characteristic of the Antioqueño, one shared by the Santandereano, was his readiness to migrate in search of better lands. Toward the close of the eighteenth century Antioqueños began to migrate to the south and southwest of the original province of Antioquia. After founding agricultural settlements at Sonsón and Abejorral, they penetrated deep into Tolima and Cauca in a process that continued at least through the first half of the twentieth century.[89] Regardless of his place of residence, however, the Antioqueño preserved his identity as a member of a unique "race."

If Santander was the heartland of Liberalism, Antioquia was the most staunchly Conservative state in Colombia. Table 7A shows heavy Conservative majorities there in the presidential elections of 1848 and 1856. In 1848 the Liberals won only 17 percent of the electoral votes cast in the province of Antioquia and carried only two of the seven cantons in the province, Amalfi (Nordeste) and Rionegro. In 1856 they received less than 23 percent of the vote and won a majority in only 12 of the 76 districts into which Antioquia was then divided. Among the twelve were Amalfi and Rionegro (see Table 7B).

One of the principal conclusions to be derived from the foregoing survey is the heterogeneity of the Liberal party, both in terms of its regional bases and the socioeconomic origins of its adherents. Among those who adopted the name of Liberal were plantation owners of the upper Magdalena Valley, provincial lawyers, Bogotá artisans, and Panamanian blacks. The party's diversity inhibited internal discipline as well as the formulation and execution of coherent party programs. Even among upper-class Liberals goals and interests were rarely uniform.

TABLE 7A

Presidential Voting, 1848 and 1856: Antioquia

Province	1848[a] Liberal	Conservative	Other
Antioquia	28	134	0

Province	1856[b] Liberal	Conservative	National
Antioquia (state)	4,351	13,978	915
Nare (district in Mariquita province)	53	56	11
Total	4,404	14,034	926

[a]Electoral votes.
[b]Popular votes.

TABLE 7B

Presidential Voting, 1848 and 1856: Selected Areas in Antioquia

Area	1848[a]	1856[b]
Amalfi (Nordeste)	4 Liberal 1 Conservative	172 Liberal 41 Conservative 0 National
Antioquia	1 Liberal 30 Conservative	96 Liberal 221 Conservative 30 National
Marinilla	0 Liberal 12 Conservative	0 Liberal 392 Conservative 67 National
Medellín	5 Liberal 39 Conservative	261 Liberal 724 Conservative 34 National
Rionegro	15 Liberal 10 Conservative	719 Liberal 34 Conservative 13 National
Salamina	0 Liberal 22 Conservative	0 Liberal 331 Conservative 66 National
Santa Rosa de Osos	3 Liberal 18 Conservative	65 Liberal 514 Conservative 6 National

[a]Electoral vote by canton.
[b]Popular vote by district.

To be sure, many Liberal supporters from the nonelite, nonliterate segments of the population undoubtedly had but the dimmest comprehension of party programs or doctrines and merely followed the political lead of patrons or employers or embraced Liberalism because their neighbors did. This does not mean, however, that the experiences of such individuals, especially participation in civil war, did not create an emotional identification with Liberalism where none had existed or strengthen a previous commitment to the party. Ernst Röthlisberger, who witnessed the revolution of 1885, pointed out: "The majority do not fight in one party or another out of conviction but because they must avenge some atrocity.

This fellow's father was killed, that one's brother was impressed, the mother and sisters of another were abused; in the next revolution they will avenge these offenses."[90]

Despite the party's heterogeneity, a few uniformities do emerge. In general, lowland areas whose populations contained large numbers of blacks and mulattoes, such as the Cauca Valley and the Atlantic coast states, were likely to be Liberal or at least not strongly committed to Conservatism. In contrast, highland zones where the Indian strain predominated, such as the areas around Pasto, Bogotá, and Tunja (the capital of Boyacá), tended to be Conservative. In areas where class or racial conflict was exceptionally severe or frequent, the disadvantaged generally perceived themselves as Liberals; the targets of their anger were likely to be Conservatives though Liberals might be included as well.

In addition, regions characterized by economic innovation, particularly directed toward the development of commercial agriculture, were usually areas of Liberal strength. This is true of northern Tolima and western Cundinamarca, which were successively major producers of tobacco, indigo, and coffee. It is also true of Santander, another leader in coffee cultivation. In the Cauca Valley, Palmira was a Liberal stronghold as well as an important tobacco-growing area.

Of course, to suggest a positive correlation between Liberalism and economic enterprise in the nineteenth century in itself offers no insight into the nature of the relationship. Did identification with Liberalism stimulate the development of entrepreneurial qualities among nineteenth-century Colombians? Or were individuals already endowed with such qualities likely to be receptive to Liberalism?

A further complication is that the correlation between Liberalism and enterprise would appear to break down in the case of Antioquia, whose inhabitants became Colombia's most dynamic entrepreneurs yet originated in a region equally celebrated for its Conservatism. This apparent paradox suggests several possible explanations which deserve further investigation. A study of the political affiliations of Antioquia's chief capitalists in the nineteenth century might show that a disproportionate number were Liberals when compared with the Antioqueño population as a whole. Francisco Montoya and Gabriel Echeverri, both leading Antioqueño businessmen, were described by contemporaries as being Liberals, though neither was actively involved in politics.[91] Sinforoso García, a native of Santander who settled in Rionegro, was a prominent businessman and Liberal, as was Luciano Restrepo, who served as chief executive of the state from 1881 to 1885.[92] It is interesting to note in this connection that a historian of Pereira, which was founded in 1863 and settled mainly by Antioqueños, found that the city's ruling classes in the early twentieth century were predominantly Liberal, chiefly because they vaguely equated Liberalism with progress and change.[93]

A second possible explanation is suggested by the fact that, despite Antioquia's staunch Conservatism, party leaders from that state were frequently at odds with their brethren from other sections of the country. It was in Antioquia, for example, that the first rumblings of Conservative opposition to the Conservative-dominated Regeneration were heard in the 1880s, and Antioqueños remained in the vanguard of Conservative dissidence in the 1890s (see chapters 7 and 8). It can be argued, therefore, that Antioqueño Conservatives differed from their coreligionists elsewhere in several important ways, one of which may have been their attitude toward economic enterprise.

Finally, it is possible that, as Safford has suggested, entrepreneurial qualities were widely distributed among nineteenth-century Colombians[94] and were not significantly linked to political orientation. If this was the case, the fact that certain regions produced more successful economic innovators than others can be attributed to such factors as access to capital, labor, and markets rather than to the prevailing political sentiments of an area or of specific groups in that area. Similarly, under this hypothesis, economic innovators would find themselves as likely to be attracted to Conservatism as to Liberalism.

3
A Liberal Profile

This chapter gives the results of a survey of biographical data pertaining to over fifty Liberals who can be said to have constituted the party's elite between 1863 and 1885. By the examination of such data we can identify uniformities which may in turn yield insights into such matters as the origins of the leaders' affiliation with Liberalism and the extent to which the leadership was representative of Colombian society as a whole or only of a small segment of that society.

Several factors were considered of special importance in this analysis: regional origins, race, and family lineage and wealth. Regional origins were deemed of importance because of the sharp socioeconomic differences among the various sections of Colombia. A party whose leaders were predominantly from one or two regions might be expected to pursue goals and adopt methods different from one whose leaders were drawn equally from all sections of the country. Race, family lineage, and wealth were considered crucial in determining the socioeconomic status occupied by party leaders at birth. The education of party leaders, as well as the political views of their fathers, also received attention in the belief that these contributed significantly to the political formation of Liberal youths.

In nineteenth-century Colombia status was determined primarily by the acquisition or possession of wealth and by political or cultural distinction. To be sure, at least a modicum of education was required for success in any of these pursuits, and in a society where schooling was available only to a small fraction of the population, elites were likely to be drawn from the ranks of those already sufficiently favored to have access to education. There appears to have been no social bias in favor of land ownership, or any stigma attached to mercantile or industrial endeavors. A. LeMoyne, who represented France in Colombia from 1828 to 1839, was impressed by the fact that he saw Vicente Borrero, a member of a distinguished Cauca family, measuring and selling cloth in his Bogotá shop the day after he had resigned as minister of foreign affairs. According to philologist Rufino José Cuervo, his mother, the daughter of a high colonial official, earned money by selling bottles of vinegar.[1] The other main determinants of status were race and family lineage, probably in that order. Of course, race and family lineage were usually closely linked to wealth. A white youth of distinguished family was not likely to be impoverished, and even if he were, more fortunately situated relatives or friends would probably see to it that he received educational or employment opportunities that would serve to improve his economic condition.

The individuals who constituted the elite of Colombian Liberalism in the second half of the nineteenth century were primarily those who held state and national office while the party was in power. After 1885, when the Liberals lost control of the national government, many of the same men occupied the top positions in the party organizations that were established from time to time, though their ranks were augmented in the 1880s and 1890s by younger Liberals. Liberals might exert influence through means other than control of governmental or party machinery, but their efforts would be effective only insofar as they made an impression on government officials when Liberals were in power or on those men generally regarded as party leaders by the Liberal community. In short, Liberal leaders were mainly holders and seekers of public office.

A composite picture of the Liberal elite would ideally be based upon an examination of the personal histories of all the men who served as national or state presidents, members of Congress or state assemblies, or cabinet members during the years of Liberal hegemony from 1863 to 1885. However, the meagerness of accessible information about all of these figures precluded the accomplishment of such a task. The following is based, therefore, on biographical data about the eleven men who governed as Liberal presidents from 1863 to 1885—Tomás Cipriano de Mosquera (1863–64, 1866–67), Manuel Murillo Toro (1864–66, 1872–74), Santos Acosta (1867–68), Santos Gutiérrez (1868–70), Eustorgio Salgar (1870–72), Santiago Pérez (1874–76), Aquileo Parra (1876–78), Julián Trujillo (1878–80), Rafael Núñez (1880–82, 1884–85), Francisco J. Zaldúa (1882–83), José Eusebio Otálora (1883–84)—and over fifty men who held other important posts in the executive and legislative branches of the national and state governments, as well as a few notable primarily for their intellectual influence. Liberals who first achieved prominence after 1885 will be touched upon only marginally here.

If regional origins are considered, Colombia's nineteenth-century Liberals tended to come from the eastern half of the country—that is, from the areas that later comprised the states of Santander, Cundinamarca, and Boyacá—and also from Tolima. Of the eleven Liberal presidents mentioned in the preceding paragraph, seven were born in the three eastern states (Acosta, Gutiérrez, and Otálora, Boyacá; Salgar, Pérez, and Zaldúa, Cundinamarca; and Parra, Santander), one (Manuel Murillo) was born in Tolima, and only three in other parts of the country (Mosquera and Trujillo in Cauca, and Rafael Núñez in Bolívar). The latter three, it should be noted, were atypical in that Mosquera and Trujillo did not join the party until long after they had reached maturity while Núñez eventually repudiated most of his early Liberal comrades and allied himself permanently with the Conservatives. A similar picture emerges if the regional origins of fifteen of eighteen Liberals who served in the cabinet from 1870 to 1875 are examined. Santander was represented by four, Cundinamarca by three, Boyacá and Bolívar by two each, and Cauca and Panama by one each; two others were each closely identified with two states, Cundinamarca and Santander in one case, and Cundinamarca and Tolima in the other.[2]

A Liberal Profile

The fact that only a relatively small number of Liberal leaders came from western Colombia (Antioquia and Cauca) or from the coastal region (Bolívar, Magdalena, and Panama) can be attributed to various causes. The eastern states, especially Santander and Tolima, were areas of Liberal strength in contrast to Antioquia and Cauca, many of the Liberal leaders in Cauca being men who had followed Mosquera into the party in 1859–60. With his deposition from the presidency in 1867 by Liberals of the so-called Radical wing, most of his supporters, regardless of their place of origin, were temporarily excluded from major positions in the federal government. The scanty representation accorded to the Coast reflected the tendency of national leaders of both parties to slight the interests and spokesmen of that region, a condition which contributed to a split in the Liberal party before the election of 1875.

The regional bias in favor of eastern Colombia is even more marked if only Radicals are considered. In a book called *El Olimpo Radical,* Eduardo Rodríguez Piñeres included a list of those Liberals whom he considered members of this group.[3] As its chief luminaries he named Manuel Murillo, Aquileo Parra, Santiago and Felipe Pérez, Felipe Zapata, Nicolás Esguerra, Luis A. Robles, and Eustorgio Salgar, along with Francisco J. Zaldúa and Florentino González, whom he called "the Precursor." He also mentioned twenty-four others who he said always remained faithful to Radicalism: Santos Acosta, Francisco Eustaquio Alvarez, Narciso Cadena, Sergio Camargo, Eugenio Castilla, Gil Colunje, César Conto, Tomás Cuenca, Gabriel González Gaitán, Bernardo Herrera, Antonio María Pradilla, Luciano Restrepo, Medardo Rivas, Rafael Rocha Castilla, Rafael Rocha Gutiérrez, Carlos Nicolás Rodríguez, Francisco de Paula Rueda, Januario Salgar, Jacobo Sánchez, Vicente Uscátegui, Germán Vargas, Florentino Vezga, José María Villamizar Gallardo, and Dámaso Zapata. Finally, he listed five besides Zaldúa who initially supported Rafael Núñez but soon returned to the Radical fold: Pablo Arosemena, Salvador Camacho Roldán, Clímaco Iriarte, Miguel Samper, and Teodoro Valenzuela.

Rodríguez Piñeres, a law partner of Nicolás Esguerra in the 1890s and the leading Colombian historian (and defender) of the Radical wing of Liberalism, was well qualified to compile such a list. The principal objection that can be made to it is that it implies a uniformity of behavior and importance over several decades that did not exist. Florentino González, for example, lived in Chile and Argentina from 1860 until his death in 1875; by the earlier date he had ended his association with Colombian Liberalism and in 1867, according to a Liberal journalist, he was even being mentioned as a possible Conservative candidate for the presidency.[4] In any event, he took no part in Colombian politics after the 1850s. Zaldúa's inclusion among the top Radical leaders can be faulted because he was not active politically between 1863 and his election to the presidency in 1882 and because he was an early supporter of Núñez. Much the same can be said of Eustorgio Salgar and Santos Acosta: while they frequently worked with the Radicals, they were by no means identified exclusively with this wing of the party. On the other hand, Rodríguez Piñeres's list excludes no prominent Radical, nor did any person mentioned ally himself permanently with Núñez and the Independent Liberals.

All but one of the thirty-nine men on Rodríguez Piñeres's list could be identified with a single state on the basis of birth or long-term residence. The results were as follows: Santander, 12; Cundinamarca, 9; Tolima, 8; Boyacá, 3; Panama, 2; Cauca, 2; Magdalena, 1; Antioquia, 1.[5] The preponderance of Santandereanos becomes even more striking when it is noted that several Radicals who were born elsewhere had close political or personal ties with that state. Teodoro Valenzuela, for example, was born in Cauca, but his father was a native of Santander.[6] Similarly, Santos Acosta, who was born in Boyacá, was the son of a Santandereano, and his great-grandfather, Juan Francisco Berbeo, played a major role in the Comunero uprising in Socorro in 1781.[7] Others became involved in Santander politics. Manuel Murillo, though a native of Tolima, was president of the state from 1857 to 1859. Eustorgio Salgar, whose birthplace is given both as Cundinamarca and Santander, divided his political career between the two states and served as president of both. Salgar was also a delegate to the Santander constituent assembly that drew up the controversial state constitution of 1857, as was Francisco J. Zaldúa, who was a native of Cundinamarca. In short, Santander, which was the cradle of Colombian Liberalism, was also the "metropolis of Radicalism," as Rafael Núñez put it.[8] Conversely, Santander provided few adherents for anti-Radical Liberals such as Núñez and Mosquera.

It is difficult to determine the racial makeup of the Liberal leadership since nineteenth-century Colombians rarely mentioned the racial characteristics of specific individuals, at least in writing. Foreigners were more likely to make comments on this subject, but the accuracy of their observations may be vitiated by prejudice or by ignorance of racial subtleties. One foreign observer, United States Minister Allan A. Burton, indicated in 1866 that Colombia's leading office-holders were of mixed racial background: "Many mulattoes hold office, also a few negroes and Indians. The present supreme court is composed of two members in which white blood is in the ascendant; one mestizo about half and half; one three-fourths negro, and one pure Indian. The other officers of the government are generally mixed. A late attorney general was a pure negro. The present, as all other congresses, is an indefinite mixture with a few pure whites."[9] On the other hand, Ernst Röthlisberger, the Swiss professor residing in Colombia from 1882 to 1885, remarked that the highest offices were, with few exceptions, monopolized by whites and mestizos.[10] According to Röthlisberger, only a few Indians had attained important positions in government; among these he cited Daniel Aldana, a former Liberal governor of Cundinamarca, who he said was universally known as "el indio Aldana," and the influential Cauca chieftain Eliseo Payán, who was known by a similar epithet. However, the same name was also applied to Juan de Dios Uribe, an Antioqueño journalist who came to prominence after 1885, and there is little evidence that he was an Indian.

In the coastal states and other areas with large black and mulatto populations, it is probable that at least some of the local leaders were of African ancestry. In 1883 the United States consul in Barranquilla found considerable racial mixture in the elites of that coastal city: "The foremost men in the mercantile, political, and literary circles are from the old Castillian families, but so changed by intermarriage, that all bloods run in their veins. In the Legislature, on the Forum or the bench, and behind the bankers desk, you will see the characteristics of all the races, from the Anglo-Saxon to the African."[11] It will also be recalled that the British consul in Panama in the 1860s stated that public offices there were filled almost entirely by "coloured or black men," who tended to be Liberals.[12] Luis A. Robles, the only Liberal of national reputation who was frequently described as being nonwhite, was a native of Magdalena. According to one contemporary, he was a black-Indian mestizo.[13]

The socioeconomic origins of the members of the Liberal elite were varied, though none of them is known to have been born of a family from the lowest stratum. Some were descended from families that had achieved distinction for wealth or public service during the colonial period. Both parents of Rafael Núñez were descendants of Francisco García del Fierro, a native of Cartagena who served as *oidor* (judge) of the *audiencia* (royal tribunal) of Puebla, Mexico, in the 1770s.[14] Medardo Rivas was the grandson of Don Juan de Rivas y Torre, a Spaniard who came to New Granada about 1714 and made a fortune in gold mining and trade besides holding various government positions.[15] According to Rivas, his forebears had owned three haciendas near Bogotá as well as gold mines in the Chocó and property in the hot country of the Magdalena Valley.[16] Even more impressive were the antecedents of Tomás Mosquera, who could trace his lineage to the nobility of medieval Spain and whose ancestors had been among the sixteenth-century settlers of New Granada.[17] At least one Liberal was the son of a father who had prospered in the early national period. The one-eyed journalist Camilo A. Echeverri was the son of Gabriel Echeverri, a wealthy merchant and agricultural entrepreneur from Antioquia who had begun life as a gold miner and peddler.[18]

The other end of the socioeconomic spectrum was represented by a number of Liberal leaders who came from families described as insignificant or impecunious or both. The Liberal firebrand from Tolima, José María Rojas Garrido, was said by a contemporary to have been a member of a poor and obscure family and to have begun his education in a second-rate elementary school.[19] José María Samper reported in his autobiography that his grandfather had lived and died in poverty and that his legacy to his son, the father of the Samper brothers, had consisted of a cot and two empty trunks.[20] It is noteworthy that four of the leading Radicals came from backgrounds of this type. The father of Manuel Murillo is said to have earned a meager livelihood by practicing medicine, though he lacked a professional degree, and was able to send his son to the university only at great financial sacrifice.[21] Aquileo Parra described his father and uncles as modest Santander farmers.[22] The parents of Santiago and Felipe Pérez were described by Felipe's son as being poor but distinguished.[23] According to a later biographer, the Pérez brothers' father, a farmer from Boyacá, was the lessee of a piece of land near Zipaquirá (Cundinamarca) at the time of Santiago's birth in 1830.[24]

It is evident, however, that lack of wealth did not prevent some of these Liberal fathers from being regarded as persons of status and influence in their communities. Murillo's father is said to have been a voracious reader of the works of Rousseau and Voltaire and a skillful politician who had helped to make Chaparral (Tolima), the younger Murillo's birthplace, a Liberal stronghold.[25] In his memoirs Parra indicated that his father and uncles were numbered among the *gente decente,* or gentry, of their Santander community, partly because of their prestigious relatives.[26] And despite his paltry inheritance and the fact that his education was rudimentary, the father of José María and Miguel Samper became a provincial governor.[27]

The political views of the fathers of all the Liberal leaders could not be ascertained, but the partial information available suggests that the majority were Liberals or were sympathetic to causes later identified with Liberalism. Several, among them the fathers of Salvador Camacho Roldán and César Conto, suffered exile or imprisonment for their complicity in the revolution of 1839–42 against the Márquez government, and the father of Aníbal Galindo, José María Tadeo Galindo, was executed in 1841 after being captured in battle.[28] An exception was Lieutenant Colonel Francisco Núñez, the father of Rafael Núñez, who distinguished himself for his services on behalf of Márquez and emerged from the conflict with the rank of colonel and an appointment to an important military post in Panama.[29] It is interesting to note, however, that the teen-aged Núñez joined the forces of the rebel general Francisco Carmona.

Most of the Liberal leaders had a similar educational background. They ordinarily attended elementary schools near their homes and were later sent to Bogotá or to a regional capital for their secondary and professional education. Since Colombian women tended to be extremely devout, a Liberal father might occasionally be induced by wifely pressure to send his sons to Catholic primary schools despite his own preference for a less sectarian education for his offspring. The fact that José María Samper's mother was a pious Catholic while his father was a freethinker may have accounted for his being enrolled in 1838 in a secondary school in Bogotá operated by José Manuel Groot, a historian and polemicist noted for his refutation of Ernest Renan's life of Jesus.[30] Miguel Samper, José María's older brother, also attended Groot's school, as did Teodoro Valenzuela, who later complained that he had learned practically nothing and had been mistreated by both teachers and pupils.[31] An outstanding private educational establishment in Bogotá was the Colegio del Espíritu Santo (1846–52, 1867–68), founded by Lorenzo María Lleras, a Liberal, where two future presidents, Santiago Pérez and Santos Acosta, were educated. Santiago and Felipe Pérez came to the attention of Lleras when he visited a public school in Zipaquirá attended by the two boys.[32] Impressed by their ability, he arranged for their enrollment at the publicly supported Colegio del Rosario, where he was rector from 1842 to 1846, and later at his own school. In 1855 Felipe Pérez married one of Lleras's daughters. One of the better known provincial schools was the Colegio de Santa Librada in Cali, which was attended by several Cauca Liberals, including César Conto and Eliseo Payán. During the 1840s the rector was Juan Nepomuceno Núñez Conto, a first cousin of Nicomedes Conto, César's father.

After spending a year at Groot's school, José María Samper entered the government-operated Colegio de San Bartolomé, where he was awarded a doctorate in jurisprudence in November 1846 after taking a two-hour examination in such subjects as civil and criminal procedure and canon law; the following April he passed a five-hour examination before the Supreme Court and was admitted to the bar.[33] A similar course was followed by most of the nineteenth-century Liberal leaders, nearly all of whom were lawyers. Most of those who had not received legal training were physicians, among them Santos Acosta and Antonio Vargas Vega; at least one, Modesto Garcés, was an engineer. The Liberal leader who probably had the smallest amount of formal education was Aquileo Parra. Left fatherless at the age of thirteen during a period of economic depression in Santander, he was forced to leave school and thereupon embarked upon a mercantile career.[34] Another Liberal president with limited schooling was Santos Gutiérrez. According to the American minister in Bogotá, Gutiérrez had had "but little education; and but little or no experience in, or knowledge of the Science of government."[35]

Although only a few Liberals, such as Manuel Murillo and Rafael Núñez, were old enough to have participated in the revolution of 1839–42, a much larger proportion of the Liberal generation studied here was directly affected by the revolution that began in 1859. Several, notably Julián Trujillo, Santos Acosta, and Santos Gutiérrez, acquired military laurels by their exploits on the battlefield. Those who did not take up arms supported the Liberal cause through the press or as officeholders in areas under Liberal control. For all who took part in this and other conflicts there were genuine risks. After a Liberal defeat at El Oratorio in Santander on 16 August 1860, virtually the entire Liberal leadership of the state was captured and imprisoned in Bogotá. The party lost several distinguished leaders during the war, the most notable being José María Obando, who was killed after being taken prisoner during a skirmish on the Bogotá savannah in 1861.

Even those too young to participate might have vivid memories of the civil wars of the nineteenth century. Fathers or other relatives might suffer imprisonment or even death. José María Quijano Wallis, who was born in 1848, recalled that in 1861 he and other students in a school in Popayán were compelled by the Conservative director to witness the execution of twenty Liberal prisoners so that the youths might develop a horror for the "reds."[36] Boys from seven to twelve years of age formed Liberal and Conservative "armies" in Bogotá during the revolution of 1876–77.[37] Armed with stones and metal-tipped sticks, they fought battles on Sunday afternoons, took prisoners, and sometimes sustained real casualties. Because of the lasting impact of such experiences, most nineteenth-century Liberals would probably have agreed with the writer who observed: "The memories of the men of Colombia are always tied to revolutions. To determine someone's age, it is enough to ask him which is the earliest civil war he remembers."[38]

Biographies of the Liberal leaders indicate that they made the transition from student to politician and public servant without great difficulty, their path often being smoothed by influential relatives and patrons. The career of Rafael Núñez, for example, was advanced by his marriage to Dolores Gallegos, who was the sister-in-law of José de Obaldía, the powerful Panamanian landowner and politician.[39] Manuel Murillo reportedly launched the political career of Nicolás Esguerra by securing his election to the state assembly of Santander and to Congress as a representative from the same state. As a young man, Murillo himself had been befriended by Esguerra's grandfather, Saturniano Ortiz, who was the patron of the future president while the latter attended secondary school in Ibagué.[40]

It is difficult to determine the reasons that led young Colombians to seek political careers. They were undoubtedly influenced by the fact that by the time they had reached their early twenties they were likely to have been highly politicized through exposure to the ideas of their fathers and relatives and their residence as students in regional capitals or in Bogotá, center of the nation's political life. Moreover, the young Liberal's commitment to his party would be reinforced by any experiences he might have undergone in the civil wars of the period.

In addition, many young graduates were probably impelled to seek public office because of the nature of their education and because of the lack of other remunerative employments of equal prestige in Colombia's sluggish economy. Contemporaries frequently averred that this was the case:

A Liberal Profile

> The higher classes of Bogotá are in general well educated, but their education is of a theoretical rather than a practical kind, unfortunately conducing mainly to render them apt at controversy, more especially on questions connected with politics, religion, and literature.
>
> Sources of profitable occupation are scanty, and, excepting trade . . . and the cultivation of the cold and temperate lands in the vicinity of the city, the remainder of the educated classes depend chiefly for a support on teaching or on political employments, the competition for which imbitters [sic] party strife in an extraordinary degree.[41]

Political careers would seem doubly attractive to those young men who came from relatively impoverished backgrounds and could not look forward to deriving an adequate livelihood from family landholdings and businesses.

On the other hand, it is virtually impossible to assess the extent to which such considerations influenced specific individuals since they were hardly likely to acknowledge motivations of this type. It should also be kept in mind that most of the Liberal leaders combined politics with one or more other activities, such as teaching or business ventures of various kinds.

There were, of course, some Liberal leaders who apparently depended almost exclusively on public employment for their livelihood. One of these was Manuel Murillo, who appears to have been in public service almost continuously from the 1830s. According to Eduardo Rodríguez Piñeres, he had little interest in money and left an exiguous estate at the time of his death in 1880.[42] An effort with a partner to launch a hacienda near Bogotá failed, and he was equally unsuccessful with a small coffee tract near Guaduas which he called "Túsculo" after Cicero's villa.[43]

Like Murillo, Rafael Núñez was also a full-time public servant as well as a wily political manipulator, though the two men differed in most other respects. Unlike Murillo, the frail, blue-eyed Cartagenero was a versifier of some competence and was notorious for his romantic entanglements. These ended, however, after his civil marriage in 1877 to Soledad Román, the forty-one-year-old daughter of a Cartagena pharmacist.[44]

Núñez is said to have been a wealthy man by the mid-1870s, with assets consisting of $100,000 in cash and stock in the Suez Canal.[45] If this account is to be believed, he must have experienced losses or spent lavishly in subsequent years, for an inventory of his property prepared after his death in 1894 indicated that his assets were considerably less, consisting mainly of $15,000 in paper currency; $17,000 in paper lent to three different individuals, with real estate as security; ten shares worth $4,000 in the Banco Internacional de Bogotá; 330 shares worth £330 in a Chilean mining company; and 1,314 gold francs in an account with Fould Frères of Paris.[46] Núñez supposedly amassed his fortune while serving as Colombian consul in Europe from 1866 to 1874, during which time most of the fees collected went to make up his salary, and he was a correspondent for *El Comercio* of

Lima.⁴⁷ However, soon after taking up the consulship in LeHavre in 1866, Núñez complained that the position had turned out to be "much ado about nothing" as far as a financial return was concerned.⁴⁸

Despite his reputed indifference to financial matters, Murillo was listed as one of the stockholders in the Compañía Colombiana de Seguros when it was founded in 1874.⁴⁹ Indeed, any list of investors in a new enterprise invariably included the names of Liberal politicians. When the first bank in Santander was founded in 1872, for example, the stockholders included Parra & Company of Vélez and several Liberals active in state and national politics: Nicolás Esguerra, Vicente Uscátegui, and Victoriano de Diego Paredes, to name a few.⁵⁰ Similarly, among the investors in the Patriotic Society of the Magdalena, established in 1872 to promote the construction of a railroad from Santa Marta to the Magdalena River, were several prominent Liberals, including Manuel Abello.⁵¹ The latter was a Santa Marta businessman who had been a founder in the 1840s of the first Colombian company to provide regular steam navigation on the Magdalena.⁵² He was also an important political figure with close ties to Murillo, who appointed him secretary of war during his second presidential term. Although Liberal politicians were most likely to invest in ventures in the fields of commercial agriculture, transportation, and banking, they did not completely ignore industrial enterprise. For example, Julio Barriga, who served as governor of Cundinamarca from 1870 to 1873, invested in an ironworks at La Pradera (Cundinamarca), which was producing over four tons of iron a day in 1884.⁵³ A few others were merchants and commission agents, such as Narciso González Lineros, whose wares ranged from agricultural implements to wines, and José María Samper, who advertised in 1867 that with his brother and partner Silvestre he purchased coffee, cinchona bark, and gold dust, and sold a variety of articles, including fabrics, buttons, and matches.⁵⁴

Of those Liberals who combined politics and business, the most prominent was Aquileo Parra—senator, cabinet member, president of the Union, and Liberal party head in the 1890s. Parra began his commercial career in 1845 when he made the first of a series of long and uncomfortable trips from Vélez (Santander) to Magangué (Bolívar), site of an annual fair, by way of the Carare River.⁵⁵ At Magangué he sold the sweets known as *bocadillos veleños* for cash or foreign products.

Parra later regretted having made Vélez the center of his commercial enterprises, for the town produced few saleable items besides the *bocadillos*, but by 1855 he had amassed "a small capital" that made further trips to Magangué unnecessary. After attending the Rionegro convention as a delegate from Santander, he decided to take advantage of the markets for Colombian cotton created by the civil war in the United States. He began buying up cotton produced near Vélez, which he ginned on his own equipment and exported by way of Honda. Although he was able to export only a small amount of cotton—a total of fifty bales of five *arrobas* each—his profits from the venture enabled him to recoup losses suffered during the recent revolution, establish a new firm, and take a trip abroad. Later Parra would become increasingly, though reluctantly, involved in politics despite the demands of his business interests.[56]

Salvador Camacho Roldán was another influential Liberal who was a businessman as well as a politician. In the 1850s he and his younger brother José developed a piece of property they owned in the hot country of Cundinamarca into a valuable hacienda called "Utica," which Salvador still owned in 1891.[57] While serving as secretary of finance under Eustorgio Salgar, Salvador encouraged the establishment of the Banco de Bogotá, and the firm of Camacho Roldán Hermanos held $2,500 of the bank's stock when it was founded in 1870.[58] In 1882 he established a commission house with his sons and others, and in 1890 he founded a bookstore called the Librería Colombiana.[59] Despite his extensive enterprises, Camacho Roldán described himself in 1884 as a "mere proletarian" who had to earn his own livelihood.[60] Although he was a delegate to the Rionegro convention, sat in Congress on several occasions, and served in the cabinet under Presidents Salgar and Trujillo, he never attained the presidency. At the age of sixty-four he delivered an embittered epitaph to his career in politics, to which he said he had devoted forty-three years of his life at considerable financial sacrifice and which he was now determined to quit. Politics, he said, is like an old painted cocotte, "fickle and unfaithful, that demands everything without giving anything in return to those of us who are not ravishers by profession."[61]

The Liberal elite also included a few men, like Nicolás Pereira Gamba and Miguel Samper, whose business activities overshadowed their political services. In 1852 Pereira Gamba, who was a member of a distinguished Cauca family, established Pereira Gamba and Company, which offered a variety of services ranging from the handling of freight on the Magdalena to the purchase and sale of letters of exchange. By 1872 branches had been opened in Honda, Barranquilla, and New York. In the 1860s he expanded his interests, importing agricultural and industrial machinery, tools, seeds, and other foreign goods which were displayed at his *quinta-modelo,* or model farm, at Paiba on the outskirts of Bogotá. That this venture was less than a complete success is indicated by the fact that in order to finance a trip abroad in 1871 he was forced to hold a lottery in which the prizes were the machines he had imported earlier but had been unable to sell.[62] In Europe Pereira Gamba familiarized himself with recent advances in industrial technology, and in Sweden he studied the problems of railroad construction in mountainous terrain, later being named Swedish consul in Colombia.[63]

Like Pereira Gamba, Miguel Samper was primarily a businessman rather than a politician. After practicing law briefly in the firm of Ezequiel Rojas,

Samper left Bogotá for the Magdalena Valley to engage in commerce and agriculture with his father and his brothers Silvestre, Antonio, and Manuel during the boom years of the 1850s. In 1855 Miguel and his associates paid $47,000 for a plantation called "La Unión" near Guaduas, where in a fruitless effort to improve the prevailing system of tobacco cultivation they permitted their tenants to sell their crops on the open market instead of to the landowners as custom dictated. Upon Samper's return to Bogotá in 1858, he founded a new firm with Manuel and was later joined by Manuel Ancízar, who was married to the Sampers' sister Agripina.[64] When the Banco de Bogotá was organized in 1870, Samper and Company was one of the largest stockholders, with an investment of $10,000, and Miguel was made an officer of the bank.[65] Although Samper was a frequent and influential contributor to the Liberal press, he rarely held high public office, no doubt because of his independence of mind and readiness to criticize his fellow Liberals. His nomination to the presidency in 1897 was a tribute to his stature among Liberals and other Colombians, but it was known that he had virtually no chance of winning the election.

For many nineteenth-century Liberals a career in politics involved not only the quest for public office but also editing or contributing to Liberal newspapers and serving as an instructor in educational institutions where Liberal doctrine was taught. Journalism, it should be pointed out, rarely brought any financial profit to the publisher or editor of a Liberal newspaper unless, as in the case of Medardo Rivas, he owned a printing plant where other publications, especially those issued by the government, could be produced. In 1879 Felipe Pérez informed Parra that he had suspended publication of *El Relator*, a leading Bogotá newspaper of which he was editor, because it cost him fifty pesos to publish each issue.[66] Liberals wanted to read it gratis or were unwilling to pay for their subscriptions, he complained, while most disagreed with his opinions anyhow. Two years later José Benito Gaitán described to Parra his unsuccessful efforts to reorganize the *Diario de Cundinamarca,* of which he was publisher, as a corporation so as to reduce the burden on himself and editor Florentino Vezga, who could no longer work without remuneration; but he had met with only a lukewarm response from fellow Liberals.[67]

Since Colombians of both parties tended to regard the country's public and private institutions of learning as vehicles for the dissemination of political ideology, the official secondary schools and the universities became a Liberal preserve during the era of Liberal domination, with Liberals monopolizing teaching and administrative posts. The intensity and duration of an individual's commitment to education varied, of course. Among those Liberals for whom teaching was a lifetime career, perhaps the most highly respected was Ezequiel Rojas, who taught courses in legislation and political economy at the Colegio de San Bartolomé for over forty years, molding the intellects of two generations of Liberal youth. Rojas himself had been taught by Francisco Soto and Vicente Azuero, two of the party's founders.[68] A few Liberals opened private schools, such as the Colegio de Pérez Hermanos, founded in 1857 by Santiago and Felipe Pérez and another brother, Rafael.[69]

Colombia's Liberal leaders were linked to each other not only by political and economic bonds but also by kinship ties produced by intermarriage among members of prominent Liberal families. These ties, often spanning several generations, may be seen very clearly in the family of Salvador Camacho Roldán. One of his sisters was the first wife of Nicolás Pereira Gamba, and another was married to Antonio Vargas Vega, for many years rector of the Colegio de San Bartolomé. In 1859 Salvador married Carmen Tamayo; one of their sons, Gabriel, became the husband of a daughter of Liberal general Gabriel Reyes Patria. Salvador's brother José, who was also active in politics, was the father of two Liberal journalists, José and Guillermo Camacho Carrizosa, who attained prominence toward the close of the century. José Camacho Carrizosa married María Luisa Lorenzana López, granddaughter of President José Hilario López, while one of her sisters became the wife of Juan Evangelista Manrique, a physician who was head of the Liberal party in Cundinamarca in the 1890s.[70]

Kinship ties among Liberals were likely to strengthen their political identity and to make affiliation with Liberalism a part of the family tradition to be passed on to future generations. Indeed, such ties may have led Liberals to assume a proprietary attitude toward the party and enabled their sons, nephews, and sons-in-law, already favored by wealth or education, to preempt positions of importance within it. Aquileo Parra appears to have been childless, but his nephew Vicente acted as his representative in Santander at the end of the century. Of forty Liberals (most of them political veterans) appointed to a party advisory council in 1897, at least three were sons or nephews of older leaders: Eladio C. Gutiérrez, the son of Santos Gutiérrez; Diego Mendoza Pérez, a nephew of Santiago and Felipe Pérez and son-in-law of the latter; and José Camacho Carrizosa, nephew of Salvador Camacho Roldán, who was also a member of the council.

To be sure, not all of the Liberal leaders married into Liberal families or produced Liberal offspring. Medardo Rivas, for example, married a daughter of José Manuel Groot; their son, José María Rivas Groot, became a well-known Conservative statesman and man of letters. Bernardo Herrera, a delegate to the Rionegro convention, became the husband of a daughter of Conservative historian José Manuel Restrepo; one of their sons, Bernardo Herrera Restrepo, was archbishop of Bogotá from 1891 to 1928.[71] It was also possible for brothers to differ in their political views. Of the five Palau brothers of Cauca, two were lifelong Liberals, two were lifelong Conservatives, and one shifted from Conservatism to Liberalism during the revolution of 1859–62.[72]

In order to enhance its sharpness, a profile of the Liberal leadership should be compared with a Conservative profile drawn along similar lines. Although information about nineteenth-century Conservative leaders has not been gathered in the same quantity as for their Liberal counterparts, a few generalizations may be advanced. For purposes of this discussion, Conservatives who held important positions in party organizations and in the two states (Antioquia and Tolima) under Conservative control during the era of Liberal dominance are considered party leaders.

If regional origins are considered, two states—Cundinamarca and Cauca—appear to have provided a disproportionate number of party leaders. This can be illustrated by the fact that two of the four Conservatives who occupied the presidency between 1885 and 1903 were from Cundinamarca—Miguel Antonio Caro and José Manuel Marroquín—while the other two—Carlos Holguín and Manuel A. Sanclemente—were from Cauca. As in the case of the Liberals, few of the Conservative leaders came from the Coast. The Conservative stronghold of Antioquia produced many notable Conservative politicians, but the region was underrepresented in national party councils. Thus, of nineteen party officers in 1879 and 1883 whose place of birth is known or who could be identified with a single state, seven were from Cundinamarca, four from Cauca, two each from Antioquia, Santander, and Tolima, and one each came from Bolívar and Boyacá.[73]

In general Conservative leaders were more likely than Liberals to be descended from families that had attained distinction during the colonial era. Sergio Arboleda and his brother Julio, for example, were descended from a seventeenth-century Spanish lawyer (*letrado*) who enriched himself through mining and settled in Popayán; his grandson, Francisco Antonio Arboleda (1732–93), established a *mayorazgo* (entailed estate) consisting of one of the finest residences in Popayán, a hacienda, and a salt mine, all of these properties being inherited by Sergio and Julio.[74] At least two Conservative leaders, Ignacio Gutiérrez Vergara and José Manuel Marroquín, were direct descendants of Francisco Antonio Moreno y Escandón, state attorney (*fiscal*) of the *audiencias* of Santa Fe de Bogotá and Lima and judge of the former in the eighteenth century.[75]

Gutiérrez Vergara's paternal grandfather, Pantaleón Gutiérrez, was a wealthy landowner who was known as the "Patriarch of the savannah." Other Conservatives whose families owned land on the savannah of Bogotá were José Manuel Marroquín and Carlos M. Urdaneta, who led a unit of Conservative guerrillas during the revolution of 1876–77.[76] One of the largest estates in nineteenth-century Colombia, located near the Saldaña River in Tolima and said to consist of over 15,000 hectares, belonged to the Caicedo family, whose noteworthy members included an archbishop of Bogotá and Domingo Caicedo Jurado, Conservative governor of Tolima in the 1870s.[77] In contrast with the Liberals, only one outstanding Conservative leader was described as being the son of poor parents; this was Pedro Justo Berrío, who was governor of Antioquia from 1864 to 1873. Despite his humble origins, however, Berrío achieved financial success through commerce and the practice of law.[78]

As in the case of the Liberals, the Conservative leaders frequently had fathers who were also distinguished proto-Conservatives or Conservatives. Antonio B. Cuervo, who was elected head of the Conservative party in 1879 and was later governor of Cundinamarca, was the son of Rufino Cuervo, a founder of the party and vice president from 1847 to 1851. Miguel Antonio Caro's father, José Eusebio Caro, was an outstanding Conservative ideologue, journalist, and poet who died while returning from self-imposed exile in 1853.[79] Rito Antonio Martínez, the father of Carlos Martínez Silva, was another distinguished Conservative and was serving as president of the Supreme Court at the time of his death in 1889. The elder Martínez had begun life as a Liberal but had adopted Conservatism because of his unhappiness over the anticlerical policies of the López administration.[80]

During the period of Liberal rule Conservatives enjoyed relatively few opportunities for public employment, though Conservative control of Antioquia and Tolima from the mid-1860s to 1877 meant that some positions both in Congress and in state government were available for party loyalists. In Antioquia these were reserved for native sons, but Tolima allowed Conservatives from other states to represent it in Congress.[81] Nor were there significant opportunities for Conservatives in public institutions of higher learning. When the National University was created in 1867, a Conservative, José María Quijano Otero, was named librarian, but the faculty was dominated by Liberals.[82]

In any event, Conservatives were likely to take a censorious view of the Liberal-controlled university and deplored the influences to which the young were exposed there and at other public institutions. To protect their sons from Liberal indoctrination in the public schools, Conservatives founded private institutions, a process that would be reversed by the Liberals after 1885. Among the better-known Conservative secondary schools were the Colegio de Pío IX, established by José Vicente Concha, father of the Colombian president (1914–18) of the same name, and the Colegio del Espíritu Santo, founded by Carlos Martínez Silva and Sergio Arboleda after the revolution of 1876–77.[83]

The pattern of the interlocking Liberal family was duplicated among the Conservatives. Only one example will be given here by way of illustration. Sergio Arboleda and his older brother Julio were maternal nephews of Lino de Pombo, one of the founders of the party. One of Julio's daughters married a brother of Carlos Urdaneta, and another became the wife of Jorge Holguín, brother of Carlos Holguín, who was himself married to a sister of Miguel Antonio Caro. The Holguín brothers were in turn nephews of Manuel María Mallarino, Conservative vice president from 1855 to 1857.[84]

The Conservative leaders differed somewhat from the Liberals in the nature and extent of their economic activities. Relatively few of the Conservative political elite became involved in business ventures to any significant extent, and those that did engaged in commerce and banking rather than in export-oriented agriculture. Among the Conservative leaders who were businessmen as well as politicians were Lázaro María Pérez and Joaquín F. Vélez. Antonio B. Cuervo engaged in cattle raising in the Magdalena Valley in the 1850s before traveling to England and Brazil in what were apparently unsuccessful efforts to enrich himself.[85]

The foregoing is not meant to suggest that Conservatives in general did not engage in business enterprise, but rather that relatively few of the party leaders did so in comparison with the Liberals. For example, Mariano Tanco, a merchant whom the American minister called "one of the wealthiest men in the republic," was a Conservative, but he played no direct role in politics.[86] The same may be said of his son Carlos, who was engaged in the production of indigo and the extraction of cinchona bark as a young man; later he was president of the Banco de Bogotá and became heavily involved in railroad construction.[87]

Indeed, the data presently available suggests that the range of economic interests represented by the Liberal leaders—either their own or those of relatives, friends, or influential constituents—was generally similar to that represented by their Conservative counterparts. In other words, there is no evidence to indicate that the Liberal leadership represented exclusively or even primarily the export-import sector (which, in any event, cannot be regarded as a single undifferentiated entity) and that this alignment constituted a fundamental difference between the Liberal party and a Conservative party that spoke for a contrary set of interests—say, those of manufacturers or traditional landowners producing mainly for the domestic market.[88] Perhaps in part because of the relatively primitive state of the Colombian economy in the nineteenth century, there was upperclass consensus on broad economic goals (though not always on the means of attaining these goals), and sectoral clashes were neither numerous nor intense. There were, of course, periodic regional conflicts with an economic dimension that might pit Liberals from one region against Conservatives from another, but such conflicts were also likely to entail divisions among Liberals as well. The controversy over the projected Northern Railroad, discussed in chapter 6, is a case in point.

Among leaders of both parties political commitments remained firm, and changes in party affiliation were extremely rare. The entry of numerous Conservatives, mainly from Cauca, into the Liberal party during the revolution of 1859–62, either because of their belief in federalism or because of their personal devotion to Mosquera, represents the only significant addition to Liberalism in the second half of the nineteenth century. Another Conservative who transferred his allegiance to the Liberal party was Jorge Isaacs, best known as the author of the novel *María* (1867).[89]

The cases of two Liberals—Florentino González and Rito Antonio Martínez—who left the party have been mentioned earlier. The only prominent Liberal who formally adopted Conservatism after 1860 was José María Samper. Several Liberals continued to support Rafael Núñez after most of his early Liberal followers deserted him in the years 1880–85 and, with the Conservatives, formed part of the National party established in 1885, but they retained their identification as Independent Liberals. Núñez himself never adopted the name of Conservative.

These exceptions notwithstanding, Liberalism was a lifetime profession for the party's leaders in the second half of the nineteenth century. In comparison with the Conservatives, they were more likely to come from eastern Colombia, especially Santander, and to be descendants of the provincial gentry rather than the colonial aristocracy. They were also more likely than their Conservative counterparts to become personally involved in economic enterprises of various sorts.

If socioeconomic origins are considered, it is clear that there was a wide gulf between the Liberal leadership and the party's rank-and-file. This gulf was enlarged by the educational opportunities available to those born in the circumstances of most of the Liberal leaders in contrast to those available to the vast majority of nineteenth-century Colombians, who remained illiterate. Further research may reveal the extent to which office-holders at levels lower than those considered here were more representative of the party as a whole and whether there were informal leaders—in urban neighborhoods and artisans' clubs, for example—who served as intermediaries between the higher party chiefs and the Liberal masses.

Liberal leaders normally acquired their political opinions and sentiments from their fathers and other close relatives and in turn bequeathed them to their own descendants. The fact that so many of the Liberal political elite underwent similar experiences as young men, such as participation in the revolution of 1859–62, tended to reinforce their Liberal predispositions, as did the familial, political, and economic bonds that linked them to one another in what was still a comparatively uncomplicated and traditional society.

4
The Evolution of Liberal Thought

It has already been seen that most Liberal leaders inherited from their fathers a predisposition toward Liberalism which was tested and strengthened by experiences shared with like-minded contemporaries. Ordinarily they acquired the philosophical underpinnings of their creed in the classroom, often from professors who were active in Liberal politics themselves, and from their extracurricular reading. In the case of many party leaders of the second half of the nineteenth century, the latter may have been especially significant because their attendance at the National University coincided with the period when the Conservative-oriented Plan of Studies instituted in 1843 was in force. José María Samper, who was a law student in the early 1840s, recalled later that he sated his thirst for knowledge of the unknown at the shop of the atheist Andrés Aguilar, who introduced him to the works of Bentham, Rousseau, Voltaire, Gibbon, and others. Travel in the United States and Europe constituted another important part of the Liberal's intellectual formation and occasionally produced changes in an individual's outlook. Samper attributed the erosion of his partisan passion and political and religious intolerance to his stay in Europe from 1858 to 1862.[1] Manuel Murillo and Rafael Núñez are also cited as Liberals who modified their views in foreign climes.[2]

Regardless of the sources of their philosophical orientation, Colombia's nineteenth-century Liberal leaders did not leave behind a body of written work which might provide the basis for a complete and systematic reconstruction of their ideas. Their writing consisted largely of official reports and newspaper articles on current issues which in some instances were collected and published in book form. This situation was probably due to several factors: the sluggishness of Liberal thought after 1850; the impediments to publication in an underdeveloped country with a small number of potential readers; and the fact that the individuals who might have been expected to produce a corpus of work expounding or refining Liberal doctrine were usually practicing politicians or businessmen and presumably had little leisure to devote to such an endeavor. The Conservative record in this respect is little better.

Throughout the nineteenth century the intellectual outlook of Colombian Liberals was strongly influenced by the writings of French and English philosophers and economists. Receptivity to non-Iberian influences, apparent at least as early as the 1820s, was a byproduct of the movement for independence from Spain, which brought with it a rejection of Hispanic values and institutions and a desire to emulate those nations, especially England, which appeared to be in the vanguard of intellectual and economic progress.³ This attitude was reflected in the favorable reception given by the precursors of Colombian Liberalism to the work of Jeremy Bentham, "undoubtedly the favorite writer of Santander and his liberal circle,"⁴ whose text on the principles of legislation was made compulsory for all law students in 1825. In the opinion of the twentieth-century historian Jaime Jaramillo Uribe, Bentham's popularity was due above all to the fact that his juridical rationalism and his defense of property and the bourgeois virtues contained an element of conservatism congenial to the nation's political leaders.⁵ Nonetheless, Benthamite utilitarianism, with its focus on pleasure and pain as the motivating forces of human behavior, was offensive to Colombian Catholics, who consistently condemned his works.

Another philosopher cherished by Colombian Liberals in the decades after independence was Antoine Louis Claude Destutt de Tracy, whose work was admired by Thomas Jefferson and by Mexican liberals as well.⁶ However, his emphasis on sensation as the source of ideas also drew the reproof of Colombian Conservatives. In 1828 Rufino Cuervo sent a copy of one of Tracy's works to Manuel José Mosquera, the future archbishop of Bogotá, who found it "bad and dangerous" and vowed to keep it out of the hands of the young. "All his ideology is mechanical," Mosquera reported. "It tends absolutely to materialism, and the spirituality of the soul in no way enters into his system."⁷ The works of both Tracy and Bentham were excluded from Colombian universities by the Conservative reform of 1843.⁸

The leading and most persistent Colombian exponent of utilitarianism and of sensationalist psychology was Ezequiel Rojas, who had become personally acquainted with Bentham while in Europe following his exile for complicity in the assassination attempt on Bolívar's life in 1828.⁹ Rojas set forth his interpretation of the ideas of Bentham and Tracy in a series of articles published in 1870 during a debate on the advisability of prescribing their works as texts in the National University.¹⁰ Two philosophical schools, Rojas wrote, were striving to dominate men's minds. One he called the "dogmatic" school, which held that ideas were innate and from this premise derived the conclusion that man's intelligence must bow before divinely appointed authority. The second school, whose chief founder was the Abbé Condillac, held that the sensations experienced by the soul constitute the source of human knowledge. Both Bentham and Tracy belonged to the latter school, the doctrines of which formed the metaphysic of all the true Liberal parties in the world. Rojas went on to assert that the sensationalist conception of human knowledge gave rise to the theory that no man is born with the right or authority to rule over his fellows and that the power of any sovereign is limited by the rights of the individual. It should be noted, however, that in upholding the natural rights of man, Rojas was defending a doctrine contrary to the position of

Bentham, who rejected the concept of human rights anterior to and above the law.

While in Europe Rojas also became a disciple of the French economist Jean Baptiste Say, whose treatise on political economy was used as a text at the Colegio de San Bartolomé in the 1820s.[11] It was probably through Say's interpretation of *The Wealth of Nations* that Colombian Liberals, like their counterparts elsewhere in Spanish America, acquired familiarity with the ideas of Adam Smith rather than through direct perusal of the Scottish economist's work.[12] Liberals often referred to the teachings of the "economists," but the name of Say was mentioned much more frequently than that of Smith, while those of Malthus and Ricardo were barely heard at all. As late as 1889 Aníbal Galindo, in pointing out the need for a new text in political economy, stated that he had been forced to use Say's treatise in his classes for twenty years.[13] While this work was sound theoretically, Galindo said, it was completely outdated; what was needed was a text that would illustrate its principles with examples taken from developments in industry unknown in Say's time.

A new wave of intellectual influences emanating almost exclusively from France broke upon Colombia in the wake of the French revolution of 1848. In the late 1840s and early 1850s Colombians, especially young men of a Liberal persuasion, were exposed to the economic optimism of Frederic Bastiat; the social theories of Saint-Simon and the Utopian socialists; the anarchistic socialism of Proudhon; Eugène Sue's anti-Jesuit novel, *The Wandering Jew;* and the works of Lamartine, among others.[14] It is difficult to determine the extent to which specific individuals came under the influence of any or all of these writers, except in the case of a few, like Aníbal Galindo and José María Samper, who left autobiographical accounts of those years, which, it will be recalled, coincided with the reformist López administration. In general, it appears that the young Liberals of the era became acquainted directly or indirectly with the French thinkers whose works were enjoying a vogue in Colombia but that they did not elaborate anything approaching a coherent synthesis of the often contradictory ideas they sampled. According to Samper, he and the other young men who frequented the *Escuela Republicana* considered themselves socialists without understanding the meaning of the term; they were infatuated with words, with political novelty, and with the extravagances of the French writers.[15] "In truth," he concluded, "we were nothing but ingenuous demagogues." Despite his disclaimer, however, Samper did give a fairly detailed outline of his conception of socialism in a speech at the *Escuela Republicana* on 30 October 1850.[16] He described socialism as the means of correcting the great inequality in the distribution of wealth which had led to the poverty of the masses and their oppression by monarchs, nobles, and priests. Socialism was not synonymous with communism, he stressed, for the latter does not recognize man's right to own property while the former not only recognizes this right but aims at the enjoyment of property by all. Specifically, socialism included the abolition of all monopolies and privileges; absolute freedom of thought; direct and universal suffrage; the imposition of a single, direct tax; the abolition of slavery and the death penalty; free education for the poor; and guarantees for the worker in his dealings with the rich. Although Samper was later to abandon many of his early beliefs, the program he set forth in 1850 proved to be an accurate delineation of some of the most cherished Liberal goals of the nineteenth century. A few of the measures advocated by Samper, such as the abolition of slavery and the institution of universal suffrage, were realized by the López administration and later Liberal governments, and in general they retained their vitality in the Liberal mind. Implicit in Samper's program, however, was not the collectivism basic to socialism but an individualism which was at all times the touchstone of Liberal thought in the nineteenth century.[17]

Until the 1880s there were no significant European additions to Liberal thought in Colombia. In fact, as late as 1870 a national debate could be sparked over a bill providing for the use in the National University of the works of Tracy in the elementary philosophy course and those of Bentham in the school of jurisprudence. The Senate passed the bill, but the session ended before the Chamber of Representatives could act on the measure; both houses, however, passed a resolution urging the president to prescribe the texts in question. The resolution was approved by large majorities, and while Ezequiel Rojas, then a senator from Boyacá, was undoubtedly motivated by purely ideological considerations in voting for the proposal, other members of Congress may have been more strongly influenced by a desire to score a victory over the Conservatives. An editorial in *El Liberal* declared: "Once the question was raised, it was necessary to triumph; otherwise, the Conservatives might just as well have defeated us on the battlefield. This was a question not only of doctrine but of honor. The uproar that the ultramontanes have raised over the adoption of this bill is in a sense the distant echo of the hatred of the sanctimonious souls of 1834 for the Benthamite school, which educated the generation that has proved most resistant to fanaticism."[18] Indeed, the Conservatives still remained hostile to utilitarianism. In 1867 José Vicente Concha, head of a Conservative secondary school, advertised a course in moral philosophy in which he would demonstrate the principles of natural law and refute utilitarianism as a standard of morality.[19] Two years later Miguel Antonio Caro published a study of utilitarianism criticizing Bentham's work on both theoretical and historical grounds.[20] Among Conservatives less learned than Concha and Caro "utility" and "utilitarianism" served as convenient labels to denote all the evils they associated with Liberalism.

By 1870, to be sure, some Liberals were no longer willing to accept the authority of Bentham and Tracy. As early as 1859 Manuel Murillo declared that, although he had once revered Bentham as an oracle, he no longer did so.[21] During the textbook debate of 1870 Antonio Vargas Vega, a medical doctor by profession and rector of the Colegio de San Bartolomé, disapproved of the bill being considered by Congress. The National University, he argued, was supposed to be a neutral ground where all doctrines would be heard, not a workshop for the production of sensationalists. He also observed that much of Tracy's work had been rendered obsolete by advances in physics, anthropology, and psychology. "That text was useful when these sciences and modern standards of judgment were in diapers," he said, "but today it is an antique in sound positivist (sensationalist) philosophy, and one wonders why the Colombian Congress has seen fit to disinter it."[22] The resolution of Congress on the matter prompted the rector of the University, Manuel Ancízar, to submit his resignation in protest.

As the authority of Bentham and Tracy began to wane, they were supplanted as sources of intellectual influence by John Stuart Mill and Herbert Spencer, both of whom found a champion in Rafael Núñez.[23] In 1880, upon the occasion of the distribution of University prizes, Núñez, who was then president of Colombia, suggested that Mill's *System of Logic* be adopted as a text at the University in order to stimulate and broaden the intellectual horizons of the students.[24] He also urged that a course in sociology be offered. Because sociology explains the laws of society, which transcend those made by governments, and enables students to understand the reasons for the existence of seemingly barbarous institutions like slavery, Núñez felt that the introduction of the discipline to the curriculum would promote greater tolerance, which he called Colombia's greatest political necessity.

On the same occasion two years later Salvador Camacho Roldán, who had been named professor of sociology at the University, delivered an address with strongly Spencerian overtones in which he held that human society is subject to laws of growth and multiplication, of the struggle for existence, and of natural selection.[25] There are, however, differences in the ways in which societies evolve, and it was the task of the new science of sociology to investigate these differences. A Conservative refutation of Camacho Roldán's address led Núñez to take up his pen in defense of sociology and of Spencer, whom he called the "true founder" of the new discipline.[26] The systems of Spencer and Comte were basically different, he said, despite similarities in their terminology. Comte emphasized the collectivity, Spencer the individual. Comte repudiated all religion except his creed of humanity, while Spencer realized that religious sentiment was the result of the mysterious origin of the universe.

The philosophy of Spencer was embraced by many young Liberals who came to maturity in the 1880s and 1890s. One of them, Carlos Arturo Torres, explained that Spencer's relativism, his affirmation of the unknowable, the breadth of his political opinions, and his belief that science and religion are not irreconcilable served to tranquilize spirits weary of intellectual strife.[27] In addition, the traditional emphasis of Colombian Liberalism on individualism, limited government, and the desirability of economic development probably made Liberals receptive to Spencer's enthusiasm for industrialization and advocacy of laissez faire.[28] Comtian positivism, on the other hand, apparently found no adherents among Colombia's Liberal leaders, who no doubt could not accept Comte's elitism and aversion to individualism.

Colombian Liberals generally viewed the political process around the world as a struggle between two competing sets of ideals, their own and those of the Conservatives, and therefore considered themselves part of an international party dedicated to the same principles, which they were likely to interpret in terms of the Colombian experience. This point of view is reflected in a statement (1887) by Rafael Rocha Gutiérrez, who asserted that the people of all Spanish America were divided into two parties reflecting conflicting philosophies:

> One of them personifies old traditions, theocratic influence, repression as the only means of government, severity in punishments, authority as the supreme guide of public or private conduct, and the centralization of authority as the basis of stability. The other represents the equality of classes, religious liberty, the will of the people as the sole instrument of government, mildness in punishments and the rehabilitation of the criminal, the decentralization of authority; in short, the democratic idea, which daily modifies the structure of society and the constitution of political power.[29]

Colombian Liberals would have immediately identified their own party with the second of the two described by Rocha Gutiérrez, and his statement is representative of the conventional Liberal attitude toward Conservatism.

The Liberal conviction that the Conservative party was the bulwark of reaction was implicit in the word *godo*, which was applied in a derogatory sense by Liberals to Conservatives, not only in Colombia but in other Spanish American republics as well. The word, which literally means "Goth," had been originally used to refer to a member of the Spanish aristocracy; in the New World it became an epithet for royalists during the independence movement. The Liberals' adoption of this term for their political adversaries probably reflected, initially at least, a desire to identify Conservatism with the colonial regime and its defenders. In 1856 Manuel Murillo spoke of the desirability of persuading the younger generation, with history book in hand, that the Conservative party was in essence the same party that had supported the king of Spain.[30]

The Liberals' use of *godo* also indicated the low esteem in which they held the colonial regime, especially in the mid-nineteenth century. At this time Liberals tended to blame Colombia's relative lack of political and economic development on what they considered the hallmarks of Spanish rule in the New World: authoritarianism, centralism, religious fanaticism, monopoly, and privilege. By the end of the nineteenth century, however, this attitude had been modified. Rafael Núñez, admittedly not a typical Liberal, asserted in 1881 that the colonial regime should be judged on the basis of whether it had improved the social and political condition of the regions that came under Spanish rule; Spain's principal error, he felt, lay in its failure to realize the need for reform.[31] In a book published in 1899 Medardo Rivas, a more orthodox Liberal than Núñez, called for an end to the heritage of hatred for Spain, which he considered a consequence of the war for independence.[32] Although the Spanish conquest, like all conquests, had destroyed the culture of the subjugated peoples, the Spaniards had brought their own civilization to America and had made the Indians subjects of the crown instead of exterminating them as had occurred elsewhere.

Related to the Liberal indictment against Spain was the conviction that the achievement of independence had brought only political emancipation and that the economic fetters imposed by Spain had remained virtually intact until the advent of the López administration in 1849. The young Salvador Camacho Roldán wrote in 1850 while explaining the need for tax reform: "The great revolution of 1810, which transformed our political system at a blow, barely touched our system of taxation, leaving . . . the monopolies, the abuses, and the inequities that . . . deserved to be labelled *organized pillage.*"[33] The principal achievement of the López administration, Liberals believed, had been to dismantle the colonial edifice. In a speech during funeral services for Murillo in 1880, for example, Gil Colunje extolled the reforms of the López era, such as the abolition of slavery and the establishment of administrative decentralization, because of their role in eradicating the remnants of the colonial regime.[34] The extent to which this interpretation took hold is illustrated by the statement of a twentieth-century economic historian of Colombia that "the historical function of Liberalism in the past century was the elimination, the extinction of the onerous and frustrating shackles that weighed upon the Granadine economy."[35]

Since Liberals believed in the 1850s that their party's reforms had freed Colombia of its colonial fetters, they reasoned that progress would henceforth be rapid because Colombia was a "new" country, endowed with vast natural resources and unburdened by the problems that afflicted contemporary Europe. About 1850 Manuel Ancízar observed that because of the fertility of the soil in America, hunger was known only from accounts of the poverty of the European proletariat.[36] In the same year Murillo expressed satisfaction that Colombians, unlike many Europeans, were not oppressed by absolutism and privilege; in their country everything still had to be created.³⁷ This optimistic attitude became less pronounced in later decades, but as late as 1874 Santiago Pérez, who was then president, in describing the tasks that faced the new generation, remarked that young Colombians had to exert no extraordinary efforts with respect to the economy, for the nation's wealth would increase provided they were industrious and thrifty.³⁸ "In this country there is no structure of privilege or monopolistic framework to halt the current of industry, to divert it or dam it against convenience or justice," he said. As a result, the struggles between capital and labor that had occurred in other lands would not be duplicated in Colombia.

The fiscal and administrative decentralization of the López administration and the fragmentation of the existing provinces had paved the way for the adoption of a federalist form of government in the 1850s, and Liberals remained theoretically committed to federalism as long as they were in power. One of the most elaborate arguments on behalf of federalism was penned in 1855 by the Panamanian Justo Arosemena in support of a bill to unite the four Isthmian provinces into a single state.³⁹ Like other Liberals, Arosemena equated centralism with despotism on the grounds that power tends to expand when it is not fragmented. At the same time he felt that overly small states or provinces were vulnerable to outside aggression, lacked the resources to be economically viable, and were likely to be dominated by political cliques. He was not impressed by the arguments of those who blamed federalism for the turbulence of the Spanish American republics, for centralized states had also experienced disorders after independence. Nor was he persuaded by those who held that federalism might be appropriate for the United States, where it involved the union of previously separate units, but not for Spanish America, where its establishment entailed the dismemberment of long united provinces. It was Arosemena's belief that the union of the Spanish American provinces had been forcibly imposed by Spain and would never have been adopted spontaneously by the people. Liberals also held that federalism permitted each section to deal more effectively with its own problems.⁴⁰ In addition, it was hoped that sectional autonomy would promote democracy by increasing popular participation in local affairs and would serve as a means of containing revolution.

Many Liberals, of course, believed that the powers granted to the "sovereign" states by the constitution of 1863 served to weaken the central government to an undesirable degree. On the other hand, while the constitution was in force, Liberal presidents did not hesitate to expand the powers of the federal government, even at the cost of encroaching upon the rights of the states.⁴¹ President Salgar declared in 1872 while praising a recent law on material improvements in which the federal government was to play a large part: "Federalism is not a selfish form of government, nor one opposed to material progress, the attainment of which is impossible through individual efforts or the isolated support of the states. Although federation breaks the chains that hinder sectional development, it does not necessarily exclude unity."[42]

In general, Liberals did not seriously question any part of their political program after 1850. The only article of the Liberal political creed that was modified was universal suffrage as several states imposed literacy qualifications for voting, while proposed amendments to the 1863 constitution, such as the extension of the presidential term from two to four years, affected form rather than substance. Instead, Liberals were more likely to be concerned with improving the economic and intellectual level of the masses, for it soon became evident that the most beneficent political institutions alone would not produce the millennium.

To ensure the proper functioning of republican institutions, most Liberals thought that three conditions were necessary. The first of these was cessation of the political disorders that had ravaged the nation since independence. Although they continued to be concerned about this problem, Liberals were optimistic about an eventual reign of peace once the two other conditions had been realized: an enlightened citizenry and economic prosperity. An editorial entitled "Needs of the Country" in 1866, for example, stressed the importance of improving primary education and hoped that at least two schools could be established in each district. "Free education for the masses—this is the motto of the true patriot and the sincere republican. Only an ignorant people can be deceived; only a brutish people can be made the victim of despotism."[43] President Salgar expressed a similar opinion while congratulating the Chamber of Representatives for appropriating $100,000 for the establishment of normal schools in 1870.[44] Emphasizing the relationship between democracy and education, he declared that the former did not exist in Latin America. Instead, more or less well-educated minorities managed affairs as they saw fit while the great majority of workers and taxpayers, who lived in rural areas, bore all the burdens of the republic but received none of its benefits. What was the point, he asked, of guaranteeing freedom and individual rights if the citizens were too ignorant to be aware of their existence?

In the opinion of Liberals, the expansion of public education was but one aspect of the struggle against ignorance. If it was to be truly successful, the hold of the clergy on the masses also had to be reduced. Liberals invariably emphasized, however, that they were not antagonistic to religion itself but to the political activity of some members of the Roman Catholic clergy and to their efforts to hinder the intellectual and spiritual enlightenment of the Colombian people. An apologist for the anticlerical policies of the mid-1870s explained: "Colombian Liberalism, far from being hostile to the true religious spirit, draws inspiration from it and seeks its protection, for it knows that freedom is in essence of divine origin and that it appears, grows, and produces its fruits only among people in whom conscience—that is, moral sense—is allowed to develop fully and with complete guarantees."[45]

Liberal leaders varied greatly in their personal religious convictions. Eustorgio Salgar and Santiago Pérez, for example, were said to be practicing Catholics.[46] When the latter was nominated for the presidency in 1873, Medardo Rivas declared that his only blemish was the fact that he attended mass; Rivas conceded, however, that this was a purely private act that in no way rendered Pérez unfit for the presidency.[47] Miguel Samper has been described as a convinced Christian who became a practicing Catholic toward the end of his life.[48] Many other Liberal leaders, however, were probably freethinkers who, like Teodoro Valenzuela, believed that the universe is governed by a supreme intelligence; organized religion had a social value, he felt, but was otherwise meaningless.[49]

Regardless of their personal beliefs, Liberal leaders could generally be divided into two camps with respect to religious issues. On the one hand were those who thought that the government should take an active role in extirpating clerical influence, both temporal and spiritual, and that in order to do so it should be invested with powers similar to those enjoyed by the Spanish crown in the colonial era. On the other were those who might deplore the power of the clergy but believed that extreme anticlericalism was not only futile but violated Liberal principle as well. Liberals of this school were likely to regard separation of church and state as the best solution for the religious question. This was the position of Salvador Camacho Roldán, who wrote in 1878: "What we seek in this country is not the repression of the Catholic idea but the complete emancipation of human thought, and this requires liberty for Catholics and non-Catholics, for those who believe and those who do not."[50]

Liberal attitudes toward the Church were shaped not only by ideological considerations but also by Conservative exploitation of clerical grievances for political ends and by Liberal suspicions about the subversive designs of the clergy, which were strengthened by the condemnation of liberalism by Pope Pius IX in 1864 and by the proclamation of the dogma of papal infallibility six years later. As a result, even Liberals who favored separation of church and state at times became alarmed by the possibility of a clerical-Conservative alliance to drive them from power. In 1874 an editorialist in the *Diario de Cundinamarca* warned that if the Conservatives attempted to use religion for partisan purposes, the Liberal party would react energetically "to annihilate completely" the political power of the clergy.[51]

The differences between these various points of view were never fully resolved while the Liberals were in power. Although separation of church and state had been decreed in 1853, the Rionegro constitution empowered the federal and state governments to exercise the right of inspection over religious cults, and the law of 23 April 1863 required of all clergymen, on pain of banishment from Colombia, that they swear to obey the constitutions, laws, and authorities of the nation and the states. By 1864, however, the belief that this law was unduly harsh and vindictive had become sufficiently widespread among Liberals to permit its substitution by a milder measure (17 May 1864), which required the oath of obedience only from prelates.[52] In addition, Manuel Murillo, who took office as president on 10 April 1864, made a conciliatory gesture by lifting the sentence of banishment decreed in 1861 against the archbishop of Bogotá, Antonio Herrán, provided he took the required oath.[53]

Relations between the federal government and the Church again deteriorated during the presidential term of Tomás Mosquera (1866-67), but after his deposition the 1864 law was repealed. This meant that in the future, relations between church and state would be governed only by the general dispositions in the constitution. In the following years tension between the Church and the federal government was at a relatively low ebb, but became increasingly severe after 1870, mainly because of clerical opposition to the educational program launched by the Salgar administration in that year. After the Conservative revolution of 1876–77, which was openly supported by some clergymen, the "hard line" temporarily gained ascendancy, winning adherents even among Liberals who had previously eschewed extreme anticlericalism.

Although Liberals often disagreed among themselves over religious policy, they were unanimous in desiring the economic development of Colombia, which they hoped would one day attain the prosperity enjoyed by the United States and thriving Latin American countries like Argentina and Chile. In 1871, for example, *El Liberal* approvingly quoted an editorial in the *Diario de Cundinamarca* which declared that Colombia had arrived at an era of "economic regeneration" and was demanding railroads, telegraph lines, education, interest in agriculture, and a postal system that would embrace every district in the Union. Above all, the nation demanded railroads "as its greatest need, . . . as the most effective antidote against its present ills." The editorial continued:

> It is indubitable that railroads will ensure peace, as they have ensured it in Chile and Peru; they will awaken this Andean population, which seems paralyzed from a commercial point of view; they will stir these towns of the savannah from the inertia and depressing status quo that afflicts them; they will introduce movement, activity, happiness, and the fruits of culture and wealth to these beautiful plateaus, which are still covered with sad and indolent thatched-roofed hamlets as in the time of the colony.[54]

In general, Liberals, having acquired their economic opinions from Say and Bastiat, were likely to view the economy of their nation and of the entire world as a harmonious and beneficent mechanism which would afford well-being for all provided the laws which governed its operation were not obstructed by unnatural obstacles to individual enterprise. From these premises were derived several conclusions, not all of which were shared by all Liberals. The most widely held belief was that the state should not erect barriers to private enterprise like the monopolies established by the Spanish crown. This position was defended in an 1849 editorial which declared:

> the legislative or administrative dispositions which directly or indirectly impede the free use of man's economic faculties and the employment of capital in the production of wealth hinder and attack commerce and industry and result in a social distress that is all the more deplorable because it would be easy to correct if government would trust to the counsels of reason and the self-interest of the individual for the sound direction of economic affairs, limiting itself to providing protection and education with equality for all and without tutelary pretensions.[55]

At the time this editorial was written Liberals generally would have endorsed government abstention from any involvement in the economy, but after 1850 unqualified laissez faire was gradually abandoned. While Liberals did not reject their commitment to private enterprise, they did conclude that in Colombia economic development could not be left entirely to the initiative of the individual because certain enterprises, such as railroad construction, demanded resources that exceeded those of native capitalists and because Colombians lacked a well-developed spirit of cooperation. President Salgar observed in 1871 that "no government that aspires to be considered enlightened and progressive can ignore economic development, especially in countries like ours, in which resources of capital, being small, are naturally timid. Material improvements require the protection of the government."[56] Aquileo Parra voiced a similar opinion while serving as secretary of finance in 1873.[57] The extent to which the government of a nation should intervene in the economy, he believed, depended upon the intellectual advancement and technical knowledge of the citizenry and, above all, on the development of their spirit of association. In a country like Colombia government support of education and of certain economic ventures was necessary; in the United States or England, however, private enterprise could manage without the state's help. In addition, a very few Liberal leaders, notably Manuel Murillo, ventured beyond the qualified interventionism endorsed by Salgar and Parra and came to the conclusion that, in view of the disparity of resources enjoyed by different segments of society, the government could not ensure equality of opportunity by total noninterference in the economic arena. On the contrary, it occasionally had to tip its weight on behalf of the less advantaged groups.

The diversity of Liberal thought can be seen by briefly examining the ideas of three influential Liberal leaders of the nineteenth century: Miguel Samper, Manuel Murillo, and Rafael Núñez. Samper was probably the most articulate and consistent exponent of classical economic liberalism. In his writings, usually signed with the initials X.Y.Z., he frequently addressed himself to the problems of economic development, which he felt should be reflected in the improvement of the material and intellectual well-being of the masses.[58] This goal, Samper believed, could be achieved if the elements of the economic structure were allowed to function in accordance with the basic laws designed for that purpose.

Although Samper was convinced that labor and thrift could guarantee prosperity for the individual and that the prosperity of the individual citizen would automatically create national prosperity, he felt that the productive capacities of Colombians had not been able to develop normally. He attributed the nation's lethargic economic growth partly to geography, partly to the nature of the colonial experience, but mainly to the insecurity bred by recurring revolution.[59] These disorders were fomented by the nonproducing members of society, "the parasites—Conservatives and Liberals alike—who do not wish to live by their labor but by rapine and fraud and whom we workers in our imbecility allow to assume control of public affairs."[60] In Samper's opinion, the two parties of Colombia encouraged the rapacity of the parasites by their fanatical devotion to uncompromising programs which served to excuse any kind of wrongdoing.[61]

According to Samper, the state had been organized to defend the interests of the productive members of the community and was, therefore, obliged to create an atmosphere conducive to labor by ensuring peace and order, which could best be attained by moderation and tolerance. Accordingly, he condemned excesses committed in the name of the majority, for he was repelled by the "deplorable sophisms" of Rousseau about the general will, which had converted justice into a mere question of numbers.[62]

Samper felt, however, that the government should avoid interference with the economic laws since such action would ultimately harm society.[63] He disapproved of any policy that seemed monopolistic or that constituted a threat to man's right to property, which he considered inseparable from man's right to liberty.[64] On the basis of these views he opposed the disamortization of Church property in the 1860s, and twenty years later he would combat President Núñez's efforts to levy a protective tariff and to establish a national bank.[65] He was not opposed to the development of manufacturing in Colombia, he wrote in the mid-1890s, but he believed that the individual, not the government, should determine which enterprises might best be undertaken.[66] The government should confine itself to eliminating tariffs on raw materials needed for industry, to establishing well-equipped technical schools, and to promoting transportation projects as an indirect means of encouraging industry.

Samper's views underwent relatively little change throughout his career. Such was not the case with Manuel Murillo and Rafael Núñez, both of whom moved away from the classical liberalism espoused by Samper. As a young man in 1847, Murillo realized that Colombia was underdeveloped economically, educationally, and culturally, but he believed that "the betterment of society is a fact of Providence and is therefore irresistible."[67] In his position as secretary of finance under López he had the opportunity to address himself to the problems of development. The objective of those who had voted for López, he said in his 1852 report to Congress, was to provide republican institutions with a solid foundation. This foundation, as a careful study of social phenomena had revealed, was the well-being of the greatest number, which was to be achieved by an increase in public wealth, equitably distributed, so that the individual might be assured of dignity and independence; otherwise, the republican form of government would be meaningless.[68] In the report Murillo went on to advocate one of his favorite schemes: the abolition of all existing taxes and the salt monopoly and their replacement by a single, direct tax, to be collected at the municipal level, with part of the proceeds being turned over to the national government.

As president of the state of Santander from 1857 to 1859, Murillo again defended the concept of the single tax in a message to the constituent assembly of the state on 10 November 1857, which accompanied a bill levying a tax on urban and rural real estate.[69] This tax, which was to be the state's sole source of income, would be equitable and relatively easy to assess and collect, Murillo said, and would stimulate economic development. As finally passed by the assembly, the tax law provided for a levy on wealth (*riqueza*), which was defined to include movable property as well as real estate.[70]

Under Murillo's leadership the state of Santander became a laboratory for Liberal reformers imbued with the doctrines of laissez faire. In his message to the state assembly in 1858, Murillo argued that the state should not assume responsibility for education, partly because each individual should have the right to determine the kind of schooling he or his children wished to receive.[71] To those who held that the poor could not pay for education in private schools, he replied that the solution was not to give their children mediocre instruction but to provide them with the means of overcoming their poverty. He also declared that the state should refrain from becoming involved in the construction of transportation projects.[72] First of all, any government-sponsored enterprise would entail a heavy financial outlay that would prove burdensome to taxpayers. Moreover, "the natural laws of development of population and wealth cannot be precipitated; . . . in this as in everything, it is wise to resign oneself to await the results of the general causes that determine the progress of the species. A road opened ahead of time is a road that will soon be closed."

It should be noted, however, that even at this early date Murillo was not an unquestioning adherent of laissez faire. In 1853, in a letter to Miguel Samper published in *El Neo-Granadino,* he referred to laissez faire as a "selfish and pernicious doctrine" which put the lambs at the mercy of the wolves.[73] In his letter to Samper, Murillo expressed his concern over the concentration of land ownership in Colombia and advocated limitations by the state on the amount of public land that might be acquired by any individual.[74] While he believed in the individual's absolute right of property in the product of his own labor, he did not think that such a right applied to those things given by Nature to the entire human race. He also pointed out that laissez faire implied injustice if it served to confirm advantages derived from an existing system of privilege.

In 1859, after he had stepped down as president of Santander, Murillo stated somewhat similar opinions while supporting a proposal before the legislature of Cundinamarca to withdraw legal protection from interest rates higher than 5 percent a year.[75] Since the capitalist had great advantages over the laborer in England and everywhere else, Murillo observed, the latter could not enjoy the economic freedom extolled by Aníbal Galindo, who opposed the measure. "You seek the law of the funnel," Murillo said, "wide for capital, which is already excessively favored because of its position, and narrow for the worker, who has no freedom." Although some steps such as the abolition of entail had been taken to lessen the gap between capital and labor, the capitalists had retaliated by upholding the gospel of economic freedom preached by economists like Say. To these economists Colombia owed the legal protection given to usury and the disappearance of municipal lands. The purpose of the law, Murillo stated, should be the attainment of justice, and he did not think that justice in the matter of interest could be left to the judgment of the individual.

Murillo again spoke in favor of limited government intervention in economic matters in 1872 when, as president of the Union, he proposed that a network of roads and railroads be constructed, largely at federal expense.[76] He also urged "truth in the debt," that is, the adoption of a proposal to pay interest on the internal debt and amortize it on the basis of its market value so that customs revenues reserved for debt service could be freed for application to transportation enterprises. According to Murillo, not only was the government burdened by this debt, but the national economy could not develop because capitalists were reluctant to invest in enterprises offering an annual return of 6 percent when they might purchase treasury notes that brought them up to 48 percent. Nor was there any point in appealing to the patriotic sentiments of the capitalists, for the new "monetary aristocracy" that dominated the world lacked the patriotism occasionally exhibited by the aristocracy of blood. The realization of this fact had gradually led Murillo to modify his earlier belief that "all progress should come from the activity of the individual and that the government . . . should confine itself to giving security." He now believed that

> the representative of the community has something more to do. He should first ask whether he himself is not responsible for the disturbances that are seen in the action of the economic laws; whether, seduced by capital, he has not inclined toward capital at the expense of labor; and whether, by offering enormous advantages to speculators in public documents, he has not withdrawn capital from industry to surrender it to the idleness, luxury, and demoralization that the easy accumulation of wealth engenders. . . .
>
> Today I am convinced that government would become an unjustifiable burden if it did not act as the prime mover of progressive enterprises that affect the community that has constituted and supports it.[77]

By the 1870s, then, Murillo had become convinced that the state had a dual responsibility: on the one hand, it sometimes had to limit economic freedom for the sake of the community and its less favored members and, on the other, it had an obligation actively to promote enterprises, especially in transportation and communications, that would contribute to national development. He had not lost his youthful optimism, however. In his annual message to Congress on 1 February 1874 he reported several promising developments, including the existence of a surplus in the federal treasury and the recent opening of a factory for the production of sulfuric acid.[78] The only enemies left to conquer, he said, were the distances and the mountains. Harking back to his earlier conception of the relationship between enlightenment and prosperity, he added that even ignorance would be defeated once the economic problems caused by inadequate means of communication had been solved. "It is vain to hope for the spread of education if well-being does not spread at the same time. A people that enriches itself and comes into contact with the rest of the civilized world automatically instructs itself."

Although Rafael Núñez was to earn the allegiance of large numbers of Conservatives, he always considered himself a Liberal and repudiated only those aspects of Liberalism which he felt had been damaging to Colombia. Prominent among the beliefs that Núñez rejected after 1860 was his youthful conviction that political institutions could determine the development of a people. By the 1880s he had learned that a republican form of government in itself could not guarantee liberty and justice and might in fact be "a deceitful cloak for the most execrable tyrannies." He had also come to believe that "laws written under the heat of enthusiasm alone have little effective power because above artificial institutions there are laws that are of decisive influence in the growth, evolution, and destiny of human societies."[79]

Núñez attributed his mature convictions to his long (1863–74) residence in the United States, England, and France. The ideas in the passage quoted above were foreshadowed in a preface to a collection of Núñez's newspaper articles published in Rouen in 1874 in which he set forth his basic beliefs. Among them were the following:

> The movement of human societies is subject to providential and permanent laws, in the same manner as the physiological life of each of its members.
> Moral development is the final synthesis of progress in all its forms.
> All great institutions, even those which seem most absurd at a distance, have had their reason for being born and for ceasing to exist.

From truths such as these Núñez believed that the following conclusion could be deduced: "reciprocal tolerance is one of the first social requirements and is all the more obligatory since the attentive study of human evolution compels us to acknowledge that we are very fallible and also persuades us that we are all seeking the same ideal in good faith, even though we follow diverse and apparently divergent paths."[80] He had reached all of these conclusions, Núñez wrote a decade later, before reading Spencer.[81]

In his 1874 collection Núñez exhibited the tolerance he defended in the preface. Writing on Spanish politics in January 1869, he said that members of the Spanish government should not be criticized for not being republicans "because all political, as well as religious, beliefs are equally pure and respectable when they are sincere. Absolute truth does not exist on earth, and relative truths necessarily depend on diverse circumstances, whose confluence cannot be counted on in every era and country." Two months later he pointed out that history had not yet given its final verdict as to the most desirable form of government, observing that the English monarchical system as it existed after 1688 was superior to the Cromwellian republic, just as the present Italian monarchy was preferable to the quarreling republics of Guelphs and Ghibbelines. The end of human history, he said, was the physical and spiritual emancipation of the human being, which had demanded above all the disappearance of inequality, first for the middle classes and now for the working classes. Governmental forms had not been able to hinder the fulfillment of this law; thus aristocratic England had freed the slaves in its colonies thirty years before the United States.[82]

Núñez also extended his concept of tolerance to religion, not to defend religious pluralism or to uphold the dogmas of the Catholic faith or the

Church as an institution, but to point out the general usefulness of religion when it served a social function. In 1873, for example, while discussing religious problems in Switzerland, he observed that contemporary Catholicism no longer had the raison d'etre it had when it represented civilization and progress and had protected right against might. In fact, the Church now represented the opposite, as the Syllabus and everything emanating from the Vatican indicated. "The truth is that the Catholic hierarchy is essentially a political power under the external guise of a spiritual power. To allow it absolute liberty of action under the pretext of the needs of conscience would be precisely the equivalent of surrendering to it part of the sovereignty of the nation."[83] Earlier, however, he had expressed the belief that the political progress of the United States had been due partly to the strength of the religious sentiments of the population. "In the absence of the principle of authority, necessarily weak in democracies, it is indispensable to seek elements of order in the moral realm."[84] Later he would seek this element of order in Colombian Catholicism.

It has already been noted that Núñez accepted Spencerian positivism partly because of his belief that the system of the English philosopher did not completely exclude traditional religion. In the last years of his life, however, Núñez apparently came to feel that the positivist approach to knowledge, based as it is on the observation and study of external phenomena, might not only lead to atheism but would also fail to lead to truth. "The objective contemplation of things gives us . . . only a portrait of appearances; it therefore follows that in order to perceive the entire truth, *the true truth,* we must engage in the study of our own souls, which are in communication with absolute truth."[85] At first glance it seems difficult to reconcile Núñez's conception of the "true truth" with his earlier assertion that "absolute truth does not exist on earth." However, both are consistent with a lifelong scepticism that convinced Núñez of the complexity, mutability, and elusiveness of human existence and institutions and of the difficulty of attaining any kind of truth by the limited means of human reason.

While Núñez reacted favorably to certain aspects of Spencerianism, especially its evolutionary view of human development, he did not accept Spencer's laissez faire principles. When discussing economic policy, Núñez was more likely to cite John Stuart Mill instead, and it is possible that the latter exerted a more profound, if limited, influence on Núñez. His 1874 collection of articles contains at least two citations of Mill and an article praising the Englishman as a philosopher, politician, and seeker of truth and justice, written upon the occasion of his death in 1873.[86]

Núñez also cited Mill on at least two occasions—once in 1883 and again in 1891—to support his contention that a moderate system of tariff protection was desirable for Colombia, specifically repudiating the authority of Say on this matter.[87] Núñez's adoption of protectionism was but one indication that he, like most of his Liberal contemporaries, had modified his commitment to laissez faire. A few years ago, he wrote in 1883, the conviction that economic freedom would solve all of Colombia's problems had reigned unchallenged, but its hold had been weakened as time passed and the expected results had failed to appear. He saw in the protectionist policy of the United States one of the reasons for its "astounding prosperity" and argued that England had adopted free trade only to protect its own interests.[88]

Perhaps more keenly than any of his contemporaries, Núñez was aware of the social and economic problems, particularly the plight of the proletariat, created by the industrial revolution in Europe and the United States and of the challenges which they posed to traditional Liberalism.[89] If Núñez was sympathetic to the concept of moderate state action on behalf of the proletariat as expounded by Pope Leo XIII in his encyclical *Rerum novarum*,[90] he did not believe that Colombia or any other Spanish American republic was faced with the problem of capitalistic exploitation as it existed in Europe or the United States. "In [Spanish America] there are no privileges of any kind that intervene, with a diminution of equity, between capital and labor," he wrote in 1892. "With the exception of a few places in the departments of Boyacá and Cundinamarca where the tenant is exploited to some extent by the landowner, it can be said that in Colombia it is the worker who lays down the law to the capitalist, not the reverse."[91] Colombia's principal problem, he said, was the uncertainty of the rule of order. At one time, in fact, Colombians had gone so far as to declare war on the religious principle, "the basis of internal order, of moral order." Colombian Conservatives were no more uniform or consistent in their thinking than Liberals, but there were several principles basic to Conservative ideology that set them apart from Liberals. The first of these principles was a belief in the universality and infallibility of the precepts of Christianity. Secondly, Conservatives regarded the Catholic Church as the sole depository and interpreter of the divine truths of Christianity. Thirdly, they considered the Conservative party as the political agency by which the teachings of Christ and the interests of the Church might best be protected and advanced in Colombia. For both clergymen and Conservatives, this last proposition occasionally raised dilemmas that could not always be satisfactorily resolved: for the clergy, the extent to which party leaders should be encouraged to act as spokesmen for the interests of the Church, and for the Conservatives, the extent to which the interests of the party were identical with those of the Church.

Conservatives also tended to feel that Catholicism and by extension the entire fabric of society were gravely menaced by Liberalism, which, by asserting that the mind is shaped only by sensory experiences, repudiated the concept of divine will as the source of human nature and institutions.

The Conservative newspaper *La América* declared in 1874 that Catholic morality was the basis of its doctrine.[92] The editorial continued:

> Today Liberalism aims to establish a school of negation [and] seeks utility or sensationalism as [the basis of] morality, and this is where the true division between the parties lies. It is natural that we who raise as a moral banner the one left to us in the Gospel by the Son of God should form ranks around the Church which received it. Those who seek in pleasure or pain the norm for their actions are the enemies of this Church, and therefore in every political question a religious question is involved.

Convictions such as these frequently led Conservatives to assert that a Catholic could not be a Liberal. Thus a Medellín newspaper stated in 1875: "the doctrinaire Liberal party is anti-Catholic, and . . . no Catholic can vote for any of its members without betraying his conscience."[93]

There were, of course, some Conservative spokesmen who did not consider defense of Catholicism or of the Church the principal, or even a primary, objective of the party. The first issue of *La Patria,* founded in Bogotá in 1867, included a discussion of "the Conservative idea," which the writer said was "the alliance of liberty with order."[94] By order he meant the assignment of each individual to the place for which his nature best suited him, and by liberty, the freedom of the individual to function within the sphere of his rights. The writer stressed that the Conservative idea did not imply a blind devotion to the past nor a rejection of all human progress. Nor was it necessary to be a Roman Catholic to be a Conservative, as the example of England showed.

This point of view was shared by Manuel María Madiedo, editor of *La Ilustración* of Bogotá, who disparaged the "sacerdotal monomanias" of some Conservatives and spurned the notion that Conservatism implied retrogression or a longing for the past. "We are for the *go ahead* of the Yankees because we believe that God has endowed man with the instinct and impulse for betterment."[95] And while an 1867 editorial in *La Prensa* acknowledged that deep philosophical differences divided the two parties, it asserted that the overwhelming majority of party members were oblivious to doctrinal considerations.[96] "Generally the interests of each family head bind his [dependents] to the party to which he belongs, and in small towns the opinion of the boss (*gamonal*) is the opinion of all the residents."

Such statements represented only a minority viewpoint, however, and the association between Catholicism and Conservatism remained close. In fact, on occasion Conservatives did not hesitate to censure publicly clerics whom they considered lukewarm in the struggle against Liberalism. One such incident in 1873—involving the archbishop of Bogotá—led to a decision of the Second Provincial Council of Colombian bishops that Catholic writers should not anticipate the judgment of the hierarchy on any issue related to the Church and that they were to submit to the authority of the prelates should they disagree with them.[97] To Miguel Antonio Caro, this ruling meant the imposition of "shackles" on Catholic writers.

Conservatives had no difficulty in accepting republican government, though they assigned a much higher priority than the Liberals to the maintenance of order and were uncomfortable with the extensive liberties enshrined in the 1863 constitution. While they affirmed the right of all citizens to equality of treatment before the law, they were likely to express hostility to those who condemned economic inequality. On 9 July 1848, for example, *El Nacional* of Bogotá declared that the achievement of de facto equality (as opposed to legal equality) would be the equivalent of robbery, for it meant elevating the lazy to the rank of the worker. Later, in the aftermath of the Paris Commune, *La Sociedad* of Medellín condemned "socialist equality," which it said was engendered by envy and based on injustice. "Its purpose is to level the human race, reducing all that is outstanding until it descends to the lowest, meanest, and most brutish level in society." This kind of equality, the newspaper asserted, was totally incompatible with Christian equality, which rested on the oneness of the human race and the universality of God's moral law.[98]

Conservatives embraced economic doctrines similar to those of the Liberals, generally endorsing the desirability of economic development. They were staunch defenders of private enterprise and of the sanctity of the right to property, which Sergio Arboleda called the barometer by which a people's moral and political development might be measured.[99] They sometimes indicated, moreover, that Liberalism represented a danger to this right and pointed to the disamortization of ecclesiastical property in 1861 as confirmation of their fears.

Conservative fears about Liberal threats to property were also aroused in 1872 as a result of President Murillo's campaign for "truth in the debt," to which reference was made earlier in this chapter. An examination of the controversy engendered by the president's proposals may serve not only to distinguish party positions but also to illustrate the kind of rhetoric employed by Colombian politicians of the era.

Murillo first raised the issue of the national debt in his inaugural address on 1 April 1872, which he devoted largely to Colombia's need for internal improvements, especially railroads.[100] An obstacle to any program of internal improvements, he said, was Colombia's "deplorable fiscal situation," which was the result of the method employed for paying interest on the national debt, that is, the assignment of virtually all of the customs revenue for this purpose. "Our customs revenue does not belong to us," the president observed, "and it is necessary to recover it . . . . Our true debt does not exceed $9 million, and we pay interest as if we owed $40 million. The present Congress . . . has the duty of dealing with this matter on the basis of truth in the debt and in consideration of the demands of the economy and the national life."

What Murillo had in mind with respect to the internal debt, which had a nominal value of $9.9 million, was its prompt amortization in cash in accordance with its market value.[101] On 10 June Congress passed a law along the lines suggested by the president which provided for the gradual amortization of the internal consolidated debt; payment was to be based on a gradually rising scale starting at 30 percent, and a specific sum was to be assigned yearly for this purpose rather than a percentage of the customs revenue.[102] The president hoped that by ending the assignment of customs revenue for service of the internal debt, the government would be able to use the sums freed to underwrite an annual guarantee of 7 percent to investors in railroad construction.

Between April and June a polemical storm raged over the capital as Liberals and Conservatives debated the president's proposal in Congress and the press. When the Industrial Society of Artisans lauded the president's position on the internal debt, Murillo's reply, cited earlier in this chapter, which condemned the "monetary aristocracy of the world," drew an indignant rejoinder from *El Bien Público*. A contributor to this newspaper, which was founded by two Conservatives and José María Samper, labeled the president's statement an "official scandal" and accused him of trying to create class antagonism.[103] How could there be class conflict, the writer asked, in a society where there was freedom of industry and education; where artisans and laborers had more than enough work, where public lands were available without charge, and where there were no monopolies or privileges?

Another journalistic tempest occurred when the head of a veterans' group expressed approval of Murillo's first acts as president. In his reply Murillo again referred to the exploitation of labor by capital, which he considered the underlying cause of the recent "communalist movement" in Paris.[104] It was his opinion that, while the government should not combat speculation and usury directly, it should not encourage them, just as it did not encourage drunkenness or prostitution. "The government has moral obligations which it must observe; it ought to be impartial and just in all its proceedings, and if it gives capital the freedom to charge as high a rate of interest as it can, it ought to concede the worker's freedom not to pay that interest, without the interference of the law in any way." *El Bien Público* again took exception to Murillo's statements, accusing the president of overstepping the limitations of his office.[105] "What does the president of the Republic have to do with the purely private matter of interest and contracts involving loans? To occupy himself with this is to intrude in an area that is none of his concern and to demonstrate clearly that what he wishes to do is to flatter envy and other evil passions."

Murillo's words also drew criticism from *El Tradicionista* of Bogotá and *El Heraldo* of Medellín, both of them Conservative organs which disapproved of the public credit plan.[106] In the opinion of the former, the plan was in complete accord with the principles of Bentham, that is, the acceptance of utility as the sole basis of morality.[107] A contributor to *El Heraldo* took a similarly dim view of the administration's ethics.

> The plan of Dr. Murillo seems like the illusion of a nightmare . . . to Christians who recognize property as an imprescriptible right, . . . who place justice above all convenience because justice is the law of God. But [Dr. Murillo] . . . does not reason according to these principles. Dr. Murillo is a utilitarian and according to the morality of this sect, a public or private act is good or evil not because it may be just or unjust . . . but in accordance with the sum of pleasure or pain it produces. Dr. Murillo has found, according to the calculations of his moral arithmetic, that to despoil the creditors of their rights and to dispose of the customs revenues to his own taste will produce more pleasure than pain; for him the action is a good one.[108]

Meanwhile, Conservative members of both houses of Congress had also been expressing objections to the proposed legislation. Sergio Arboleda, who represented Tolima in the Senate, argued that the bill was unfair to the creditors of the nation, that the government's financial resources were not nearly so exiguous as Murillo had implied, and that in any case it should not harbor ambitious plans for economic development.[109] "The mission of government is not to populate the wilderness, . . . nor to build railroads . . . nor to do anything that can be executed by private citizens. . . . The mission of the government is to see to it that justice reigns in society and that all the citizens, protected by the government, may feel that they may enjoy their rights and the full exercise of their faculties." In the Chamber of Representatives Lázaro María Pérez also indicated doubts about the alleged penury of the federal treasury. Nor did he approve of references to the exploitation of labor by capital which he felt were irrelevant to Colombia, where there was a shortage of laborers and whoever was willing to work could earn enough to live.[110] "These communist themes of capital and labor have been awakened among us on account of the issue of public credit, and we have seen that the president has made them an obligatory topic in his speeches. The *utility* of the tactic is clear to me, but I declare that at present, when each artisan can count on at least one disappointment, the maneuver seems to me not only evil but futile."

Another Conservative congressman, Carlos Holguín, was also concerned about the "socialistic speeches praising the Paris Commune" which emanated from the presidential palace, "arousing the evil passions of the poor against the rich."[111] These speeches merely represented an attempt to mobilize popular support on behalf of the public credit bill; as in 1850, the Liberals were using the masses for their own political ends, but times had changed, and the people no longer had their former faith in the Liberal party. It was Holguín's opinion that the public credit bill represented a revolution against anyone who had property and against the present organization of society, which guaranteed to all the enjoyment of the fruits of their labor, economy, and intelligence.

Medardo Rivas, a Liberal who represented Cundinamarca in the Chamber of Representatives, offered a rebuttal to Holguín.[112] The cry of socialism was always raised when an injustice was about to be corrected, Rivas asserted, but he and other supporters of the public credit bill were not socialists. "We are simply Liberals who work for the destruction of monopolies and of artificial barriers established by law that prevent the nation's wealth from spreading everywhere like water and favor only the capitalists, so that the labor, morality, and efforts of the workers will always be futile, and the people will always have to purchase with a tear the grain of wheat with which they nourish themselves." Rivas denied that the Liberal party was the enemy of property; on the contrary, it wanted the extension of property. In fact, he claimed that the number of proprietors had increased since the Liberal party had put its doctrines into practice, removing monopolies and other obstacles to progress.

When the public credit bill became law in June, *El Tradicionista* expressed the belief that the measure, which it said constituted the "official spoliation of public creditors," together with the "socialistic inclinations" of the president, had discouraged foreigners interested in railroad construction in Colombia, for they could have little confidence in the promises of a government guilty of such a "scandalous" proceeding.[113] Unmindful of the gloomy forebodings of *El Tradicionista,* Murillo was pleased by the results of the law. In his message to Congress on 1 February 1874 he reported that the law had contributed to the improvement of the nation's fiscal condition.[114] A surplus of $850,000 had remained at the end of the previous fiscal year, and a surplus of at least $1.4 million was expected in the current fiscal year. With this encouragement, the government was ready to embark on several railroad projects, one of which, the Northern Railroad, proved to be even more controversial than the public credit law.

As this episode illustrates, Liberals and Conservatives disagreed on policy issues as well as on several basic principles, and significant consequences often flowed from the implementation of Liberal as opposed to Conservative prescriptions. To be sure, some matters might be agitated by either party at a given moment primarily for political gain, but for both parties there were ideological boundaries that limited and shaped the content and direction of debate. For the Liberals, these boundaries encouraged an outlook toward human society that was secular, meliorist, and individualistic. Such a world view could have little significance for established elites or for the plebeians at the base of the social pyramid. It was most likely to be acceptable to the upwardly mobile like the provincial gentry from whose ranks so many Liberal leaders had sprung.

5
The Political Process in a Federal Setting

If one accepts the definition of a political party given by Leslie Lipson—"a group of people who are sufficiently like-minded to work together in order to secure control of the government and apply the policies that promote their interests"[1]—then Colombia's nineteenth-century Liberals clearly constituted a party. This definition is so broad, however, that it can encompass other kinds of associations, such as factions or interest groups. Another set of defining characteristics has been identified by Karen L. Remmer. These have the merit of permitting a distinction to be made between parties and "other social structures seeking power within the political arena": "(1) a set of consciously shared perspectives, opinions or beliefs; (2) continuing and regularized connections or relationships between political leaders at the center and local leaders or party activists; (3) a durable base of popular support; and (4) coordinated activity to win popular support in order to exercise control over the selection of government authorities and the formulation of public policy."[2]

On the basis of these criteria, Colombian Liberalism cannot be said to have fully constituted a political party by the 1860s. The preceding chapters have shown the existence of "consciously shared perspectives, opinions or beliefs" and "a durable base of popular support." However, while connections or relationships between political leaders at the center and local leaders or party activists were continuing, at this time they were not yet regularized through permanent committees or other organizations. The extent to which the party of the 1860s and 1870s met the fourth requirement depends partly on the interpretation of the term *popular support* in this context. Liberals directed their appeals not so much to a generalized public as to their already committed constituency. Moreover, party activity was coordinated to some extent, but since the political life of the nation revolved around the electoral process, such organized party effort as occurred was in evidence mainly during campaigns. The second half of this chapter will be devoted to a discussion of the electoral process and the party activity that it generated. First, however, it is necessary to consider some of the political forces that most strongly influenced the electoral process while the Rionegro constitution was in effect: the relationship between the federal and state governments, intraparty dissension, and the actions and inclinations of the Conservative opposition.

Because of the powers assigned to the states by the Rionegro constitution, the state governments were highly desirable prizes, and in most states there was vigorous competition for control of the government. In fact, the independence and power of the states led Miguel Samper in 1881 to liken Colombian federalism to the feudalism of medieval Europe. In his opinion, the state governments were similar to the great baronies, while the federal government, like the monarchies of the Middle Ages, exercised only nominal authority.[3]

Samper was only partly correct, however. While the states were theoretically sovereign and exercised great powers, particularly with respect to the election of the president of the Union, the federal government was by no means a creature of the states. There was continual tension between the federal government and the states, and one of the principal grievances of Conservatives and dissident Liberals in the mid-1870s was that Liberal administrations had flagrantly violated the rights of the states, especially by trying to impose on them governments that would be subservient to the national executive.

Perhaps no issue better illustrated the complexity of federal-state relations in the political sphere than the perennial controversy over what was known as "public order"—that is, the course to be followed by the federal authorities when a state government was threatened by rebellion. The issue was of considerable importance, for any state government might be confronted with an armed insurrection led by members of the opposing party or by a dissident faction of the ruling party. If the federal government was authorized to intervene on behalf of the beleaguered government, the likelihood of its defeating the insurrection would probably be increased. Conversely, federal neutrality or nonintervention might have the effect of aiding the revolution.

The Rionegro constitution said nothing on the subject of public order, providing merely that the president of the Union was "to watch over (*velar*) the preservation of general order" (Article 66, clause 19). In 1867, however, Congress passed a law enjoining the federal government to observe strict neutrality between the contending parties whenever a revolution broke out in any one of the states. This law was in large measure a byproduct of the controversy then in progress between Congress and President Mosquera, and its desirability was soon questioned. In 1868 Carlos Martín, secretary of the interior and foreign relations and a leader in the conspiracy that effected Mosquera's deposition on 23 May 1867, called for repeal of the law in his annual report to Congress.[4] He felt that the law was unconstitutional, contrary to "the doctrines of science," and unconducive to the prosperous development of the nation. He found it incomprehensible that under the terms of the law the entire nation could be engulfed by war while the federal government had to maintain the fiction that peace reigned. What Martín proposed was replacement of the current law with legislation patterned on Section 4, Article 4, of the

Constitution of the United States, "the model nation in theory and practice of the federal republican system," which protects the states against domestic violence.

No change was then forthcoming, but three years later, on 19 April 1871, Martín, now serving as a senator from Cundinamarca, introduced a bill providing for repeal of the 1867 law and adoption of Section 4, Article 4, of the United States constitution.[5] Martín's bill failed of passage, as did several others on the same subject introduced during the 1871 session of Congress, but the Senate did vote to repeal the 1867 law, thereby giving the president a freer hand when a critical situation arose.[6] In the Chamber of Representatives, however, the repeal bill was defeated by a vote of 28 to 16, with the Conservative delegations from Antioquia and Tolima voting solidly against it.[7] Conservative strategists presumably felt that the preservation of existing restraints on the federal government might serve to abet Conservative revolutions against Liberal states.

Despite the fact that the 1867 law remained on the books, there were frequent charges that the federal government did not remain neutral with respect to state revolutions. It was claimed, for example, that a revolt which overthrew Felipe Pérez as president of Boyacá in 1871 had had the indirect support of the Salgar administration in Bogotá. According to Pérez and others, Salgar had tacitly endorsed the aims of the Boyacá revolutionists by refusing to sell arms to the state government and by removing a batallion of the federal army, or Colombian Guard, from the state capital at Tunja at a time when the plot against Pérez was common knowledge.[8] Salgar's successor, Manuel Murillo, was accused of direct intervention in the internal affairs of a state in May 1873 when troops of the Colombian Guard stationed in the city of Panama restored Gabriel Neira to the presidency of Panama, from which he had been ousted only the month before. The Colombian Guard had acted, it was alleged, on Murillo's instructions in order to insure the vote of Panama for Santiago Pérez, the presidential candidate whom Murillo was backing.[9]

The 1867 law remained in force until June 1876 when it was repealed shortly before the start of the Conservative revolution of that year. This move, according to one Conservative commentator, was a transparent stratagem to permit federal assistance to the administration of César Conto in Cauca, where the Conservative uprising was brewing.[10] As the Liberal party was increasingly gripped by internal division in the late 1870s, federal intervention in state conflicts, no longer explicitly banned, became more common. The culmination of this trend was reached in May 1880, during the first administration of Rafael Núñez, when Congress passed a law authorizing the federal government to act on behalf of state governments facing domestic violence. In the opinion of United States Minister Ernest Dichman, passage of the law did not augur an era of political tranquility for

Colombia. "My knowledge of the political development of this country, and of the character of its politicians," he wrote, "leads me to entertain the opinion, . . . that the Colombian law . . . will be used merely as an instrument for the selfish purposes and personal aggrandizement of the politicians who, for the time being, may wield the power of the federal government."[11] Without adopting Dichman's arrogant tone, it may be agreed that the law did serve as a means of maintaining in power state governments friendly to Núñez and the Independent Liberals.

An important weapon in the hands of a president who wished to influence political events in the states was the Colombian Guard. Between 1863 and 1875 the army consumed an average of 12 percent of the federal budget and ranged in size from 1,000 to 2,500 men.[12] By 1880 the figure had risen to 5,000 men; at this time about 1,000 were employed as a garrison in the capital, and another 500 were ordinarily stationed in Panama, supposedly to prevent interruption of Panama Railroad service.[13]

It is clear that the officers of the Colombian Guard did not constitute a professional body with a sense of corporate identity that might encourage them to defy civilian authority. "The National Army is merely nominal," Minister Scruggs reported in 1875. "Indeed, it can scarcely be said to exist. By constitutional provision, any citizen can be created an officer of any grade, from the lowest to the highest, without the slightest military experience or education."[14] Several years later an American army officer engaged to help organize Colombia's school of civil and military engineering, which began operations in 1880, expressed the belief that few, if any, of the officers of the Colombian Guard had received professional military training.[15]

Although all the states were supposed to furnish contingents for the Guard in accordance with their population, contemporaries believed that the army was composed mainly of "Indians" from Boyacá and Cundinamarca, who were impressed into service "very much in the same manner that a Texas herdsman lassos his cattle."[16] Although the recruitment of soldiers by this method was routinely deplored by Colombians, it was still in use at the end of the century. The soldiers themselves rarely deserted and often displayed great bravery in battle; if captured, however, they would fight just as readily for the enemy.[17]

One reason for the preponderance of soldiers from the interior in the Guard is suggested by an exchange between Manuel Murillo and Buenaventura Correoso, the president of Panama, in 1872.[18] Murillo, then president of the Union, inquired with some asperity why the Panamanian authorities did not provide recruits for the batallion stationed on the Isthmus, for it was "impossible" to keep on sending soldiers from the interior, most of whom went there to die. Correoso replied by proposing that soldiers from Cartagena or Santa Marta be sent to Panama since "people here are very reluctant to serve in the national batallion because they are fearful of being sent out of the country."

The political role of the Guard was limited but varied, becoming more prominent during the period of intraparty strife starting in 1875. The endorsement of a presidential candidate by officers of the Guard might serve to discourage rivals.[19] In addition, soldiers of the Bogotá garrison might be instructed to vote for candidates favored by the federal government. Finally, the Guard might intervene directly in the political affairs of a state.

Nowhere was the Guard more active in politics than in Panama. Its role in restoring President Gabriel Neira to power there in 1873 has already been mentioned. This was not an isolated case, for in 1865 a company of the Guard took part in the bloodless overthrow of another Isthmian government. After a mutiny of Guard troops in the interior of Panama shortly afterward, the *Star and Herald* was moved to exclaim: "For many years, in our memory, the Isthmus of Panama was the quietest portion of the Republic, and people never dreamt of revolutions, though in those days we had but a little police force of twenty-five men; but ever since large bodies of national troops have been kept here, the Isthmus has, we may say, been constantly in a state of revolution."[20] Similarly, Minister Dichman commented in 1878 that the role of the Colombian Guard in Panama was "to make and unmake" presidents of that state.[21]

To be sure, the political relations of the federal government with the states varied in accordance not only with the responsiveness of the latter to the national government but also with local conditions, for there were great differences in political style and behavior among the states. Panama and the two other coastal states were probably the most turbulent and frequently experienced revolutionary movements, usually involving an effort by one Liberal group to displace another. United States Minister Allan Burton, stationed as he was in Bogotá, did not observe Costeño politics directly, but the grievances of American citizens hurt by the turmoil in the region in the 1860s led him to take a censorious view of politics there. "It is indeed difficult to imagine a more melancholy specimen of government than the authority exercised by the petty heads of the coastal states, among the worst of which is the present one of Panama," he wrote in 1865. "These states are almost uniformly in the hands of men whose chief incentive to intrude themselves into office is the opportunity it affords to secure selfish and unworthy ends."[22] Once in power, he added, such men could be dislodged only by force. Fourteen years later Conservative Carlos Martínez Silva echoed Burton's opinion of Panamanian politics. "The politics of Panama is *sui generis*. There, more than in any other state of the Union, the Liberal factions lack principles and dignity in their conduct. The struggle for power, carried on with scandalous rapacity, is not even between circles but between families; it seems like Peru in miniature or a caricature of the Italian republics of the Middle Ages."[23]

At the other extreme were Santander and Antioquia, both of which were remarkable for their political tranquility. Of Santander, a Conservative newspaper in Medellín reported in 1871:

> Here is a state which forms a contrast to . . . other Liberal states. The government of Santander proceeds with regularity; it attends with interest all branches of public administration, especially popular education and the means of communication; it is not the scene of shameful dissensions or electoral frauds. Santandereanos are proud, fond of liberty and work, and respectful of the law. . . . For this reason they are not divided into infernal circles . . . like those which constantly appear in Bolívar, Panama, Magdalena, and Cundinamarca.[24]

In his reference to Cundinamarca the writer was undoubtedly alluding to that state's Liberal political machine, the most notorious in nineteenth-century Colombia, founded by Ramón Gómez, a professor of law who was nicknamed *El Sapo* ("the toad"). Because of the nickname, the machine and the young lawyers who constituted it became known as *sapos* or *sapistas*. The *sapista* machine originated in 1861 when the results of a state election held while the Liberal revolution was still in progress gave Gómez and his followers a majority in a constituent assembly that met in August 1862.[25] They proceeded to draft a state constitution that enabled them to remain dominant by concentrating power in the legislature and the judiciary. The constitution provided for the election by the legislature of the *procurador,* or attorney general, and of judges of the superior court of the state. The court in turn named circuit judges, notaries, and registrars of public documents; the *procurador* appointed district attorneys (*fiscales*); and the circuit judges appointed lower court magistrates. The constitution also provided that the *juntas escrutadoras,* or examining committees, which inspected election returns, be composed of circuit judges, notaries, registrars, and district attorneys. By means of this system, therefore, the men who determined the membership of the state assembly were themselves creatures of that body.

By the time the constituent assembly ended its labors on 18 July 1863 it had nominated Gómez to the Supreme Court of the Union, and several other *sapos* were appointed to the state tribunal.[26] Daniel Aldana, who was sometimes identified as a *sapista,* was named attorney general. Although they controlled two-thirds of the state legislature, the *sapos* came into conflict with the president of the state, the popular revolutionary hero and future president of the Union, Santos Gutiérrez, and were forced to convoke another constituent assembly for 1 January 1865. However, *sapos* again dominated the assembly, and the new constitution did not differ markedly from its predecessor.[27]

Sapista influence in Cundinamarca was checked somewhat in 1867 when Aldana, then serving as state president, removed pro-Mosquera *sapos* from office a few days after Mosquera had been deposed as president of the

Union. By 1870, however, the *sapos* had made a comeback of sufficient strength to provoke a coup by young Liberals against the assembly and Cundinamarca's president, Justo Briceño, who was accused of excessive submissiveness to their will.[28] Thereafter their influence seems to have waned, but as late as 1876 anger at *sapista* rule in the department of Ubaté prompted one Antonio Nieto M. to write a letter to the president of the Union, Aquileo Parra, in which he excoriated "that purely personal circle which has done nothing but exploit public office, especially the judicial power; which prostituted the right of suffrage; and which is a continuous threat to property."[29] More specifically, Nieto charged that criminals with money or the right connections were able to avoid prosecution and that most of the qualified voters in Ubaté had been stricken from the rolls. Since the departmental prefect, a physician, was concerned only with his practice, the government was actually in the hands of his secretary, a man who could descend no lower on the scale of political degradation.

By the time Nieto made his complaint, Conservatives and Liberal dissidents were regularly depicting the *sapos* as allies of the Radicals, and the term *sapismo* eventually became a general label of opprobrium for the electoral abuses to which Liberal rule and the Rionegro constitution had supposedly given rise.[30] The association of *sapismo* and Radicalism was only partly correct, however. Ramón Gómez supported the Radical presidential candidates in 1875 and 1879, but other *sapos* became adherents of Rafael Núñez. In 1881 José María Samper, by then an avowed Conservative, fulminated against the "*sapista* maneuvers" of fellow-Conservative Manuel Briceño which had prevented Samper's selection as a delegate from Tolima to a forthcoming Conservative convention.[31] Samper's words indicate that the term *sapista* was also being used to characterize political practices of which one disapproved, regardless of the party to which the culprits belonged. Likewise a 1973 article called the machine of a twentieth-century Conservative boss one of "*sapista* perfection."[32] It should be noted that at no time did critics of the *sapos* identify them with any class, interest, or region of the state, though an artisans' newspaper did assert in 1867 that *sapo* domination had brought to public office men who were fit only for the manual labor of peons.[33]

Competition among Liberal factions on the state level usually, though not invariably, involved nothing more than the pursuit of office and personal gain by local party chiefs and their followers. On the national level, however, the party was at times divided into two factions which not only sought to monopolize public office but also had significant policy differences and were marked by divergent regional orientations.

Bifurcation of the Liberal party became evident several times after 1850, notably in 1854, 1866–67, and 1875–78. In each case the specific issues which prompted the division were different, but contemporaries frequently felt that the leadership and tendencies of each of the two groups at the time of each division established a link between them. This perception of continuity is shown by the use of the same labels to designate the contending factions in different periods.

The first major split in the Liberal party, briefly described in chapter 1, saw the emergence of the *Gólgota* and *Draconiano* factions and culminated in the coup d'ètat of 17 April 1854, led by *Draconiano* General José María Melo, who was soon ousted by a coalition of *Gólgotas* and Conservatives. By 1855 the *Gólgotas* were being called Radicals on some occasions, though the specific reasons for this designation are not clear.[34]

In the following decade many Radicals distinguished themselves for their opposition to Tomás Cipriano de Mosquera, who led the Liberals in the successful revolution of 1859–62 and served as president of the Union in 1863–64 and 1866–67. Although the latent hostility between the Radicals and Mosquera had flared at the Rionegro convention, the struggle was not joined until he assumed the presidency on 20 May 1866. The principal battleground was Congress, where the anti-Mosquera members were able to form a majority with the help of the Conservative delegation from Antioquia.

Numerous issues arose to exacerbate the relations between the two Liberal factions. The first of these was a contract for a $7.5 million loan for internal improvements which Mosquera had negotiated with the English firm of Robinson & Fleming while serving as Colombian minister in London after his retirement from the presidency in 1864.[35] The opposition criticized the contract on many grounds, but their principal argument was that the annual service of $800,000 would impose too heavy a burden on the nation. A second source of conflict was the public order bill described earlier in this chapter, which was passed despite the president's opposition.

An even more explosive issue involved the relations of Colombia with Peru, then at war with Spain, a conflict in which Colombia had adopted a policy of neutrality. When the appearance of a mysterious warship of uncertain origin led to disclosure of a secret treaty with Peru and the congressional majority made clear its intention of investigating the matter, Mosquera responded on 29 April 1867 by declaring the republic in a state of war and ordering the closure of Congress for the current year.[36] To the opponents of Mosquera the events of 29 April heralded the imposition of a dictatorship upon the nation, and that very night plans were laid for the deposition of the president, which took place in the early morning hours of 23 May.[37] The same day presidential alternate Santos Acosta was installed as chief executive for the remainder of Mosquera's term.[38]

The coup of 23 May met with little resistance anywhere in the republic, except for Bolívar, where the state president, Antonio González Carazo, initially refused to recognize the Acosta administration. Later in the year Mosquera was tried before the Senate on a number of charges, including the negotiation of the Peruvian treaty, which had been designed to help Peru evade the neutrality laws of other nations and acquire arms with Colombian connivance. He was found guilty and sentenced to two years' imprisonment, but was allowed to go into exile in Peru, where he remained until 1871, when he returned to Colombia to resume his political career by serving as president of Cauca.[39] Meanwhile, he and his followers remained hostile to the Radicals, whom they attempted unsuccessfully to unseat in 1869 and 1873, and in 1875 the Mosqueristas supported the candidacy of Rafael Núñez almost to a man.

To nineteenth-century Liberals of Radical sympathies, the support of the Mosqueristas for Núñez and his adherents was not surprising, for they asserted that both groups, along with the *Draconianos* of the 1850s, were cut from the same ideological cloth. It was the opinion of the Radicals that the same two groups could be discerned in the periodic divisions of the party. One, made up of the *Gólgotas* and their successors, was devoted to Liberal principles, specifically to civilian and constitutional government, with strong limitations on the power of the executive. The other, which one writer called a "pretorian faction,"[40] had a predisposition toward authoritarianism, personalism, and militarism. As a Radical spokesman explained in 1867, what divided Mosquera's foes from other Liberals was that "some of us uphold certain doctrines which we believe to be true, while others uphold men whom they believe to be necessary."[41]

In reality, only one charge in the Radical indictment—the accusation of personalism—holds up under scrutiny, in that Obando and Mosquera did at times evoke a popular adulation and loyalty that was never conferred upon any single Radical chieftain. While the Radicals are often described as doctrinaire extremists by unfriendly historians, they were no more consistent or immoderate than their Liberal adversaries. On religious matters, for example, as indicated in chapter 1, the Radicals were in general considerably less anticlerical than the Mosqueristas in the 1860s, though they would shift their position after 1876.

The Radical-Mosquerista conflict has been viewed from another perspective by Indalecio Liévano Aguirre, a modern Colombian defender of Mosquera. According to Liévano Aguirre, Mosquera was a populist whose opponents, concerned mainly with the protection of private property, were galvanized to action by a decree (11 August 1866) indicating that Mosquera planned a drastic agrarian reform in Colombia.[42] However, this argument is vitiated by a number of considerations, among them the fact that Mosquera himself rescinded the decree the following February, that he did not portray himself as a friend of the landless in the various statements he made in his defense, and that he reacted with horror to land seizures in Cauca a decade later (see chapter 6). In addition, Liévano Aguirre's depiction of Mosquera as a nationalist, in contrast to his foes, is weakened by the fact that the Robinson & Fleming contract, which he defended so vigorously, contained an article providing for the appointment of foreign nationals as collectors of Colombian customs. This article was criticized by opponents of the contract and was rejected when the contract was approved, with other important modifications, on 28 June 1866.

What did distinguish the Radicals from their Liberal opponents, as stated in chapter 3, was their origin in eastern Colombia, especially Santander. Their opponents, on the other hand, tended to come from Cauca and the Coast, especially Bolívar, and enjoyed considerable popularity in these regions. In the presidential election of 1856, for example, Mosquera came in a distant third behind Conservative Mariano Ospina Rodríguez and Liberal Manuel Murillo Toro, but he won a plurality or majority not only in his native province of Popayán but also in the state of Panama and in the three provinces that later comprised the state of Bolívar as well as in one of the provinces out of which Magdalena was formed.[43] These were, moreover, the only areas carried by Mosquera. Similarly, in the presidential election of 1869, when Mosqueristas and some Conservatives united to work for the election of Mosquera, the former president won the votes of both Bolívar and Cauca. In the elections of 1871 and 1873 Bolívar voted for Radical candidates, but Cauca cast its ballot for Julián Trujillo, a native son and close associate of Mosquera, on both occasions.

Mosquera also expressed resentment at the supposed domination of the country by the eastern states and appealed to such resentment elsewhere. In 1868, for example, in commenting on Buenaventura Correoso's accession as president of Panama, Mosquera expressed satisfaction that the Isthmus had been returned to native control and was no longer "a colony" of the "Santandereano *Gólgotas.*"[44] Three years later he complained to Correoso that there was a desire in Bogotá to invest all the nation's financial resources in the eastern states and suggested a "cordial union" of the western states in order to make themselves respected.[45] On another occasion he revived the idea that the national capital should be moved to a federal district in Panama.[46]

Two points deserve emphasis. Although Liberal factionalism was not infrequent and sometimes had dire consequences for the party, it did not prove sufficiently severe to inflict a mortal wound. Liberal factions, whether national or local, readily patched up their differences when they perceived a serious threat to the party. Secondly, despite the vigor of the periodic attacks against the hegemony of the Radical leadership and despite the fact that they permanently lost control of the federal government in 1878, they were and continued to be the pivotal figures of Colombian Liberalism. When disenchantment set in among many of Núñez's earlier followers, it was to Radical chiefs like Aquileo Parra that they turned for leadership, and after the definitive fall of the Liberals in 1885, it was Parra and other erstwhile Radicals who were acknowledged as party directors. To be sure, they encountered almost as much opposition after 1886 as they had in previous decades, but they or those who considered themselves their political heirs never lost their dominant position in the party.

The Colombian party system was, of course, a two-party system, and the existence of the Conservative party inevitably affected Liberal policies and practices. As the party out of power from 1862 to 1885, the Conservatives in turn plotted their course in accordance with their perceptions of Liberal strategy and goals, though their aim was to regain control of the national government either in the short or the long run.

Three avenues toward this objective were open to Conservative strategists, all of which were followed after 1862, at times simultaneously. First of all, the Conservative party could function as a loyal and pacific opposition party, competing with the Liberals at the polls and by means of the written and spoken word. A second alternative was the formation of alliances with dissident Liberals, especially for electoral purposes, through which Conservatives might win positions in the state or federal governments or attain other ends, such as constitutional reform. The third course was armed revolt, either on the state or national level, aimed at overthrowing the Liberals by force.

Conservatives were by no means agreed as to which of these courses should be adopted or given priority at any specific moment. Some, for example, were opposed in principle to any policy involving the use of violence while others simply felt that revolution, especially against the federal government, was bound to fail. Well-to-do Conservatives were sometimes described as being adverse to revolution because of its economic ravages. Minister Burton reported in 1863, shortly after the revolution that brought the Liberals to power: "The wealth of this country is mainly in the hands of the Conservatives and this class does not favor agitation; but will mostly acquiesce in the rule of either party for the present, rather than jeopardize their property."[47]

Among the most reluctant to assist their coreligionists in revolutionary endeavors were the Conservative leaders of Antioquia, who themselves came to power by violence in 1864. In January of that year the forces of the Liberal state government were decisively defeated on the battlefield by Conservatives led by Pedro J. Berrío. Although Berrío, who became provisional governor, affirmed his fidelity to the Rionegro constitution and to the federal government, some Liberals were alarmed by the Conservatives' success, particularly because they feared that the Antioqueños might encourage similar uprisings in Cauca and Tolima.[48] Berrío tried in vain to obtain federal recognition of his government from the Mosquera administration, and it was not until after Manuel Murillo took office as Mosquera's successor on 10 April 1864 that a formal agreement was reached.[49] Berrío's commissioners pledged that the state government would carry out its obligations as prescribed by the Rionegro constitution, would grant a general amnesty, reduce its army to 200 men, and secure the withdrawal of Caucanos living in Antioquia who were deemed dangerous by the governor of Cauca to points at least fifteen leagues from the border. On 19 April President Murillo hailed the agreement, which he said ensured peace, the most important goal of his administration.[50] It has been suggested, however, that Murillo's willingness to accept the Conservative regime in Antioquia was due less to a desire for peace than to a desire to weaken the Mosqueristas, with whom the fallen Liberals of Antioquia were associated, to warn Liberals in other states that they could not expect federal help if they allowed themselves to be overthrown, and to sow seeds of future discord between the Antioqueños and their Conservative brethren elsewhere.[51]

Elected to a four-year term as governor of Antioquia in 1865 and reelected in 1869, Berrío left an outstanding record, and at the time of his death in 1875 both houses of Congress passed a resolution lamenting his demise.[52] Meanwhile, relations between Antioquia and the Radicals remained amicable. On 19 September 1865 the state legislature paid tribute to "the moderation, probity, and skill" with which President Murillo had directed national policy, giving security to the governed, striving to end partisan hatred and violence, and guiding Colombia along the path of order and peace.[53] During Mosquera's conflict with Congress in 1866–67, the delegation from Antioquia supported the Radicals, and Governor Berrío actively opposed the president's dictatorial measures after 29 April 1867.[54]

Relations between the Radical-dominated federal government and the Antioquia Conservatives were not uniformly harmonious, however. Although the semiofficial *El Heraldo* of Medellín spoke favorably of the auguries for Murillo's second term on the basis of his past record, it strongly opposed his plan for paying the internal debt in 1872.[55] In 1874 the same newspaper attacked a speech by the president in which he referred to the "bitterness" he had experienced when he had recognized in 1864 a sectional government that was to be "a permanent nucleus of conspiracy against the Union."[56] The speech was seen by *El Heraldo* as a bid by Murillo to win the approbation of *Draconianos* within the Liberal party.[57] A short time later the newspaper's ill will was dispelled when Congress passed legislation granting Antioquia public lands and an annual subsidy for ten years of $100,000 to aid in construction of a railroad linking Medellín with the Magdalena.[58]

Despite Murillo's description of Antioquia as "a permanent nucleus of conspiracy," it appears that the Conservative leaders of the state did remain aloof from revolutionary plots hatched by their coreligionists elsewhere. In 1865, while discussing the possibility of a nationwide Conservative uprising, Conservative José María Quijano Otero noted in his diary his conviction that Berrío felt obliged to remain loyal to Murillo because of Murillo's support the year before. "This, together with the selfishness of the Antioqueños, has led us to have little faith in the help they might give us should the need arise."[59] For his part Berrío seems to have felt little dissatisfaction with the status quo. In a message to the state legislature in 1873, he stated that Antioquia had acquired federalist habits in colonial times and pointed out how difficult it would be for the region to adapt to centralism.[60] For this reason, he continued, Antioquia had accepted the Rionegro constitution in good faith and defended it with enthusiasm. "I have said before, and I will now repeat, that this constitution is generally good . . . its only objectionable features are its tyrannical dispositions regarding ecclesiastical matters." With Berrío dead, however, the state government reluctantly became a participant in the Conservative revolution of 1876–77, and the Liberal victory that followed meant a temporary end to Conservative domination of Antioquia.

Conservatives were able to make gains in two other states as a result of the events of 23 May 1867. Tolima, which was controlled by Mosquerista Liberals, fell under Conservative control and remained a Conservative state until 1877. In Cundinamarca a Conservative, Ignacio Gutiérrez Vergara, was elected governor in 1867 but was soon at loggerheads with the state legislature, where the Liberals had a slim majority.[61] When Gutiérrez Vergara issued a decree on 9 October 1868, convoking a constituent assembly and setting up procedures for the election of delegates, the Liberals claimed that his action constituted an assumption of dictatorial power, and he was removed from office by the federal authorities the following day.

According to Carlos Holguín, who had been secretary of government in Gutiérrez Vergara's administration, the Conservatives who had aided the Radicals in their struggle against Mosquera felt betrayed by the treatment accorded the governor.[62] The result was a decision by Holguín and other Conservative leaders to join followers of Mosquera in supporting Mosquera's candidacy for the presidency in 1869, primarily as a means of indicating the extent of their dissatisfaction with Radicalism and the recent conduct of the federal government.

The alliance, or *liga,* of the Mosqueristas and Conservatives was formalized in a fifteen-point agreement signed on 5 April 1869 by three Conservatives—Recaredo de Villa, Luis S. Silvestre, and Leonardo Canal—and by three Mosquerista Liberals—José María Rojas Garrido, Ramón Mercado, and Angel María Céspedes.[63] According to the terms of the pact, both parties would vote for Mosquera in the coming election; they would try to obtain equal representation for both parties in Congress and in the legislatures of all the states except Tolima and Antioquia; upon his election Mosquera was to divide public offices equally between Liberals and Conservatives. Both parties also agreed to seek speedy negotiation of a concordat that would permanently settle the religious question and to convoke a convention to reform the constitution. Mosquera, still in exile in Lima, received a copy of this agreement and gave his approval on 5 July.[64]

As might be expected, the *liga* was denounced by most Liberal leaders, who backed the candidacy of Eustorgio Salgar, and many Conservatives also rejected it.[65] Most important of all, Antioquia cast its presidential vote for former President Pedro A. Herrán, thereby nullifying the April agreement, which was to be invalid if either Tolima or Antioquia failed to vote for Mosquera. However, even before the April agreement was signed, the federal government was concerned enough about the threat of a Mosquera candidacy to order the transfer of 150 troops of the Colombian Guard from Cartagena to Panama to prevent Mosquera's return to Colombia via Panama. The *Star and Herald* remarked on this occasion: "That [Mosquera] has many supporters in Panama is . . . evident, and it is probable if he were to land here that he would carry the state against Salgar."[66] As it turned out, Salgar won the vote of Panama as well as those of Boyacá, Cundinamarca, Magdalena, and Santander, while Mosquera carried only three states: Cauca, Bolívar, and Tolima.

Carlos Holguín, the architect of the 1869 *liga*, realized that Mosquera would not win the presidency but considered the effort a success because it brought the Conservatives into contact with dissident Liberals with whom they could cooperate.[67] The *liga* thus paved the way for similar understandings between Conservatives and Independent Liberals in the following decade, a strategy with which Holguín continued to be identified and which eventually bore fruit in the Conservative triumph of 1885–86.

During the period of Liberal rule elections for both state and federal offices were held regularly and were normally contested by both parties or at least by factions of each one. As already seen in this chapter, state leaders occasionally came to power as a result of revolution, but in general elections constituted the accepted method of filling public office. Accordingly, of the eleven men who occupied the federal presidency between 1863 and 1886, only one—Santos Acosta in 1867—attained the position by irregular means.[68] Party leaders might manipulate elections in order to ensure a favorable outcome, the balloting might be marred by violence or fraud, a large proportion of the populace might be excluded from participation because of apathy or illiteracy, but nonetheless the electoral process was the central feature of the Colombian political system.

At times it seemed as if the electoral process were never ending. Because of the large number of posts to be filled in the state and federal governments and because terms were short, the country appeared to be engulfed in unceasing political strife. In 1873 an editorialist making an appeal for electoral reform observed that since each state held its presidential election at a different time, the Colombian people endured constant agitation for eight or ten months of every election year.⁶⁹ Moreover, he said, the fact that the stock of the various candidates rose or fell as each state cast its ballot encouraged unsavory intrigues and bargains and inflicted great pressure on the states which had not yet held elections. Although greater uniformity was achieved by the constitutional reform of 1876, which provided that presidential elections be held on the same date throughout the country, a writer in an Independent Liberal newspaper still found fault with the system in 1882:

> Every two years we have a war or feel the effects of one. When blood is not shed, or forced loans are not exacted, or property is not confiscated, there is at the very least profound agitation affecting even the lowest levels of society; business is paralyzed, industries decay, and capital flees to where it can find better guarantees—that is, in four or six months of agitation we destroy the good we have done in the previous two years.⁷⁰

The agitation to which the writer referred was concentrated in the national capital. Not only was Bogotá the residence of the president and other influential party leaders, but it was also the place where politicians from all the Liberal states met in Congress and incidentally plotted electoral strategy. Indeed, much of the important preelectoral activity, such as the selection and endorsement of candidates, took place while Congress was in session.

In the capital political unrest was further aggravated by an unfettered and occasionally irresponsible press and by the proliferation of broadsides, which, according to Nicolás Esguerra, had a wider circulation than the newspapers since they were given away free.⁷¹ The fact that broadsides were often anonymous or emanated from vaguely identified sources encouraged the spread of rumors and inaccurate information. Another breeding-ground of rumors in Bogotá was the *altozano,* or raised terrace, in front of the cathedral, which was the favored spot for postprandial political discussions. Said Esguerra: "This *Peripatos* of Colombian politics is the place that draws everyone who wants to make a good digestion by speaking of Greeks and Trojans and magisterially deciding all the questions of the day, both foreign and domestic."⁷²

The Liberals' lack of a permanent party organization during the period in question probably accounted in part for their failure to standardize procedures for the selection of presidential candidates. This question was discussed with some concern in 1865 by Salvador Camacho Roldán, who observed that candidacies were left almost to chance, to the preference of a few individuals, or to the inspiration of the party press.⁷³ Although he admired the nominating conventions of the United States, he felt that the difficulty of travel made such a system impractical in Colombia and concluded that candidates ought to be selected by Congress, whose Liberal members did in fact often take the lead in making nominations.

As each presidential election approached, the names of various individuals were advanced by their friends around the country, often with considerable anticipation, for it was felt that an aspirant to the presidency could strengthen his position by getting into the race before other candidates made their bids; such an early-bird candidacy was known as a *madrugada,* or early rising.[74] Candidacies were "proclaimed" publicly by members of Congress and state legislatures, by informal groups of prominent Liberals, by the press, or by a combination of these. At some point in this process the president made his own preference known; presumably he might also have a hand in initiating a candidacy.

The role of the president in the initial stages of the contest should not be overemphasized, however. Although he might have the power to ensure the victory of a candidate, the selection of candidates was made in consultation with other Liberals, and the final choice was likely to be someone who it was hoped would be acceptable to large segments of the party. Aquileo Parra related, for example, that since Mosquera's Conservative-backed candidacy of 1869 was objectionable to "doctrinaire" Liberals, Eustorgio Salgar was chosen to oppose him not only because of his merits and services to the Liberal cause but also because his close personal and political ties to Mosquera made it probable that he would attract support among the latter's followers.[75] After Salgar had taken office, he confided to Buenaventura Correoso, the president of Panama, that he was unenthusiastic about the emergence of Manuel Murillo as the strongest Liberal candidate to succeed him in 1872:

> You probably know already that the question of the candidacy has been reduced to Murillo and [Julián] Trujillo, for although the candidacy of General [Santos] Acosta has been proclaimed, he is supported only by a small group in Bogotá. It is a pity that stubborn pretensions do not allow one to choose among the best, and I, like you, must give up so worthy a candidacy as that of Dr. Camacho R[oldán]. The Murillo candidacy has been acclaimed here and in the North not because it is free of blemishes, but because it is the least objectionable and the one that . . . is most conducive to unity and has the greatest likelihood of triumph.[76]

After Murillo became president, he was initially circumspect regarding the succession. "Try not to commit yourself regarding the presidential election," he advised Correoso on 4 August 1872. "Let us wait until the horizon clears up in order to see whom it will be desirable to elect. It is not good to hasten the matter and resolve it by whims."[77] By October Murillo was willing to be more specific:

> I will tell you confidentially that I like the candidacy of Dr. [Carlos] Martín, but I do not want to appear active in this sense. I would like to see the states produce candidates and the appearance of a spontaneous choice. I will

express an opinion later when the opinion of the people has made itself felt so that I may follow the current insofar as my own judgment will permit.

You say that you wish to hasten and proclaim the candidacy of Dr. Martín or that of Dr. [Teodoro] Valenzuela, and I think that you should do as you see fit. It is more probable that Dr. Martín's candidacy will find an echo than Dr. Valenzuela's. In Magdalena they seem to accept Dr. Martín's. In Bolívar they want the candidacy of Mr. Rafael Núñez. I do not find myself at this point in a position to judge with precision the strength of any of these fledgling candidacies, and therefore I have not wished, nor do I wish, to give a definite opinion on the matter. I can only say to you that I like Dr. Martín's candidacy, but his absence hurts him because people here are working for others. . . . There is no active agent here to work [on his behalf], and I can do nothing because of my duties. I do not wish to appear to impose my successor, and I can only express my preference. The army will vote with entire freedom.[78]

Two of the candidacies mentioned by Murillo surfaced publicly before the year was out. On 1 December the candidacy of Núñez was proclaimed in Cartagena, and that of Carlos Martín in Santa Marta two days later.[79] Martín was a Bogotano, but the Núñez candidacy was undoubtedly a reflection of Costeño desire to see a native son in the presidency.[80] There were also efforts on behalf of other Liberals as well. On 19 October twenty-six members of the Santander assembly held a meeting at the instigation of several "political friends" and agreed to propose the name of Felipe Zapata.[81] In November the candidacy of Mosquerista José María Rojas Garrido was also proclaimed.[82] Finally, on 1 January 1873 the *Diario de Cundinamarca,* considered the most authoritative spokesman for proadministration Liberals, announced that it was supporting Santiago Pérez for the presidency. The next day's issue contained an endorsement of Pérez by a group of Liberal notables which included Salvador Camacho Roldán and Miguel Samper.

It gradually became evident that Pérez was the candidate favored by the administration, though the reasons for this development are not clear. According to Parra, Murillo's personal relationship with Pérez was not particularly warm.[83] Although Pérez had served in the cabinet under Santos Gutiérrez and as minister to Washington, his reputation was based more on his abilities as an educator and intellectual than on his political prowess. In 1870 the American minister described him as "a very quiet, retired scholarly man."[84] It is probable, of course, that the other candidates, such as Martín, did not generate sufficient enthusiasm throughout the country; certainly Rojas Garrido would be objectionable because of his Mosquerista connections and his record of intemperate anticlericalism.[85] Pérez, on the other hand, was a practicing Catholic and led so impeccable a personal life that even *El Tradicionista* was moved to praise him on this score.[86]

The candidacies of Martín and Núñez soon faded, and Zapata explicitly withdrew in favor of Pérez.[87] Rojas Garrido remained in the race, but he was soon overshadowed by the emergence of a much more formidable rival to Pérez: Julián Trujillo, newly elected president of Cauca, whose candidacy was first proclaimed in April 1873. Trujillo won substantial Conservative support, to the consternation of pro-Pérez Liberals, who charged that another *liga* had been formed, and received the votes of Antioquia and Tolima along with that of Cauca. Pérez carried the six remaining Liberal states, but Murillo was criticized for allegedly interfering in Panama and Boyacá to assure Pérez victories there.

Candidates for the state presidencies, for Congress, and for other elective offices were usually chosen by the state legislatures or by Liberal juntas meeting in various districts throughout each state. The meeting of such a junta in a district did not necessarily preclude the meeting of rival juntas in the same locality with the selection of different candidates and the circulation of competing lists of office-seekers. There was, however, a desire to achieve harmony wherever possible. In 1866 Liberals of two opposing factions in Cartagena formed a five-man central committee and agreed that each group should be allowed to choose one-half of the candidates for the state assembly.[88] As one of the movers of the unity drive explained, if the party was divided at election time either the Conservatives would triumph or the Liberals would have to resort to fraud in order to win.

After a candidate had been nominated for a state presidency, his backers usually formed a state committee with local branches through which to carry out their electioneering activities. In some cases the state committee was an offshoot of the junta which had met to nominate the candidate. On 4 June 1873 a junta of Liberals met in Bogotá, unanimously chose ex-President Eustorgio Salgar as their candidate for the governorship of Cundinamarca, and appointed five of its members to an electoral directory which was to manage the campaign and encourage the formation of similar bodies on the local level.[89] At least one such directory was formed, in the department of Ubaté, after a meeting attended by twenty-two persons had been held on 1 July and all but one of those present had agreed to support Salgar.[90] Normally it was state and local organizations such as these which promoted Liberal candidates for the federal presidency, for party leaders did not ordinarily establish national committees for this purpose.

State and local organizations rarely outlived the elections that had prompted their formation. More permanent were the democratic societies, or *democráticas,* that continued to be vehicles for the mobilization of nonelite support for Liberal candidates. They were most influential in Cali and other towns in the Cauca Valley, being described in 1868 as indispensable to the party's activities in that region.[91]

Almost immediately after a candidate for the federal presidency had been nominated, endorsements or declarations of support known as *adhesiones* began coming in from state legislatures, Liberal election committees, democratic societies, and unorganized groups of Liberals throughout the country. A typical *adhesión* endorsing Santiago Pérez in 1873 read as follows: "We, the undersigned, residents of the district of Manta, State of Cundinamarca, will in the coming elections for President of the Union vote and work for the learned and honorable citizen, Dr. SANTIAGO PEREZ, who fully satisfies the country's aspirations for peace and prosperity."[92] The *adhesión* bore the names of seventy persons. Between 1 January and 31 October 1873 the *Diario de Cundinamarca* printed *adhesiones* supporting Pérez from members of Congress and the Cundinamarca and Boyacá assemblies, the democratic societies of Cali and Ibagué (Tolima), and the residents of over 150 different towns and cities in all nine states.

In a country still lacking adequate means of communication, *adhesiones* were useful in identifying the extent and nature of a candidate's following. Occasionally an individual would protest that his name had been affixed to an *adhesión* without his consent or, after signing an *adhesión* on behalf of one candidate, would suffer a change of heart and declare his preference for another. Nor was the negative *adhesión* unknown. Shortly after the proclamation of Murillo's candidacy by the Liberal press in 1871, thirty-seven members of Congress affirmed that they had had no part in his nomination.[93]

The abuses to which the practice of gathering *adhesiones* might give rise were revealed by the tribulations of Rafael Olaya Ricaurte, mayor of Suesca (Cundinamarca), who was removed from his post in 1873, reportedly for signing an *adhesión* supporting state gubernatorial candidate Eustorgio Salgar after previously signing one on behalf of his opponent, Octavio Salazar.[94] Olaya himself attributed his ouster to the machinations of one David Cortez, who wanted to avoid facing trial for horse stealing and other crimes.[95] Olaya disparaged Cortez's political influence and said that the *adhesión* Cortez had prepared for Salazar contained the names of only five qualified voters, the others being illiterates, children, or nonexistent persons.

In the interval between the proclamation of a presidential candidacy and the election in the states, the candidate's cause was taken up by one or more newspapers; sometimes newspapers were founded solely to promote a particular candidate and might be given away free of charge. Along with a stream of *adhesiones,* each newspaper would carry polemical articles extolling the candidate's merits and the policies with which he was associated and attacking the opposition. Editorial endorsements were often vague. A statement supporting Murillo for the presidency in 1863, for example, gave a lengthy list of his virtues, which included the following: "the humility of his origins, a democratic circumstance of the first order;

the nature of his political studies, which were made in adversity and were crowned not only with Liberal beliefs in every respect but also with excellent and abundant results; his experience as an administrator; the noble firmness of his political convictions; the poverty of his estate and the austerity of his habits."[96]

The candidates themselves made few public bids for votes, usually remaining aloof from the exertions of their followers. In fact, when the Liberal directory of Cundinamarca asked Eustorgio Salgar for an explicit acceptance of the gubernatorial nomination in 1873, its request was described as an unusual one.[97] It was not even necessary for a presidential candidate to be in Colombia during an election; Manuel Murillo, for example, was serving as minister to Washington when he was nominated for the presidency in 1863 and did not return until just before he took office the following year. Presumably, however, Murillo, unlike Carlos Martín, had active agents in Bogotá and other parts of the country who promoted his candidacy.

While the candidate ostensibly remained on the sidelines, his supporters were urged to "work" on his behalf. The nature of this work was never clearly spelled out, but it would ordinarily involve such chores as communication with influential persons in different areas who might be induced to support the candidate, the compilation of *adhesiones,* and the preparation of ballots. If a Liberal held a politically significant office, the boundaries between his partisan and official duties might become blurred before an election. Liberal members of municipal corporations, for example, might see to it that Conservatives or unfriendly Liberals were excluded from the voting lists. Or state officials might combine electioneering with official inspections of their districts. Thus when President Venancio Rueda of Boyacá, accompanied by his secretary and the state director of public instruction, began a tour of the state's Western Department early in 1873, *El Tradicionista* commented that the visit signaled the start of electoral operations.[98] The same year a prefect of a Cundinamarca department was accused of employing his time during an inspection in offering jobs in exchange for support for the gubernatorial candidate he was backing.[99] The federal president himself might also "work" to ensure the election of an acceptable successor, as Murillo was accused of doing in 1873. It was also alleged that before his own election in 1871 he offered a cabinet post to a leading Bolívar politician, Ramón Santo Domingo Vila, in return for the latter's support.[100] Of course, the limited functions of the federal government and the relatively small number of favors and positions at his disposal restricted the president's activities in this regard.

Preelection efforts, it might be noted, were aimed at encouraging the party faithful or wooing dissident members of the party. Since it was assumed that there were no independent voters or leaders and that party lines were rigid, there were no attempts to attract the uncommitted or to win the support of members of the opposing party. On those occasions when Liberals backed Conservative candidates, or Conservatives backed Liberals, such support was forthcoming only after agreement had been reached by party leaders who then authorized the crossing of party lines.

The fact that little information is available regarding the financing of party activities during this period suggests that political leaders did not consider it a major problem. This situation may have stemmed from the fact that the kind of electioneering carried out in nineteenth-century Colombia required the expenditure of relatively small sums and that the overlapping of partisan and official duties mentioned above resulted in the disbursement of public funds for party ends. In the 1890s, after the Liberals had lost control of the government, the more affluent members of the party were expected to subsidize party activities, particularly the publication of party newspapers, and it seems likely that the same was true for both parties in earlier decades. In 1856, after Mariano Ospina Rodríguez had been nominated for the presidency by a caucus of the Conservative members of Congress, the committee formed to direct election activities named two persons to solicit funds from Conservatives deemed in a position to contribute.[101] The money raised was to be used for a variety of purposes, including the publication of a newspaper to be distributed gratis and the printing and distribution of circulars and ballots.

Although each of the nine states had its own constitution and electoral code, both of which were frequently modified, there was considerable uniformity in election procedure. Ordinarily popular elections were held for president of the Union, state president or governor, representatives to the lower house of Congress, and deputies to the state legislature. In some states senators were also chosen by popular vote; thus in the election year 1873 senators were popularly elected in Magdalena, Santander, Cauca, Antioquia, and Tolima, but were elected by the state assemblies in Bolívar, Boyacá, and Cundinamarca.[102]

Voting requirements varied from state to state, but by the 1870s the earlier Liberal ideal of universal manhood suffrage had been considerably modified. The Boyacá constitution of 1869, for example, restricted the ballot to literate males who were at least eighteen years of age or were married.[103] The constitution adopted in Cundinamarca in 1870 allowed only literate males over eighteen to vote.[104] By 1875 these two states, together with Santander, had a literacy requirement while Bolívar, Cauca, Magdalena, and Panama still adhered to universal suffrage for males who were over eighteen or twenty-one, or who were or had been married. The constitution promulgated by the Conservatives in Antioquia in 1864 gave the vote to male Antioqueños who were over twenty-one or were married, provided they lived on income derived from their property or labor, while the Tolima constitution of 1870 enfranchised males who were over twenty-one or were married and were literate or possessed property worth at least $1,000.[105]

The various stages in the electoral procedure of each state were minutely outlined in laws replete with safeguards to eliminate fraud. First came the compilation and publication of lists of the eligible voters in each electoral district, a step usually carried out by the *cabildo* of the district. Once the list was completed there followed an interval during which additional voters were to be enrolled if qualified, and nonexistent or ineligible voters removed. According to the Boyacá election laws of 1869 and 1872, this procedure was to be supervised by the *cabildo,* meeting from 10 A.M. to 3 P.M. for two weeks from 1 June of the year in which elections were to be held.[106] In order to prove literacy, a prospective voter had to be able to read any printed work or manuscript presented to him and to write an article of the election law. No person could be removed from the voting list unless adequate proof of his ineligibility was presented and he was notified in person. In some states, such as Cundinamarca, this step was carried out by special juries, or *jurados.*

After the final list of voters had been prepared, the electoral juries that would supervise voting on election day were formed, usually with the inclusion of citizens chosen by lot. The Bolívar election code of 1870, for example, stated that each jury was to consist of five principal members and five alternates chosen by lot from the literate residents of the district.[107] According to the Boyacá election law of 1869, the jury of each district was to be composed of the mayor and four individuals selected by lot. This provision of the law aroused so many protests, however, that it was amended three years later. Henceforth each jury was to be made up of the members of the *cabildo,* the state tax collector, and two persons chosen by lot from the voters of the district, but in no case was the mayor to be included.[108] Where the voters in a district exceeded a certain number, provision was made for the selection of two or more juries.

Because of the importance of these juries, politicians often sought to control their composition. An example of such manipulation was given by Andrés J. Macías, director of the public school of Punta de Piedras (Magdalena), in a letter published in the state's official newspaper.[109] According to Macías, the public meetings required by law to supervise the drawing of lots for membership on the electoral juries of Punta de Piedras were never held; indeed, there were some villages in the district in which there was not a single person qualified to serve on the juries. Although the minutes of such a meeting in 1872 had been printed in the state newspaper, the local boss (*gamonal*) had merely forged the names of those who had supposedly been present, including Macías, and filled the juries to suit his own interests.[110] Since the newspaper never reached Punta de Piedras, there was little likelihood that the residents would become aware of the fraud.

Elections were held on Sundays, with the federal president, state presidents, and members of Congress usually being chosen on one day and deputies to the state assembly on another. In most states the popular votes cast for the federal president and state president were totaled, and the office awarded to the candidate who had received at least a plurality. Cundinamarca and Cauca used different systems. As of 1873 Cundinamarca was divided into ninety-seven districts, each of which had one electoral vote for every 1,000 inhabitants and any fraction in excess of 500, and the candidate who received a plurality of the popular vote in each district received all the electoral votes of the district.[111] Cauca was divided into sixteen municipalities, each of which was allotted from two to six votes.[112]

Although senators and representatives were elected on a statewide basis throughout the country, deputies to the state assemblies were ordinarily elected from electoral circles or districts. In 1872, for example, Boyacá was divided into twenty-two electoral circles, each of which sent from one to four deputies to the assembly.[113] In Antioquia, however, the thirty members of the state assembly were elected from a single list.[114]

Voting in Boyacá, according to the laws of 1869 and 1872, was to take place between 10 A.M. and 3 P.M. in public places previously designated by the mayor of each locality; the start of the balloting was to be signaled by the roll of a drum.[115] A barrier was to be used to separate members of the electoral jury and voters from spectators, who were to be kept at least two meters away from the jury's table and from the points at which voters were to enter and leave the polling place; the spectators were to use other means of entrance and egress. The members of the jury were to station themselves around three sides of a table bearing a wooden box with an opening eight centimeters long and one centimeter wide. Before the voting began, the ballot box was to be opened for public inspection.

As each voter arrived, the president of the jury was to ask him his name. After the jury had ascertained that the prospective voter was included in its list of qualified electors, he had to prove his identity and sign his name in the jury's register. The voter would then cast his vote on a folded piece of paper, which the president of the jury was to examine to make sure that only one ballot was being inserted; under no circumstances was the president to unfold the paper. Upon voting, the elector was to leave the polling place and not return. Immediately after the conclusion of the balloting, the jury was to count the votes cast, seeing to it that the number of ballots corresponded to the number of voters.[116] The results were to be inscribed in a register, copies of which were to be sent to the state president and the next examining group. This group would also receive the ballots, the notebook in which the voters had signed their names, and the jury's original voting list.

Despite such legislative safeguards, however, fraud and disorders frequently occurred just before or during the balloting, sometimes at the instigation of the authorities. Local officials might try to keep known opponents from the polls by threatening them with impressment into the state military force just before an election or by declaring that they owed money to the state (which would disqualify them from voting) and then refusing to accept payment. Liberals in Tolima complained in 1873 that they had been victims of both of these stratagems, even though the state's election law specifically stated that on election day no elector was to be required to pay any tax or perform any public service that would interfere with his voting.[117] On 23 August 1883 the American consul in Barranquilla reported that shortly after midnight the previous evening soldiers and policemen had awakened some 300 men from their slumber and had impressed them in an "election farce."[118] "This morning and all day," he said, "there has been a crowd of weeping women in front of the soldiers' barracks." In Bogotá soldiers of the Colombian Guard were sometimes instructed to cast ballots for candidates favored by the federal government. In 1881 Camacho Roldán estimated that the soldiers' ballots represented one-eighth of the votes cast in Cundinamarca and determined the outcome of elections in the national capital.[119]

Such heavyhanded methods were not always employed, however. The members of an electoral jury might force the cancellation of an election in their district simply by failing to meet. Another approach is shown in a fictional account of the last-minute preparations for an election in a small Santander town.[120] The *gamonal,* shown in consultation with local officials and candidates, is heard inquiring after a ballot box with a false bottom and instructing his henchmen to reward cooperative voters with all the liquor they can drink.

In addition, elections were sometimes disrupted by spontaneous outbursts of violence. In the fictional account cited above, the election proceeds in an orderly fashion at first. Suddenly, however, an uproar arises at one jury when a voter whose name appears on the public list of electors is rejected because it does not appear on the jury's list. This altercation is cut short by another disturbance at the next jury where onlookers are arguing over a prospective voter's right to cast his ballot. Clubs, knives, and pistols are produced despite the appeals of the jury's president for order, and serious trouble is averted only by the sound of the drum, which signifies that the voting is at an end. According to Ernst Röthlisberger, arguments over the eligibility of would-be voters were frequent.[121] Further light on this kind of electoral dispute is shed by a Bogotá newspaper's account of some children, none over ten years of age, who played at election on a real election day in 1883.[122] The props for the game included a cannon, and when one child accused another of already having voted, someone put a match to the cannon, and a young "voter" was seriously injured.

Contemporary accounts suggest that Colombians of both parties frequently stayed away from the polls. In Conservative-controlled Antioquia and Tolima, qualified Liberal voters often abstained out of fear of intimidation or because of the certainty that their votes would not be counted honestly; there was, of course, widespread Conservative abstention in Liberal areas for the same reasons. Newspaper references to Liberal apathy or indifference indicate that Liberals sometimes failed to vote in localities controlled by their own party. In general abstention seems to have been highest among the nonpolitical members of the "better" classes, who undoubtedly found the potential or actual disorders of election days distasteful.

It should be noted, however, that the official returns of some states indicate considerable variation in electoral participation from year to year. Antioquia, for example, recorded 9,497 votes in the presidential election of 1871; 11,504 in 1873; and 24,807 in 1875. A similar pattern is evident for Santander—7,433 votes in 1871; 5,597 in 1873; and 9,360 in 1875—and for Bolívar: 29,585 votes in 1871; 37,589 in 1873; and 44,126 in 1875.[123] The 1875 increase may have been due partly to the passions aroused by the bitter presidential contest of that year, but fraud was probably at work also, especially in Bolívar, where only fourteen votes were credited to candidates other than Rafael Núñez. The prevalence of fraud, together with the lack of statistics on literacy and age structure, makes it virtually impossible to determine accurately the level of electoral participation during the Liberal era.

After the voting had ended and the ballots had been counted by the local juries, the next step in the electoral process was the official examination, or *escrutinio,* of the juries' registers, which was followed by the announcement of the winners in the various contests. In general, state assemblies conducted the *escrutinio* of votes in elections for the federal president, state presidents, and members of Congress, while the *escrutinio* of elections for deputies to the state assemblies was entrusted to special groups. In Boyacá, for example, as of 1872 this *escrutinio* was conducted by a junta that met in the principal town, or *cabecera,* of each electoral circle and that consisted of the local electoral jury and the presidents of the *cabildos* of the districts in that circle.[124]

Further opportunities for fraud existed before this final *escrutinio*. During the gubernatorial election in Cundinamarca in 1873 an editor supporting opposition candidate Eustorgio Salgar warned that agents of the state government were planning to assault carriers of registers so that they would not be delivered to the examining body before the legal deadline.[125] If they did arrive at their destination, they could be annulled for real or fictitious irregularities if a majority of the examining body so agreed. Or the registers might simply disappear before they could be inspected.

After the final *escrutinio* or indeed at any time during an election, the supporters of a candidate might attempt to secure his victory by armed violence, which was an integral part of the electoral process in nineteenth-century Colombia. In 1872–73 there were at least four local outbreaks—in Panama, Cauca, Tolima, and Bolívar—all of which were related to the elections held in the latter year. Only the first had any national implications, however; the others were minor affairs, easily contained by state authorities.

The electoral process in nineteenth-century Colombia cannot be described as democratic as the word is normally used, and it served mainly to advance the interests and aspirations of elites. Despite its many defects, however, it provided a mechanism for the regular and more or less orderly alternation of officeholders under civilian direction and for the politicization and recruitment of future leaders. Only in the last quarter of the century, as subsequent chapters will show, did the electoral process appear to break down as holders of political power, both Liberals and Conservatives, proved less flexible in dealing with serious challenges. Even then the legitimacy of the electoral process remained unquestioned, and critics, regardless of party, sought only to correct its abuses and flaws. Meanwhile, although party organization remained embryonic during the federal era, party activity associated with the electoral process helped to preserve and strengthen political ties between Liberal leaders in Bogotá and their counterparts in the states and served as a basis for efforts to establish a more durable network of party organizations later on.

During the 1860s and 1870s the federal organization of the nation helped to determine the electoral strategy of party leaders connected with national administrations in Bogotá. State leaders enjoyed considerable independence because of the powers accorded the states by the Rionegro constitution, especially in presidential elections, and because of the limited military and financial resources at the disposal of the federal government. Yet Liberals in Bogotá were by no means helpless before the "sovereign" states and could frequently manipulate the course of events in Panama and other states to suit their interests. For the Conservatives, so long as unfriendly Liberals remained in control of the national government, federalism offered certain advantages, notably the opportunity to gain power in one or more states, as they did in Antioquia and Tolima. Accordingly, as the next chapter will show, by the mid-1870s critics (dissident Liberals and Conservatives alike) of recent administrations did not complain about the weakness of the central power but rather lashed out at what they considered excessive federal intervention in state affairs.

6
The Crisis of Liberalism

The decade 1875 to 1885 was a time of troubles both for Colombia and for the Liberal party. For much of this period the party was rent by dissension, and at the end of the decade it lost control of the government and was forced to witness the destruction of the institutions created by the 1863 constitution. However, party leaders could take some consolation from the fact that by 1885 the Liberal schism had been in large measure healed and that the party itself, though driven from power, would survive the debacle of 1885. This chapter does not attempt a complete account of political events during these turbulent years. Instead, it focuses on the evolution of Liberal dissidence and in particular on three aspects of this theme: the issues that provoked the Liberal split, the rise and decline of the Independent Liberal faction, and the response of the Conservatives to the conflict within Liberal ranks.

As was to be expected, differences within the Liberal party emerged in 1875 within the context of a presidential election. Party leaders had never been able to achieve total harmony before 1875, but dissension within party ranks had been muted and confined to one or two states. In 1875, however, all those Liberals who had grievances against recent federal administrations united behind the candidacy of Rafael Núñez, thereby mounting a serious challenge to the incumbent, Santiago Pérez, and to the man whom he supported as his successor, Aquileo Parra.

Among the earliest Núñez supporters were Liberal politicians from the three coastal states of Bolívar, Magdalena, and Panama who felt that the resources of their region were being drained for the benefit of the states of the interior and resented the fact that no one from their region had ever been elected to the presidency. They believed, as a writer in the *Estrella de Panamá* declared in 1874, that "the time has come for justice to be done to the coastal states by conferring the first magistracy of the nation on a Costeño."[1] With a native son like Núñez in the presidency, the Costeños could look forward not only to the satisfaction of regional pride but also to increased federal spending for public works projects in the coastal states, such as the improvement of the *dique*, or canal, linking Cartagena with the Magdalena River.

Coastal support for Núñez was made clear on 5 January 1875 when nine Liberal politicians from Bolívar, Magdalena, and Panama unanimously adopted him as their standard-bearer at a convention in Barranquilla.[2] To be sure, the Núñez candidacy did not have the backing of every prominent Liberal from the Coast. The president of Magdalena, José Ignacio Díaz

Granados, refused to name deputies to the Barranquilla convention, and the state was represented by an unofficial delegation led by Joaquín Riascos.³ The coolness of Magdalena's president to the Núñez candidacy can perhaps be explained by that state's traditional support for Liberals of Radical orientation and by the fear that a Núñez victory might bring preferential treatment for Cartagena and Bolívar which would aggravate the economic decline of Santa Marta.⁴

The belief that a Costeño should occupy the presidency was not held only by Liberals from the coastal states. On 2 December 1874, ex-President Mosquera informed César Conto that this was one of the reasons why he was working on behalf of the Núñez candidacy.⁵ In 1875 Núñez had the backing not only of Mosquera himself but also of most of his followers. While data on the preferences of all the leading Mosqueristas in the 1875 contest is not available, there can be no doubt that the Liberals most closely associated with him in the 1860s—Julián Trujillo, José María Rojas Garrido, Froilán Largacha, and Andrés Cerón, to name but a few—were Nuñistas in 1875. On the other hand, the only prominent Liberal identified as a Mosquerista in the 1860s who is known to have opposed Núñez in 1875 was Ramón Gómez, the *sapista* chief of Cundinamarca.

Núñez's strength in 1875 was not derived solely from the adherence of disgruntled Costeños and Mosqueristas still chafing at the treatment meted out to their leader in 1867. The dissatisfaction of these groups had, after all, been made evident in past years. The Nuñista challenge in 1875 was serious precisely because Núñez had the backing not only of those who might have been considered chronic malcontents but also of many influential Liberals, such as Carlos Martín, Salvador Camacho Roldán, and Teodoro Valenzuela, who had been Radical stalwarts in the 1860s and had supported recent federal administrations. In addition, Núñez won the endorsement of two former presidents of the Union, Santos Acosta and Eustorgio Salgar.

In a letter to Conto on 13 January 1875 Mosquera stated another reason for supporting Núñez. "It is intolerable," he said, "that a circle should want to dominate the nation from Bogotá, centralizing power and corrupting the electoral system."⁶ In this sentence Mosquera was giving utterance to one of the charges hurled most frequently by all segments of the Nuñista opposition at Pérez, Parra, and others associated with them, particularly Manuel Murillo, who was often depicted as the archmanipulator of the group.⁷ Collectively, these men were dubbed "oligarchs" by the Nuñistas. A newspaper in Barranquilla, for example, maintained that the opponents of Núñez constituted "an oligarchical circle that took possession of the government in 1867 with the hypocritical pretext of saving the republic, when it had only the sinister aim of making the nation its property and sinking it into the abyss in which it now finds itself."⁸

It was the contention of the Nuñistas that the oligarchs had used their positions in the federal government to interfere shamelessly in the affairs of the states in order to ensure the establishment of friendly regimes, even to the extent of using the Colombian Guard for this purpose. More specifically, bitter criticism was directed at Murillo's conduct during the 1873 presidential election when Santiago Pérez's candidacy had been challenged by Julián Trujillo. At that time Trujillistas in Boyacá had claimed that their candidate had been cheated of his rightful triumph by the machinations of Murillo.[9] Now such Boyacá Trujillistas as José Eusebio Otálora and Antonio Roldán became partisans of Núñez.

In addition to attacking the oligarchs' political practices, the Nuñistas mounted a strong offensive against a project with which the Murillo and Pérez administrations and Parra himself had become closely identified— the Northern Railroad, which was to have linked Bogotá with the lower Magdalena River by way of Boyacá and Santander. In fact, Parra had accepted the position of secretary of finance in Murillo's cabinet in 1872 primarily to devote himself to the Northern Railroad, which Murillo called "the greatest and most important enterprise for our country and above all for the state of Santander."[10]

Plans for the Northern Railroad had taken shape during Murillo's second term in the presidency after he addressed a message to Congress on 27 April 1872, in which he outlined his hopes for the construction of a great interoceanic highway to be financed at least in part by the federal government and made up of both roads and railroads.[11] Murillo believed that two portions of the highway could be undertaken at once: a railroad from the Pacific to the Cauca River near Cali, for which a preliminary contract had already been signed, and a railroad from Bogotá to the lower Magdalena, which had already been declared an enterprise worthy of preferential attention in Law 69 of 1871. It was to help provide funds for these projects that the foreign debt had been refunded and steps taken to amortize the internal debt in 1872; in addition, a surcharge of 25 percent was imposed on import duties in 1874.

The Northern Railroad quickly became the project on which the federal government lavished its greatest concern, and in 1874 Minister Scruggs called it "the pet scheme of the Murillo administration, as it is also of its successor."[12] In 1873 the government was authorized by Congress to borrow up to $20 million abroad to finance construction of the railroad, and negotiations toward this end were begun in Europe.[13] On 24 June 1874 President Pérez issued a decree providing for the formation of a national corporation to direct the building of the railroad.[14] The federal government was to subscribe up to three-fourths of the company's stock and could convert up to $1 million of its stock into $100 shares to be made available to workers and small property-owners; both these shares and those held by the private stockholders were to be guaranteed an annual return of 7 percent by the government. Meanwhile, on the advice of William Ridley, an engineer employed by the Public Works Construction Company of London, it was decided to build the railroad from Bogotá to a point on the Carare River near its confluence with the Magdalena.[15] Since Parra owned land near the Carare and had previously been involved in an unsuccessful effort to open a road from Vélez to the river, it was charged that he had been responsible for the selection of the Carare route for the railroad, but he denied that this was the case.[16]

Despite the enthusiasm of Presidents Murillo and Pérez and of Secretary Parra for the railroad, many Liberals voiced strong opposition to the project for a variety of reasons, both before and during the campaign of 1875. Some of the criticism was directed not so much at the concept of the railroad but at the choice of the Carare route. In 1872 a newspaper was founded in Boyacá to urge the adoption of another route which its proponents said would pass through more densely populated regions and would serve domestic as well as foreign commerce; it is interesting to note that the editors supported Núñez for the presidency as early as 1873.[17]

Others fought construction of the railroad regardless of the route selected on the grounds that such an enterprise was beyond the financial capabilities of the nation and that even if it could be built, it would be of value only to three states (Cundinamarca, Boyacá, and Santander) or a portion of them while consuming virtually all of the resources of the federal government. In 1874 Salvador Camacho Roldán pointed out in the Chamber of Representatives that the government was in no position to assume responsibility for a $20 million loan and that the railroad would directly benefit no more than 10 percent of the nation's population.[18] In the opinion of another Nuñista, Juan de Dios Restrepo, Parra's record as secretary of finance rested on the tariff increase and on the Northern Railroad project, but "the strong rise in tariff rates is counterproductive and detrimental to revenue, and the Carare railroad is an outrageous injustice toward all the taxpayers of the nation."[19] What Restrepo, along with other Nuñistas, favored was a "realistic" program of railroad construction, including the building of a short, direct line from Bogotá to the Magdalena. Another argument was advanced by J.M.B., who maintained that the projected loan, which would permit the federal government to finance construction of the railroad, would be a disaster for the nation. In his opinion governments should not become entrepreneurs; the development of transportation should be left to private enterprise, for the true spur to economic growth was self-interest.[20]

Nor were opponents of the Northern Railroad impressed by the apparent support of the Murillo and Pérez administrations for the Cauca railroad project. They asserted, in fact, that the federal government had signed contracts for the construction of the railroad in 1872 and 1874 in the full knowledge that the entrepreneurs would be unable to fulfill their obligations and with the expectation that the Northern Railroad would then be able to absorb all the funds appropriated for the interoceanic route.[21]

It is difficult to evaluate the validity of the charges of the Nuñistas against the Murillo and Pérez administrations. That no Costeño had ever occupied the presidency is, of course, true, but that the resources of the coastal states were drained for the benefit of the interior or that the federal government had discriminated against them is less clear. While most of the federal government's revenue from tariffs was collected in Barranquilla, Cartagena, and Santa Marta, the exports that financed Colombian imports came predominantly from the interior. Moreover, nearly all the revenue derived from the federal government's salt monopoly, which followed customs receipts in importance, came from salt works in Cundinamarca and Boyacá.[22] On the other hand, it does appear that the Panamanians had a legitimate grievance when they complained about the fact that the state received only $25,000 of the $250,000 annuity paid to the Colombian government by the Panama Railroad Company. Panama seems to have gained very little in return from the government except for the dubious benefits obtained from the presence of federal troops on the Isthmus.

It is also true that when railroad enthusiasm reached its peak in the early 1870s two of the four major projects approved by Congress were in eastern Colombia and that the most ambitious of these, the Northern Railroad, would have devoured the nation's resources.[23] If one ignores the Northern Railroad, however, the charge of federal preference for eastern Colombia rings less true. First of all, the federal structure of the government and the limitations of the regular sources of federal revenue, which never surpassed $4 million in any year between 1865 and 1874, precluded excessive financial largesse to any region, and federal spending for public works during this period was meager.[24] In addition, neither of the two principal projects to receive federal assistance before 1874 was in eastern Colombia. In 1863 the Rionegro convention authorized Mosquera to contract a $1 million loan in London, the proceeds of which were spent in a futile attempt to build a road from Buenaventura to the Cauca River.[25] Construction of the Bolívar Railroad, which was opened to traffic in 1871, was backed by a federal guarantee of an annual return of 7 percent on the capital invested in the project.[26]

The one Nuñista charge that does hold up is that the oligarchs wished to monopolize the federal presidency. In 1875 they preferred to risk a serious and perhaps permanent party split in order to ensure the succession of Parra. Such conduct contrasts with the course followed in 1869 when party division was averted by the selection of the widely acceptable Eustorgio Salgar as the Liberal standard-bearer.

Crisis of Liberalism

That Rafael Núñez was highly qualified to be president of Colombia is unquestionable. Before his departure from the country in 1863 he had ably filled a number of important positions and had avoided complete identification with any of the factions of the 1850s; on some occasions he had acted in concert with the *Gólgota* Radicals, but he had also served in the cabinet under Obando in 1852 and under Mosquera in 1862. During his years in the United States and Europe he had regularly contributed newspaper articles to the Liberal press which gave evidence of his powerful and far-ranging intellect. The fact that he was a native of Cartagena made him ideally suited to be the candidate of the Costeños, while his long absence from Colombia freed him of any responsibility for the policies objectionable to Liberal dissidents. His only possible drawback was the unconventionality of his private life.

Aquileo Parra, whose candidacy was announced by the *Diario de Cundinamarca* on 25 January 1875, was described by a Conservative contemporary as "a perfect gentleman, completely devoted to the cause of Liberalism; honorable by any standard; . . . an exemplary family man of impeccable public and private virtues."[27] While Parra's services to the Liberal party were as meritorious as those of Núñez, he lacked the latter's intellectual prestige. A further disadvantage was that, in contrast to Núñez, he had been in the forefront of Liberal politics during the past decade and therefore had a record to defend.

In endorsing Parra, the *Diario de Cundinamarca* laid special emphasis on the fact that he had overcome poverty and adversity to reach his present eminence.[28] The writer of the editorial—presumably Florentino Vezga, like Parra a native of Santander—also observed that Parra had been born in a region where there had never been slaves, where all men treated each other as equals, and where no form of labor was considered dishonorable. This statement, which was undoubtedly meant as a slur against Núñez's place of birth, was perhaps one of those which led him to recall in 1881 "the hateful designations of a personal character relative to the race and industrial habits" of the Costeños that had been made during the 1875 campaign.[29] Whether the oligarchs did in fact give themselves "airs of superiority" as Núñez charged remains a matter for speculation, but if such an attitude did exist it could have only exacerbated Costeño grievances. One of Núñez's biographers has indicated that Santiago Pérez did harbor a special antipathy for Costeños.[30]

It has been asserted by some writers that the oligarchs regarded Núñez himself with an obsessive hatred that accounted for their opposition to his political ambitions in 1875 and throughout the rest of his life. On this point there is no conclusive evidence. Parra relates in his memoirs that neither he nor Murillo felt especially hostile toward Núñez though they considered him something of an opportunist.[31] Despite the acrimony of the campaign, Núñez was able to write friendly letters to Parra in 1877, praising the latter's conduct in the presidency and stating that the two shared identical ideas and sentiments.[32] Whatever his true feelings toward Parra may have been, Núñez clearly thought little of Murillo. As early as 1866 he called Murillo a "fanatic worshiper of popularity" whose "selfish policy" had left the party in a state of anarchy; a decade later he described Murillo as "corruption incarnate."[33]

In 1875 Parra's supporters tended to be Liberals who were identified with recent federal administrations. Of thirteen individuals who served in the cabinet between 1870 and 1874 and whose preference in 1875 could be ascertained, only four supported Núñez while nine, including Parra himself, were Parristas.[34] If the Parristas are studied on the basis of regional origins, no clear-cut national pattern emerges, but it is apparent that Parra had the support of most Liberal politicians from his home state of Santander. On the other hand, few Parristas came from Bolívar, Panama, or Cauca.

Although some historians have depicted Murillo, Pérez, and Liberals associated with them as unwavering adherents of laissez faire, this issue was not raised by the Nuñistas in 1875. To have done so would hardly have been an effective tactic in view of their attacks on the Northern Railroad. Nor did the Nuñistas express any desire to carry state interventionism beyond the point favored by the oligarchs. If anything, articles in the Nuñista press were more likely to assail the oligarchs for violating traditional Liberal principles, both in the political and the economic spheres. Thus *La Unión Colombiana* of Bogotá claimed that recent Liberal policy had been "openly *reactionary,* going directly against the spirit and letter of our *federalist constitution,*" while *El Correo de Colombia* denounced the oligarchs for moving toward centralism and for being advocates of the doctrine of "doing everything" (*hacerlo todo*).[35] An editorial entitled "Where is Radicalism?" maintained that the Radicalism of the 1850s was extinct and that the Parristas did not even deserve the name of Liberals: projected federal expenditures were larger than at any time since 1859, tariffs were nearly unendurable, and Santiago Pérez was outwardly at least as devout a Catholic as any Conservative.[36]

The reference to Pérez is indicative of the role played by the "religious question" in the campaign of 1875. Although relations between the federal government and the Church were strained and Conservatives would soon rise in revolt under a religious banner, ecclesiastical matters occupied a relatively minor place in the campaign. This was probably a result of the fact that both of the contending camps held individuals of diverging views on the religious question. Many oligarchs were strongly anticlerical, but President Pérez was a practicing Catholic, and neither he nor Parra had ever been known for intransigence toward the clergy. Some Nuñistas, such as Salvador Camacho Roldán, were moderates on the subject of church-state relations, and Núñez himself stated that he was not anti-Catholic.[37] On the other hand, many Nuñistas were noted for their anticlericalism; Mosquera, for example, had not only been responsible for the most severe anticlerical measures enacted in Colombia to date, but in 1874 he was still exhibiting concern over what he called "neo-Catholic fanaticism" in Cauca.[38] Another Nuñista, the Antioqueño Camilo A. Echeverri, claimed that the Pérez administration was a "subject" of the Catholic spiritual power, which he described as the strongest and most unyielding enemy of Liberal institutions; Echeverri viewed Núñez as a man who would respect the religious beliefs of the masses but would end the "adulterous union" of church and state.[39]

The Conservatives, meanwhile, did not remain impassive before the Liberal donnybrook. Many Conservatives were sympathetic toward Núñez, and he made overtures to the Conservative leadership of Antioquia, promising, among other things, to seek constitutional reform giving the states control over primary education and religious matters and to appoint Conservatives to certain key positions.[40] In the end, however, the Conservatives of Antioquia, who were themselves beset by internal division, decided to remain neutral in the struggle between Núñez and Parra and named Bartolomé Calvo, a Cartagena native, as their presidential candidate. Tolima followed the example of Antioquia.

The elections of 1875 unfolded in a climate of abnormal tension and violence. The Nuñistas accused Pérez of toppling the government of Panama in order to win that state's vote for Parra and of using similarly underhanded tactics in Cundinamarca. For their part the Parristas held that the Nuñistas were preparing to launch a revolution should their candidate be defeated, and President Pérez dismissed the secretary of war, Ramón Santo Domingo Vila, and the commander of the Colombian Guard, Solón Wilches, both of whom were Nuñistas, when they refused to sign a statement pledging the Guard to neutrality in the election.

Since neither Núñez nor Parra won the five state votes needed for election, the contest had to be decided by Congress. After three weeks of uncertainty and intrigue, the balloting took place on 21 February 1876 and resulted in a victory for Parra, who received forty-eight votes; Núñez received eighteen, as did Conservative Bartolomé Calvo.[41] Parra tried to steer a conciliatory course as president, but the election had engendered such bitter feelings within the Liberal party that the Conservatives rose in revolt the following July in the expectation that the Nuñistas would refuse to support the government.[42] Although Conservatives hopes in this respect proved unfounded and nearly all the Nuñistas actively aided the government in its successful attempt to crush the revolution, the fissure in the Liberal party was not closed permanently, for the Nuñista grievances of 1875 remained unsatisfied. Indeed, the party's division was deepened by several new sources of controversy which arose in the wake of the Liberal victory over the Conservatives. At the same time the failure of the Conservative attempt to regain power by force of arms convinced the leaders of that party that their best chance for success lay in an alliance with one of the two Liberal factions.

The most inflammatory of the issues which emerged after the Conservative defeat in 1877 was related to the ever-recurring religious question, itself an important factor in bringing about the revolution. Since 1870 relations between the federal government and the clergy in many parts of the country had deteriorated because of the government's assumption of an expanded role in primary education and the establishment of several normal schools headed by Protestant professors imported from Germany.[43] Provision was made for religious instruction in the primary schools, and some prelates, notably Archbishop Vicente Arbeláez of Bogotá, proved willing to accept the secular schools provided they were not used for the dissemination of anti-Catholic doctrine.[44] In Cauca, however, there was vociferous clerical opposition to the Liberal educational program, and Bishop Carlos Bermúdez of Popayán forbade parents to send their children to public elementary schools.[45] Fanatic Liberals in that state, meanwhile, claimed that the furor was part of a Conservative conspiracy to regain political power. On 15 March 1876 César Conto, president of the state, informed Parra that the Conservatives had joined the clergy in an effort to make federal education laws unenforceable in Cauca and warned that if the federal government did not take action to make itself obeyed, the entire nation would find itself in the hands of the Papal Curia.[46]

In Cauca, where the revolution began, the conflict resembled a Catholic crusade as well as a struggle for political ends. Indeed, the religious character of the war was what persuaded two prominent Nuñistas to come to the aid of the Parra government.[47] After the conclusion of the war the triumphant Liberals resolved to end clerical interference in political matters once and for all.

In his 1877 report to Congress, which was now composed exclusively of Liberals, Secretary of the Interior Carlos N. Rodríguez called for the imposition of legal curbs on clerical freedom. Although he acknowledged that Colombia's revolutions had been caused by many factors, he felt that the "excessive pretensions of the clergy, abetted by the religious fanaticism of the masses," had been a major source of the present conflict.[48] The clergy's appeal to arms, despite the freedom they enjoyed in Colombia, was not to be wondered at in view of the tendencies of the Catholic Church, which aspired not to liberty but to domination. "In its exorbitant pretensions of possessing infallible authority and of therefore being the only depository of truth, it considers that it has the exclusive right to be dominant everywhere without any counterweight." Rodríguez, who believed that the separation of church and state established in 1853 had proved to be a "dangerous" experiment, hoped that government patronage over the Church could be restored with some modifications; for the present he urged the enactment of legislation that would give the federal executive adequate means of controlling the reactionary turbulence of the clergy. Ex-President Mosquera, now serving as a senator from Cauca, also favored strong legislative restraints on the clergy. "[P]ublic tranquility cannot be guaranteed," he wrote, "except by forcibly subduing the enemies of the true republic, who . . . are trying to establish a theocracy in Colombia, . . . maintaining that to achieve this end all kinds of methods can be used, even those condemned by the very religion whose defenders they claim to be."[49]

On 4 May 1877 the Chamber of Representatives passed a bill along the lines suggested by Rodríguez by a secret vote of thirty-six to four.[50] The Senate passed the bill the following day and after it received President Parra's signature, it became known as Law 35 of 9 May 1877.[51] Based on Article 23 of the constitution, it declared that clergymen would be guilty of violating public security and tranquility if, while acting in their capacity as priests, they incited or caused disobedience of any state or national law or of any act of public authority by means of sermons, pastorals, speeches, or writings of any kind. Earlier in the session Congress had passed a law (number 8 of 19 March 1877) cancelling the annual payments made to the Church for the property disamortized in 1861.[52]

The members of Congress were also determined to punish the bishops of Popayán, Pasto, Antioquia, and Medellín, whom José María Quijano Wallis called the "principal promoters of the rebellion."[53] Accordingly, they enacted Law 37 of 12 May 1877, which provided that the four bishops were to be exiled for ten years and were forbidden ever again to exercise priestly or episcopal functions in Colombia. When the government issued a general amnesty the following month, the four bishops were excepted, as were all clergymen who had taken up arms or encouraged rebellion against federal or state authorities.[54] In addition, anticlericalism was revived on the state level, especially in Cauca, where President Conto had anticipated the federal government by ordering on 4 February 1877 the expulsion of the bishops of Popayán and Pasto from the state.[55]

Another source of controversy was the collection of forced loans from Conservatives during the revolution to raise funds to support the government's military effort. The usual procedure was to demand a fixed sum from a Conservative; if he was unable or unwilling to pay the required amount in cash—and in some cases, even if he was—portions of his property were bound over to the state or nation and might then be auctioned off at a fraction of their value to a deserving Liberal.[56] Such practices were, of course, a familiar byproduct of civil war in nineteenth-century Colombia, but contemporaries seemed to feel that the spoliations of 1876–77 exceeded anything that had occurred in the past, perhaps because, as one writer observed, in previous conflicts only movable property had been seized while real estate had remained untouched.[57] Núñez later commented that during the revolution "the abuses committed with respect to real estate reached such alarming proportions that it could be perceived that the country was rapidly approaching the state of barbarism where this matter was concerned."[58]

Forced loans were decreed in all the areas affected by the revolution, that is, throughout the country except the three coastal states, which remained relatively tranquil. It was in Cauca, however, that the greatest turmoil occurred, partly because the victorious Liberal troops and politicians there felt that their services on behalf of the cause merited tangible rewards at the expense of the Conservatives. In addition, economic conditions in the state were especially poor, not only because of the ravages of the war but also because of an incursion of locusts and a prolonged drought.[59]

Mosquera, who left Bogotá for Cauca on 21 June 1877, was appalled by the violations being committed against the property rights of Conservatives.[60] From both Cali and Popayán he reported that many families were being ruined because of the forced loans and the low prices for which their property was being auctioned. Although Sergio Camargo, who acted as chief executive of Colombia from 14 May to 15 August 1877, while Parra stepped down temporarily for reasons of health, had officially declared on 7 August that order had been restored and tried to halt the collection of forced loans, his decrees were being ignored in Cauca's southern municipalities because of Liberal greed for Conservative property. Only the presence of a federal battalion had prevented the southerners from rebelling against the local authorities, Mosquera said, but the commander of the battalion, one Figueredo, was an ally of those involved in the auctions of Conservative property and had himself acquired a valuable piece of land. Mosquera also deplored the fact that the returning soldiers were being led astray by demagogues who filled them with communistic notions about land distribution. "The immorality that the revolution has caused," he remarked, "forebodes evils for the future."

Meanwhile, on 1 June 1877 the Cali *democrática* had submitted to President Conto a petition in which the members requested that any individual be permitted to settle anywhere in the state and to cut in the state's natural forests provided he did not seriously harm the rights of others.[61] The *democráticos* conceded that their request might seem extreme, but they thought it unjust for the defenders of the state to be deprived of homes after they had fought off repeated invasions by Antioqueños who were abetted by those who owned most of the land in Cauca. Observing that the petition had been turned over to the state legislature for consideration, Felipe Pérez stated that to grant the request of the *democráticos* would be to incite another revolution of a different and more fearsome character.[62] The legislature presumably did not act favorably on the petition, but Conto later approved a measure freeing residents of the state from the obligation of paying rents or making interest payments on debts due between 12 July 1876 and the date of the promulgation of the law.[63] In October the attorney general of the nation declared the law to be flagrantly unconstitutional.[64]

Modesto Garcés, who succeeded Conto as president of Cauca on 1 August 1877, admitted that he found it difficult to curb the unruly Liberals of the state. He had been unable to comply fully with Camargo's order that the collection of forced loans be suspended for fear of arousing Liberal opposition; the tendency in Cauca was to impoverish the Conservatives, and all the leading Liberals were involved in the property auctions.[65] "I am struggling here to contain unrestraint and demagoguic tendencies," he observed somewhat plaintively. "The social milieu in which I live must be taken into account."

Division within the Liberal party reappeared during the administration of Julián Trujillo, a Nuñista in 1875, who had added luster to his military reputation during the recent revolution. Although he was elected as a unity candidate, dissension began almost immediately after he took office on 1 April 1878. It was during his term that his supporters and those of Núñez became known as Independents while their Liberal adversaries revived the Radical label for themselves, presumably to suggest a parallel between contemporary conditions and the struggle against Mosquera in 1866–67.

Núñez gave the Independent movement a sonorous if vague slogan in a speech delivered on the occasion of Trujillo's inauguration when he warned that catastrophe threatened Colombia unless a "fundamental administrative regeneration" was undertaken.[66] Shortly afterwards Trujillo gave the Independents a program in a series of messages to Congress dealing with the most pressing issues of the day: railroad policy, church-state relations, and forced loans.

On 25 April 1878 he delivered a message to Congress on "material improvements" in which he extolled railroads as a means of stimulating economic development and suggested that a "moderate" loan be negotiated to finance railroad construction.[67] He pointed out, however, that all of the states should share equally in the benefits to be derived from such a loan and that the states rather than the federal government should assume the primary responsibility for railroad construction. Trujillo's message presaged the abandonment of the Northern Railroad so cherished by Parra, who had kept the project alive during his administration, though it had undergone numerous modifications, including a change in route.⁶⁸ In 1878 legislation was enacted which reflected the new emphasis on decentralization and authorized the government to borrow up to $2 million abroad for railroad building.⁶⁹ In addition, efforts were to be directed in the future at the construction of a short, direct railroad link between Bogotá and the Magdalena, a goal realized with the start of work on the Girardot Railroad in 1881.⁷⁰

Trujillo next addressed himself to the religious question. On 27 April he asked Congress for changes in the ecclesiastical laws, including the extension of amnesty to the proscribed bishops and the repeal of certain provisions of Law 35 of 1877.⁷¹ The Senate, in which the opposition had a majority, refused to consider Trujillo's requests, voting on 13 May that it would be inopportune to legislate on religious matters at the present moment; the Chamber of Representatives passed a similar resolution the following day, but both houses reiterated their support and respect for the president.⁷² It was not until 1880, when the Independents controlled Congress, that the sentence of exile against the bishops was revoked; Law 35 was repealed in its entirety two years later. It should be noted, however, that although the Independents became champions of the clergy in 1878, the anticlerical measures of 1877 had received the blessings of at least a few Nuñistas at the time of their enactment. When Congress unanimously adopted a resolution congratulating the Cauca government for expelling the bishops of Popayán and Pasto, among those voting aye were José María Quijano Wallis and Antonio del Real, both of whom had been Nuñistas in 1875.⁷³ Ricardo Becerra, a leading Independent, wrote a pamphlet refuting Chilean criticism of the anticlerical laws and justifying them on the grounds that the Colombian clergy had sought to destroy educational freedom, restore the religious intolerance of the colonial period, and subordinate the state to the Vatican.⁷⁴

In a third message to Congress, Trujillo called for an end to the collection of forced loans and requested authorization to return auctioned real estate to the original owners with reasonable compensation to purchasers and upon payment to the national treasury of the loan that had brought about the auction.⁷⁵ Congressional action was not forthcoming, but the president ordered a halt to the collection of forced loans by decree on 24 September 1878.⁷⁶ In 1879 he was still asking for legislation on the matter. "It is necessary to recognize that the respect for property is one of the fundamental bases of any good government which seeks the progress and well-being of its citizens," he told the legislators. "This being the case, there is no reason why the confiscations that took place in some parts of the nation during the war in the heat of passion should continue."⁷⁷ Congress finally acted in 1882, passing a law that provided for the return of property that had been auctioned as a loan or contribution during and after the revolution of 1876–77. Meanwhile, when Eliseo Payán, an Independent, became chief executive of Cauca in 1879, one of his first acts was to order the unconditional return of all the real estate acquired by the state or purchased by private individuals as a result of the revolution.[78]

The Independent program was expanded in 1880 when Núñez succeeded Trujillo in the presidency, having been elected with the support of the Independents and a sizable portion of the Conservative party. In his inaugural address on 8 April Núñez called for establishment of a protective tariff to stimulate domestic industry and for the creation of a national bank to serve as a spur to economic growth.[79] Although duties had been raised in the 1870s, the Radicals now expressed opposition to a frankly protectionist policy, primarily for two reasons: the belief that Colombia was destined to remain an exporter of agricultural products, at least in the foreseeable future, and the undesirability of granting preferential treatment to the artisans of Bogotá at the expense of the consumer.[80] The Radicals directed even heavier fire at the proposed national bank, which they declared would be monopolistic and would drive private banks out of business.[81] Despite the objections of the Radicals, bills creating a protective tariff and a national bank were passed by Congress in 1880.

It was the hope of Núñez that the national bank would help lift the Colombian economy from the depressed state into which it had fallen in the late 1870s. To some extent a reflection of unfavorable conditions in other parts of the world, the Colombian depression was largely the result of the low prices which the nation's exchange-earning exports, especially tobacco and cinchona bark, were commanding in European markets.[82] As a result of the mounting trade imbalances, gold was drained from the country and became increasingly scarce. The federal government, burdened by the costs of quelling the revolution of 1876–77 and its commitment to public works expenditure, found its revenues diminishing because of the economic slump, and deficits piled up inexorably. Although the national bank, which went into operation on 1 January 1881 as a completely official institution issuing notes redeemable in silver, did not destroy the private banks as the Radicals had predicted, it did not produce an economic upturn. Shortly after Núñez became president for the second time in 1884, he reported to Congress that the federal treasury was running a monthly deficit of at least $100,000 and that the nation was in the midst of "the most serious industrial and monetary crisis" it had ever known.[83]

The Radicals were also critical of other policies adopted during Núñez's first administration, such as the public order law of 1880 and what they called the unnecessary expansion of the armed forces and the bureaucracy, to which they said he appointed mainly relatives and political friends.[84] Jibes directed at the president's Costeño heritage were voiced on occasion too. One editorialist, for example, asserted that when Núñez arrived in

Bogotá to take over the presidency, he was guarded by "Costeño locusts" who were "so ugly, so black, and so repugnant that many doubted that they belonged to the human race."[85]

Núñez in turn was resentful of those who suggested that he favored Costeños or that lowlanders were drones.[86] During his first year in office, however, he did spend three months in the coastal region. The official explanation for the trip was the need to settle a boundary dispute with Costa Rica, but the United States minister felt that the real reason was the president's desire "to gratify the harmless vanity of his friends and relatives at the Coast who have never before seen a Colombian President among them."[87]

In 1882 Núñez retired from the presidency but not from politics, and he was reelected the following year, again with Independent and Conservative support. In his 1884 inaugural address, he called himself an "irrevocable member of Colombian Liberalism" and pledged to reconstitute the party's scattered forces.[88] Despite the president's avowal of his devotion to Liberalism, by 1884 he had lost the support of most of the top-ranking Liberals who had backed him in the 1870s, and the Independent party had been reduced to a shadow of its former self.

In part dissension within the Independent movement can be ascribed to the personal ambitions of leaders who emerged as potential rivals to Núñez. In 1883 two leading Independents—José Eusebio Otálora, who was acting chief executive of the Union in his capacity as second *designado,* and Solón Wilches, president of Santander since 1878—launched presidential candidacies in defiance of Núñez, and Wilches won the endorsement of the Radical leadership.[89]

Other Independents found themselves in disagreement with the policies adopted by Núñez during his first presidential term. Liberals with commercial interests and ties to the Banco de Bogotá and other private banks could be expected to be critical of the legislation of 1880 and hope for a reversal of policy with an end of Independent rule. Miguel Samper, for example, was a Nuñista in 1875, but he later condemned the protective tariff and the national bank.[90]

But the most important factor in the disenchantment of many erstwhile Nuñistas was undoubtedly their fear that the Independents would allow the federal government to fall into the hands of the Conservatives. Nuñista-Conservative cooperation was discussed by a few individuals as early as 1876,[91] and the Conservative defeat in the revolution of 1876-77 made such a strategy seem even more attractive. By 1879 the leading Conservative chiefs, particularly Carlos Holguín and Antonio B. Cuervo, had concluded that revolution had to be discarded as a method of regaining power and that the most feasible route to this end would be through cooperation with the Independents.[92] Although this policy encountered resistance from individual Conservatives who mistrusted Núñez and the Independents, the party gave him significant support in the presidential election of 1879 and officially endorsed his candidacy in 1883.[93] The Independents, of course, had to balance their animosity toward the Radicals against the hazards of cooperation with the Conservatives. In 1876 Núñez himself had indicated that he was undecided as to the proper course. "Should we lean toward the oligarchs out of fear of the Conservatives?" he asked one of his supporters. "Or should we unite as much as possible with the latter even though we may later be dominated by the theocratic element?"[94] To most Independents, if not to Núñez, the second alternative was unacceptable.

The disintegration of the Independent movement was signalled as early as 20 July 1880 when two former chief executives, Santos Acosta and Eustorgio Salgar, both of whom had been Nuñistas in 1875, joined Radical ex-presidents Santiago Pérez and Aquileo Parra in a committee formed to direct the activities of Liberals willing to recognize their authority.[95] An even more impressive set of defections took place the following year when the Radicals were able to capture the presidential candidate selected by Núñez and the Independents, Francisco Javier Zaldúa, and proclaim him as their own choice as well.[96] This attempt at Liberal union had the support of such prominent Independents as Julián Trujillo and Salvador Camacho Roldán, though not that of Núñez himself. In a manifesto to Independents on 30 April 1881 Trujillo and Camacho Roldán warned of the dangers inherent in Conservative support for one of the Liberal factions and pointed out that the original reasons for the party's split had disappeared: both of the presidential aspirants of 1875 had served as chief executive; respect for religious beliefs was now the order of the day; and public funds were being spent on internal improvements of the second rank that would pave the way for the great enterprise that would some day link the states of the interior, this last statement being a reference to the new railroad policy then in effect.[97]

Many Independents remained loyal to Núñez. These included individuals from all states, but especially from the Coast (Felipe Paúl, Felipe Angulo, and José María Campo Serrano, for example) and from Boyacá (Luis Carlos Rico, Aristides Calderón, and his nephew Carlos Calderón Reyes, for example). With but a few exceptions they had not been in the forefront of Liberal leadership before 1875 but had been obscure or at best secondary figures. The major exceptions to this generalization were three men—Daniel Aldana, Ramón Santo Domingo Vila, and Eliseo Payán— who supported Núñez during the crisis of 1885 but lost their political influence in the years immediately afterward. In short, by 1884 the Independents constituted neither a party nor a movement but may best be likened to a group of satellites orbiting around the figure of Núñez.

Despite the fact that the Liberal rift was slowly being healed by the gradual union of erstwhile Independents and Radicals, the Liberal party evinced serious weaknesses in the 1880s. By the end of 1879 Radicals had been ousted from most of the states they had controlled, leaving only Antioquia and Tolima under Radical rule; the others, with the exception of Santander, remained staunchly in the Independent column. Moreover, the Independents' control of the electoral machinery made it unlikely that they could be easily dislodged; the prospects for successful revolutionary action seemed equally slim, given the existence of the 1880 public order law.

Another source of weakness was the death of Manuel Murillo in 1880, which deprived the party of its most experienced and respected figure. Aggravating the loss was the fact that there was no single individual who could readily take his place. In the period after 1885 Aquileo Parra would emerge as the most influential Liberal spokesman but earlier in the decade he lacked the prestige or even the desire to assume a dominant position. After the conclusion of his presidential term in 1878, Parra returned to his native Santander and continued to spend much time there despite pleas that he move permanently to Bogotá in order to play a more commanding role in party affairs.[98]

Perhaps paradoxically, the 1880s also saw the first halting efforts by Liberal leaders to organize the party on a national basis. The initial step took place in 1880 with the formation of the Central Committee composed of Parra, Santiago Pérez, Santos Acosta, and Eustorgio Salgar. At the same time the committee's secretary urged Liberals in the various states to form similar bodies and to correspond regularly with the Bogotá committee.[99] Soon the pages of *La Defensa*, which was edited by Santiago Pérez, were filled with statements from towns throughout the country supporting the Central Committee.

The attempt to forge Liberal union by Radical endorsement of the Zaldúa candidacy in April 1881 was spearheaded by the members of the Central Committee. In June Liberals were instructed to form unionist committees on the state and municipal levels.[100] Such committees were to meet frequently and to correspond with their counterparts elsewhere in order to exchange opinions and ideas. In addition, these committees were to select Liberal candidates for public office and to identify Liberals in the principal towns. A party organ, *La Unión*, was founded in May and reported the creation of committees of Liberal union in Medellín, Tunja, and other places. By 1883 Liberal committees were active in at least two states: Antioquia and Tolima. The Central Committee evidently expired, for in 1884 Parra was asked to serve on a new Liberal body organized by the minority members of Congress.[101]

Meanwhile, auxiliary groups were not neglected. *La Defensa* reported a meeting on 29 May 1881 attended by over six hundred Liberals to unify and reorganize the Democratic Society of Cali.[102] Tomás Rengifo, a one-time Nuñista whose presidential candidacy was supported by the Radicals in 1879, was elected president of the society. A new organization, the Society of Public Safety, was formed in Bogotá on 4 December 1881, the anniversary of Melo's defeat in 1854.[103] The purpose of the society, whose first president was Teodoro Valenzuela, another former Nuñista, was to defend Liberal principles and institutions, which were said to be threatened by the Núñez administration. By early January the Bogotá society reportedly had 382 members, and similar groups were being organized in other Cundinamarca towns as well as in other states.[104] Despite the fact that prominent Liberals served as officers of the Bogotá society, it acquired a reputation for violence and was blamed for assassination attempts against Independents Ricardo Becerra and Daniel Aldana in 1882.[105]

Although it can be argued that the repeated Liberal efforts at organization and mobilization were a response to the party's precarious situation and particularly its expulsion from the seats of power it had formerly occupied, it should also be noted that the Conservatives, who could look to the future with greater optimism, pursued a similar course. A party convention was held in Bogotá in April 1879 and created an elaborate national organization headed by a supreme director, Antonio B. Cuervo.[106] A party constitution was drawn up, to which all officers were to swear an oath, and *El Deber* of Bogotá was temporarily designated as the party's official newspaper, being supplanted by a new organ, *El Conservador*, in June 1881.[107] The organization created in 1879 was retained in subsequent years with some modifications, the most notable of which was the substitution of a three-man directory for a single party head.

The Conservatives' success in maintaining a continuous form of party organization can be attributed at least in part to the relatively favorable circumstances which they enjoyed after 1879. A few Conservatives continued to be uneasy about the strategy of cooperation with Núñez and the Independents because of their Liberal origins and because of their support of the Parra government during the revolution of 1876–77. On the other hand, proponents of Conservative-Independent collaboration such as Cuervo and Holguín could argue that it had borne fruit not only in Núñez's appointment of Conservatives to the cabinet and other positions but also in legislative action favored by Conservatives, such as repeal of the anticlerical legislation of 1877 and the enactment of the public order law of 1880. Both of these had been described as Conservative objectives in a party platform endorsed by the principal Conservative leaders in 1878.[108] The program said nothing about an expanded government role in the economy and in fact called for a reduction in taxes and an end to the "socialist" policy of direct government sponsorship of public works. Some Conservatives, therefore, might be unhappy about the policies of the Núñez administration, but not to the point of jeopardizing the possibility of future political advancement under his leadership.

When Núñez made his commitment to Liberalism in his inaugural address on 11 August 1884, the political and economic situation of Colombia was marked by uncertainty and distress. The tension had been aggravated by the fact that Núñez failed to arrive in Bogotá to take office on 1 April as scheduled; it was learned later that he had gone to Curaçao for medical treatment.[109] His absence was felt most strongly by the Independents, who depended on his guidance, but according to Conservative Carlos Martínez Silva, their confusion was symptomatic of conditions in general: "commerce, agriculture, all industry, politics, domestic life itself, everything is impaired by the uncertainty and anguish in which we find ouselves."[110]

In the weeks that followed his inauguration Núñez's intentions remained unclear, perhaps even to himself, as was suggested by his first cabinet appointments: two Independents, two Conservatives, and two Radicals (Eustorgio Salgar and Napoleón Borrero, both of whom had supported Núñez in 1875).[111] Yet in less than five months the Radicals would rise up in arms against the Núñez government, and he in turn would appeal to the Conservatives for assistance in quelling the revolution. It is this action, along with his subsequent declaration that the Rionegro constitution was defunct, that led Liberals both then and later to denounce Núñez as a traitor to his party and to the institutions with which it was identified.

Students of the political crisis of 1885 have usually focused on three subjects in attempting to explain the course of events: the possible influence on Núñez of his wife, Soledad Román; the issue of constitutional reform; and the developments in Santander that preceded the president's request for Conservative assistance. Núñez wed Soledad Román by proxy in a civil ceremony held in New York in 1877.[112] However, his first wife, Dolores Gallegos, whom he had married according to the Roman Catholic rite, was still alive. Therefore, while Núñez's second marriage might be valid in the eyes of the state, he was guilty of adultery in the eyes of the Church and of devout Catholics.

Núñez appears to have been concerned about his anomalous marital situation. During his first presidential term Soledad Román remained in Cartagena instead of accompanying him to Bogotá. Unfriendly writers have charged that as president Núñez allowed his desire for ecclesiastical sanction of his domestic arrangement to impede a religious settlement with the Vatican.[113] No such sanction was forthcoming, and it was not until after the death of Dolores Gallegos in 1889 that Núñez and Soledad were married in a religious ceremony. Meanwhile, when he had at last taken her to Bogotá in 1884, the Conservatives had presumably swallowed their religious scruples and greeted her in the company of their wives while the Radicals had come alone.[114]

Forty-one years old at the time of her marriage, Soledad Román was an intelligent and well-read woman, extremely devout, and Conservative in her political inclinations.[115] In the opinion of some writers, Núñez's drift toward the Conservatives was in part the result of her influence.[116] Late in life she herself denied that she had modified her husband's views in any important way, though she did admit that she occasionally gave him advice.[117]

There has been considerable disagreement among historians over Núñez's views regarding reform of the constitution in 1884 and over the extent to which the Radicals were willing to support constitutional changes. There is no evidence that before 1875 Núñez's dissatisfaction with the Rionegro constitution exceeded that expressed by many other Liberals after 1863. By 1876, however, he had come to the conclusion that modification of the constitution to strengthen the federal government was necessary, and in 1881 he informed Congress that "the fundamental institutions of our country are no longer in harmony with its needs or with the opinion of the Colombian people."[118] He indicated his continuing commitment to federalism and offered the Argentine constitution, with its indirect elections and six-year presidential term, as an appropriate model for Colombia. Núñez frequently returned to this theme in the years that followed, reiterating his preference for a more powerful national government but continuing to reject a highly centralized system.

According to Núñez and writers sympathetic to him, the Radicals obstinately refused even to consider reform of the Rionegro constitution, the implication being that he was forced to resort to more drastic measures to achieve his ends.[119] Parra rejected this argument as early as 1889, noting that in July 1884 the Radical minority in the Senate supported a resolution asking the state legislatures to petition Congress to take up the matter of constitutional reform in 1885. According to Parra, the Radical leadership also approved a list of proposals prepared by Núñez as a basis for reform but found him uninterested in pursuing the matter further.[120] However, it hardly appears likely that given the years of antagonism between Núñez and the Radicals and his ties with the Conservatives, consensus could have been easily reached, even if the political atmosphere had been less feverish than it was in the latter half of 1884.

It was a series of events in Santander that produced the crisis of 1885.[121] Radicals in that state had never been reconciled to the rule of Solón Wilches despite the national leadership's endorsement of his presidential candidacy in 1883. With the economy of the state reeling from the effects of the collapse of the *quina* market and a drop in coffee prices, Wilches had rekindled opposition with the imposition of new taxes in 1883. Radical hostility was further exacerbated by the state government's use of fraud and violence to control the outcome of state elections held on 27 July 1884. The result was a Radical revolution against Wilches in mid-August, which ended with his retirement from the state government and with the convocation of a convention to settle "the questions of legality" stemming from the disputed election. When the convention—made up of 19 Radical delegates, 13 Independents, and 3 Conservatives—met on 10 November the Radicals attempted to invest it with the character of a constituent assembly in the hope of regaining control of the state. At this the Independent and Conservative delegates withdrew, depriving the convention of a quorum, and the acting president of the state, backed by federal troops, decreed its dissolution. The Radical delegates then met on their own and named Sergio Camargo president of the state. Their choice for second alternate was Daniel Hernández, who a few days later rebelled against the state government, then entered Boyacá with the aim of widening the war.

Before the meeting of the Santander convention, the Radicals of that state had praised President Núñez for his contribution to the apparent restoration of peace, but the unhappy outcome of the convention brought renewed suspicions of the president's intentions.[122] Even so, many Liberal leaders outside of Santander were unenthusiastic about the prospect of revolution. Both José María Quijano Wallis and Foción Soto, a Santander Radical, describe meetings of party leaders in Bogotá during which most showed themselves to be opposed or at best lukewarm toward the activities of the revolutionaries.[123]

Luciano Restrepo, the Radical governor of Antioquia, was another who doubted the wisdom of the revolutionaries' actions. He informed Parra on 24 December 1884 that the Liberals of Antioquia were determined to defend their beliefs if the state was attacked; his government would do what it could for the triumph of Liberalism and the reestablishment of peace, but his efforts were hampered by the fact that news arrived late and distorted in Antioquia.[124] The governor of Tolima, Gabriel González Gaitán, was more blunt. He deplored the futile sacrifices being made by Hernández and the other insurgents in Santander. Before acting in such a precipitate fashion, they should have realized that they were gambling not only with their own destinies but also with that of the entire Liberal party.[125]

Even as González Gaitán was writing the letter cited above, however, Núñez was contemplating action that would convince the Tolima governor and other vacillating Liberals to rally around their comrades in arms. On 23 December 1884 Núñez named Leonardo Canal, a veteran Conservative general, commander of a reserve force which was to be mobilized "for the defense of the nation's institutions."[126] Canal accepted the appointment on 3 January 1885, declaring that 3,675 men, of whom 1,641 were armed, had already been billeted in Bogotá and nearby towns. Three days later the decisive step was taken as two divisions of this force, led by Carlos M. Urdaneta and Antonio B. Cuervo, were incorporated into the federal army.[127]

Núñez's appeal to the Conservatives was followed by the expansion of the war, which now spread throughout the country. The governors of Tolima, Antioquia, Boyacá, and Bolívar eventually cast their lot with the revolutionaries, as did many officers and men of the Colombian Guard. To be sure, some of those who took up arms did so reluctantly, like Luis

Lleras, destined to lose his life in the conflict, who wrote to a friend: "War is . . . madness . . . and turns the kindliest men into wild beasts; . . . but when one takes up arms, one cannot, one ought not, lay them down in the moment of peril, [and] one cannot turn one's back on one's friends . . . without committing the basest of actions, without being a cowardly wretch."[128]

With the help of the Conservatives and those Independents who remained loyal, Núñez was able to crush the revolution by the end of August 1885. On 10 September, during an extemporaneous speech, he announced that the constitution of 1863 had ceased to exist.[129] "Soon," he is reported to have said, "the people will give themselves a new one which will satisfy their true needs and will reflect the inclinations of the great majority of the Colombian people. The constitution will begin with an invocation to Almighty God." Thus the Rionegro constitution had come to an ignominious end, slain by one who had pledged to defend it.

Some Colombian historians have portrayed Núñez as a reluctant and even peripheral actor in these events, noting that he took to his bed with dysentery on 8 January 1885, and arguing that during his month-long illness the federal government was actually directed by Secretary of War Felipe Angulo, an Independent, and Soledad Román.[130] This interpretation is complemented by the depiction of Núñez after 1886 as a man disillusioned by the course of the regime he had fathered.[131] That Núñez felt some uncertainty in 1884-85 is suggested by his overtures to the Radicals upon assuming the presidency. However, in view of his increasingly close ties with the Conservatives and his oft-stated belief that the Rionegro constitution had outlived whatever usefulness it may have had, it is not surprising that he felt no compunction about extinguishing the Liberal regime, especially since by rising in revolt his enemies had provided him with a superb opportunity for taking this drastic step.

The events of 1884-85 above all represented a victory for Conservatism, particularly for those party leaders who had advocated the strategy of collaboration with the Independents. It is fitting that Carlos Holguín, who had perceived the potential efficacy of such a strategy as early as 1869, should become one of the leading figures of the Regeneration, as the new regime was called. The Independents, on the other hand, had few reasons for self-congratulation. Although they had succeeded in realizing some of their initial goals, such as abandonment of the Northern Railroad project and expulsion of the Radicals from the state governments, they had eased the way for a Conservative restoration even as their own movement disintegrated. Moreover, as will be seen in the next chapter, their position in the Regeneration would at best be a precarious one. The Radicals also had ample reason for self-reproach. Their initial error in vetoing the Núñez candidacy in 1875, supported as it was by a large and respectable segment of the party leadership, was compounded by subsequent mistakes, such as the enactment of the anticlerical legislation of 1877, for which they bore the major responsibility. Although the Radicals had previously been relatively moderate on religious issues, after 1877 they found themselves cast in the uncomfortable role of persecutors of the faith.

What is perhaps the most remarkable feature of the decade 1875–85 is the survival of the Liberal party despite the gravity of the schism of the 1870s and the erosion of Radical strength in the state and federal governments after Trujillo assumed the presidency in 1878. The result might well have been the permanent eclipse of the Radicals as a political force, accompanied by the disappearance of Liberalism or by the appropriation of the Liberal heritage by Núñez and the Independents who remained loyal to him. That neither of these eventualities occurred can be attributed to the heterogeneity of the Independents and to the changing, diverse, and sometimes contradictory goals which they espoused. As a result, the movement was soon eviscerated by defections because of frustrated personal ambitions, as in the cases of Otálora and Wilches, or because of discontent over the direction of the movement, particularly its increasingly close ties with the Conservatives. Not only did the Independents fail to develop an integrated program, but they also failed to create a mythology and organizational structure that would have enabled them to compete more successfully for the loyalties of Colombian elites and masses alike. These failures were probably inevitable considering the limited aims of the movement at the time of its inception in the mid-1870s, when a repudiation of Liberalism was not contemplated, and its dependence on the leadership of the enigmatic Núñez. The economic difficulties of the era, particularly as they affected the federal treasury, may have constituted another constraint on the Independent movement by limiting the financial rewards that could be offered to supporters in the federal and state governments. Although federal expenditures increased dramatically from 1879 to 1883, they declined sharply after that, especially in the area of public works.[132] Even so, government employees complained of not being paid on time.[133] In any event, the best evidence of Independent debility is the fact that in 1885 Núñez was forced to call upon the Conservatives in order to deal with the revolution and to effect the political transformation he desired. Meanwhile, despite their blunders and defeats, the Radicals, their ranks augmented by the ever-increasing number of repentant Independents, met no effective challenge as they draped the mantle of Liberalism around themselves, evoking the memory of past struggles and aspirations and warning of the "common enemy" that lurked behind Núñez and his followers. As a result, the Liberal party, though relegated to the political wilderness for decades, would remain the only alternative to Conservatism.

7
In the Role of the Vanquished

The defeat of the revolutionaries of 1884–85 marked the beginning of a new era for the Liberal party. Whereas the Liberals had constituted the dominant party of Colombia after 1863, now they would be cast in the role of the vanquished, and the energies of party leaders would henceforth be directed toward the reconquest of power. Like their Conservative counterparts in the two preceding decades, Liberals would consider several strategies as they surveyed the political scene: they might rely on the ballot box, seek alliances with Conservative dissidents, or raise the flag of revolution. And, as the Conservatives had done, the Liberals would adopt each of these strategies, or a combination of them, at one time or another. Meanwhile, deprived of their hold on governmental machinery, Liberal leaders would begin to convene assemblies of party notables and establish party organizations in order to develop and articulate party policy.

The formal governmental structure created in 1886 differed greatly from that of Rionegro and in many respects hampered Liberal efforts at resurgence. Just as the constitution of 1863 had come in the wake of the Conservative defeat of 1862, so the Liberal debacle of 1885 was followed by a thorough revamping of the country's political institutions. The device of a constitutional convention having been rejected by the victors, an eighteen-man council of delegates, composed of an equal number of Conservatives and Independents, met on 11 November 1885 to draw up bases for constitutional reform which were then submitted to the municipalities for approval.[1] The council, now considering itself invested with the necessary authority, then proceeded to the writing of a new constitution.

President Núñez presented his recommendations for the new document in an exposition to the Council of Delegates on 11 November 1885.[2] He declared, first of all, that "enervating particularism" should be replaced by "vigorous generality." The individual's sphere of activity should be limited by the rights of others and of the community at large, and the educational system should be based on the teachings of Christianity, which was the alma mater of world civilization. In the past, he said, Colombians had been unable to establish stable governments because they had ignored certain realities, such as the fact that republics ought to be authoritarian, in contrast to monarchies, which need centrifugal institutions to counteract their tendencies toward concentration. More than any of its predecessors, the Rionegro constitution had given rise to disorders and civil wars that had not only littered the nation with corpses but had prevented economic development as well. However, a new constitution had gradually been engraved in the hearts of the people. "Thus," Núñez concluded, "the political reform known as fundamental *Regeneration* shall not be a copy of foreign institutions, nor the creation of the isolated speculations of feverish brains; it shall be the simple and natural codification, as it were, of the thoughts and desires of the nation."

Although the new constitution, which was promulgated on 7 August 1886, reflected the guidelines laid down by Núñez, its chief architect was Miguel Antonio Caro, who represented Panama in the Council of Delegates and was a member of the drafting committee.[3] Another of the delegates, José María Samper, who had submitted a constitutional draft of his own, found the new document "excessively reactionary" and more suited to a monarchy than a republic.[4] Carlos Martínez Silva, however, was lavish in his praise of the constitution, which he predicted would have a long and robust life because it reflected the social and political reality of Colombia and was not inspired by exclusivism.[5]

The constitution of 1886, which was decreed "in the name of God, Supreme Source of All Authority," stated explicitly that Colombia was a unitary republic and that sovereignty resided only in the nation.[6] The once-sovereign states were reduced to the status of departments, which were subdivided for administrative purposes into provinces and municipal districts. The departments were to be administered by governors appointed by the president for three-year terms and by departmental assemblies which were given limited jurisdiction over primary education and matters affecting the local economy. The department of Panama, however, was to be subject to the direct authority of the central government. All the departments retained the boundaries they had had as states, a decision supposedly taken at the insistence of Cauca's Eliseo Payán.[7] In addition, the constitution made it extremely difficult to dismember the departments by creating new ones.

The president, who was to be elected indirectly for a six-year term, could be called to account only for acts of violence or coercion in elections, high treason, and acts intended to hinder Congress or other public bodies in the execution of their duties. Moreover, Congress was authorized to invest the president with extraordinary faculties "as necessity may require or the public convenience demand." The office of vice president was restored, and in case of the absence of both the president and vice president, executive duties were to be discharged by a presidential alternate (*designado*) chosen by Congress for a two-year term. While the Council of Delegates was in session, its members elected Núñez president for the 1886–92 term, and Payán was chosen vice president.

In order to be elected president, vice president, or senator, a man had to be a native Colombian with an annual income of at least $2,000. Senators were to be elected for a six-year term by the departmental assemblies, and representatives to Congress were to be elected for a four-year term by citizens who could meet certain literacy or property qualifications. Congress was to meet every two years.

There were other departures from the constitution of 1863 in the section dealing with civil rights. The right to import, manufacture, and possess arms and munitions was restricted exclusively to the government. Although the death penalty could not be imposed for political offenses, it was restored for certain crimes, such as treason in times of war and parricide. According to Article 42, the press was to be free in time of peace, but it was responsible under law for injury to personal honor and for disturbances of public peace and social order. Transitory Article K, however, declared that until a press law was enacted, the government was empowered to prevent and punish abuses by the press.

Important modifications were also made in the relationship between the state and the Roman Catholic Church. Although Roman Catholicism was declared to be the religion of the nation and public authorities were empowered to enforce respect for it, the practice of all cults not contrary to Christian morality and law was permitted, and no person was to be molested because of his religious beliefs or compelled to profess any creed or perform rites against the dictates of his conscience. Public education, which was to be free of charge but not compulsory, was to be directed in accordance with the Catholic religion. The government was also authorized to enter into negotiations with the Vatican, which led to the signing of a concordat on 31 December 1887.[8]

The government of the Regeneration was not only more centralist and authoritarian than its predecessor, but it also attempted to exert a greater direct influence upon the course of the Colombian economy. This goal was pursued by a variety of means, including the imposition of protective tariffs, the establishment of new fiscal monopolies, and above all by the government's assertion of the exclusive right to issue money and by its adoption of a monetary system based upon inconvertible paper.

Notes issued by the national bank had originally been redeemable in silver, but the government suspended specie payments in January 1885 as a result of a run on the bank.[9] This action took place at a moment of political crisis, but its underlying causes were the continuing outflow of specie from the country and the ever-mounting deficits of the government. In 1886 the bills of the national bank were declared inconvertible and of forced currency and were made the sole legal tender of Colombia.[10]

By Law 124 of 1887 the maximum amount of paper money which could be issued was set at $12 million, but by September 1892 over $9 million in excess of that figure had been emitted without legal authorization.[11] A Congressional investigation of these "clandestine emissions" in 1894 produced a minor scandal, particularly over an unauthorized issue of $2,206,319 in 1889 which was used to retire over $3 million in documents of the internal debt. While the government profited from the transaction, the fact that the public creditors received a sum nearly 15 percent in excess of what they had paid for the documents provoked considerable criticism of the officials involved, notably Carlos Martínez Silva, who was minister of the treasury at the time.[12] The criticism may have been at least partly motivated by political considerations since by 1894 Martínez Silva was moving rapidly into the ranks of the Conservative opposition to the government.

In 1894, shortly after the investigation into the "clandestine emissions," Congress ordered the liquidation of the national bank, which lost its theoretically autonomous status and became a section of the Ministry of the Treasury.[13] Although Congress and the government hoped eventually to retire the paper money in circulation, additional emissions had to be authorized during the 1890s. By 7 August 1898 approximately $31.4 million had been issued.[14] Meanwhile, the value of the Colombian peso in relation to foreign currencies declined steadily after 1885, as can be seen in Table 8:

TABLE 8

Rate of Exchange, Colombian Pesos per 100 U.S. Dollars

1880 = 111
1885 = 130
1890 = 193
1895 = 265
1898 = 291

Source: William Paul McGreevey, "The Economic Development of Colombia" (Ph.D. dissertation, Massachusetts Institute of Technology, 1965), p. 60.

Another feature of the fiscal policy of the Regeneration was the establishment of monopolies in several areas where they had never existed or had been abandoned in previous decades. Among the industries reserved exclusively for the disposition of the government were the supply of ice to Panama (1889), the importation and manufacture of cigarettes (1893), and the manufacture and sale of matches (1897).[15]

Another major economic change after 1886 was the emergence of coffee as Colombia's leading export, a development that was clearly related to the system of paper money. Exports of coffee climbed from 107,589 bags of 60 kilos each in 1880 to 475,356 bags in 1896, and by the latter year coffee represented 55 percent of the total value of Colombian exports.[16] Although Colombian coffee growers faced high transportation costs in comparison with producers elsewhere, they benefited from the decline in the value of Colombia's currency, for they could use depreciated paper money to meet their expenses while being paid in gold from abroad. Therefore, as long as the international market was expanding and the price of coffee remained relatively high—as it did until the late 1890s—they were able to derive a profit margin that was more than satisfactory and encouraged further investment in the industry.[17] Indeed, during a congressional debate over an export tax on coffee in 1896, the minister of foreign relations, Jorge Holguín, argued that the government had in effect subsidized the coffee industry through its emissions of paper money.[18]

In the 1880s and 1890s the principal coffee-growing regions of Colombia were located in the eastern part of the country, especially in the areas around Cúcuta and Ocaña in Santander and in the *tierras templadas,* or temperate zones, of Cundinamarca and Tolima. In the 1890s coffee cultivation began to shift to western Colombia, notably Antioquia, but as late as 1913 the region that comprised the old department of Antioquia accounted for only 35 percent of Colombia's coffee.[19] At the beginning of the surge in coffee cultivation Santander was the leading producer, but its share of total production declined from almost 90 percent in 1874 to about 55 percent in 1888. Meanwhile, thousands of acres of land, especially public lands, were being planted in coffee in Cundinamarca and Tolima, where the large coffee plantation was the norm.[20]

Perhaps because the principal coffee zones of the period were in areas where Liberalism had traditionally been strong, a large number of the leading coffee growers of the 1880s and 1890s were members of Liberal families or were active in Liberal politics themselves. Nicolas Sáenz Pinzón, a coffee grower in Cundinamarca and manager of the Banco de Exportadores, which he helped found in 1897 to provide credit for coffee sales abroad, was a member of a Liberal advisory council created in 1897, as was Sixto Durán, also a coffee grower and merchant.[21] Eustacio de la Torre Narváez, who was an important figure in Liberal politics in the 1890s, established the first large-scale coffee plantation in Cundinamarca, and was said to derive an annual income of $100,000 from coffee.[22] When a petition requesting that the export tax on coffee be lowered or repealed was presented to the government in 1897 by individuals and firms connected with the coffee industry, the signers included not only Sáenz in his capacity as head of the Banco de Exportadores but also José María and Enrique Cortés, who had long been active in Liberal politics; Luis E. Villar, who was the brother of the party's director in Santander; and the firm of Camacho Roldán & Tamayo, of which Liberal elder statesman Salvador Camacho Roldán was a partner.[23] Another possible explanation for the prominence of Liberals in the coffee industry was offered by Luis Ospina Vásquez, who suggested that Liberals denied political careers during the Regeneration turned to coffee cultivation instead; it was considered a nice touch of Liberalism (*una buena nota de liberalismo*) to do so.[24]

The coffee boom of the late 1880s and 1890s and the depreciation of the currency produced a steady increase in the cost of living which was one of the most distinctive features of the period. In 1888 British consular officials estimated that the price of food in Bogotá had doubled in recent years (see Table 9).

TABLE 9

Food Prices in Bogotá, 1878–88

Article	Price per Cwt. in Pesos in Bogotá	
	1878–86	1888
Wheat	$ 3.00	$10.00
Potatoes	2.00	4.50
Maize	3.00	6.00
Sugar (white, coarse)	14.00	22.00
Cacao (beans)	24.00	52.00
Rice	7.00	16.00
Lard	25.00	50.00
Barley	2.00	4.50
Coffee	12.00	20.00–24.00

Source: Great Britain. Foreign Office. *Report on the Agricultural Condition of Colombia.* Reports on Trade and Finance. Annual Series No. 446. London, December 1888, pp. 17–18.

The inflationary trend abated in 1891–92 but resumed in 1893.[25] While wages for some workers also rose during this period, in general they did not keep pace with the increase in prices, and a recent student of the era has concluded that national income became more concentrated than it had been earlier.[26]

Increases in the prices of food and other necessities were fully observed in the contemporary press. A Liberal newspaper in Bogotá complained in 1889: "Society in general is resentful. There is little business activity; wages do not rise while merchandise is becoming more expensive; meanwhile, taxes are drowning us, and new ones are being considered."[27] A nonpolitical newspaper in Bogotá voiced a somewhat similar lament in April 1891: "We are going through a period of dearness and scarcity rarely experienced not only here but in any other country in the world."[28] The following month a Conservative organ calculated that 80 percent of the population in the capital could barely afford the necessities of life.[29] In 1893, *El Espectador* of Medellín remarked that the basic foods in the Antioqueño diet—maize, beans, meat, and *panela* (coarse brown sugar)—had risen beyond the reach of the day laborer.[30]

El Espectador, a Liberal publication, attributed the high price of food in Antioquia to the financial policies of the Regeneration. This was the usual explanation offered by Liberal journalists and political leaders, who regularly inveighed against Regeneration economics despite the fact that

Liberal coffee growers and exporters were benefiting from the government's policies. To some, such as Miguel Samper, the dependence on paper money, the establishment of monopolies and other measures constituted a violation of sound economic principle and deserved castigation on this score alone.[31] In addition, party leaders calculated that exploitation of economic issues would yield political dividends.

While Liberal critics lambasted the Regeneration's economic policies, President Núñez adhered to a position similar to the one he had held before 1886. The basic causes of the nation's economic problems, he wrote in 1886, were the relatively low value of Colombian exports and the nation's dependence on foreign agricultural and industrial goods.[32] He continued to defend the use of paper money as a means of stimulating economic development and upheld the right of the government to specify legal tender without making any exceptions.[33] Núñez was cautious, however, about the emission of large sums of paper money unsupported by specie and, after the legal limit was raised to $26 million in 1892, he expressed his certainty that no government or Congress would ever exceed that figure.[34] Miguel Antonio Caro, who succeeded Núñez as president, shared his opinion that paper money was the recourse of the modern state, but he was inclined to be more venturesome in monetary matters than his predecessor.[35]

The political arm of the Regeneration was the National party, composed of Conservatives and Independents, which had taken shape during the revolution of 1884–85 and raised as its banner Núñez's exposition to the Council of Delegates and the constitution itself.[36] Leaders of the new party made an effort at first to discard the old partisan labels forever, as did Rafael Reyes, a hero of the recent revolution and a member of the Council of Delegates, when he declared in Cali on 19 August 1886: "The political denominations that engender hate, jealousy, and rancor have been forgotten. There are no longer Independents and Conservatives: we are all Nationals!"[37]

Despite Reyes's rhetoric, however, relations between Independents and Conservatives were uneasy from the very dawn of the Regeneration, the difficulties stemming from both personal and ideological motives. In these conflicts the Conservatives invariably emerged the victors. Among the earliest Independent casualties were Daniel Aldana, who was removed from his post as governor of Cundinamarca on 7 November 1885, and Solón Wilches, who was offered diplomatic assignments in Venezuela and Italy which were later withdrawn when he proved dilatory in taking them up.[38]

The misfortunes of Aldana and Wilches can be attributed to suspicions that they wished to cling to their sectional influence in Cundinamarca and Santander, respectively. Vice President Payán, always a potential threat because of his strength in Cauca, also fell from the good graces of the

Regeneration, but his misstep was to show signs of receptivity toward the blandishments of his former Liberal comrades.[39] On 19 December 1887 Payán, who had assumed the presidency six days earlier after Núñez had departed for the coast, issued a decree freeing the press of all restrictions except those specified in Article 42 of the constitution. On 1 January 1888 he granted amnesty to all persons in exile, and the following day the Liberal party publicly tendered the vice president its good wishes and thanks.[40] Alarmed by Payán's flirtation with the Liberals, Núñez cut short his stay in Cartagena and hurried back to the capital, announcing as soon as he set foot in Cundinamarca that he was reassuming the presidency.[41] Payán was banished to Medellín and was stripped of the vice presidency the following May.[42] Núñez wielded the executive power himself for only a few months. On 7 August 1888 Carlos Holguín, who had recently been elected *designado*, took office as chief executive while Núñez retired to Cartagena.[43] He never returned to Bogotá.

In his inaugural address upon taking power in 1888, Holguín pledged obliquely to preserve the status of the Independents,[44] but their position remained weak. Later that year Núñez tried to assuage the fears of Luis Carlos Rico, an Independent from Boyacá, regarding the future of the Independents. "Dr. Holguín will do everything possible to save the Independent element from complete eclipse," Núñez wrote.[45] "It is true that there is intransigence among some, but the thinking part of the old Conservative party is fully aware of the need for a counterweight as well as of the justice of not discarding those who provided such efficacious service. But there must also be sincerity in the adoption of the new doctrines since the previous ones left nothing after half a century of trial." Rico's reply to Núñez suggests that the Independents had little confidence in Holguín.[46] "We expect everything from you as our leader and friend," Rico asserted. "We put our fortunes in your hands many years ago." In general, the Independents had no personal ambitions, he added. "They desire only that importance be given to the party to which we belong because of deep conviction and all kinds of bonds and historical precedents." Rico also indicated that the Independents viewed the "new doctrines" somewhat differently from Núñez. "I have spoken with several of them regarding [present] institutions. They are in agreement with you, but they would like them to be put into practice with more generosity than severity, taking into account the demands of the times in which we live and the special customs of the country."

Despite Núñez's assurances to Rico, the position of the Independents continued to deteriorate, and a list of ten Cabinet appointments made by Holguín on 1 October 1890 contained eight Conservatives and only two Independents. According to the American minister in Bogotá, John T. Abbott, a great distinction was made between Independents and Conservatives, and "no Independent would for a moment have any share in the government were it not for the persistence of Dr. Núñez, who insists on their retention, and the weakness of the real Conservatives who could not sustain themselves unaided."⁴⁷ As the foregoing remarks suggest, the Independent movement would soon be extinct as an autonomous political force, though a few individual Independents continued to play important roles within the Regeneration.

Liberal journalists, as might be expected, chortled at signs of dissension within the National party. By 1888, in fact, César Conto was arguing in *El Liberal* that the National party had died aborning and that only the two traditional parties were left.⁴⁸ Political parties, he asserted, could not be cultivated like fruit in a greenhouse; they were natural and spontaneous productions.

> A party is the association or aggregation of various individuals bound by the profession of similar principles with respect to the organization, policy, and administration of the State. This association or aggregation is formed by a kind of crystallization, for which doctrines serve as the nucleus. These [doctrines] are very clearly defined in the political world and are synthesized in two large groups; from this stems the division which exists in all civilized countries between Liberals and Conservatives.

Party splits, he added, might be frequent, but they were not lasting.

Of course, Liberals might well have regarded dissension within the National party as a double blessing, for it meant not only a weakening of their political adversaries but also the return to Liberalism of Independents who had strayed from the flock but had now seen the error of their ways. The task of reincorporating former Independents into the Liberal party at this stage was a delicate one, to be sure, for they could easily be blamed for its present cheerless plight.⁴⁹ The party labels used by the Liberal and progovernment press during this period illustrate the complexity of the political situation. Although some Liberals regularly referred to themselves as Radicals, the term was regarded by others as one likely to hinder the achievement of party unity. Supporters of the government, on the other hand, consistently referred to their opponents as Radicals in order to indicate that the Conservative-Independent fusion remained intact and perhaps, as César Conto suggested, to perpetuate division within the Liberal party.⁵⁰

Until the last years of the century, however, party leadership would remain largely in the hands of one-time Radicals like Aquileo Parra, Santiago Pérez, and Luis A. Robles. Several other familiar faces had been removed by death: Manuel Ancízar had died in 1882, José María Rojas Garrido and Julián Trujillo in 1883, and Eustorgio Salgar in 1885. Some retired from politics or sought foreign exile, among them Felipe Zapata, who lived in Europe until his death in 1902. Zapata apparently took no part in Colombian politics, but other Colombian expatriates, especially those in Venezuela and Central America, plotted tirelessly for their party's return to power, an end for which they sought to enlist their hosts' moral and financial support. From the safety of exile, moreover, a few Liberals dipped their pens in vitriol to denounce the Regeneration and its servitors, especially Núñez, who was branded an apostate and an adulterer.[51]

Meanwhile, veteran party leaders were joined, and sometimes challenged, by younger Liberals such as Diego Mendoza Pérez, a nephew and son-in-law of Felipe Pérez who became editor of *El Relator* upon the latter's death in 1891, and Fidel Cano, who founded *El Espectador* in 1887 in his native Medellín. Another Antioqueño destined to achieve great prominence within the party was Rafael Uribe Uribe, born in 1859 and the son of a landowner who was an ardent Liberal.[52]

Nor was the instruction of the future generation of Liberals neglected, for several educational institutions were founded under Liberal auspices after the public secondary schools and the national university came under Conservative influence. In 1886 the Externado was established by Nicolás Pinzón Warlosten as a school for professional and secondary instruction. By 1891 it had conferred sixty degrees in law, political science, and commerce and took special pride in its courses in philosophy and natural history; two years later, however, it was shut down by the government.[53] The attitude of the devout toward the Externado can be illustrated by the remark of the mother of a young man whose father, a Liberal, wanted him to study there: "Better for you to go to heaven with your ignorance than to be damned with your learning."[54] Two other well-known Liberal institutions were founded in the 1890s: the Liceo Mercantil, which consisted of a preparatory school and faculties of commerce and literature, and the Universidad Republicana, established by José Herrera Olarte and others.

The faculties of these schools boasted such Liberal notables as Salvador Camacho Roldán, Luis A. Robles, and Francisco E. Alvarez, while the student bodies included the sons of Robles, Modesto Garcés, and Daniel Aldana, as well as youths, such as Enrique Olaya Herrera, who would be Liberal luminaries of the twentieth century. In 1899 a newspaper debate on the merits of the instruction at the Colegio de San Bartolomé, which had been under Jesuit control since 1887, led to several brawls on the streets of Bogotá between the Bartolinos and students from the Universidad Republicana, the Liceo Mercantil, and the Colegio de Araujo, another Liberal school.[55]

During the early years of the Regeneration the government and its agents considered the Liberal party a subversive element whose members were bent on destroying the new order. Their activities, therefore, had to be strictly controlled. Thus when a small group of Liberal leaders—fewer than ten, according to Parra—met in Bogotá in 1887 and agreed to work for the reconstruction of the party, the government used the meeting as a pretext to exile Parra, Daniel Aldana, Carlos Martín, and several others.[56] According to the American minister, the banishments "aroused a deep feeling throughout the country," and there was "much suppressed excitement" despite the apparent political calm.[57]

Government agents in the departments also observed the actions of Liberals and were on the alert for possible conspiracies. For example, one Abraham C. Rodríguez, evidently an army officer stationed in Magdalena, reported on 18 February 1889 to Minister of War Antonio B. Cuervo that the residents of La Ciénaga were extremely hostile to the government and tried to extract as much money as possible for the food and laundry services which they supplied to the garrison. Only six days earlier a group of townspeople had paraded through the streets, accompanied by the local band and carrying a picture of Ricardo Gaitán Obeso, the dead Liberal hero of the 1885 revolution.[58] From Panama on 30 January 1889 General J. V. Aycardi informed Cuervo that Radical officers and sergeants still remained in his batallion and that signs reading "Viva Gaitán!" and "Down with the *godos!*" could be found in the barracks.[59] Colonel Tomás C. Varona, another officer stationed on the Isthmus, was indignant over the reception given to César Conto in Panama City while he was en route to foreign exile and over the fact that the government-supported band had taken it upon itself to play for him.[60] When Varona had remonstrated with the band's director, the latter had replied that he had been a Liberal before he had been director of the band, and that once the band had fulfilled its obligations to the garrison and the government, it could play for whomever it wished. In Cauca, José María Domínguez E. wondered about the inclinations of the former vice president, Payán, who had recently returned to his native region and was reported to be deeply hurt and vengeful.[61]

In this period the administration was able to use two legal weapons against Liberals who were considered a threat to the regime. The first of these was a decree governing the press, issued on 17 February 1888, shortly after Núñez had recovered the reins of government from Payán.[62] The decree defined as subversive any publications that were harmful to society, including those that encouraged disobedience of the law, attacked the Roman Catholic Church or the armed forces, offended the dignity and privileges of civil and ecclesiastical authorities, incited one social class against another, or impugned the monetary system. Penalties for violation of the decree ranged from compulsory retraction to permanent suspension of the offending publication. Numerous Liberal publications fell afoul of this decree. In April 1888, for example, *El Liberal,* which was edited by César Conto, was forced to cease publication. Conto was arrested and jailed, later being allowed to seek exile in Guatemala, where he remained until his death in 1891.[63] Nicolás Esguerra brought out one issue of *El Liberal* after Conto's arrest, but the newspaper was suspended for six months, and Esguerra was subsequently exiled.[64]

The second legal instrument of the Regeneration was the "Law of the Horses" (number 61 of 15 May 1888), so called by Liberals because it originated in a report from the governor of Cauca that some decapitated horses had been found near Palmira, leading supporters of the administration to believe that a conspiracy was afoot.[65] Based on the right of Congress to grant extraordinary faculties to the chief executive, the law authorized him to prevent and repress crimes or offenses against public order and property and to impose the penalties of imprisonment, confinement, expulsion from the country or loss of political rights. The president was also empowered to remove from the military list members of the armed forces who showed themselves to be unworthy of the confidence of the government, as well as to exercise the right of inspection over scientific and educational institutions and to suspend any establishment that became the source of revolutionary or subversive propaganda. An effort to repeal the law was made in the Chamber of Representatives in 1892, but it was defeated by a vote of fifty-seven to six.[66]

After the 1887 meeting which had been followed by the exile of Parra and other Liberal leaders, no formal effort was made to reorganize the party until 1891, and Liberals generally abstained when elections were held in 1888 and 1890 to fill departmental and municipal offices. Spurred by the fact that a presidential election was scheduled for December 1891 and by the hope that disaffection in National ranks might facilitate Liberal gains, a convention of delegates from the various departments met in Bogotá on 5 April and voted to form a three-man committee to assume direction of party affairs.[67] Parra, Camacho Roldán, and Sergio Camargo were named principal members of the committee, which became known as the Liberal Center, while Robles, Teodoro Valenzuela, and Januario Salgar were chosen as alternates. Camargo, however, did not serve, his place being taken by Robles. To a group of Liberals in Santander, Parra indicated that he would have preferred the naming of a single person to act as party head; he had not, however, attended the Bogotá meeting, nor did he know how the decision to establish plural leadership had been reached.[68]

On 2 May the Center issued a statement of party policy to be circulated confidentially in each department which provides considerable light on the thinking of the Liberal leaders at the time.[69] The statement began by rejecting the idea that the party should refuse to recognize the legitimacy of the government: "Every society needs some political regime to serve as a bulwark for public order and the security of the individual. Regardless of whether the government is good or evil, of pure or impure origin, it is better to obey it than to remain in a state of impotent struggle. Remedies should be sought through the pacific means which every political system, no matter how perverse it may be and even to its own regret, leaves open to its citizens." Although the party leaders thus repudiated the strategy of armed violence against the government, they pointed out that an unexpected political convulsion might occur after the presidential election and that the party should be prepared for such an eventuality through thorough organization and discipline. Efforts should be made to identify the Liberals in each locality, party organizations should become active on the local level, party newspapers should be established wherever possible, and Liberals should register to vote. Funds were also needed, primarily to support the party press and to pay for the printing of party statements.

With respect to the press, the Center pointed out that the revival of old quarrels and grudges should be avoided so as not to discourage former adversaries who wanted to rejoin the party. "We especially urge that in our press the terms *Radical* and *Independent* be omitted. We ought to recognize only Liberals." The Center also stated that the weakest point of the Regeneration lay in its fiscal practices, such as its extravagant spending and high taxation, and recommended that Liberal journalists aim their fire in that direction. The first goal of the party should be the restoration of freedom of the press, as it would serve as a base for the attainment of other objectives. They further advised that the "religious question" be ignored for the time being; when abuses involving the clergy or the Church occurred, they should be denounced, but criticism should fall only on the guilty parties, not on the entire Catholic community. Finally, the Center asserted that for the present Liberals should maintain an attitude of neutrality with respect to the presidential contest.

The presidential campaign had already gotten underway when the Liberal convention met in April 1891, and dissension within the National party was plainly visible. In fact, cracks in the edifice of the Regeneration had become evident as early as October 1888 when the Holguín administration proposed to Congress the adoption of a constitutional amendment providing for the division of each of the departments except Panama into two or more provinces. In a message to Congress defending the proposal, Holguín pointed out that at present division of the departments was almost impossible and argued that this step was necessary to wipe out lingering traces of federalism in Colombia.[70] "The federation, with its sovereign states, had sunk such deep roots in our soil that it was not possible to extirpate it completely at the first attempt.... But it is up to you, honorable senators and representatives, to protect the work of the National Constituent Council and apply the scalpel with a firm hand to the corruption which still remains and out of which may still be reborn the anarchic and disuniting regime of the federation." The constitution of 1886, according to Article 209, could be altered by an act of Congress approved by majority vote in one session and approved again in the following session by a two-thirds vote in both houses. Two years had to elapse, therefore, before Holguín's proposal could become law. In the meantime, however, the proposal touched off the first serious internal dispute among Conservative supporters of the Regeneration. It also proved to be a portent of future conflict since those Conservatives who opposed departmental division in 1888–90 would remain in the forefront of opposition to the regime.

When the proposed amendment was voted on in first debate in the Chamber of Representatives on 16 October 1888, it was approved by a vote of 36 to 13.[71] Of the 13 representatives voting against the administration, 6 were from Antioquia and Cauca, where opposition to departmental division was strongest. The bill was passed with some modifications by large majorities in second and third debate in the following months, but 25 legislators, representing all 9 departments, issued a statement declaring that they were opposed to departmental division and had voted for it only in the interests of party unity and because they realized that it could not become law until 1890.[72] The bill was approved in the Senate on 13 November.[73] Of the 3 senators who went on record as voting against the proposal, 2 were from Antioquia and one was from Cauca.

Starting in October 1888, departmental division was the subject of heated controversy in the press. It seems clear that the administration's principal concern in pressing for the elimination of the existing departments was the desire to reduce the actual or potential influence of regional *caudillos* who might seek to subvert the existing order. An article from a newspaper in Pasto stated:

> The governors of the departments are sovereigns, though the term is no longer used, and they enjoy influence and powers capable of disturbing order and maintaining the Republic always in a state of intranquility. . . . They exercise authority in the entire territory of each of the old federal states; they count, just as they did before, on immediate and direct agents in the provinces, now called provincial prefects; they dispose of their own treasury, and if their revenue is smaller, so are their expenses.[74]

An editorial in *La Nación,* "organ of the principles of the Regeneration," maintained that departmental division was a device to permit the establishment of true administrative decentralization and would strengthen the municipalities. The reform would in no way alter the distinctive character of Colombia's regions.[75]

Opponents of the proposal were convinced that it was aimed primarily at Cauca and Antioquia, where there was already unhappiness about the forced retirement of private bank notes.[76] A Medellín newspaper opposed to departmental division also complained that while the national government had financed public works in Cauca, Bolívar, Cundinamarca, and Santander, Antioquia had received no aid toward completion of a vital railroad.[77] This newspaper went so far as to threaten secession if the Holguín proposal became law. "If the government insists on carrying out this measure and succeeds in imposing division, the result will be secession. . . . Cauca and Antioquia will not return to the exaggerated centralism of former times."[78] What the editors envisioned was the creation of a republic of Tolima, composed of the departments west of the Magdalena.[79]

Although Núñez had endorsed the Holguín proposal in 1888, the controversy it aroused led him to have second thoughts on the matter. When *El Telegrama* of Bogotá suggested that he was a strong proponent of departmental division because of his belief in the need for "vigorous" centralism, he wired from Cartagena on 25 November 1889: "Vigorous political centralism is not, in my opinion, annihilation of sections."[80] On 1 December he wrote an article in *El Porvenir* of Cartagena in which he spelled out his views at greater length.[81] While the division of one or two departments might be desirable, he said, he did not consider it a matter of urgency and therefore favored maintaining the status quo, partly because he did not regard as opportune any legislative innovation that might hurt the sentiments or interests of respectable individuals or communities. He felt that absolute calm was the fundamental requirement of the moment and that any division of the type proposed would be more likely to cause displeasure than satisfaction, for it was clear that for every friend of the reform, there would be many adversaries who would carry it out with annoyance. Finally, he pointed out that the proliferation of small provinces would mean an end to the sectional powers and responsibilities preserved in the constitution.

Although *La Nación* argued that the Núñez article indicated that the titular president was opposed only to the creation of small provinces and not to the breakup of the existing departments, the antidivision *La Tarde* reprinted the article under the headline: "We have won!"[82] In the ensuing months the proposed reform would indeed be gently laid to rest, but in the meantime it became intertwined with another important matter facing Congress in 1890—the election of a *designado* to succeed Holguín as acting president. On 17 March 1890, José Manuel Goenaga, former governor of Bolívar, and Enrique P. Román, a nephew of Núñez's second wife, were among those issuing a statement in Cartagena which called both for the reelection of Holguín and for the postponement of departmental division since "serious traditional interests" insisted on preserving the status quo.[83] On 11 April Rafael Reyes, who had previously spoken in favor of departmental division and was considered a possible candidate for Holguín's post, also endorsed his reelection and suggested the desirability of burying the question of the proposed amendment to the constitution.[84] He warned, moreover, that dissension within the National party might eventually lead to "the triumph of demagoguic and atheistic Radicalism." Four days later a trio of distinguished Antioqueño Conservatives—Marceliano Vélez, Abraham Moreno, and Alejandro Botero U.—indicated their acceptance of the Holguín candidacy in accordance with the terms of the Cartagena statement of 17 March.[85] These events suggest that at least a tacit agreement was reached whereby Holguín and his backers agreed to abandon the proposed amendment in exchange for support for Holguín's reelection on the part of the opponents of departmental division.

When Congress met on 20 July 1890, Holguín delivered a message in which he too agreed that it would be prudent to postpone departmental division for the present because of the differences of opinion it had aroused.[86] Six days later he was reelected *designado* by a vote of 70 to 14, a blank ballot being cast by his brother Jorge.[87] The 14 dissenting votes went to Marceliano Vélez, the veteran chieftain from Antioquia. At least 8 of the 14 who voted against Holguín had been opponents of departmental division.

Despite the hopes of Núñez, the demise of departmental division and the reelection of Holguín did not usher in an era of harmony within the National party. Indeed, dissension was deepened by the presidential election of 1891, which was to see a significant number of Conservatives in opposition to Núñez.

According to Title 17 of the constitution and the basic election law (number 7 of 31 January 1888), presidential electors were to be chosen on the first Sunday in December of an election year; the following February they were to gather in electoral assemblies to cast their ballots for president and vice president. Citizens who were literate, who had an annual income of $500, or who owned immovable property worth $1,500 were eligible for vote for electors. One elector and one alternate were to be chosen for every 1,000 inhabitants in a given district.

At first the right of Núñez to head any ticket was unquestioned by Conservatives and Independents. At the same time it was known that Núñez would remain in retirement in Cartagena. Interest, therefore, centered on the vice presidential nomination, but it was understood that Núñez would have the final word on his running-mate. The question of the vice presidential nomination had been debated by National party leaders after the Congressional session of 1890, but no genuine agreement had been reached.[88] The candidacy of Marceliano Vélez then began to win support, and when it was endorsed by a Committee of Vigilance in Cartagena early in 1891, it was assumed that the nomination had Núñez's blessing.[89] Vélez's supporters in Bogotá hurriedly completed an *adhesión* endorsing him, which was published in Carlos Martínez Silva's *Correo Nacional* on 9 March 1891.[90] Only a week later, however, a recently founded newspaper, *La Prensa,* which was owned by Jorge Holguín, advanced the vice presidential candidacy of Miguel Antonio Caro.[91]

From the very beginning Caro was depicted by his supporters as the person best suited to defend the cause of the National party, which, according to *La Prensa,* was pledged to uphold the Roman Catholic religion, centralism, the use of paper money so long as a favorable balance of trade was not achieved, restrictions on the licentious and revolutionary press, and in general all the doctrines identified with the Regeneration.[92] This newspaper admitted that all was not perfect in Colombia, but it argued that the Regeneration had brought great benefits:

> The nation has been at peace for six years and during this time, even if everything has not been done well and every evil has not been avoided, at least the lash of anarchy and the explosion of demagoguery have not been felt; young people have not been hurled into the mire of materialism, public buildings have not been shamefully mortgaged in order to meet the most necessary expenses, and workers have not had their labors interrupted by the report of cannon or by the clash of swords and bayonets on bloody battlegrounds.[93]

Another Bogotá newspaper declared that Caro had for the constitution of 1886 the love which the craftsman has for his handiwork while Vélez was basically an opposition candidate.[94] Unlike Vélez, Caro was a truly national candidate who had no "fief" or "favorite department" which he was bound to prefer.[95] It is clear that at the time of its promulgation the Caro candidacy was supported by those Conservatives closest to the regime and by most of the major Independent leaders, among them Luis Carlos Rico and Minister of Government Antonio Roldán.[96]

The Vélez candidacy, on the other hand, had the backing of Conservatives, particularly from Antioquia and Cauca, who had challenged the administration on the issue of departmental division. The fact that the Velista organ *La Paz* found it necessary to refute the charge that the supporters of Vélez were hostile to the Independents serves to indicate the weakness of Velismo among them.[97] *La Paz* claimed that Caro was undesirable for a variety of reasons, among them his relationship to Carlos Holguín (his brother-in-law) and his lack of political experience, but above all because his was an official candidacy, hatched within the government and lacking popular support outside of the ranks of officeholders.[98]

In the early stages of the contest Núñez professed neutrality toward the rival vice presidential candidates and expressed the hope in a letter to Rico that the administration would be circumspect in charting its course during the election.[99] It gradually became clear, however, that Vélez was indeed opposed to certain features of the Holguín administration. On 16 May 1891 Vélez addressed a letter to Núñez in which he referred to national concern over possible revival of the issue of departmental division, the intervention of the government in past elections, the use of the executive's extraordinary powers to imprison and exile citizens in time of peace, and speculation with the national treasury.[100] In view of this concern, he concluded, "it can be seen why the free and spontaneous current of public opinion wishes to see the direction of the government in the hands of men completely alien from these errors, or, if you will, from these practices." He concluded by asking Núñez to indicate his attitude toward Vélez's candidacy.

The president did not make his sentiments known until 8 September. In a telegram to Vélez, he stated that the language of the Velistas made it clear that they were in disagreement with his policies and that, despite his initial pleasure at the Vélez candidacy, he could not allow the Antioqueño's name to appear alongside his. He added that reports of a Radical alliance with the Velistas and his own concern for a cause to which he had dedicated great efforts might impose on him obligations incompatible with the neutrality he had hitherto displayed. Vélez replied on 17 September by again condemning the administration's political practices and by stating his desire to remove himself from the electoral contest.[101] Vélez's statement, the American minister remarked, was "the first public defiance of Dr. Núñez which has ever been given by a Conservative."[102] Many of Vélez's original backers, such as Martínez Silva and Rafael Reyes, now transferred their allegiance to the Núñez-Caro ticket, but others proceeded to nominate Vélez for the presidency in the name of the Conservative party late in October.[103] José Joaquín Ortiz, a journalist and educator noted for his proclerical views, was selected as his running-mate.

Meanwhile, the Liberal Center had continued its operations in the expectation that the Liberal party would profit from the divisions in National ranks. Party committees were formed on the departmental, provincial, and municipal levels, and Liberals were urged to inscribe themselves on the electoral rolls. The Center acknowledged that many Liberals were reluctant to take any part in the election because of their fear of harassment and fraud, but it repeatedly advocated peaceful participation in the contest "because the Republic consists essentially in the exercise of the ballot, and whoever evades the fulfillment of this duty, either voluntarily or because of intimidation, will appear to be renouncing this form of government, which our forefathers acquired and established for their descendants at the cost of so much suffering."[104]

The Liberal Center molded its strategy in accordance with developments in the enemy camp. The nomination of Liberal candidates for the presidency and vice presidency was evidently never considered seriously. Such a course, Camacho Roldán declared on 18 August 1891 in a letter to Uribe Uribe, who was vice president of Antioquia's Liberal directory, would be almost ridiculous.[105] Camacho Roldán felt, however, that Liberals had a duty to vote in the election; to permit without Liberal opposition the triumph of Caro, whom he likened to Francia of Paraguay, would make the party the laughing-stock of America. At the same time he did not believe that Liberal support should be given to Vélez or to any other Conservative so long as Núñez's name headed the ticket.

Núñez's disavowal of the Vélez candidacy in September and the proclamation of the Vélez-Ortiz ticket the following month opened the way for Liberal cooperation with the Velistas. On 13 October the Liberal Center instructed departmental directors that Liberals should vote for Liberal electors in areas where they were in the majority; elsewhere they should try to form mixed slates in agreement with opposition Conservatives.[106] On the same date Parra informed Liberal leaders in Panama that should Vélez be nominated for the presidency, the Liberal party would support him. Vélez would probably not win the election, but the position of the party was bound to improve in any event.[107]

According to Parra, the decision to endorse Vélez was accepted by Liberals everywhere, except in Barranquilla,[108] but many were reluctant to support his running-mate José Joaquín Ortiz. "The Ortiz candidacy can satisfy no Liberal," Parra admitted on 18 November 1891 in a letter to Fidel Cano, head of the Antioquia directory, "but it . . . should not deter us from the object we had in mind in accepting the candidacy of General Vélez; and since denying votes to Mr. Ortiz would be equivalent to favoring the Caro candidacy, there should be no vacillation in supporting that of the former. After all, Mr. Ortiz is also affiliated with the opposition."[109]

Liberal support for the Vélez-Ortiz ticket did not mean, however, that the Liberals had effected an alliance with the opposition Conservatives, or that relations between them were friendly. In the letter to Cano cited above, Parra complained about the coolness of the Vélez directory toward the Liberals. "It seems as if these gentlemen [the members of the directory] harbor the strange pretension—not to give it another name—of appearing *forced* by the Liberals to accept their support in the election of General Vélez. The singular aloofness of these gentlemen has not permitted up to now the understanding that is natural between two parties who are going to struggle against a common adversary tomorrow." And the hope expressed in the circular of 13 October that Liberals would be able to join with Velistas in drawing up mixed slates of candidates in areas where the Liberals lacked a clear majority proved unfounded. No agreement could be reached with the Velistas in Cartagena and Bogotá, and in Antioquia Liberals were instructed by the departmental directory to vote for the Velista slate of electors.[110]

After the balloting took place on 6 December, the *Correo Nacional* reported that the Núñez-Caro ticket had won a widespread victory,[111] but Liberals charged that they had been intimidated while attempting to register and to vote.[112] There is also evidence that, despite the exhortations of the Liberal Center, party members had abstained in large numbers. In letters to Uribe Uribe and Belisario Zamorano in Cauca, Camacho Roldán reported that the Liberal turnout had been poor in most of the larger towns in the country. Liberals had stayed away from the polls because of fear or because of unwillingness to concede the legitimacy of the regime, and in some areas Liberal committees had even advised abstention.[113] Only in Antioquia and in a few places in Boyacá and Bolívar had the Liberals made a good showing.

On 19 December the Center informed the departmental directors that Liberal electors were to cast their ballots for Vélez and Ortiz in the electoral assemblies in February.[114] The Velistas merited Liberal support, the circular said, and the party would betray its weakness if the electors were to vote for other candidates. These instructions were made public in a circular to the electors dated 1 January 1892.[115] By voting for the opposition candidates, they would be expressing the party's willingness to contribute to the establishment of a legal regime that would guarantee the rights of the citizens and permit political parties to operate freely. Moreover, if Vélez were elected president, some reforms might be made, such as repeal of the Law of the Horses and removal of restrictions on the press. When the electoral assemblies met on 2 February, Núñez and Caro received 2,075 and 2,082 votes, respectively, and Vélez and Ortiz received 509 and 503, respectively; 347 of Vélez's votes came from Antioquia.[116] Precise figures on the number of Liberal electors chosen in December are not available, but party leaders themselves indicated that it was very small.[117]

After the conclusion of the presidential contest, the Liberal Center began its preparations for the May 1892 elections for seats in municipal councils, departmental assemblies, and the Chamber of Representatives. All citizens were eligible to vote for municipal councilors and deputies to the assemblies, who served two-year terms. Voting qualifications for the Chamber of Representatives were the same as for presidential electors. For election purposes, municipal districts containing at least 50,000 inhabitants were considered electoral districts, each of which was entitled to elect one or more representatives and from two to five deputies.

In March the Center petitioned the government for the correction of certain electoral practices so that voters' lists different from those used in December might be compiled.[118] The government's equivocation or silence, coupled with the probability of official intervention in the elections, put the members of the Center in a perplexing position. To advise Liberals to go to the polls, where they might be exposed to intimidation by the authorities, might ignite a revolution. On the other hand, to advocate abstention would mean the surrender of the most precious of republican rights. Accordingly, the Center instructed Liberals to vote in those areas where the authorities seemed disposed to hold honest elections, that is, in places where there was no recruitment or increase in the armed forces just before the balloting and where voting lists had been made public so as to permit appeals. Elsewhere, Liberals were to abstain.[119]

The Center had initially hoped that Liberals might collaborate with the Velistas in the selection of candidates for the May elections, but the latter had refused to support Liberals. This was the substance of a communication from Camacho Roldán to the Bolívar directory, which was authorized to draw up slates of Liberal candidates in full freedom.[120] The Antioquia directory, reversing its policy of the previous December, also decided to back Liberal candidates.[121]

The balloting itself was notable mainly for the fact that it brought to Congress the first Liberal representative since the beginning of the Regeneration. In Antioquia, where the Conservative split was most profound, Luis A. Robles was elected to the Chamber of Representatives from Medellín.[122] Liberals were also elected to the departmental assembly and won control of several municipal councils.[123]

In the months since its foundation, the Liberal Center had not been preoccupied exclusively with electoral matters. Another subject which had aroused considerable concern was the matter of party finances, particularly the raising of funds to help support the Liberal press. In September 1891 Parra spoke of the desirability of converting *El Relator*, the official organ of the Center, into a daily, but the party could not supply the monthly subsidy of $500 that would be needed.[124] The problem would be solved if subscribers outside of Bogotá paid for their subscriptions promptly, Parra said, but very few did so. In his correspondence with Uribe Uribe, Camacho Roldán also referred to the party's financial plight. When Uribe Uribe suggested that Liberal agents be sent to the departments to combat apathy among the rank and file, Camacho Roldán pointed out that the only persons available for such a chore were bibulous military men; an even more serious obstacle was the scarcity of money, for most of the Center's funds were being spent on *El Relator*, which everybody criticized but nobody read.[125] Camacho Roldán indicated some displeasure with the editors of *El Relator*, who he said were a drain on the Center's resources but claimed to be suffering losses.[126]

By September 1892, when the Liberal Center was disbanded, it had raised the sum of $8,178.70 from Liberals in four departments: Cundinamarca, $4,645.50; Santander, $1,656.00; Bolívar, $1,104.00; and Tolima, $773.20. Of this sum, $6,953.35 had been disbursed by the Center, the largest share being devoted to the press: $3,197.50 had been spent on *El Relator;* $1,805.00 had been used to subsidize *El Espectador* and other newspapers; and $700 had gone to pay fines for *El Relator* and the *Diario de Cundinamarca*.[127] The balance had been used for office expenses and the salary of a secretary ($430.25), the printing of signs, circulars, etc. ($680), and election expenses in Bogotá ($140.60).

A problem potentially more serious than the inadequacy of party funds also presented itself to the Center early in 1892. Although some militant Liberals had always favored an attempt to overthrow the Regeneration by force, it was not until after the 1891 election that their arguments began to sound increasingly cogent to Liberals unhappy over their virtual exclusion from public life or distressed by unsatisfactory economic conditions. In

March 1892 the entire departmental directory of Cundinamarca resigned after the Center refused to approve a set of resolutions it had adopted indicating a desire to resort to violence.[128] According to Camacho Roldán, Liberals in Cauca also favored revolution.[129] He ridiculed those restless Liberals who fancied that it would be easy to overthrow a regime that controlled the nation with an army of 7,000 men, forbade traffic in arms, and banned the gathering of five persons or more. In his opinion, an attempt to regain power by force would require a civil war of several years, at the conclusion of which Liberals might find themselves faced with a government worse than the present one. "I will never accept barracks revolts," he declared. "Isolated movements that serve only to spill blood and strengthen usurped powers are counterproductive. An appeal to arms can only be made when the ripened fruit is ready to fall from the tree of its own weight."[130]

That Camacho Roldán's fears were well founded became clear in September 1892 when Liberals from all the departments gathered in Bogotá to plan the party's future course. Perhaps because of the fear of government reprisals, the Liberal convention of 1892 was conducted in an atmosphere of secrecy, and relatively little information about it was reported in the contemporary press. According to historian Eduardo Rodríguez Piñeres, who had access to the unpublished memoirs of one of the delegates, Inocencio Cucalón, he and two others, Modesto Garcés and Juan Félix de León, prepared a plan for the acquisition of weapons and the military organization of the party so that it might be prepared should war be deemed necessary at some future date.[131] The delegates apparently approved this proposal but greatly softened its impact by selecting Santiago Pérez, a well-known pacifist, as party head.[132] They also approved on 3 October a manifesto indicating their determination to fight the regime primarily by means of the press since the rights of free suffrage and of association had been suppressed.[133]

The decision to replace the party's plural leadership with a single party director was evidently made at the instigation of Parra, speaking on behalf of the old Liberal Center.[134] It was also decided to pay the director an annual salary of $6,000 and to establish a new Liberal organ, the editorship of which would be entrusted to Pérez and would constitute his principal duty as party head.[135] Funds for Pérez's salary and the newspaper were to come from a $100,000 loan to be raised in the various departments, each of which was assigned a quota. A special committee was appointed to administer party funds and to pass on financial requests in consultation with Pérez and party treasurer Garcés.[136] On 14 February 1893, however, Pérez stated that there was no need for continued efforts to gather funds since the plans to launch a new periodical had been dropped; neither he nor contributors to *El Relator,* which was to continue as the principal Liberal organ in Bogotá, would receive remuneration for their services.[137]

The real reason for the change of plans may have been that, as Pérez reported a few days later, the money had not been forthcoming, and some departments had not contributed a cent.[138]

Despite the selection of Pérez as party head, the more militant Liberals did not desist from their plans to prepare for an armed struggle against the Regeneration. Pérez was handicapped, therefore, not only by the vigilance of the authorities but also by the fact that there was substance to the government's suspicions about the subversive intentions of some Liberals. Indeed, he considered himself a hostage of the government, for he was held accountable for the activities of all Liberals regardless of whether they were following instructions or not.[139]

Nevertheless, he continued to voice his opposition to revolution privately and publicly, and suggested that he be replaced if it seemed that his views were damaging to the party's interests. In a note to departmental directors asking them to prevent acts of violence by Liberals, he acknowledged the need for change but stressed that it had to be achieved by means of sustained and peaceful protests. "Armed struggles have cured none of our ills," he declared, "and the proof of this is that after so many of them, often crowned with Liberal triumphs, the position of Colombia with respect to political rights and public liberties is in many ways worse than it was before 1810."[140]

In May 1893 Pérez made public a ten-point program which he said was aimed at the restoration of basic civil rights and represented the wishes not only of Liberals but of all Colombian republicans.[141] First of all, he appealed for freedom of the press, restricted only by dispositions enacted into law, and for electoral legislation to guarantee freedom of suffrage. He also called for abolition of the national bank and for a permanent halt to the emission of paper money, together with the amortization of all paper money already in circulation. The government's fiscal monopolies were denounced; when money was urgently needed by the treasury, it should be raised by means of increased indirect taxes or by the establishment of equitable direct levies. Among the other policies of the Regeneration censured by Pérez were the extraordinary faculties granted to the president, which he said undermined republican institutions by their very existence, and the arbitrary recruitment of soldiers. Finally, Pérez raised the old federalist banner in modified form by calling for administrative and fiscal decentralization so that no department or region would be deprived of its resources and the right to plan its own development.

Shortly afterward Pérez's program, as well as his pacifist policy, was endorsed by nine prominent Liberals, including Camacho Roldán, Robles, Santos Acosta, and Miguel Samper.[142] Although they felt that the Pérez program concentrated on Colombia's most urgent needs and that the nation's institutions could be improved by reforms other than those mentioned by Pérez, they did not think that any of his recommendations could fail to win Conservative acceptance. Indeed, a manifesto issued by Marceliano Vélez the following month closely paralleled Pérez's program.[143]

Despite the pacifist avowals of Pérez and other Liberal leaders, the government, now headed by Caro (who had taken office on 7 August 1892), remained apprehensive of possible Liberal subversion and suspected that the reorganization of the party and the fund-raising activities undertaken after the 1892 convention were a prelude to insurrection. Its fears were undoubtedly sharpened by a serious outbreak of rioting by the lower classes of Bogotá in January 1893. The immediate cause of the disturbances was the publication in a weekly periodical called *Colombia Cristiana* of four articles by José Ignacio Gutiérrez, who described the working classes of the capital as being immoral, thievish, and deceitful, and blamed their poverty on excessive consumption of alcoholic beverages.[144] During the peak of the disorders on 16 January mobs attacked all but one of the police stations in the city, invaded the Asilo de San José, a house of correction with which Gutiérrez was associated, and freed all the prisoners there. In addition, the Gutiérrez home was attacked, as were the homes of the mayor of Bogotá, Higinio Cualla, and of Antonio B. Cuervo, governor of Cundinamarca. It was estimated that fifty persons died as a result of the rioting.[145]

With the authorization of Caro, who was not in Bogotá, Governor Cuervo decreed a temporary state of siege on 16 January which was not lifted until 24 February.[146] Although the government charged that a *Sociedad Filantrópica* had instigated the disorders,[147] the rioters clearly lacked organization and leadership. According to a report in the *Correo Nacional,* some denounced the army and the upper classes while others praised them; the one universal target of the rioters seems to have been the police.[148] It was also conceded that the riots had no directly political character. "It is evidently not a matter of a political movement nor of any plan comparable to those which socialism and the spirit of anarchism are accustomed to engendering in society," Cuervo reported on 17 January.[149] "The events which we have witnessed are the explosion of passions maliciously stirred up by those who try to deceive the laboring masses, for whom the authorities and all social classes have every consideration." To Núñez, the disorders showed that the "socialist scourge" had penetrated Colombia despite the absence of aristocracy, privilege, monopoly, or trusts such as those in the United States.[150]

In the ensuing months the government remained on the alert for signs of revolutionary activity. Tensions were kept high by a newspaper debate between Pérez and Carlos Holguín, which "excited the public . . . in a most remarkable manner,"[151] and by a spirited defense by Santos Acosta of his role in the deposition of President Mosquera in 1867. By August the Caro administration had determined to crack down on the entire Liberal party leadership, justifying its actions by citing recent newspaper attacks on the government and by vague references to a conspiracy in Barranquilla and efforts by Inocencio Cucalón to purchase arms in New York.[152] Immediately after the publication of the 4 August issue of *El Relator* the newspaper was suspended, and the party's funds—a total of $13,467.87—were confiscated.[153] Santiago Pérez, Santos Acosta, Modesto Garcés, and the members of the party's finance committee were apprehended, and Pérez and Garcés were banished from Colombia.[154] Several Cauca Liberals were also imprisoned, and *El Espectador* was shut down.

These events left the party without a formal structure, a condition in which it remained until 1896. The absence of a national organization to restrain the militant Liberals probably contributed to the outbreak of a revolution which began in Cundinamarca in January 1895 and was crushed by the government in three months.[155] Although Diego Mendoza Pérez asserted that the revolt had come as a surprise to most Liberals,[156] the American minister, Luther F. McKinney, had predicted the early outbreak of a revolution in a dispatch dated only two days before the first pronouncement.[157] "[T]here is general uneasiness among the people and especially the working people of the country," he explained. "While the premium on exchange has . . . increased within the last two years, there has been no perceptible increase in wages, and the laboring people are consequently very poor. There is no money in the Government Treasury, and no prospect of any change for the better in financial matters, and the people hold the Government responsible for their present condition." The defeat of the revolution did not in any way dampen the ardor of Liberals who felt that the restoration of Liberalism would be achieved only by the forcible overthrow of the government. On the contrary, their arguments would sound increasingly more persuasive in the years ahead.

8
Road to Revolution

In the years after 1895 the Liberal party moved inexorably toward armed revolt against the Regeneration. Although the government became less repressive in the last years of the century, Liberal exclusion from public office remained nearly complete. In addition, several other circumstances—increasing Conservative dissension, the onset of an economic depression caused by a drop in coffee prices in 1896, and the emergence of the charismatic Rafael Uribe Uribe as spokesman for those who spurned peaceful opposition to the regime—combined to swell the ranks of the Liberal militants and to strengthen their belief in the government's vulnerability. The result was the outbreak of a revolution in October 1899 that proved to be the most destructive of Colombia's nineteenth-century conflicts.

In *Coffee and Conflict in Colombia, 1886–1910,* Charles W. Bergquist offered a detailed account of the events preceding the war, emphasizing the primacy of economic motives in arousing opposition to the Regeneration by the Liberal leadership and Conservative dissidents. His argument rests on three principal contentions. (1) Liberals and Conservatives linked to the export-import sector fought the Regeneration mainly because of their unhappiness with its statist fiscal and economic policies, especially its reliance on paper money. (2) Conservative leaders who opposed the Regeneration on economic grounds readily cooperated with like-minded Liberals. (3) Liberals who tried to discourage an appeal to arms were tied to the export-import sector in contrast to the militant Liberals, who were younger and were more frustrated over their exclusion from public office and therefore emphasized political rather than economic reform.

While it is true that deteriorating economic conditions contributed to the start of the war, Bergquist's arguments seem flawed in several ways. The most serious weakness in his analysis is his failure to deal systematically with the question of who gained and who lost from the regime of paper money. He merely states that traditional agriculturalists may have benefited (p. 51) while export-import merchants and holders of liquid capital (p. 37) as well as coffee producers suffered. To the argument made by Caro and Jorge Holguín that paper money had in fact subsidized coffee cultivation, Bergquist replies that the growers did not see things that way because they had a doctrinaire commitment to laissez faire, because most of them were also importers, and because they believed that paper money would discourage foreign investment (pp. 75-76n). Little evidence is brought forward to support any of these assertions.

That critics of the Regeneration mounted vehement attacks on its economic and fiscal policies is of course true. It also seems safe to assume that the new monopolies, the ban on the issue of notes by private banks, and other Regeneration measures did injure numerous interests. However, it is by no means clear that those adversely affected can be categorized as neatly as Bergquist indicated. Indeed, the inflation that began in the 1880s probably hurt most Colombians in the money economy. The political opposition would have hardly overlooked such conditions in their indictment of the Regeneration. This does not necessarily mean that criticism of the economic and fiscal policies of the Regeneration reflected an unwavering belief in laissez faire or was designed primarily to further the interests of a particular group. In any event, few of the Liberal leaders could be described as firm adherents of laissez faire by the end of the century.

Bergquist's analysis also exaggerates the dissension within the Conservative and Liberal parties in the late 1890s as well as the possibilities for collaboration between the Liberals and the Conservative opposition, whose members continued to regard Liberalism with the "aloofness" of which Parra had complained in 1891. Finally, he fails to appreciate the significance of the establishment of Cipriano Castro's regime in neighboring Venezuela as a factor in the start of the war.

Dissension among Conservatives, as we have seen, became evident as early as 1888 with the debate over departmental division and intensified during the presidential election of 1891. By the time Congress met on 20 July 1894, Conservative disunity had reached such proportions that appeals were sent to Rafael Núñez in Cartagena urging him to return to the capital in the hope that he might be able to heal the breach.[1] The ailing president was reluctant to exchange the tropical calm of Cartagena for the turmoil of Bogotá, but after some hesitation he began making preparations for the journey. They were never completed: he collapsed during a visit to the home of a favorite sister-in-law and died a few days later on 18 September 1894.

The Conservative dissidents of the mid-1890s claimed to uphold traditional Conservative principles and reserved the name of Conservative for themselves; by historians they are usually known as Historical Conservatives. Those Conservatives who continued to give wholehearted support to the Regeneration became known as Nationalist Conservatives or simply Nationalists. The latter designation also embraced the Independent Liberals who had joined in the formation of the National party, which was moribund in fact if not in name by the mid-1890s. The nucleus of the Historical Conservative faction was made up of those who had supported the Vélez-Ortiz ticket in 1891, but their ranks were continuously augmented by other Conservatives, such as Carlos Martínez Silva, who attracted official displeasure with an article in the *Correo Nacional* in April 1894. Soon afterward he came under severe personal attack as a result of disclosures regarding "clandestine emissions" of paper money while he was minister of the treasury. In November 1894 the *Correo Nacional* was suspended for six months; it was allowed to resume publication only under another editor.

The grievances of the Historical Conservatives against the government can be found in a document (January 1896) signed by Martínez Silva and twenty other Conservatives and known as "Motives of Dissidence."[2] Acknowledging that the Regeneration had brought two definite benefits to Colombia—national unity and the restoration of harmony between church and state—the signers pointed out, however, that the safeguards to civil liberty in the constitution of 1886 had not been respected. They were critical of many other policies of the Regeneration: its excessive centralization, its systematic exclusion of the Liberals from Congress and the departmental assemblies, its mishandling of the nation's finances and virtual repudiation of the foreign debt, its neglect of education, and its failure to stimulate realistic and useful transportation projects. They also stressed the responsibility of the Conservative party for both the benefits and failings of the Regeneration because in their opinion the National party no longer had any significance, and the Independents, with a few exceptions, constituted merely a profit-making enterprise totally subservient to the government.

For his part Caro did not deny that the Regeneration was alien to Conservatism. The National party, he maintained in 1896, was Conservative insofar as it defended constituted order, respect for authority, and harmony with the Church, but he asserted that the constitution of 1886 and that of 1858, which had been promulgated under a Conservative government, were antagonistic.[3] Another defender of the Regeneration, Marco Fidel Suárez, argued that for the present it was the only regime suitable for Colombia. "The policy and governments of the Regeneration have proposed and in part have realized the patriotic object of preparing the field for rational parties, causing the disappearance of the anomaly of Radicalism," which he described as "a revolutionary school determined, as its name indicates, to uproot the foundations of political and civil society."[4]

Caro's imperviousness to the concerns of the Historical Conservatives was illustrated in March 1896, when he stepped down from the presidency, presumably to preserve his eligibility for election as chief executive for the following term.[5] He was succeeded by *designado* Guillermo Quintero Calderón, a Conservative who had served in the cabinet and as governor of Santander. Upon taking office, Quintero Calderón appointed several Nationalists to his cabinet, but to fill the key post of minister of government he named Abraham Moreno, an Antioqueño and follower of Marceliano Vélez.[6] At this Caro hurried back to the capital from his retreat at nearby Sopó and relieved Quintero Calderón five days after the latter had assumed the presidency. Caro proceeded to organize a solidly Nationalist cabinet in the belief, as he remarked to a correspondent, that "the harmony of Christian elements is not obtained by naming Protestant cardinals."[7]

Despite Caro's apparent imperturbability, his administration came under increasingly heavy fire from Conservatives as the election of 1897 approached. By 1897 the Nationalist leadership had been reduced to the surviving Independents, whose fate was inextricably linked with the Regeneration and who were unlikely to find a comfortable haven among the Liberals or the Historical Conservatives, and some traditional Conservatives, such as Caro and Manuel Casabianca. In addition, the Nationalist leadership included younger men like Rafael Reyes, who had had an opportunity to rise from obscurity under the tutelage of the Regeneration. Others were Marco Fidel Suárez, the illegitimate son of a washerwoman, who became acting minister of foreign affairs in 1891, and Aristides Fernández, who had begun as a doorman in the National Academy of Music in 1887 and reached the position of director of police in November 1898.[8] According to Bergquist, what divided the Historical Conservatives from the Nationalists in 1897 were their conflicting economic and ideological interests. "Nationalists represented bureaucratic, ecclesiastical, and apparently (although the evidence is largely circumstantial) traditional agricultural interests who benefited from the statist economic policies and centralist, pro-Catholic political policies of the Regeneration governments." The Historical Conservatives, on the other hand, are seen as representatives of import-export interests. Bergquist also maintains that during the presidential campaign of 1897 the various political groups in Colombia "consistently pursued their interests."[9]

Bergquist's assertions rest on a tenuous foundation. First of all, statements about the economic interests of the members of the Conservative factions are extremely difficult to substantiate because of the continuing defections from the ranks of the Nationalists. Today's Nationalist might well be tomorrow's Historical Conservative: Carlos Martínez Silva is a case in point. To support his arguments, Bergquist makes much of the occupational differences between Historical Conservative and Nationalist electors chosen in Bogotá in 1897, and particularly of the fact that 30 of the 114 Historical Conservative electors identified by occupation were merchants while there were only 7 merchants among 92 Nationalist electors so identified.[10] On the other hand, 33, or more than one-third, of the Nationalist electors were *empleados,* a term which Bergquist himself admits was generally applied to government employees. This result would seem to suggest above all that by 1897 Nationalist strength in Bogotá was limited in large measure to government employees whose jobs depended on the perpetuation of the Nationalist-dominated regime. That there were fewer *empleados* among the Historical Conservative electors than among the Nationalists is not surprising given the tendency of Colombian political groups to exclude their foes from the bureaucracy. It should also be noted that both Conservative factions counted approximately the same number of landowners among their electors: 7 for the Historical Conservatives and 8 for the Nationalists. Finally, the statement that Colombian political factions "consistently" pursued their interests in 1897 is puzzling, especially if applied to the Conservatives. As will be seen in the following pages, both Conservative groups exhibited great confusion and uncertainty while choosing their presidential and vice presidential candidates, and the Historical Conservatives ended by instructing their electors to vote for the Nationalist candidates instead of their own.

If Caro remained inflexible in the face of Conservative disaffection, he could not ignore the economic and fiscal crisis which gripped the country as coffee prices began to fall in 1896 as a result of overexpansion in Brazil. The Colombian growers, who had also expanded in the 1890s, encouraged by the abundance of money and favorable market conditions, now found themselves unable to meet interest payments on loans and to pay rising transportation costs and still make a profit.[11] The state of the industry was described on 30 June 1897 in a petition to Caro from individuals and firms engaged in coffee cultivation in Santander, Tolima, Cundinamarca, and Antioquia.[12]

The petitioners pointed out that the coffee industry had been the primary agent of Colombian development in recent years, helping to maintain the value of the nation's paper currency and to preserve political peace. Now, however, these benefits were jeopardized by the recent decline in the price of coffee in foreign markets. "This depreciation has produced . . . a great economic perturbation in business, which, if it is not contained or at least normalized, is capable of causing a complete and noisome commercial crisis, a decline in the value of paper money, and difficulties for the government which can bring with them, in a country exalted by political passions, war itself, which would be the culmination of all our evils and misfortunes." The petitioners requested the government to lower or eliminate the export tax on coffee and to use its influence to induce the railroads and the firms engaged in navigation of the Magdalena to reduce their freight rates.

Caro suspended the export tax on coffee on 13 July 1897, but coffee prices continued to decline, and the consequences foreseen by the petitioners became a reality. The drop in coffee prices and the resulting deterioration in Colombia's terms of trade were accompanied by sharp fluctuations in the rate of exchange which greatly impeded business transactions. Government revenue plummeted, and by mid-1899 the condition of the national treasury was being described as "desperate" by the American minister and "terrifying" by the Colombian minister of finance.[13] As the Caro administration and that of his successor attempted without success to improve the government's financial situation—by introducing a match monopoly, by requesting authority for new emissions of paper money, and by seeking loans from both foreign and domestic sources—the political opposition used the economic crisis to demonstrate further the failure of the Regeneration and especially of its financial policies.

The Liberal party, meanwhile, had embarked upon a two-pronged strategy. In the year following the 1895 revolt party leaders began to prepare for the renewal of armed conflict by attempting to raise funds and by sending Luis A. Robles abroad to join Colombian exiles in neighboring Latin American countries in obtaining arms and in arranging for their entry into Colombia.[14] In addition, Parra and other Liberal leaders formed a national election committee to direct party activity during the 1896 election in the belief that the party would be permitted to gain limited representation in Congress. The committee, whose members included Parra, Uribe Uribe, and Diego Mendoza Pérez, urged Liberal participation in order to obtain the election of representatives who would cooperate in Congress with reform-minded members of both Conservative factions. As in the past, the reforms most strongly advocated by the committee included repeal of the law on extraordinary faculties, passage of legislation to free the press from the jurisdiction of the executive power, and changes in the electoral system.[15] As its official organ, the committee founded *El Republicano* under the editorship of Mendoza, Uribe Uribe, and Carlos Arturo Torres, a young graduate of the Externado.

For the 1896 elections the National Election Committee made serious efforts to establish uniform organization throughout the country. It named committees in each of the departments except Panama, where Liberal electoral activities were obstructed by the authorities, and the departmental bodies were instructed to organize groups in the *cabecera,* or principal town, of each electoral district, which would in turn select municipal committees.[16] These committees were to choose candidates for seats in the municipal councils in consultation with local Liberals; candidates for the assemblies were to be selected by provincial committees, subject to approval by the departmental organizations, which were to name the candidates for Congress.[17]

The members of the national committee soon became convinced, however, that the government's promises of electoral freedom would not be honored by its agents in the departments, whom they accused of hindering the efforts of Liberals to register, to assemble peacefully, and to communicate with each other by telegraph.[18] Liberals in Antioquia complained that departmental authorities had gerrymandered electoral districts in order to minimize the impact of votes cast in heavily Liberal communities.[19] Despite these unpromising developments, on 11 April the national committee again urged Liberals to vote except in areas where registration lists could not be legally verified or where violence might occur.[20] Soon afterwards it was reported that Liberals in Boyacá, Bolívar, and Santander had decided upon total abstention, and an election-eve editorial in *El Republicano* stated that abstention would be the rule nearly everywhere; nevertheless, the newspaper encouraged Liberals to attempt to vote in Bogotá and other areas where abuses were unlikely to be flagrant.[21]

In 1896 elections for municipal councilors and deputies to the departmental assemblies were scheduled for Sunday, 26 April, and for members of the Chamber of Representatives for 3 May. On the first of these days the elections in Bogotá were orderly despite Liberal charges of abuses at some tables. Elsewhere in Cundinamarca local authorities were accused of intimidating Liberal voters: in Cáqueza and Zipaquirá, Liberals were told by party leaders to withdraw from the polls at 11 A.M., and the conduct of officials in Guaduas and Subachoque led Liberals there to decide to abstain on 3 May.[22]

In Bogotá on 3 May there was considerable harassment of opposition voters by policemen and soldiers, as a result of which at 9 A.M. the Cundinamarca committee ordered Liberals to stay away from the polls.[23] Later some 10,000 Liberals and "republican Conservatives" protested formally that they had been deprived of their right to vote in Bogotá.[24] Liberals in Medellín also claimed that on 3 May soldiers had intimidated voters and had excluded government foes from the voting tables. In other parts of Antioquia, the Conservative split worked to the Liberals' advantage, as in 1892. Two Liberal representatives to Congress were elected: Santiago Pérez from the district of Santo Domingo and Rafael Uribe Uribe from Sopetrán.[25]

Because of the government's failure to keep its promise to conduct a free election, the members of the national committee proposed that Pérez and Uribe Uribe refuse to take their seats in Congress in protest.[26] They may also have been loath to give Uribe Uribe the opportunity to air his views in so prominent a forum as the Chamber of Representatives. Not only was the high-spirited Antioqueño emerging as the spokesman of Liberals who chafed under the committee's discipline, but he had also come to favor a military solution to the party's difficulties. Uribe Uribe eventually occupied his seat, but Pérez did not.

Although the decision to participate in the 1896 elections had yielded but a slim return, Liberals could hope for some gains from the 1897 presidential contest because of the continuing conflict between Nationalists and Historical Conservatives. The campaign was launched in September 1896 when the candidacy of Rafael Reyes was announced by a Bogotá newspaper in the name of the National party. Although Reyes had the support of Caro at this time, some Nationalists of Independent origin were unenthusiastic about the Reyes candidacy and put forth the name of Caro, who would have to step down from the presidency by 2 August 1897 in order to be eligible for election. Caro's candidacy served only to alienate even more Conservatives, and he was forced to declare himself out of the running in July. Meanwhile, many Historical Conservatives had also endorsed Reyes in the belief that he was committed to reform. Reyes, who wanted to seem acceptable to both factions, added to the confusion by sending cryptic telegrams to his various supporters from Paris, where he was serving as Colombian minister.[27]

In the first part of 1897 the policy of the Liberal leadership was one of watchful waiting with the aim of seeking some advantage from the rivalry between Historical Conservatives and Nationalists. In February Parra, speaking as president of the Liberals' national organization, which was now known as the Liberal Directory, instructed Liberals to refrain from expressing a preference for any candidate and from entering into any kind of agreement with other political groups without the authorization of the directory.[28] The likelihood of an armed conflict between supporters of Caro and Reyes, in which the Liberal party could not remain an idle bystander, prompted the national leadership on 11 April to urge the departmental directors to take discreet action to provide for the military organization of the party and to instill a sense of strict discipline among their followers.[29]

A month later the national leadership issued a call for a party convention to meet in Bogotá on 20 August to determine Liberal policy in the forthcoming election. Each departmental director was to select two delegates, each one from a different locality in the department; their expenses were to be paid with funds collected from wealthy Liberals.[30] The convention met as scheduled under the name of the National Electoral Convention, though the departmental directors were added to the original complement of eighteen delegates. Present were the members of the directory, which now consisted of Parra, Camacho Roldán, Nicolás Esguerra, and Gil Colunje, as well as some of the most eminent members of the party, including veterans like Sergio Camargo and Pablo Arosemena, and younger men, such as Fidel Cano, Diego Mendoza Pérez, and the physician Juan Evangelista Manrique, who was party head in Cundinamarca.[31] Among the absent were Robles and Uribe Uribe, both of whom were abroad attempting to obtain arms for the Liberal cause.

The serenity of the proceedings was soon broken by a debate over the possibility of forming an electoral alliance with Caro and the Nationalists. Efforts toward such an *evolución* had originated after the publication of a letter written to Parra on 30 March 1897 by José C. Borda, who believed that the party would do well to support Caro's presidential candidacy.[32] The letter did not receive a favorable response from Liberals, but Borda and others had persisted in their quest for an accommodation with Caro. Sergio Camargo, who was a personal friend of Caro, discussed the matter with the president; from their conversation there emerged a proposal for Liberal support for Antonio Roldán, a Nationalist and one-time Independent governor of Santander. According to Parra, the party leadership had neither authorized nor given serious consideration to these discussions, but the question of Liberal endorsement for a Roldán-Caro ticket was put before the convention, presumably by Camargo. The proposal aroused some enthusiasm among the delegates from the coastal departments, but the Antioqueños were adamantly opposed.[33]

Although the possibility of an alliance with the Nationalists was not completely ruled out, the delegates turned to other matters. They restored one-man national leadership by choosing Parra as sole party director with authority to delegate his functions to other individuals, to organize an advisory council if he deemed it necessary, and to solicit funds from party members. The convention also decided that Liberals should exercise their right to vote in the forthcoming presidential election, but the advisability of nominating Liberal presidential and vice presidential candidates was left to the director, who was to study Liberal opinion in the departments on the matter. The director was authorized to enter into agreements with other political groups on the basis of mutual concessions.[34] The convention also gave him secret instructions to issue a call to arms if a war could be undertaken in conjunction with another party or faction, or if specific routes for the introduction of arms to Colombia were available.[35] Parra, however, stipulated that he would make use of this authorization only if Liberals could count on the support of the Historical Conservatives or if the arms were to enter Colombia by way of Venezuela.[36]

On 11 September the delegates drew up what they considered a moderate program which might win the endorsement of Conservatives as well as Liberals. As on previous occasions, the party called for constitutional reform to protect civil liberties, repeal of the Law of the Horses and of other measures conferring discretionary powers on the executive, and the creation of an independent agency to supervise elections. In line with traditional aims, they sought a reduction of the presidential term to four years, political and administrative decentralization, absolute freedom of the press, the abolition of capital punishment, and the reorganization of public elementary education so that it would be free of charge and benefit all social classes. Their economic demands included the suppression of export taxes, the gradual amortization of the paper money in circulation and prohibition of any further emissions, together with reestablishment of the freedom to specify legal tender in contracts and the freedom of private banks to issue money. The delegates also declared, in deference to the religious beliefs of the majority of the Colombian people, that relations between church and state were best regulated by the concordat method.[37] In a manifesto on 15 September they further explained that while they still believed that the solution to the religious question lay in the separation of church and state, they did not wish to impose their opinions on the nation, for they realized that laws and institutions must reflect the convictions of the people if they were to be effective.[38] In adopting this position, the party once again committed itself to moderation on the religious issue, as it had since 1891, at least partly in the hope of reassuring Conservatives who might be contemplating an alliance with the Liberals.

By the time the convention adjourned in mid-September, Reyes had become the candidate of what was called the "reintegrated" Conservative party, whose leaders included Quintero Calderón, Marceliano Vélez, and Martínez Silva. Because of Caro's withdrawal from the race and Reyes's non-committal attitude, on 14 October the directory of the National party presented a new ticket, nominating Manuel A. Sanclemente for the presidency and José Manuel Marroquín for the vice presidency.[39] Since Sanclemente, a Conservative from Cauca who had served as secretary of government under President Ospina in the 1850s, was over eighty years old, it was assumed that he would be a figurehead president, while the country was to be governed by Marroquín. Marroquín, however, was himself a septuagenarian and was known primarily as an educator and man of letters rather than an active politician. The fact that both had impeccable Conservative credentials would presumably increase their acceptability to Conservatives wavering between the Historical and Nationalist camps.

At the insistence of his Conservative supporters, Reyes finally returned to Colombia and on 3 November issued an ambiguous statement in which he lauded the national unity and religious tranquility produced by the 1886 constitution but promised to work for fiscal and electoral reform.[40] Reyes's statement satisfied the opposition Conservatives, but they were soon chagrined by the publication of a letter written by Reyes on 13 November to three Barranquilla Nationalists in which he explained that he had made his 3 November declaration only to prevent proclamation of a Vélez-Quintero Calderón ticket that would have won Liberal support and would probably have been successful.[41] The letter led the Conservatives to abandon Reyes and to nominate Quintero Calderón for the presidency and Vélez as his running-mate.

Parra continued to press Liberals to vote for Liberal electors on election day, 5 December, if only to preserve discipline and unity of action, though many party members were undoubtedly reluctant to brave the hazards of the polls. It was also decided that the party should nominate presidential and vice presidential candidates of its own. After requesting authorization from the departmental directors, Parra summoned the advisory council which he had been empowered to create by the convention. On 28 November the 45-man council, whose members included Camacho Roldán, Nicolás Esguerra, Juan Evangelista Manrique, and Diego Mendoza, met at the home of Eustacio de la Torre Narváez to choose the party's standard-bearers. Parra himself was the unanimous choice of the council on the first ballot, but he refused the nomination with the explanation that his candidacy would be incompatible with his position as party head.[42] Santiago Pérez and others were also considered, but on the second ballot Miguel Samper won a plurality of the votes, and he was declared the presidential candidate, while Foción Soto was chosen as his running-mate, a combination said to have been suggested by Parra.[43] The choice of Samper—a Liberal noted for his abhorrence of political passion, orthodox economic views, and acceptance of Christianity—was designed to appeal to the Historical Conservatives,[44] as he himself suggested in accepting the nomination on 30 November. The selection of Soto, on the other hand, was obviously intended to mollify the militants, for he had spent most, if not all, of the years since 1885 in Venezuela seeking aid for a Liberal revolution in Colombia.

The nomination of Samper immediately drew protests from Liberals hostile to Parra's leadership who argued that Samper was unrepresentative of the Liberal party. According to Juan Manuel Rudas, Samper's only link with Liberalism was his opposition to paper money, and the fact that he was a practicing Catholic made him unfit to be the standard-bearer of the party.[45] Statements by Samper that he was willing to accept the 1886 constitution and disapproved of unrestricted press freedom also stirred opposition.[46] Defenders of the Samper candidacy countered that these attacks were inopportune at such a critical moment, but Rudas retorted that blind obedience to the party's leadership was antithetical to Liberalism. For his part Samper publicly assured Parra of his readiness to step aside if it seemed that his nomination would provoke dissension within the party or impede an agreement with the Conservatives.[47]

While the controversy over Samper's nomination still raged in the Liberal press, the presidential and vice presidential electors were chosen on 5 December. The government once more promised Liberal leaders that there would be no interference in the election, perhaps in the hope that a Nationalist-Liberal agreement might yet be worked out, but the departmental governors, especially in Santander, Tolima, Bolívar, and Panama, did not abide by the assurances given in the capital.[48] After the balloting took place in Bogotá, however, *La Crónica* hailed the election there as one of the most orderly and "civilized" that had ever taken place in Colombia. According to Liberal voting inspectors, 3,788 votes were cast for Liberal electors, 2,385 for the Nationalists, and 1,162 for the Conservatives.[49] Elsewhere, Liberals again complained of fraud.[50] In Medellín, for example, they contended that 500 Liberals had been illegally removed from voting lists and that over 900 of the 1,576 votes won by the Nationalists had been cast by policemen and soldiers.[51]

Although electors were chosen on 5 December, the winning presidential and vice presidential candidates would not be elected until the electoral assemblies met on 1 February 1898. There was some uncertainty as to whether the Liberal electors should participate in the electoral assemblies, but a special committee appointed by Parra to study the question recommended on 10 January that the electors attend the assemblies and vote for Samper instead of casting blank ballots.[52] Some Liberals, including José C. Borda, continued to believe that the party's salvation lay in joining with the Nationalists and proposed that the Liberal electors cast their ballots for Caro as vice president without exacting concessions in advance.⁵³ Parra, however, consistently opposed any kind of negotiation with the Nationalists.

At virtually the eleventh hour the Conservative party instructed its electors to vote for the Sanclemente-Marroquín ticket, supposedly because of fear that Nationalist electors were planning to substitute Caro's name for Marroquín's. Reyes advised electors loyal to him to do likewise.⁵⁴ Carlos Martínez Silva was highly critical of this decision and particularly of its timing, for it implied that the Conservative party approved of the frauds perpetrated during the election. According to the *escrutinio* of votes cast in the electoral assemblies, Sanclemente received 1,606 votes, Samper 318 (two-thirds of them from Cundinamarca and Antioquia), and Reyes, 121, all of them from Cauca.⁵⁵

Despite the fact that the election had brought no gains to Liberalism, Parra steadfastly defended the decision to take part in the voting. In a manifesto on 15 February 1898 protesting the conduct of government agents during the election, he stated that abstention would have indicated cowardice or conformity with the existing regime. Moreover, the Liberal leadership had not sought to gain control of the government but had hoped to form an electoral alliance with the Historical Conservatives and obtain representation in the administration so that the reforms desired by both parties could be achieved. However, the Conservatives had placed the unity of their party above republican principles. In light of the abuses committed during the presidential contest, Parra and the advisory council had decided to instruct Liberals to take no part in local elections scheduled for 1898.⁵⁶

The frustration engendered by the presidential election gave additional fuel to Liberals who advocated an appeal to arms at an early date and were critical of the party leadership for its willingness to temporize in the illusory hope that reforms might be achieved with Conservative help. In 1898 Rafael Uribe Uribe would openly repudiate Parra and become the undisputed chief of the militant Liberals.

The immediate source of the conflict was Uribe Uribe's conduct during his absence from Colombia in 1897–98. In a letter to Nicolás Esguerra on 27 January 1897, Uribe Uribe requested that he be sent abroad on an arms-procuring mission and promised to work only under the direction of Foción Soto and Luis Robles, both of whom were carrying out similar assignments. Although Parra doubted Uribe Uribe's loyalty to the party leadership, he and the other members of the directory decided on 24 February to grant his request. He was, however, given precise instructions. He and the other two agents were authorized to borrow funds and to purchase weapons individually but only after unanimous agreement had been reached. Whenever possible they were also to seek the approval of Santiago Pérez, and Pérez, as well as the directory, was to be regularly informed of their activities. The agents were also empowered to introduce weapons to Colombia, and to notify the directory of such an operation so that it could then decide when the revolution was to begin.[57]

After Uribe Uribe's departure, Parra and the other party leaders in Bogotá quickly became convinced that he was bent on violating his instructions. He had been told to stop in Cauca before leaving Colombia to stimulate party sentiment in that department; he performed this task, but, without informing the directory, also laid plans for an uprising in Cauca with arms to be obtained in Ecuador. Uribe Uribe then proceeded to Ecuador, despite the fact that Parra and Robles were opposed to his going there. Robles, who was in Nicaragua and had been seeking a definite pledge of assistance from Eloy Alfaro, president of Ecuador, stated that Alfaro did not want to see Colombian Liberals in Ecuador.[58] Upon arriving in Quito, however, Uribe Uribe informed Alfaro on 2 November 1897 that his trip to Ecuador had the approval of Robles.[59] Although Uribe Uribe was traveling incognito he was soon recognized by the Colombian minister in Ecuador, and Alfaro, finding himself in a compromising situation, withdrew the promises of aid that he had made earlier.

Uribe Uribe next traveled to Guatemala, whose president, José María Reina Barrios, apparently promised to give arms to the Colombian Liberals, but was prevented from fulfilling his pledge by his assassination in mid-1898.[60] Uribe Uribe hoped that his successor, Manuel Estrada Cabrera, would carry out Reina Barrios's promises, but Estrada Cabrera artfully deceived the Colombians.[61]

Meanwhile, Robles and Soto had obtained commitments from other sources, presumably from Venezuelans, and had scheduled a meeting in Jamaica in March 1898 with Uribe Uribe to plan the revolution. They also asked Parra for authorization to set the date for the opening of hostilities. In acceding to their request, Parra asked only that he be informed of the date two months in advance so that he might have time to notify the departmental directors. Uribe Uribe, however, who felt that he was being ignored by Parra, refused to heed the summons to attend the meeting. It was never held, partly because of the war in the Caribbean (presumably the Spanish-American War) and the outbreak of a revolution in Venezuela.[62]

On 20 June the party leadership informed the departmental directories of the current situation, warning that impetuous persons might revolt against the government on their own initiative without the military equipment necessary for success. It was emphasized that neither of the conditions set by the 1897 convention for an appeal to arms had been fulfilled; at present a peaceful policy should be maintained, while war was to be considered an alternative if the party's rights were not restored and if a propitious occasion presented itself.[63]

Two days later Juan Evangelista Manrique and Francisco de la Torre were also made members of the foreign delegation and were told to attempt to persuade Uribe Uribe to adhere to his instructions. They met with him at Puerto Limón, Costa Rica, but failed to accomplish anything. In any case, by that time Uribe Uribe was already en route to Colombia to begin his ultimately successful drive to unseat Parra.[64]

Uribe Uribe's intentions became evident immediately after his return to Colombia. On the night of 25 July he was welcomed to his native land at a rally in Barranquilla attended by over five hundred Liberals. When it was his turn to speak, he launched into a diatribe against the party leaders, whom he accused of cowardice and hypocrisy for failing to call Liberals to arms against the government immediately after the December election. He also had harsh words for the Liberal rank and file, declaring that the party had sunk into such abjectness that it would be relegated to oblivion. Uribe Uribe's speech attracted widespread notice, and Parra hastened to retaliate by informing the departmental directors of the Antioqueño's insubordination during his foreign tour.[65] To press his campaign against Parra, Uribe Uribe established a newspaper in Bogotá called *El Autonomista,* the first issue of which appeared on 20 September under the nominal editorship of Maximiliano Grillo and Alejandro Rodríguez F. The name of the newspaper reflected the editors' belief that the best formula for political behavior was personal autonomy and not a "degrading submission" to discipline.[66]

The opening of Uribe Uribe's campaign against Parra coincided with the start of the Sanclemente-Marroquín administration. As was expected, Sanclemente's failing health prevented him from taking office on 7 August 1898, and he was replaced by the vice president, Marroquín. Marroquín's Conservative affiliations, together with the fact that the Conservative opposition had increased to the point that it could now command a majority in the Chamber of Representatives, fostered hopes that reforms might be enacted during the congressional session. In a message to Congress on 26 September Marroquín himself expressed approval of proposals to repeal the Law of the Horses and to pass legislation to ensure the integrity of elections; he also asked for a press law that would combine freedom with responsibility and for creation of a tribunal to supervise the national treasury.[67]

In a manifesto on 22 September Parra had asked Liberals to support the efforts of Congress to secure reform. He also listed a series of measures whose enactment he said would satisfy the aspirations of the Liberal party. These included repeal of the Law of the Horses, jurisidiction by the judiciary over press offenses, reduced public spending with the aim of gradually retiring the paper money in circulation, and, most important of all, reform of the election law.[68]

Parra's manifesto drew considerable criticism from *El Autonomista,* which stated that the party director had gone too far in asserting that Liberal grievances would be assuaged by enactment of the reforms which he had mentioned. It also wondered whether the members of the advisory council, particularly Juan Manuel Rudas, had been consulted before publication of the manifesto. Rudas promptly replied that he had not been consulted and that he did not approve of the manifesto.⁶⁹

In a communication to the departmental directors on 3 October Parra explained that his manifesto of 22 September had been designed to bolster the reform movement in Congress, for he did not want it said that the lack of such a statement from him had contributed to the failure of the movement. He also observed that consultation with the advisory council was not mandatory.⁷⁰ The following day he again wrote to the departmental directors, giving additional insight into his strategy. He indicated that he had not deemed it prudent to demand as a condition of peace all the reforms advocated by the 1897 convention, simply because his demands would not have been met and the party would have found itself in an extremely difficult position, for its efforts to obtain foreign assistance had not yielded the expected results. Thus the party would have been pressured into war without being adequately prepared. He asked the directors to make his views known to local leaders but without publicizing the party's difficulties; if the directors found themselves in disagreement with Parra, they were to communicate their opinions only to him.⁷¹

All the departmental leaders except those of Santander gave their approval to the 22 September manifesto. Parra wrote to the Santandereanos on 13 October, pointing out that if the desired reforms were not enacted and faithfully executed, the party would be free of all moral commitments and would have full liberty of action in the future.⁷² The extent of the party's military weakness was made clear in a "very confidential" letter to Carlos J. Delgado, Liberal director of Santander. Letters from Foción Soto had indicated that Colombian Liberals should expect no help from the Venezuelan government in getting arms across the border. Robles, who had written from Caracas in a similar vein, had also observed that "we must tell our friends frankly not to expect redemption from outsiders; the sacrifices must be exclusively ours." Within Colombia, Liberals in Cauca and the coastal departments favored a peaceful policy, undoubtedly because of a lack of weapons, while only a group in Cundinamarca had some arms and was determined on war.⁷³

Meanwhile, the anti-Parra campaign in *El Autonomista* continued unabated. Although Parra had been attacked for ignoring the advisory council in September, Rudas was claiming by 6 October that it had been designed merely to disguise Parra's immense power.⁷⁴ The newspaper also charged that the party was being contaminated by the Caesarism implanted by the Regeneration and that Colombian Liberals were undermining their party's ideals by meekly following its leaders.⁷⁵ According to *El Autonomista*, the party needed leaders who had definite aims and faith in the vitality of the rank and file. The newspaper did not suggest that Parra's place be filled by Uribe Uribe or by any specific individual; it merely wanted to raise to prominence the youthful and vigorous elements in the party.⁷⁶

Parra's principal defender, *La Crónica,* scoffed at charges that Liberals who adhered to his instructions were guilty of *incondicionalismo,* or unthinking submission to his will. Indeed, Parra's critics were accused of trying to impose upon the party a "Draconian personalism" foreign to its nature, for Liberals followed ideas, not men.[77] On 17 November thirteen members of the advisory council issued a lengthy defense of Parra's conduct as party director. They began by pointing out that the Liberal party was basically a civilian party committed to the rule of law; accordingly, it could not consider war as anything but a last, desperate resort in its efforts to restore republican government to Colombia. In any event, Parra had had no alternative but to follow a peaceful policy aimed at seeking reforms. An alliance with the Nationalists, as some proposed in 1897, would have been immoral, and the Historical Conservatives had been unwilling to join the Liberals. The possibility of revolution had also been considered but had been dismissed as foolhardy.[78]

Carlos Nicolás Rodríguez, the son of the Liberal politician of the same name from Santander, was unimpressed by the council's statement. In forming the council, he said, Parra had supposedly given representation to all elements in the party but had actually chosen persons who shared his opinions. Therefore, Rodríguez asserted, the spirit of exclusivism that had given rise to the Independent movement of the 1870s was still being displayed by the same individuals who were guilty of it then. Parra was also accused by Rodríguez of deceiving Liberals by letting them believe that he intended to launch a revolution when he became president of the Liberal directory. Instead, he had systematically discriminated against the revolutionaries of 1885 and 1895, and the only policy he had advanced was the search for union with the Historical Conservatives, a policy which most Liberals found repugnant and which the Conservatives themselves disdained.[79]

Distrust of the Historical Conservatives and of the congressional reform effort was especially strong in Santander. As a young man from Suaita put it, the members of Congress were the very men who had driven Liberals away from the polls at rifle point; in short, they were the same old dogs in new collars.[80] Parra's nephew Vicente reported to the party director that Liberals in Santander were convinced that only war could alter the current situation and that they would be willing to accept any ally who could supply arms, even the Nationalists. "They [the Santander Liberals] consider an alliance with the Historical Conservatives as dirty and repugnant as one with the Nationalists; but they say that the implements of war are not contaminated, and they will be of use no matter where they come from."[81]

To be sure, many Liberals believed that Uribe Uribe's attacks on Parra were motivated mainly by personal ambition or feared that he would weaken the party by encouraging divisiveness. Pablo Arosemena was a close friend of Uribe Uribe, but he assured Parra that he considered war a policy to be resorted to only in the most desperate extremity and only if the means necessary for victory were available; to do otherwise would be to play into the enemy's hands. "I am convinced that there has never been a revolutionary who has not repented the day after, when it is too late," he added, "[and] I include those of 1810."[82] Even Max Grillo, Uribe Uribe's collaborator on *El Autonomista,* privately advised him to mitigate the severity of his criticism against Parra and against the party in general for accepting Parra's leadership.[83]

Grillo went on to remind Uribe Uribe that both he and the party leadership shared the same goals—restoration of the party's rights and the regaining of power—and indeed the two Liberal factions of the late 1890s appear to have been divided over tactics and strategy rather than ultimate objectives or the propriety of revolution as a political weapon. Both Parra and the delegates to the 1897 convention had approved a revolution in principle, it will be recalled, attaching only two not unreasonable conditions: Liberals were not to be summoned to arms unless an alliance with one of the Conservative factions had been reached or means found to bring arms into Colombia. Moreover, the party leadership itself had authorized efforts to acquire arms abroad and to obtain assistance from friendly Latin American regimes. And, as will be seen later in this chapter, when the revolution did break out, even Uribe Uribe had misgivings about the party's preparedness.

Bergquist argues that the Liberal militants were more youthful and less affluent than other party members and were more likely to live in rural areas.[84] This may well have been the case, for such people probably suffered most from the economic distress and sporadic repressiveness of the 1890s and were likely to expect improvements from a change in government. Nor is it surprising that they turned to the handsome and articulate Uribe Uribe and were ready, as one of his supporters said, "to close our eyes and, clinging to your coattails, follow you wherever you decide to take us."[85] He in turn seemed to enjoy the adulation he aroused. In 1897 he told his wife that his progress through Cauca had been a "prolonged ovation": "a reception and banquet in Buga; a large number of people to accompany me when I entered Palmira and a sumptuous banquet that night; serenades in both places; a reception fit for a bishop in this city [Cali] in the midst of some 6,000 persons; innumerable visits, [calling] cards, fetes, and greetings. You cannot imagine the popularity I have encountered in Cauca."[86] He found similar enthusiasm while traveling in Cundinamarca in 1899. "Some 200 horsemen went to meet me in Sutapelado, and about 100 artisans were waiting for me on the outskirts of this settlement [Ubaté]. There was a serenade, a dinner, shouting and revelry until late at night."

Whatever the characteristics of the rank and file among the Liberal militants, their leaders were not especially youthful, impoverished, or obscure. Uribe Uribe himself, though only thirty-nine in 1898, was the son of a landowner and the owner of a rural property valued at $80,000 in that year.[87] Another of Parra's foes, Juan Manuel Rudas, was in his fiftieth year in 1898 and had been a high customs official and rector of the Colegio del Rosario while the Liberals were in power. Also prominent among the militants were José María Ruiz and Marco A. Wilches, both of whom were kinsmen of Solón Wilches and had been active in pre-Regeneration politics in Santander. Another militant, Cenón Figueredo, was probably the same man mentioned in chapter 6 as a Colombian Guard officer involved in property seizures in Cauca after the revolution of 1876–77; later he had served as Colombian envoy to Belgium. The fact that Ruiz, Wilches, and Figueredo were Santandereanos does point up the extent of dissatisfaction in that department and the eagerness of Liberals there to take up arms against the government.

In discussing the leadership of the Liberal factions in the late 1890s, it is misleading to convey the impression that a clear line divided the Liberal militants from those sympathetic to Parra's more cautious strategy. Members of both groups were in frequent contact as they mulled over the implications of each new development, and an individual might lean toward peace one day, toward war the next. Justo Villamizar, a Santandereano who corresponded with both Parra and Uribe, informed Parra on 4 October 1898 that he had diminished the discontent of Ruiz and others by explaining Parra's views to them, only to see their impatience revive as a result of Parra's manifesto of 22 September.[88] In 1898, when José Santos, a Nationalist general from Santander, proposed to join the Liberals in an uprising against the government, he found a receptive audience among militants in that department, but leaders from both factions, including Carlos J. Delgado, the party head appointed by Parra, took part in discussions about the conspiracy, which eventually fell through.[89]

It has been seen that Parra's peace strategy was based on his hopes that significant reforms might be effected by Marroquín and the Historical Conservatives, who had a majority in the Chamber of Representatives. These hopes received a setback, however, when the Nationalists prevailed upon Sanclemente to leave his home in Buga and to travel to the capital to take office as president. He was sworn in before the Supreme Court on 3 November while the Conservatives in the Chamber of Representatives, abetted by the Liberal leadership, plotted unsuccessfully to disavow him. *El Autonomista* characterized the conduct of the Liberal and Conservative leaders on this occasion as "pathetically inept" because of their lack of foresight in failing to prepare for just such an opportunity.[90] Two days after taking office, Sanclemente left Bogotá to seek a more salubrious climate; he never returned to the capital, functioning as president in Anapoima, Tena, and Villeta, three hot-country towns in Cundinamarca.

Although the departure of Marroquín and the opposition of the slim Nationalist majority in the Senate stalled efforts to pass reform legislation, several important measures had been enacted by the time ordinary and extraordinary sessions came to an end on 6 December. The Law of the Horses had been repealed and a new press law passed which placed offenses under the jurisdiction of the courts. In addition, Congress had repealed the export tax on coffee and greatly weakened the monopoly system by voting to indemnify individuals engaged in industries subsequently placed under government monopoly. The all-important election bill failed to come to a vote, however, because of the obstructionist tactics of the Nationalists. In time even they came to favor passage of the bill, and a three-day extension of the congressional session was requested of Sanclemente. A refusal immediately came from Anapoima.[91]

Despite the fact that several Liberal demands had been met by Congress, so much emphasis had been placed on passage of a new election law that those who challenged Parra's leadership could now claim that his hopes of reform had been ill founded. Thus *El Autonomista* accused the Chamber of Representatives of not being genuinely interested in reform and charged the Conservatives with duping the Liberals, just as they had on so many other occasions.[92] Parra could only admit that, with the end of the reform movement in Congress, the party had no alternative but to resort to force for the recovery of its rights. Nevertheless, he continued to argue that a revolution at the present moment would be disastrous to the Liberal cause because the party lacked the military leadership and organization needed for such an undertaking, and the opposition of some Liberals to violence would endanger the entire movement.[93]

The fact that Parra could no longer offer anything but patience made it unlikely that he would be able to maintain either his position as party head or his policy of peace much longer. Indeed, Parra had been considering resignation at least since 18 November 1898. On that date he reminded the departmental directors that, according to rules laid down by the 1897 convention, the party leader could be replaced by one of several alternates appointed by him. However, the alternates that he had named either refused to serve or resided outside the capital, and the party would find itself without a leader if the present director was unable to remain in the post. Accordingly, he now asked the delegates to the 1897 convention to suggest the names of possible alternates. He also inquired whether a new convention should be held to reorganize the party and whether plural or unitary leadership was more desirable.[94]

The replies received indicated that there was little enthusiasm either for a convention or for plural leadership because of the fear that the existing dissension would thereby be aggravated. For example, Paulo Emilio Villar, party head in Santander, reported that he had consulted his predecessor, Carlos J. Delgado, his brother Luis Eduardo Villar, and José

María Villamizar Gallardo, and all had agreed that neither a convention nor a plural directory would solve the party's problems. If both factions were represented, the party's division would be exhibited before the nation, and if one were to be excluded, the old cry of "oligarchy" would again be raised.[95]

Although most of his correspondents urged Parra not to relinquish his post, he submitted his resignation to the advisory council on 4 February 1899.[96] A commission appointed by the council to make recommendations regarding future policy proposed that Parra remain in office until a provisional directory could be selected to govern the party while opinion regarding permanent organization was studied.[97] In view of Parra's determination to quit the leadership immediately, however, the council was forced to seek a new leader at once. Its unanimous choice was the veteran Sergio Camargo, who not only refused the appointment but questioned the right of the council to make it.[98]

At this point the council decided to name a provisional directory, and on 31 March it appointed Siervo Sarmiento, Juan Evangelista Manrique, and Medardo Rivas as principal members, and Venancio Rueda, José Benito Gaitán, and Francisco de la Torre as alternates.[99] Five days earlier *El Autonomista* had proposed that Sarmiento, a native of Boyacá and a hero of the 1895 revolt, be named as party director.[100] On 12 May Sarmiento, who was in London, wrote to refuse the nomination. He also informed the provisional directory that he would accept appointment to that body but that his business interests made it necessary for him to remain in Europe, where he had spent two years studying coffee markets.[101] Although he did not mention it, his business interests also included the purchase of arms for the Liberal cause.

One of the first acts of the directory was to issue a manifesto to Liberals which stressed the need for unity and called for the passage of a new election law. The manifesto, which as a whole was characterized by a stridently partisan tone, did not make an explicit disavowal of revolution.[102] The directory also prepared an elaborate plan for a complete reorganization of the party, starting at the municipal level. After departmental directories had been formed, representatives from the municipalities would select the new party leadership.[103] According to Manrique, it was hoped that the reorganization would end division within the party and still the perennial charges of "olympus" and "sanhedrin" once and for all.[104]

Although the provisional directory remained opposed to any attempt at revolution until the party's reorganization had been completed and until all hopes of obtaining reforms peacefully had been exhausted,[105] the danger of an unauthorized uprising increased as the year progressed. On 12 February in Bucaramanga Uribe Uribe, José María Ruiz, and other militants promised to begin the revolution on a date to be set by Paulo Emilio Villar; he in turn pledged not to give the order for the revolt until there was certainty that it would be supported by responsible leaders in other parts of the country.[106] Another event that encouraged the champions of revolution was the start in May 1899 of an insurrection against President Ignacio Andrade of Venezuela led by Cipriano Castro and launched from Colombian soil in the name of Venezuela's Liberal party.

The possibility of Venezuelan assistance to would-be Colombian revolutionaries, coupled with disclosure of the 12 February agreement, led the government to declare the disturbance of public order in Santander and Cundinamarca on 28 July. The same day Governor Marceliano Vargas of Cundinamarca, a son-in-law of Vice President Marroquín, ordered the arrest of several Liberals identified with the anti-Parra wing of the party, including Uribe Uribe and José María Ruiz. When news of the arrests became public, a mob stoned the offices of *La Crónica*. The aggrieved editors saw in the attack the appearance of a new adversary for "the sacred and generous cause of Colombian Liberalism," namely, "the Draconianism that substitutes force for right."[107] *El Autonomista* deplored the incident but asserted that the Liberals of Bogotá were justifiably angry with *La Crónica* for having singled out Uribe Uribe and the others as potential rebels.[108] Uribe Uribe and Ruiz remained in captivity until 17 August when they were released after sharing a bottle of champagne with Governor Vargas at the home of his secretary.[109]

Meanwhile, a new Liberal committee for Bogotá in which Uribistas were prominent had nominated Gabriel Vargas Santos for the party leadership, and his candidacy was endorsed by *El Autonomista* late in July.[110] Since Vargas Santos was, like Parra, a septuagenarian and had long been living in retirement on the plains of Casanare, he seems an incongruous choice for the militants, who had stressed the need for youthful leadership, but his military record dating back to the 1860 war and his ties with the one-time Radicals made it likely that he would be acceptable to both factions in the party. On 14 September Parra informed Manrique that he would agree to the selection of Vargas Santos as party director provided he named a council of delegates composed of five principal members, three of whom would be chosen by Parra.[111] Manrique replied that the imposition of such a condition would be offensive to Vargas Santos and that, since the party leadership was no bed of roses, he might well refuse the position, thereby deepening the party's division.[112] Manrique's advice may have influenced Parra, for it was announced less than a week later that after a series of conferences he and José María Ruiz had both agreed to recommend the candidacy of Vargas Santos. On 30 September they also stated that Vargas Santos would have the authority to choose his alternates and other associates.[113]

In October Uribe Uribe and Ruiz met with Vargas Santos in Casanare and persuaded him to accept the candidacy. Another topic of discussion was the movement planned in February with Villar. Villar had already set 20 October as the starting date of the revolution, but in the opinion of Uribe Uribe the party was not yet ready. In fact, early in October he and Cenón Figueredo had sent Villar a telegram designed to prevent the uprising by referring to it openly.[114] In Casanare Vargas Santos and Uribe Uribe agreed that the revolution should be delayed at least until the end of the year. However, while Uribe Uribe was hurrying to Bucaramanga to try to forestall the uprising, Juan Francisco Gómez Pinzón, acting on Villar's orders, raised the flag of revolt near Socorro at midnight on 17 October. At the same time Ramón Neira, another signer of the 12 February agreement, rebelled in Ráquira (Boyacá) and Figueredo issued a pronouncement in Nocaima (Cundinamarca).[115]

The provisional directory had evidently been informed that Villar was not to be deterred from striking as planned and called a meeting of party leaders on 16 October to determine the policy it should follow. The result of their deliberations was a telegram, adopted only after much discussion and printed on 17 October in *La Crónica,* exhorting Liberals to maintain a peaceful attitude and to ignore any instructions that did not emanate from the directory.[116] The telegram was signed by Manrique and Medardo Rivas on behalf of the directory and by thirty-eight party notables. Although most of the signers had been supporters of Parra and his policies, at least one, Juan Manuel Rudas, had been an opponent of the former director; now he felt that it was not right "to sacrifice a cause to the impulsiveness of a few lunatics." Another signer, Lucas Caballero, would soon take up arms on behalf of the revolutionaries. On 19 October Vargas Santos wired the directory from Casanare emphasizing the necessity for the preservation of peace and expressing his desire to hinder any "hare-brained" plan for immediate revolution.[117] His pleas and those of other party leaders went unheeded, however, as the revolution spread throughout the country.

Thus the revolution began in the face of opposition not only from those who had been reluctant to go to war but also from militants like Uribe Uribe who questioned the timing of the revolt. The outbreak of the revolution at this time seems all the more paradoxical when it is recalled that in 1899 the Liberal leadership and the party press enjoyed considerably more political freedom than had been the case in the early years of the Regeneration, and that several major Liberal goals, such as repeal of the Law of the Horses, had been realized as a result of the work of the Congress of 1898. These gains, of course, had to be set against the continuing exclusion of Liberals from government and the likelihood, in view of Congress's failure to pass a new election law in 1898, that this condition would not be significantly modified in the near future.

But other forces were also at work to spark the conflagration at this particular time. It seems likely that the economic depression of the late 1890s contributed significantly to the start of the revolution. In addition to

Bergquist, Joaquín Tamayo, a Colombian historian, has identified economic conditions as constituting the major cause of the war, though Tamayo emphasizes the monetary instability of the era and Bergquist the crisis in the coffee industry.[118] A Colombian writing for a North American audience in 1902 also saw the origin of the conflict in the country's financial condition. "Would the Liberal Party have gone to war," he asked, "if there had been sound money in the country, if the finances were scrupulously managed, and if the public wealth were not evaporating daily in the hands of speculators and people without a conscience?"[119]

The prominence of Liberals in the coffee industry and the fact that the principal growing areas—Santander, Tolima, and western Cundinamarca—were Liberal strongholds indicate that Liberals would be most severely and directly affected by the decline in coffee prices. According to Bergquist, "the fall in prices was particularly devastating in Santander, where profit margins were lower,"[120] and it was here that revolutionary sentiment was strongest in 1898. Santander, along with Tolima and Cundinamarca, would become a major battleground of the revolution.

In addition, the economic gloom had been deepened by a sudden plunge in the value of the Colombian peso in mid-1899. Starting in May drafts on London at ninety days' sight began to be quoted at figures in excess of 400 percent whereas the average for the previous December had been 217—that is, over 400 pesos were now required to purchase a bill for £20 which had cost 217 pesos in December 1898.[121] "Our country is today subject to the action of all the causes capable of producing complete financial catastrophe," *La Crónica* reported on 11 August, "because everything combines to produce an increase in the price of gold. The paralysis of business becomes greater each day, and the disappearance of credit is absolute. Public revenue is declining, and customs duties . . . are nearly extinguished."[122] By October there had been no improvement in the situation.

Regardless of whether they favored an early armed uprising against the government or not, Liberals were unanimous in blaming the country's economic difficulties on the Regeneration and had consistently emphasized this theme since 1886. Leaders reluctant to resort to war might be content to urge government economies and reforms in the monetary system, especially if they felt capable of riding out the crisis, but, as noted earlier, others less favorably situated were likely to evince greater impatience. This is clearly shown in the letters of a Liberal in El Banco (Magdalena) who wrote to Uribe Uribe in 1898 giving a plaintive account of his troubles: prices were outrageously high because of the fiscal policies of the Regeneration, his children could not go to school because they lacked clothing, and in any case the government did not pay its teachers. The national party leaders could, like the Jews, afford to await the coming of the Messiah because they were all men of substance, but in the correspondent's opinion, the present situation was intolerable, and war was preferable to talk of reform or similar nonsense.[123]

In some areas moreover, economic grievances were exacerbated by local discontents. The American minister, for example, asserted that "intense dissatisfaction" had existed in Tolima before the war, stemming from the operations of the *aguardiente* monopoly in that department.[124] In Panama, which would also be the scene of much fighting during the revolution, separatist sentiment had increased rapidly in the late 1890s, and "the general feeling of dissatisfaction among the Panamanians . . . was reflected in the unprecedented popular support given to the revolution."[125] Soon after the outbreak of the war the American consul in the city of Panama reported that seven out of eight residents were believed to be opposed to the government.[126]

The Liberals who took up arms against the government were also influenced by the hope that the Historical Conservatives would remain neutral or perhaps even come to the aid of the revolutionaries. This hope had been nourished not only by years of mounting Conservative opposition to the Nationalists but also by several recent statements in which Conservative leaders had threatened to withhold support from the government in the event of a Liberal revolution and had suggested the possibility of an alliance with the Liberals.[127] After the revolution broke out, however, traditional party loyalties overcame the Conservatives' rancor against the Nationalists. Despite the efforts of Marceliano Vélez and others to maintain Conservative neutrality, nearly all the Conservative leaders eventually came to the assistance of the administration, two notable exceptions being Vélez himself and Carlos Martínez Silva.[128] Liberals disappointed by the conduct of the Conservatives should have recalled the revolution of 1876–77 when the Nuñista Liberals had been guilty of similar behavior toward the Conservatives.

What was probably the decisive event in bringing the outbreak of the war in late 1899 was the success of the Venezuelan revolutionaries led by Cipriano Castro, who entered Caracas on 22 October 1899. A native of Táchira, the Venezuelan state bordering Santander, Castro was educated in Santander like many of his Andean compatriots and spent several years there while exiled from Venezuela.[129] Belisario Porras, the future president of Panama, and Antoine Rougier, a French lawyer whose account of the Colombian and Venezuelan conflicts was published in 1904, are among those who assert that Castro received considerable assistance from Colombian Liberals in mounting his invasion of Venezuela and promised to aid them in return once he had triumphed.[130]

Both the Colombian government and Liberal leaders saw Castro's movement as a boon to the Liberal cause almost from its inception. On 18 June 1899 Juan Evangelista Manrique dispatched the party's funds—£19,295—to Foción Soto, observing that the Venezuelan war might make it possible to introduce arms to Colombia by way of Táchira.[131] Possible collaboration between the Venezuelan and Colombian Liberals was cited by the Colombian government in its declaration of a state of siege in Cundinamarca and Santander on 28 July 1899, and the subsequent arrest of Uribe Uribe and other Liberals was attributed by the American minister to the fact that "they were known to be in communication with Venezuelan revolutionaries, many of whom are Colombians and ready to take part in a movement to overthrow the present Colombian government."[132]

Castro later redeemed his pledges to his Colombian coreligionists, and Rougier goes so far as to attribute the survival of the Liberal revolutionary effort to the aid provided by Venezuela.[133] Castro's assistance to the Colombian insurgents embroiled him in difficulties with the Colombian government, which apparently authorized a raid into Venezuela by Venezuelan exiles and Colombian soldiers on 26 July 1901. Diplomatic relations between the two countries were severed on 16 December 1901.

Once the die had been cast in Santander, Liberal support for the war grew as a result of some early victories by the revolutionaries and of government moves against party members which presented them with the alternatives that confronted Uribe Uribe: "the camps of friends or the dungeons of the enemy." Accordingly, as he wrote later, he sacrificed his better judgment and joined the war effort, even though he knew what the outcome would be.[134] Most party leaders eventually took up arms or gave the insurgents moral or financial support, and Parra probably summed up the feelings of many once-hesitant Liberals when he wrote to Manrique on 19 December: "the torrent is dragging us, and it would be neither sensible nor patriotic to insist on opposing it."[135]

Thus, with a few exceptions, Liberals swallowed their misgivings and heeded the call of party loyalty.[136] That they should have done so in view of all the circumstances is not surprising. Despite the creation of a national organization, party chiefs in Bogotá had been unable to elicit unflagging obedience even from their departmental counterparts; it was, after all, the party's official head in Santander who defied the Bogotá leaders to launch the revolution. That others should be reluctant to heed their edicts was only to be expected, given the worsening state of the economy, the likelihood of continued Liberal exclusion from public office, and the prospect of Venezuelan assistance in the introduction of weapons to Colombia, which meant that one of the conditions set by the 1897 convention for an appeal to arms was on the verge of realization. Moreover, in 1899 Liberals still regarded revolution as an integral part of the political process in Colombia, and very few were prepared to repudiate it out of hand. It was not until after the War of the Thousand Days (1899–1902), which surpassed all of its predecessors in carnage and devastation, that Liberals generally renounced revolution as an instrument of political change.

The circumstances under which the revolution began should not obscure the fact that the Liberal party did not suffer any serious attrition during the Regeneration and that it gained in terms of improved organization despite its long banishment from public office. The foundation of Liberal secondary schools and colleges, the regular appearance of Liberal newspapers, and the ability of party leaders to obtain financial contributions from well-to-do Liberals all testify to the continuing appeal of Liberalism, at least to the literate, more affluent segment of the population. It will also be recalled that the Liberals claimed a majority of the popular vote cast in Bogotá in the Presidential election of 1897. Although it is much more difficult to estimate how Liberalism fared among the population as a whole, the fact that the party was able to mount a revolution against the government for nearly three years suggests considerable strength. The continuing links between the party and the artisans of Bogotá can be seen in the formal participation of a group of artisans in the selection of the new Cundinamarca directory during the party reorganization of 1899.[137]

Party identification was probably strengthened by the fact that for much of the period from 1891 to 1899 party organization exhibited a degree of continuity and penetration unseen in previous years. Individuals were officially designated as party leaders and in turn gave way to their successors; party conventions attended by delegates from all the departments met twice to consider policy; and interaction between national and departmental leaders was extensive and sustained. If there was an element of self-perpetuation in the selection of party officials and if discipline was imperfect, it is also true that efforts were usually made to reconcile conflicting viewpoints, as when Manrique, a peace Liberal, and Siervo Sarmiento, a favorite of the militants, were both named to the provisional directory of 1899 and when Gabriel Vargas Santos, who was acceptable to both factions, was named party chief.

In addition, it should be kept in mind that despite periodic outbursts of repression, the Regeneration did not make extended or coordinated efforts to destroy the Liberal party or to modify the political system in a radical fashion—for example, by dispensing with Congress or by permitting a single individual to rule indefinitely. Núñez was reelected in 1891, to be sure, but he did not rule. More instructive in this regard is the unhappy experience of Caro when he explored the possibility of remaining in the presidency in 1897. Liberals did not normally languish in prison for years during peacetime because of their political writings or activity, and many of those who remained in exile did so voluntarily. One result of the limited freedom accorded the party was that a new generation of leaders could be recruited to take the place of the patriarchs of Liberalism, some of whom had begun their political careers during the López administration.

Liberalism also benefited from the failure of efforts to create in the National party an alternative to the two traditional parties. This was perhaps inevitable in view of the weakness of the Independents vis à vis the Conservatives, which was aggravated by Núñez's abandonment of the day-to-day management of political affairs. The National party was meaningful only insofar as it represented a genuine union of Independents and Conservatives, but the former, already enfeebled by 1885, suffered additional losses afterwards while the Conservatives quickly gained an ascendancy over the Regeneration which they never relinquished despite their internal quarrels. Meanwhile, Núñez, the father of the National party, remained in Cartagena, too remote both physically and intellectually to give his offspring the care it required. Consequently, it can be argued that while the "hereditary hatreds" between the Conservative and Liberal parties remained as strong as ever—strong enough, indeed, to prevent cooperation between the Liberals and the Historical Conservatives in the 1890s—and were to vent themselves with unaccustomed fury in the War of the Thousand Days, the survival of the Liberal party was made possible in part by the continued existence of its traditional foe.

Conclusion

The civil war that began in October 1899 and lasted until the latter part of 1902 became known in Colombian history as the War of the Thousand Days.[1] It proved to be the bloodiest conflict in Colombia's first century of independence, with the number of deaths from combat or disease estimated at between 75,000 and 100,000. The war also surpassed any of its predecessors in the devastation it wrought both on property and on the social fabric. "The country was completely ruined," Jorge Holguín recalled later. "Agriculture gave no sign of life. Since business was paralyzed, bankruptcies multiplied in an extraordinary fashion. . . . The sight of devastated towns, of burned-out plantations, of abandoned fields, of entire families wandering everywhere without homes, food, or clothing was heartrending. . . . A gust of death had passed over the entire country."[2] The secession of Panama in November 1903 after Colombia's rejection of the Hay-Herrán treaty the preceding August was but another demonstration of the nation's enfeeblement.

For the Liberal revolutionaries the war ended in frustration and failure with the Conservatives still in control of the government. Hampered by inadequate supplies and matériel and by acrimonious squabbles among the chief commanders, the revolutionaries were unable to mount a sustained campaign against the government after suffering a major defeat at Palonegro (Santander) in May 1900. Even so, the government was still harried by the operations of Liberal guerrillas, especially in Cundinamarca and Tolima, who briefly posed a threat to Bogotá itself early in 1902. By that time too Benjamín Herrera, who had emerged as one of the most successful revolutionary generals, had invaded Panama and was in the process of winning control over the entire Isthmus, except for the cities of Panama and Colón.[3]

In short, the government, while too strong to be defeated, was unable to crush the revolutionaries completely and was beset by serious economic and political problems of its own. In order to finance the war, the government was forced to resort to a variety of expedients, including the time-tested method of exacting forced loans from the opposition and the extension for six years of the concession of the New Panama Canal Company in return for five million gold francs.[4] Mainly, however, the government relied on the printing presses, which produced at least $600 million in paper currency between 16 October 1899 and 28 February 1903.[5] Meanwhile, the value of the peso plummeted: while the exchange rate with the United States gold dollar was approximately four to one in mid-October 1899, by October 1901 it had dropped to nearly fifty to one and reached a hundred to one the following September.[6] To be sure, the government's distress was a source of profit to some, and fortunes were made in currency speculations and in loans and the sale of supplies to the government.[7]

Another impediment to the government war effort was the continuing dissension among Conservatives. By mid-1900 some of those connected with the Historical faction, always lukewarm in their support of the Sanclemente administration, had become convinced that the aged president, who had not returned to Bogotá after his departure in 1898, had become a pliant instrument in the hands of unscrupulous advisers. They were also concerned about the mounting ferocity of the fighting and believed that the war should be brought to a rapid end even if some concessions had to be made to the Liberals. Accordingly, they concocted a plot that resulted in the deposition of Sanclemente on 31 July 1900, and the installation of Vice President Marroquín in his place.[8]

Although Marroquín had cooperated with the Historical Conservatives in 1898 and had been informed of the plans to remove Sanclemente, he now repudiated the conspirators and refused to make any concessions to the revolutionaries except to promise their political and civil rights would be respected if they laid down their arms. To offer more, he felt, would have been an admission of defeat and a betrayal of Conservative principles. With the active collaboration of the *éminence grise* of his administration, Aristides Fernández, who successively became governor of Cundinamarca, minister of war, and minister of government, Marroquín proceeded to prosecute the war with greater vigor. This can be seen in a series of decrees in 1900–1902 which provided that recalcitrant revolutionaries were to be treated as common criminals and subject to increasingly harsh penalties to be imposed by military courts. Conservatives who ventured to criticize the administration found that they too risked exile or imprisonment.

By mid-1902 Marroquín's policy of severity had seriously weakened the revolutionaries, though Herrera was still entrenched in Panama, and the vice president evidently felt his position to be secure enough to permit some new overtures toward the Liberals. After several Liberal civilians publicly urged Marroquín to extend peace terms to the revolutionaries, he responded with a decree on 12 June offering a pardon to most of those in arms. The two principal Liberal commanders in the field, Herrera and Uribe Uribe, refused to come to terms so long as Fernández occupied the war ministry, but after he retired temporarily in October 1902, both of them negotiated settlements with the government that implicitly recognized the revolutionaries as belligerents.[9]

Uribe Uribe had called for an end to the war in 1901 but had returned to the battlefield and had recently suffered a series of defeats in Magdalena. On 24 October 1902 he signed the controversial Nerlandia treaty which provided for the dissolution and disarming of the revolutionary forces of Magdalena and Bolívar and for the release of political prisoners in both departments but made no political concessions. Uribe Uribe also agreed to urge Herrera to adhere to the treaty. The exhortations of Uribe Uribe and the warnings of the American consul-general that fighting would not be permitted in the cities of Panama or Colón or along the railroad convinced Herrera that he had no alternative but to make peace. He reluctantly accepted Rear-Admiral Silas Casey's offer of the U.S.S. *Wisconsin* as a conference site, and a treaty was signed there on 21 November 1902.[10] It provided for the immediate restoration of public order and for the holding of a special election for a Congress to study the reforms proposed by Marroquín in 1898, the Panama Canal question, and changes in the monetary system. The signing of the two treaties brought the fighting to a virtual end, though Marroquín did not declare that public order had been restored until 1 June 1903, and the lack of guarantees led Liberals to boycott the congressional elections of that year.

Although the Liberals had failed to drive the Conservatives from power, the party once more survived a defeat on the battlefield. Indeed, after the Panama crisis, when prominent Liberals rallied around the government, Marroquín himself made a conciliatory gesture by naming Carlos Arturo Torres minister of the treasury and revolutionary Lucas Caballero to a mission headed by Rafael Reyes which was dispatched to the United States. Liberals did not take part as a party in the presidential election of 1903, but they were encouraged by the victory of Reyes, who had been absent from Colombia during the war.[11] He disavowed partisanship in his inaugural address, included two Liberals in his first cabinet, and in general, as one writer put it, accustomed Colombians to seeing the cat and the mouse at the same dish.[12]

Meanwhile, intraparty quarrels—between Uribe Uribe and his rivals, between revolutionaries and civilians—continued. In December 1903, however, party leaders patched up their differences and began the task of reorganization with the creation of a provisional directory composed of Uribe Uribe, Nicolás Esguerra, Juan Evangelista Manrique, Diego Mendoza Pérez, and Manuel W. Carvajal.[13] It instructed Liberals to form directories in the municipalities which would appoint members to provincial bodies; these in turn would choose members to sit on departmental directories which would eventually select the permanent national leadership. By the end of June 1904 the party's reorganization had been completed on the Coast and in Antioquia, Cauca, and Santander, and the provisional directory dissolved itself on 28 June.[14] Thus the party not only survived its defeat but emerged from the recent conflict with sufficient strength to undertake organization on the national, departmental, and municipal levels. Henceforth, such structures would remain a permanent part of party activity.

Soon after its formation the provisional directory also asked Liberal organizations throughout the country to strive for effective Liberal participation in the municipal, departmental, and congressional elections scheduled for mid-1904.[15] Steps were to be taken to identify Liberals and to determine which ones were eligible to vote so that protests might be made if qualified voters were excluded from official voting lists. Liberals were also urged to vote despite the discouragement they might feel because of their recent defeat.

When the elections took place in April and May, local authorities in many places violated the administration's promises that the voting rights of Liberals would be respected. In Bogotá, a Liberal newspaper complained, on the day of elections for the municipal council, voting tables reserved for civilians were monopolized by soldiers.[16] However, in Antioquia and some other areas the balloting was conducted honestly, and Liberals were elected to the Chamber of Representatives as well as to departmental assemblies and municipal councils.[17]

If factional disputes, efforts at party organization, and frustration at the polls were reminiscent of the prewar era, in other respects there were differences. First, the war years saw the demise of many of the remaining Liberal chiefs of the federal period: Luis A. Robles died in 1899; Santiago Pérez, Salvador Camacho Roldán, and Aquileo Parra in 1900; and Medardo Rivas in 1901. By 1904 the only major figure of that generation still active in politics was Nicolás Esguerra, who survived until 1923. The disappearance of the Liberal patriarchs meant that the party would now be dominated by men like Uribe Uribe, who had first come to prominence after 1886, and others who had won national reputations by their exploits during the war. Outstanding among the latter was Benjamín Herrera, a man of modest origins, born in Cali of northern Colombian parentage, who would become the party's presidential candidate in 1921. Contemporaries were aware of this renewal of leadership, and one journalist was critical of Liberals who continued to venerate the "old idols." He reminded them that "unfortunately Felipe and Santiago Pérez today live only in the Temple of Glory, and they will not leave it, like the ancient gods, to take part in the battles of human beings."[18]

The postwar period also saw Liberal leaders generally condemn violence as a means of effecting political change. This position was adopted not only by Liberals who had taken no part in the revolution but also by the most articulate prewar militant, Rafael Uribe Uribe, who in December 1902 called the recent conflict "Colombia's last civil war" and admitted that the length and cost of the war had taught him a bitter lesson.[19] The provisional directory also acknowledged the inefficacy of extralegal methods in correcting the country's ills.[20] Although some Liberals grumbled at this repudiation of violence and there would be occasional outbursts of revolutionary sentiment in later years, Uribe Uribe's prediction that the 1899–1902 war would be Colombia's last proved to be accurate. Violence did not disappear from the country's political life, however, and reached extraordinary levels in the 1940s and 1950s. It is probable that the antagonism between Liberals and Conservatives, especially in rural areas, was intensified by the war, which was fought with increasing savagery after Palonegro, and by its aftermath, when the defeated revolutionaries were once more subject to the control of Conservative authorities.

Conclusion

Finally, in the postwar period Liberal leaders, continuing the process begun at the 1897 convention, explicitly turned their backs on the Rionegro constitution. Calling for the convocation of an extraordinary legislative body on which Liberals would be represented and which would undertake constitutional reform, the provisional directory affirmed that it did not seek the abrogation of the 1886 constitution or a return to the Rionegro charter.[21] In the directory's opinion, the most essential changes were the reestablishment of sectional autonomy in certain fields such as economic development; adoption of an electoral system, independent of the executive power, that would guarantee proportional representation to all parties in all public bodies; and the reduction of the presidential term to four years and abolition of the vice presidency.[22] The directory also recommended that the concordat be preserved, that military conscription be ended, and that preferential attention be given to primary instruction, which should receive the funds being expended on professional education. This program, like that of the 1897 convention, made it clear that by the beginning of the twentieth century party leaders had drastically modified their mid-nineteenth-century commitment to federalism and that they were willing, if only for tactical reasons, to accept the privileged position of the Catholic Church.

The Liberals' abandonment of federalism and acceptance of the concordat were in keeping with the intellectual flexibility displayed by party leaders in the second half of the nineteenth century. Liberals would not have gone so far as to favor the complete suppression of sectional autonomy or to embrace authoritarian political doctrines, but they had proved willing to revise the principles they had upheld in the 1850s. The erosion of their devotion to federalism was initially manifested in the centralizing aspects of the educational and transportation programs of various administrations during the 1870s; support for federalism was further weakened during the Regeneration. Although Liberals had fought to lessen the influence of the Catholic Church since the early nineteenth century, a respectable proportion of party leaders (the size of which varied according to circumstances) had always doubted the efficacy of extreme measures. After 1886 the position of this group prevailed for a variety of reasons: the Liberals' exposure to Spencerian positivism, which undermined the intellectual rationale for anticlericalism; the negative political consequences of the vindictive policies of the late 1870s; and the hope of enlisting Conservative allies in the struggle against the Regeneration.

The Liberals' commitment to laissez faire had also been diluted during their years in power, as shown in their programs for federal support of railroad construction. After 1886 Liberals would vociferously denounce the economic and fiscal policies of the Regeneration but without reverting to the dogmatic preachments in favor of laissez faire characteristic of the López era.

In the realm of ideology, it is vain to seek perfect consistency among nineteenth-century Liberals. To some Liberals ideas mattered a great deal; to others not at all. Among the former, there were those like Manuel Murillo who altered their beliefs in the light of newly received ideas and experiences. Others refashioned their convictions to correspond to changing political and economic realities. Thus Aquileo Parra, who had voted against Mosquera's harsh anticlerical proposals at Rionegro, signed equally harsh legislation fourteen years later. Similarly, Nuñistas who inveighed against the statism and centralism of the oligarchs in 1875 praised the national bank and the public order law five years later.

If the behavior of nineteenth-century Liberals was shaped in part by doctrinal considerations, an equally powerful force was regionalism. In the second half of the century the party was dominated by leaders from eastern Colombia, especially Santander, a state of affairs that provoked resentment and occasional challenges, notably from Mosquera of Cauca and the Costeño Rafael Núñez. Regional conflict within the party reached a peak in 1875 when Núñez was nominated for the presidency as a frankly regional candidate and his supporters attacked the proposed Northern Railroad on the grounds that the project would benefit only three states at the expense of the other six. In 1874 Minister Scruggs, though cautiously optimistic about the prospects for construction of the railroad, astutely grasped the political importance of the project: "since it has become the chief measure of the party in power, its failure would, in all probability produce a revolution in the administration, and possibly also in the constitution of government."[23] Scruggs's prophecy, however, reversed the order of events as they actually occurred. The end of the Radical ascendancy in the federal government during the presidency of the Caucano Julián Trujillo also brought the end of the Northern Railroad.

In view of Santander's importance as a stronghold of Liberalism, the economic vicissitudes it experienced after 1850—especially the collapse of the *quina* boom in the 1880s and the coffee crisis of the 1890s—were bound to have an impact on the rest of the party. Although the entire nation suffered hard times in the 1880s and late 1890s, the severity of conditions in Santander contributed to the fact that it was there that restless Liberals raised the first cries of revolt in 1884 and 1899. In both instances many Liberals resident in Bogotá and other parts of the country expressed dismay over what they considered the rashness of the Santandereanos, but most eventually followed their lead.

Among the Conservatives Antioquia corresponded to Santander as the party's principal stronghold. Unlike Santander, however, Antioquia did not play a role within the Conservative party in keeping with its relative wealth and solidly Conservative population. Antioqueños exhibited considerable independence from their coreligionists in eastern Colombia or Cauca, who ultimately proved to be more influential in determining national party policy. For over a decade, from 1864 to 1876, relations

Conclusion

between the Conservative state government and the Liberal administrations in Bogotá were generally correct and at times cordial, and the governor of the state was but a reluctant participant in the revolution of 1876–77. Later, after the Conservatives had returned to power, it was in Antioquia that discontent with the Regeneration first appeared and remained strongest. The Antioqueños may, as some critics charged, have been guilty of excessive self-esteem and preoccupation with the welfare of their own section. If so, federalism as interpreted by the Liberal administrations of Murillo and Salgar gave the Antioqueños the freedom to plot their own course with relatively little interference from Bogotá; in this light Governor Berrío's encomiums to the Rionegro constitution are understandable. With the restoration of centralism under Conservative auspices in 1886, regional self-interest would impel the Antioqueños to seek greater influence over the national party in order to be in a position to steer the government along paths they favored.

During the nineteenth century the Liberal party remained a federation of state or departmental parties. This situation prevailed not only while the Rionegro constitution was in effect but also, though to a lesser extent, under the 1886 constitution. While the Liberals were in power, the presidents and congressional caucuses gave a measure of centralized direction to the party; afterward, this task was performed by formal party organs. Even so, lack of discipline was inevitable in view of the diversity of interests to be satisfied and the limited sanctions and rewards at the disposal of party leaders, first because of the federal government's limited resources and later because of the party's exclusion from power.

In these circumstances the conciliation of opposing views came to be the preferred mode of settling intraparty conflicts. Thus Mosquera was permitted to return to Colombia after a few years of banishment and to resume his political career as governor of Cauca, while Eustorgio Salgar, the first regularly elected president after Mosquera's deposition in 1867, was acceptable to both the friends and the foes of the exiled *caudillo*. This tendency toward accommodation and cooptation often produced programmatic incoherence and a diminished capacity for coordinated action, as it did in the late 1890s when the party leadership prepared for war and for peace simultaneously. At the same time the quest for consensus probably helped prevent the disintegration of the party.

Meanwhile, by the end of the nineteenth century party chiefs had succeeded in forging a loose but viable system of linkages that embraced political leaders throughout the country and penetrated to the lower sectors of the population. These linkages, duplicated as they were among the Conservatives, were sufficiently strong to enable the two parties to control the enlarged electorate of the twentieth century and to assert themselves successfully as the only vehicles through which the demands voiced by this electorate might be met.

Notes

Abbreviations and Short Titles

AC Archivo Correoso
ACH Academia Colombiana de Historia
AM Archivo Manrique
AP Archivo Parra
AUU Archivo Uribe Uribe
BL-AA Biblioteca Luis-Angel Arango
CAP Correspondencia de Aquileo Parra
CP Copiador Parra

Despatches Barranquilla—Despatches from United States Consuls in Barranquilla, 1883–1906
Despatches Cartagena—Despatches from United States Consuls in Cartagena, Colombia, 1882–1905
Despatches Panama—Despatches from United States Consuls in Panama, 1823–1906
Diplomatic Despatches—Despatches from United States Ministers to Colombia, 1820–1906

Preface

1. John A. Peeler, "Colombian Parties and Political Development: A Reassessment," *Journal of Interamerican Studies and World Affairs* 18 (May 1976):204.
2. Indalecio Liévano Aguirre, *Rafael Núñez*, 3d ed. (Bogotá: Ediciones Librería Siglo XX, 1946); William Paul McGreevey, *An Economic History of Colombia, 1845–1930* (Cambridge: Cambridge University Press, 1971). For a critique of McGreevey's book see Frank Safford, *Aspectos del siglo XIX en Colombia* (Medellín: Ediciones Hombre Nuevo, 1977), pp. 201–84.
3. Cf. Maurice Duverger, *Political Parties: Their Organization and Activity in the Modern State,* translated by Barbara and Robert North (London: Methuen & Co., Ltd., 1954), pp. xv–xvi.
4. Eric A. Nordlinger, "Political Development: Time Sequences and Rates of Change," *World Politics* 20 (April 1968):494–520. It should be mentioned that Nordlinger cites Colombia "as a telling Latin American case in which the suffrage was expanded 'too far and too fast'," for the "overnight introduction of universal male suffrage" in 1853 "was followed by two tumultuous civil wars" (p.517, n.48). This may well be true. However, universal male suffrage remained in force on a nationwide basis for only a few years. The adoption of federalism soon afterward meant that each state was free to determine its own electoral legislation, and by 1875 only four of Colombia's nine states still extended the ballot to all male citizens (see chapter 5). The constitution of 1886 imposed literacy or property qualifications, and it was not until 1936 that universal male suffrage was reestablished.
5. Mario Latorre Rueda, *Elecciones y partidos políticos en Colombia* (Bogotá: Universidad de los Andes, Departamento de Ciencia Política, 1974), pp. 274–275.

Chapter 1

1. The modern republic of Colombia was known by various names in the nineteenth century, reflecting changes in its political organization. From 1819 to 1830 it was called New Granada and, with Venezuela and Ecuador, formed part of the republic of Colombia, usually known as Gran Colombia. After the disintegration of Gran Colombia in 1830, it became the independent nation of New Granada. From 1858 to 1861 it was called the Granadine Confederation, and from 1861 to 1886 the United States of Colombia. In 1886 the name of Republic of Colombia was adopted. For the sake of clarity, the name Colombia will be used wherever possible.

2. For an account of the revolution from the Liberal point of view, see Felipe Pérez, *Anales de la Revolución, escritos según sus propios documentos* (Bogotá: Imprenta del Estado de Cundinamarca, 1862). An account written by a Conservative participant is Angel Cuervo, *Cómo se evapora un ejército,* Biblioteca de Autores Colombianos (Bogotá: Editorial Cromos, 1953).

3. A somewhat incoherent account of the convention can be found in Ramón Correa, *La convención de Rionegro* (Bogotá: Imprenta Nacional, 1937), which contains many documents. The recollections of two anti-Mosquera delegates are presented in Salvador Camacho Roldán, *Memorias* (Bogotá: Librería Colombiana, 1923), and Aquileo Parra, *Memorias* (Bogotá: Imprenta de "La Luz," 1912).

4. Joaquín Tamayo, *Nuestro siglo XIX,* vol. 1, *La Gran Colombia* (Bogotá: Editorial Cromos, 1941), pp. 272–73.

5. On the policies advocated by Santander and his associates, see David Bushnell, *The Santander Regime in Gran Colombia* (Newark, Del.: University of Delaware Press, 1954).

6. Robert Louis Gilmore, "Federalism in Colombia, 1810–1858" (Ph.D. dissertation, University of California, Berkeley, 1949), pp. 110–11; José de la Vega, *La federación en Colombia,* Biblioteca de Autores Colombianos (Bogotá: Editorial A B C, 1952), pp. 106–08.

7. Joaquín Posada Gutiérrez, *Memorias histórico-políticas,* Biblioteca de Historia Nacional, 4 vols.(Bogotá: Imprenta Nacional, 1929), 1:28–29; Ignacio Gutiérrez Ponce, *Vida de Don Ignacio Gutiérrez Vergara y episodios históricos de su tiempo (1806–1877)* (London: Imprenta de Bradbury, Agnew & Cía., 1900), pp. 183–88.

8. Gilmore, "Federalism," p. 114.

9. Ibid., pp. 138–39. See also Gutiérrez Ponce, *Ignacio Gutiérrez,* pp. 208–11; José María Samper, *Los partidos en Colombia* (Bogotá: Imprenta de Echeverría Hermanos, 1873), pp. 22–25; Estanislao Gómez Barrientos, *Don Mariano Ospina y su época,* 2 vols. (Medellín: Imprenta Editorial, 1913–1915), 1:128–30.

10. Angel and Rufino José Cuervo, *Vida de Rufino Cuervo y noticias de su época,* 2 vols.(Paris: A. Roger y F. Chernovez, 1892), 1:292; José Manuel Restrepo, *Historia de la Nueva Granada,* 1 (Bogotá: Editorial Cromos, 1952): 148.

11. Horacio Rodríguez Plata, *José María Obando, íntimo (Archivo-epistolario-comentarios),* Biblioteca Eduardo Santos (Bogotá: Editorial Sucre, 1958), pp. 56–57. For an analysis of the events surrounding Sucre's death, see Thomas F. McGann, "The Assassination of Sucre and Its Significance in Colombian History,

1828–1848," *Hispanic American Historical Review* 30 (1950): 269–89, as well as a rebuttal by Colombian historian Luis Martínez Delgado and a rejoinder by McGann, ibid., 31 (1951):520–29.

12. Gustavo Arboleda, *Historia contemporánea de Colombia*, 2 (Bogotá: Librería Colombiana de Camacho Roldán & Tamayo, 1919):92–93; José María Samper, *Historia de un alma*, Biblioteca Popular de Cultura Colombiana, 2 vols.(Bogotá: Editorial Kelly, 1946–48), 1:118.

13. Samper, *Alma*, 1:185; Gutiérrez Ponce, *Ignacio Gutiérrez*, pp. 471–72; Camacho Roldán, *Memorias*, pp. 195–96; Aníbal Galindo, *Recuerdos históricos: 1840 a 1895* (Bogotá: Imprenta de "La Luz," 1900), p. 31.

14. Joseph Leon Helguera, "The First Mosquera Administration in New Granada, 1845–1849" (Ph.D. dissertation, University of North Carolina, 1958), p. 248.

15. Miguel Urrutia, *The Development of the Colombian Labor Movement* (New Haven: Yale University Press, 1969), pp. 7–11. On the origins of this society, see also Camacho Roldán, *Memorias*, pp. 75–76.

16. *El Aviso*, 18 June 1848.

17. Biblioteca de Historia Nacional, *Correspondencia y otros documentos del General Tomás Herrera* (Panama: Tipografía y Casa Editorial "La Moderna," 1928), p. 379.

18. Helguera, "Mosquera," pp. 259–67; Eduardo Rodríguez Piñeres, "Proceso del 7 de marzo," *Boletín de Historia y Antigüedades* 36 (July–September 1949):421–22.

19. An account of the balloting favorable to the Liberal position is given in Rodríguez Piñeres, "Proceso," pp. 424ff. The research of Helguera tends to substantiate the Conservative version ("Mosquera," pp. 290–301).

20. Urrutia, *Labor*, p. 13; José Manuel Restrepo, *Historia de la Nueva Granada*, 2 (Bogotá: Editorial El Catolicismo, 1963):136.

21. Galindo, *Recuerdos*, p. 43; Robert Louis Gilmore, "Nueva Granada's Socialist Mirage," *Hispanic American Historical Review* 36 (May 1956):200–03. A society of Conservative artisans, the *Sociedad Popular*, was established on 17 December 1849 (Restrepo, *Nueva Granada*, 2:134).

22. Helguera, "Mosquera," pp. 350, 525.

23. Theodore E. Nichols, "The Caribbean Gateway to Colombia: Cartagena, Santa Marta, and Barranquilla and Their Connections with the Interior, 1820–1940" (Ph.D. dissertation, University of California, Berkeley, 1951), pp. 52–53.

24. Helguera, "Mosquera," pp. 354–59.

25. Gilmore, "Federalism," p. 212.

26. Restrepo, *Nueva Granada*, 2:149–50.

27. A law passed by the Congress of Cúcuta in 1821 provided for the gradual division of the *resguardos*, but it was not carried out until 1832 (Bushnell, *Santander*, pp. 175–76). The breakup of the *resguardos*, at least in the state of Boyacá, had begun in the mid-eighteenth century as a result of pressure on the land by middle-class whites and mestizos. See Orlando Fals Borda, *El hombre y la tierra en Boyacá: Bases sociológicas e históricas para una reforma agraria* (Bogotá: Ediciones Documentos Colombianos, 1957), pp. 84–85.

28. Luis Eduardo Nieto Arteta, *Economía y cultura en la historia de Colombia*, 2d ed. (Bogotá: Ediciones Tercer Mundo, 1962), pp. 160–64.

29. [Manuel Murillo Toro], *Informe del secretario de estado del despacho de hacienda de la Nueva Granada al Congreso Constitucional de 1851* (Bogotá: Imprenta del Neo-Granadino, 1851), pp. 2–5.

30. Frank Safford, *The Ideal of the Practical: Colombia's Struggle to Form a Technical Elite* (Austin: University of Texas Press, 1976), pp. 134–35.

31. There is no full-length work that thoroughly explores both the Mosquera and López administrations. Germán Colmenares's slender volume, *Partidos políticos y clases sociales* (Bogotá: Ediciones Universidad de los Andes, 1968), covers the period in question but does not adequately relate the subjects of the title—political parties and social classes—to each other. Gilmore provides an excellent discussion of Liberal thought in the mid-nineteenth century in "Federalism," pp. 185–206, and in "Mirage." Economic aspects are emphasized in William Paul McGreevey, *An Economic History of Colombia, 1845–1930* (Cambridge: Cambridge University Press, 1971), pp. 67–96, and the conditions of the artisans are discussed in Urrutia, *Labor*, pp. 17–44. For a Marxist version of the mid-century revolution, see Alvaro Tirado Mejía, *Introducción a la historia económica de Colombia*, 3d ed.(Medellín: La Carreta, 1974), pp. 101–08. Jay Robert Grusin, "The Revolution of 1848 in Colombia" (Ph.D. dissertation, University of Arizona, 1978), came to my attention too late to be considered here.

32. Nieto Arteta, *Economía*, pp. 263–75; William Paul McGreevey, "The Economic Development of Colombia" (Ph.D. dissertation, Massachusetts Institute of Technology, 1967), p. 43. On the tobacco industry, see Luis F. Sierra, *El tabaco en la economía colombiana del siglo XIX* (Bogotá: Dirección de Divulgación Cultural, Universidad Nacional de Colombia, 1971), and two works by John Parker Harrison, "The Colombian Tobacco Industry from Government Monopoly to Free Trade, 1778–1876" (Ph.D. dissertation, University of California, Berkeley, 1951), and "The Evolution of the Colombian Tobacco Trade, to 1875," *Hispanic American Historical Review* 32 (May 1952): 163–74.

33. Gilmore, "Mirage," p. 198.

34. Galindo, *Recuerdos*, pp. 53–54; Cuervo, *Rufino Cuervo*, 2:190–92; Camacho Roldán, *Memorias*, pp. 195–96.

35. Gilmore, "Federalism," pp. 224–25.

36. Restrepo, *Nueva Granada*, 2:169–72, 193–94, 209.

37. Gilmore, "Federalism," p. 221.

38. Samper, *Alma*, 1:254–56.

39. Gilmore, "Mirage," pp. 193–94; Camacho Roldán, *Memorias*, pp. 196–97; Salvador Camacho Roldán, *Escritos varios*, 3 vols. (Bogotá: Librería Colombiana, 1892–1895), 2:508–09.

40. Rodríguez Plata, *Obando*, p. 467.

41. Obando received 1,548 electoral votes while his nearest opponent, Tomás Herrera, who had *Gólgota* support, received only 329. Miguel Urrutia and Mario Arrubla, eds.,*Compendio de estadísticas históricas de Colombia* (Bogotá: Dirección de Divulgación Cultural, Universidad Nacional de Colombia, 1970), p. 277.

42. Restrepo, *Nueva Granada*, 2:310–11.

43. Cuervo, *Rufino Cuervo*, 2:255–57; Carlos Lozano y Lozano, "El golpe de cuartel del 17 de abril de 1854," *Boletín de Historia y Antigüedades* 31 (November-December 1944):1085; Venancio Ortiz, *Historia de la revolución del 17 de abril de 1854* (Bogotá: Imprenta de Francisco Torres Amaya, 1855), pp. 22–25.

44. For a discussion of Obando's conduct on 17 April, see Lozano y Lozano, "Golpe," pp. 1088–92.

45. Gilmore, "Federalism," pp. 238ff.

46. Ibid., pp. 350–51; Vega, *Federación*, pp. 164–65.

47. The designation of Radical began to be applied to the *Gólgotas* in the mid-1850s. Cf. Gilmore, "Federalism," p. 191. On Radical rule in Santander, see Marco A. Estrada, *Historia documentada de los primeros cuatro años de vida del Estado de Santander*, vol. 1, *Años de 1857 y 1858* (Maracaibo: Tipografía de "Los Ecos del Zulia," 1896), pp. 184–92; David C. Johnson, "Social and Economic Change in Nineteenth Century Santander, Colombia" (Ph.D. dissertation, University of California, Berkeley, 1975), pp. 46–153.

48. Gustavo Arboleda, *Historia contemporánea de Colombia* 4 (Cali, 1933):428–29.

49. Antonio Pérez Aguirre, *25 años de historia colombiana, 1853 a 1878: Del centralismo a la federación*, Biblioteca Eduardo Santos (Bogotá: Editorial Sucre, 1959), p. 114.

50. Camacho Roldán, *Memorias*, pp. 290, 291.

51. [Bernardo Torrente], "Fastos de Bogotá," *Boletín de Historia y Antigüedades* 17 (June 1928–January 1929): 56–57.

52. Correa, *Rionegro*, pp. 224ff.

53. Camacho Roldán, *Memorias*, pp. 384–85. For an English translation of the constitution, see William Marion Gibson, *The Constitutions of Colombia* (Durham, N.C.: Duke University Press, 1948), pp. 273–96.

54. Cf. Camacho Roldán, *Memorias*, pp. 299, 312–13; Galindo, *Recuerdos*, pp. 207–15; Justo Arosemena, *Estudios constitucionales sobre los gobiernos de la América Latina*, 2 vols., 2d ed. rev. (Paris: Librería Española i Americana de E. Denne, 1878), 2:58ff. A proposal to move the national capital to the city of Panama received some support at the convention. According to Aquileo Parra, who was one of the sponsors of the proposal, it was defeated after critics pointed out the distance between the Isthmus and the interior, the unhealthful climate of the former, and its vulnerability to foreign aggression (*Memorias*, pp. 328ff.; Correa, *Rionegro*, pp. 197ff.).

55. For a discussion of this issue of "public order," see chapter 5.

56. *La América*, 9 March 1874.

57. *Diario de Cundinamarca*, 8 May, 24 May 1877.

58. *El Tradicionista*, 9 June, 4 July 1876.

Chapter 2

1. For a discussion of the problems of explaining the origins of party affiliation in the first half of the nineteenth century, see Frank Safford, "Social Aspects of Politics in Nineteenth-Century Spanish America: New Granada, 1825–1850," *Journal of Social History*, Spring 1972, pp. 344–70.

2. The growth of the telegraphic network is shown in [Evaristo Delgado], *Informe del ministro de gobierno de Colombia al Congreso Constitucional de 1892* (Bogotá: Imprenta de Antonio María Silvestre, 1892), pp. 192–93.

3. The last official census in the nineteenth century took place in 1870. For the merits and defects of this census, see Miguel Urrutia and Mario Arrubla, eds.,

Compendio de estadísticas históricas de Colombia (Bogotá: Dirección de Divulgación Cultural, Universidad Nacional de Colombia, 1970), pp. 16–18. Population figures for the nine Colombian states in 1870 are taken from Table 13, p. 30, of this work. Later estimates of population are given in Ricardo S. Pereira, *Les États-Unis de Colombie: Précis d'Histoire et de Geographie Physique, Politique et Commerciale* (Paris: C. Marpon et E. Flammarion, Editeurs, 1883), p. 80, and Clímaco Calderón and Edward E. Britton, *Colombia, 1893* (New York, 1893), pp. 59–60.

4. According to the constitution of 1843 only citizens could vote. To be a citizen, an individual had to be male, twenty-one years of age or older, and own property worth $300 or receive an annual income of $150 (Title 2, Article 9). To be eligible to serve as an elector, one had to be a citizen at least twenty-five years of age, literate, and a resident of the canton from which he was to be elected (Title 5, Section 2). The constitution of 1853 conferred the right to vote on all male Colombians who were twenty-one years of age or were or had been married (Title 1, Article 3; Title 2, Article 13). English translations of the constitutions can be found in William Marion Gibson, *The Constitutions of Colombia* (Durham, N.C.: Duke University Press, 1948).

5. The development of the three Coastal cities is traced in Theodore E. Nichols, "The Caribbean Gateway to Colombia: Cartagena, Santa Marta, and Barranquilla and Their Connections with the Interior, 1820–1940" (Ph.D. dissertation, University of California, Berkeley, 1951).

6. Thomas M. Dawson, #115, 10 November 1884, in *Despatches Barranquilla*.

7. By a contract signed on 15 April 1850, the Panama railway company was given an exclusive right to build and operate a transisthmian railroad for forty-nine years.

8. See Arosemena's pamphlet, *El Estado Federal de Panamá*, Biblioteca de Autores Panameños (Panama: Editora Panameña, S.A., 1965).

9. All sums of money mentioned in this work will be given in Colombian pesos unless otherwise noted. Until the early 1880s the peso was roughly equivalent to the United States gold dollar. Thereafter there was a gradual depreciation of the currency, caused partly by the introduction of paper money after 1880. By January 1892 the peso was worth 69.1 cents in U.S. currency (Calderón and Britton, *Colombia*, p. 79).

10. Robert Louis Gilmore, "Federalism in Colombia, 1810–1858" (Ph.D. dissertation, University of California, Berkeley, 1949), pp. 152–56.

11. Pereira, *Colombie*, p. 216. See also William Paul McGreevey, "The Economic Development of Colombia" (Ph.D. dissertation, Massachusetts Institute of Technology, 1967), Table I-C-1, and Eliseo Reclus, *Colombia,* translated and annotated by F. Vergara y Velasco (Bogotá: Papelería de Samper Matiz, 1893), pp. 379–80.

12. For the number of foreigners in Santander, see *Censo de la población del Estado Soberano de Santander en el año de 1870 aprobado por la lei nacional de 19 de mayo de 1871* (Socorro: Imprenta del Estado, n.d.).

13. See the list of Barranquilla's businesses, with the nationality of their owners, in #28, 6 November 1888, in *Despatches Barranquilla*.

14. José Manuel Groot to Bishop José Telésforo Paúl, 6 April 1876 (Ms. #97, BL-AA).

15. Quoted in *La Sociedad* (Medellín), 26 October 1872.
16. *La Estrella de Panamá* (Panama), 17 October 1865.
17. In preparing Table 2A and other tables based on the presidential election returns for 1848 and 1856, the vote for each state was compiled by totalling the results in the provinces or parts of provinces which were later joined to constitute the state in question. Electoral votes cast in 1848 for José Hilario López were counted as Liberal votes, as were those cast for Florentino González. Electoral votes cast in 1848 for Rufino Cuervo and Joaquín J. Gori, both of whom were major contenders, were counted as Conservative votes, as were the scattered votes cast for Mariano Ospina Rodríguez and Eusebio Borrero. Joaquín María Barriga, who was appointed minister of war in 1846 by the incumbent president, Tomás Cipriano de Mosquera, was Mosquera's choice to succeed him. Barriga, however, was uninterested in the presidency and was not a serious candidate. He cannot be identified with either party, and electoral votes cast for him have been listed separately as "Other."

Popular votes cast for Manuel Murillo in 1856 have been counted as Liberal votes, and those for Mariano Ospina Rodríguez as Conservative votes. Ex-President Mosquera ran as the candidate of a shortlived National party, and votes cast for him are so listed. A small number—seventy-six in all—of votes cast for unidentified other candidates has been ignored. The election of 1856 attracted approximately 40–46 percent of the eligible voters, a rate of participation that has been described as "remarkably high" by David Bushnell in "Voter Participation in the Colombian Election of 1856," *Hispanic American Historical Review* 51 (May 1971):237–49. The results of both elections appear in Urrutia and Arrubla, *Estadísticas,* pp. 258–66, 279–310.

18. Ramón León Sánchez, #31, 24 July 1851, in *Despatches Cartagena.*
19. See his statement (2 August 1859) ff. #16, 7 August 1859, ibid.
20. Edmund W. P. Smith to John Davis, #134, 29 January 1885, ibid.
21. On the *arrabal,* see Rubén D. Carles, "Apuntes sobre la historia de Panamá," *Estrella de Panamá,* 9 August 1970, p. 2.
22. Ignacio Quinzada, "Apuntamientos para la historia de Panamá (1868–1922)," *Lotería,* 2d ser., 10 (May 1965):63.
23. Charles Toll. Bidwell, *The Isthmus of Panama* (London: Chapman & Hall, 1865), p. 181.
24. *Star and Herald,* 19 July 1862; *Estrella de Panamá,* 26 July 1862.
25. See *Estrella de Panamá,* 3 December, 29 December 1863; 14 January, 16 January, 19 January 1864.
26. Armando Aizpurúa, "José Leonardo Calancha, escritor, periodista, poeta, estadista, orador, político y revolucionario," *Lotería* 12 (October 1967): 68–72; *Star and Herald,* 6 October, 17 November 1868. José Domingo de Obaldía, another of the elder Obaldía's sons, and José Clemente de Obaldía, a nephew, were both associated with the Conservative-dominated Regeneration in later years. José Domingo also served as president of Panama (1908–10).
27. Joaquín F. Vélez to the Conservative Committee of Cundinamarca, 14 October 1868 (Ms. #66, BL-AA).
28. One of the wealthiest men in Magdalena was Manuel J. de Mier, son of the Spaniard in whose home Bolívar died in 1830, but he is said to have been nonpolitical. He was appointed United States consular agent in 1883 after Thomas

M. Dawson, the American consul in Barranquilla, recommended him for the post, describing him as "a man of wealth, position, and influence who speaks our language." See Dawson, #11, 3 April 1883, in *Despatches Barranquilla*.

29. *El Liberal* (Bogotá), 12 August 1870.

30. See, e.g., Felipe Pérez, *Jeografía física i política de los Estados Unidos de Colombia* (Bogotá: Imprenta de la Nación, 1862–63), 1:384–85, and Pereira, *Colombie*, p. 159.

31. On the Chocó during the colonial period, see William Frederick Sharp, "Forsaken but for Gold: An Economic Study of Slavery and Mining in the Colombian Chocó, 1680–1810" (Ph.D. dissertation, University of North Carolina, 1970).

32. Raymond E. Crist, *The Cauca Valley, Colombia: Land Tenure and Land Use* (Baltimore: Privately printed, 1952), pp. 14ff. According to Luis F. Sierra, *El tabaco en la economía colombiana del siglo XIX* (Bogotá: Dirección de Divulgación Cultural, Universidad Nacional de Colombia, 1971), p. 98, in 1875 Palmira accounted for 260,000 of the 511,000 *arrobas* of tobacco produced in Colombia that year. An *arroba* is equal to 12.5 kilos, or 27.5 pounds.

33. Pereira, *Colombie*, p. 170.

34. On transportation between Cali and Buenaventura, see James H. Neal, "The Pacific Age Comes to Colombia: The Construction of the Cali-Buenaventura Route, 1854–1882" (Ph.D. dissertation, Vanderbilt University, 1971).

35. Sharp, "Chocó," pp. 257–58; Crist, *Cauca Valley*, p. 43.

36. On the Cali *ejidos*, see [Ramón Mercado], *Memorias sobre los acontecimientos del sur de la Nueva Granada durante la administración del 7 de marzo de 1849* (Bogotá: Imprenta Imparcial, 1853), pp. xlv–xlix; [Avelino Escobar?], *Reseña histórica de los principales acontecimientos políticos de la ciudad de Cali, desde el año de 1848 hasta el de 1855 inclusive* (Bogotá: Imprenta de Echeverría Hermanos, 1856), pp. 9–36; Gustavo Arboleda, *Historia contemporánea de Colombia*, 3 (Popayán: Imprenta del Departamento, 1919):151–52; Miguel Urrutia, *The Development of the Colombian Labor Movement* (New Haven: Yale University Press, 1969), pp. 34–37.

37. [Escobar?], *Reseña*, pp. 36–37; Arboleda, *Historia*, 3:152–54.

38. José Manuel Restrepo, *Historia de la Nueva Granada*, 2 (Bogotá: Editorial El Catolicismo, 1963):193.

39. [Mercado], *Memorias*, pp. iv–viii.

40. *Estrella de Panamá*, 15 March 1864.

41. Fr[iedrich] von Schenck, *Viajes por Antioquia en el año de 1880*, Archivo de la Economía Nacional (Bogotá: Imprenta del Banco de la República, 1953), p. 52.

42. List of known members of the Liberal party resident in the center of Buga, around 1903–04, signed by Régulo Domínguez (AUU, ACH).

43. For a discussion of conditions in Tolima, see a series of five articles on "La cuestión del Tolima" by José María Samper, a native of Honda, in *El Republicano* (Bogotá), 14 September 1867 to 28 September 1867.

44. Frank Robinson Safford, "Commerce and Enterprise in Central Colombia, 1821–1870" (Ph.D dissertation, Columbia University, 1965), pp. 286–92; Medardo Rivas, *Los trabajadores de tierra caliente*, Biblioteca Popular de Cultura Colombiana (Bogotá: Prensas de la Universidad Nacional, 1946), pp. 261–65.

45. Urrutia and Arrubla, *Estadísticas*, p. 210.
46. William L. Scruggs, *The Colombian and Venezuelan Republics, with Notes on Other Parts of Central and South America* (Boston: Little, Brown and Company, 1905), p. 103.
47. Scruggs to Hamilton Fish, #26, 27 December 1873, and *Separate*, ff. #71, 7 November 1874, in *Diplomatic Despatches*.
48. J. M. Vergara V. and J. B. Gaitán, *Almanaque de Bogotá i guía de forasteros para 1867* (Bogotá: Imprenta de Gaitán, 1866), p. 299.
49. Comte [Alexis] de Gabriac, *Promenade a travers L'Amerique du Sud: Nouvelle-Grenade, Equateur, Pérou, Brésil* (Paris: Michel Levy Frères, Libraires, Editeurs, 1868), p. 45.
50. Miguel Samper, "La miseria en Bogotá," *Escritos político-económicos*, 4 vols. (Bogotá: Editorial de Cromos, 1925-1927), 1:8–12.
51. Scruggs to the Secretary of State, #152, 17 March 1876, in *Diplomatic Despatches*.
52. Samper, "Retrospecto (1896)," *Escritos*, 1:136–57.
53. Manuel M. Zamora, *Guía de la República de Colombia* (Bogotá: Imprenta Eléctrica, 1907), pp. 49–50.
54. Reclus, *Colombia*, p. 384n.
55. F. J. Vergara y Velasco, *Nueva geografía de Colombia* (Bogotá: Imprenta de Vapor, 1901), pp. 709, 739.
56. Edouard André, "América Equinoccial (Colombia-Ecuador)," *América pintoresca: Descripción de viajes al Nuevo Continente* (Barcelona: Montaner y Simón, Editores, 1884), p. 531.
57. Miguel Cané, *Notas de viaje sobre Venezuela y Colombia* (Bogotá: Imprenta de "La Luz," 1907), p. 173.
58. Gabriac, *Promenade*, pp. 47–48; Charles Saffray, *Viaje a Nueva Granada*, Biblioteca Popular de Cultura Colombiana (Bogotá: Ministerio de Educación, 1948), pp. 398–99; Pierre d'Espagnat, "Souvenirs de la Nouvelle-Grenade," *Revue de Deux Mondes* 152 (November–December 1900):849.
59. *La Alianza* (Bogotá), 25 January, 8 February 1868.
60. Ibid., 1 January 1867.
61. Ernst Röthlisberger, *El Dorado: Estampas de viaje y cultura de la Colombia suramericana*, translated by Antonio de Zubiaurre, Archivo de la Economía Nacional (Bogotá: Banco de la República, 1963), p. 103.
62. Charles W. Bergquist, *Coffee and Conflict in Colombia, 1886–1910* (Durham, N.C.: Duke University Press, 1978), pp. 70–71.
63. *¿Qué cosa es el empréstito?* (Bogotá: Imprenta de Gaitán, 11 June 1866). Critics of the loan argued that because of discounts, commissions, etc., Colombia would receive only $5,095,875.00. The reference to the legacy that would have to be mortgaged stemmed from Article 13 of the loan contract, which committed the Colombian government, as security for the loan, to pledge its right to purchase the Panama railroad in 1875 for $5 million.
64. *La Alianza*, 1 October 1866.
65. Bergquist, *Conflict*, pp. 161–62.
66. Pereira, *Colombie*, p. 141; Vergara y Velasco, *Geografía*, p. 875.
67. Pereira, *Colombie*, p. 142. Cf. figures giving the estimated population and annual income for 1878 of each state in Joaquín Esguerra O., *Diccionario jeográ-*

fico de los Estados Unidos de Colombia (Bogotá: J. B. Gaitán, 1879). Only Magdalena had an income lower than Boyacá's $172,100, yet its population was about one fifth that of Boyacá.

68. Pereira, *Colombie,* pp. 142–43.
69. Pérez, *Jeografía,* 2:336.
70. Pedro Fermín de Vargas, *Pensamientos políticos y memoria sobre la población del Nuevo Reino de Granada,* Biblioteca Popular de Cultura Colombiana (Bogotá: Ministerio de Educación, 1944), p. 100; Joaquín Camacho, "Relación territorial de la provincia de Pamplona," in Francisco José de Caldas, ed., *Semanario del Nuevo Reino de Granada,* Biblioteca Popular de Cultura Colombiana, 2 (Bogotá: Editorial Kelly, 1942):8.
71. Vargas, *Pensamientos,* pp. 55, 103–04; Luis Ospina Vásquez, *Industria y protección en Colombia, 1810–1930* (Medellín: E.S.F., 1955), pp. 67–71.
72. Horacio Rodríguez Plata, *La antigua provincia de Socorro y la Independencia,* Biblioteca de Historia Nacional (Bogotá: Publicaciones Editoriales, 1969), p. 409.
73. Ospina Vásquez, *Industria,* p. 224; David C. Johnson, "Social and Economic Change in Nineteenth Century Santander, Colombia" (Ph.D. dissertation, University of California, Berkeley, 1975), pp. 205ff.
74. Vergara y Velasco, *Geografía,* p. 762.
75. Johnson, "Santander," pp. 194ff.
76. Salvador Camacho Roldán, *Escritos varios,* 3 vols. (Bogotá: Librería Colombiana, 1892-1895), 1:619–624.
77. Vergara y Velasco, *Geografía,* p. 762; Ospina Vásquez, *Industria,* p. 264.
78. McGreevey, "Development," p. 167.
79. Johnson, "Santander," p. 199.
80. Ibid., p. 192. It should be noted that of the 319,858 artisans in the Colombian work force in 1870, 227,511, or more than 70 percent, were women. See Urrutia and Arrubla, *Estadísticas,* p. 29.
81. Johnson, "Santander," p. 190.
82. Safford, "Commerce," pp. 281–82.
83. Johnson, "Santander," pp. 183–85.
84. Ibid., pp. 303, 305.
85. Rodríguez Plata, *Socorro,* pp. 40-46.
86. Safford, "Commerce," pp. 385–86; J. M. Restrepo, "Ensayo sobre la geografía, producciones, industria y población de la provincia de Antioquia en el Nuevo Reino de Granada," in Caldas, *Semanario* 1 (Bogotá: Editorial Minerva, S.A., 1942):271.
87. Schenck, *Viajes,* pp. 18–19.
88. On the various explanations for the Antioqueño's qualities of enterprise and industry, see James J. Parsons, *Antioqueño Colonization in Western Colombia,* Ibero-Americana (Berkeley and Los Angeles: University of California Press, 1949); Everett E. Hagen, *On the Theory of Social Change: How Economic Growth Begins* (Homewood, Ill.: Dorsey Press, 1962); and Frank Safford, "Significación de los antioqueños en el desarrollo económico antioqueño: Un examen crítico de las tesis de Everett Hagen," *Anuario Colombiano de Historia Social y de Cultura* 2 (1965): 49–69.
89. On the migration of the Antioqueños, see Parsons, *Colonization.*

90. Röthlisberger, *El Dorado*, p. 358.
91. "Emiro Kastos" [pseud. of Juan de Dios Restrepo], *Un recuerdo al Sr. Francisco Montoya* (Bogotá: Imprenta de la Nación, 1862); Teodomiro Llano, *Biografía del señor Gabriel Echeverri E.* (Bogotá: Casa Editorial de Medardo Rivas & Cia., 1890), pp. 73–74.
92. Luis Latorre Mendoza, *Historia e historias de Medellín* (Medellín: Imprenta Oficial, 1923), pp. 159–60, 213.
93. Jaime Jaramillo Uribe, "Historia de Pereira, 1863–1963," in Luis Duque Gómez, Juan Friede, and Jaime Jaramillo Uribe, *Historia de Pereira* (Pereira: Club Rotario de Pereira, 1963), pp. 408–09. Pereira was founded in the state of Cauca in 1863 on lands donated by Guillermo Pereira Gamba.
94. Safford, "Commerce," pp. 385–86.

Chapter 3

1. A. Le Moyne, *Viajes y estancias en América del Sur, la Nueva Granada, Santiago de Cuba, Jamaica y el Istmo de Panamá*, Biblioteca Popular de Cultura Colombiana (Bogotá: Ministerio de Educación de Colombia, 1945), p. 128; Rufino José Cuervo, "Noticia biográfica de D. Angel Cuervo," in Angel Cuervo, *Cómo se evapora un ejército* (Paris, 1900), p.xix. See also Frank Safford, *The Ideal of the Practical: Colombia's Struggle to Form a Technical Elite* (Austin, Texas: University of Texas Press, 1976), pp. 34–35.
2. The fifteen cabinet members in question were in office on 1 February—the date of the opening of Congress—in the years from 1870 through 1875: Narciso González Lineros, Aquileo Parra, Antonio María Pradilla, Felipe Zapata, Santander; Salvador Camacho Roldán, Medardo Rivas, Jacobo Sánchez, Cundinamarca; Manuel Amador Fierro, Ramón Santodomingo Vila, Bolívar; Sergio Camargo, Felipe Pérez, Boyacá; César Conto, Cauca; Gil Colunje, Panama; Eustorgio Salgar, Cundinamarca and Santander; Nicolás Esguerra, Cundinamarca and Tolima. Three cabinet members could not be identified with any state: Januario Salgar, José M. Caro, and Francisco Agudelo.
3. Eduardo Rodríguez Piñeres, *El Olimpo Radical: Ensayos conocidos e inéditos sobre su época, 1864–1884* (Bogotá: Talleres Editoriales de Librería Voluntad, 1950), p. 147.
4. *El Mensajero*, 8 January 1867.
5. The one Radical who could not be identified with any state was Januario Salgar. The other thirty-eight and their states are as follows: Santander—Narciso Cadena, Florentino González, Aquileo Parra, Antonio María Pradilla, Carlos Nicolás Rodríguez, Francisco de Paula Rueda, Vicente Uscátegui, Germán Vargas, Florentino Vezga, José María Villamizar Gallardo, Dámaso Zapata, Felipe Zapata; Cundinamarca—Salvador Camacho Roldán, Tomás Cuenca, Nicolás Esguerra, Santiago Pérez, Medardo Rivas, Eustorgio Salgar, Miguel Samper, Jacobo Sánchez, Francisco J. Zaldúa; Tolima—Francisco E. Alvarez, Eugenio Castilla, Gabriel González Gaitán, Bernardo Herrera, Clímaco Iriarte, Manuel Murillo, Rafael Rocha Castillo, Rafael Rocha Gutiérrez; Boyacá—Santos Acosta, Sergio Camargo, Felipe Pérez; Panama—Pablo Arosemena, Gil Colunje; Cauca—César Conto, Teodoro Valenzuela; Antioquia—Luciano Restrepo; Magdalena—Luis A. Robles. Although Felipe and Santiago Pérez were brothers, they were born

in different states—the former in Boyacá, the latter in Cundinamarca—and have been so listed. Except for periods of residence abroad, Santiago seems to have lived his entire life in Cundinamarca; Felipe was president of Boyacá from 1868 to 1871.

6. Gustavo Arboleda, *Diccionario biográfico y genealógico del antiguo departamento del Cauca* (Bogotá: Biblioteca Horizontes, 1962), pp. 452–53.

7. *Diario de Cundinamarca,* 21 July, 5 August 1882.

8. Rafael Núñez, *La reforma política en Colombia,* Biblioteca Popular de Cultura Colombiana, 2 (Bogotá: Editorial A B C, 1945):85.

9. Enclosure A following Allan Burton to William H. Seward, #219, 14 February 1866, in *Diplomatic Despatches.*

10. Ernst Röthlisberger, *El Dorado: Estampas de viaje y cultura de la Colombia suramericana,* Archivo de la Economía Nacional (Bogotá: Banco de la República, 1963), p. 93.

11. Thomas H. Dawson, #53, 21 August 1883, in *Despatches Barranquilla.*

12. Charles Toll. Bidwell, *The Isthmus of Panama* (London: Chapman & Hall, 1865), p. 181.

13. Eduardo Rodríguez Piñeres, *Hechos y comentarios: Nova et vetera,* Academia Colombiana de Historia, Biblioteca Eduardo Santos, 11 (Bogotá: Editorial Sucre, 1956), p. 189.

14. Nicolás del Castillo, *El primer Núñez,* 2d ed. (Bogotá: Ediciones Tercer Mundo, 1972), pp. 12–13.

15. José María Restrepo Sáenz, *Documentos sobre la familia Rivas* (Bogotá: Editorial Minerva, S.A., 1930), pp. 99–100.

16. Medardo Rivas, *Los trabajadores de tierra caliente,* Biblioteca Popular de Cultura Colombiana (Bogotá: Prensas de la Universidad Nacional, 1946), pp. 282–83.

17. Arboleda, *Diccionario,* pp. 280–81, 288.

18. Teodomiro Llano, *Biografía del señor Gabriel Echeverri E.* (Bogotá: Casa Editorial de Medardo Rivas & Cia., 1890), p. 37.

19. Salvador Camacho Roldán, *Memorias* (Bogotá: Librería Colombiana, 1923), p. 319.

20. José María Samper, *Historia de un alma,* 2 vols., Biblioteca Popular de Cultura Colombiana (Bogotá: Editorial Kelly, 1946–1948), 1:18–23.

21. Rodríguez Piñeres, *Olimpo,* pp. 195–98.

22. Aquileo Parra, *Memorias* (Bogotá: Imprenta de "La Luz," 1912), p. l2.

23. Enrique Pérez, *Vida de Felipe Pérez* (Bogotá: Imprenta de "La Luz," 1911), p. 5.

24. Antonio José Rivadeneira Vargas, *Don Santiago Pérez: Biografía de un carácter* (Bogotá: Editorial "El Voto Nacional," 1966), p. 2.

25. Rodríguez Piñeres, *Olimpo,* pp. 195–98.

26. Parra, *Memorias,* pp. 11–12.

27. Samper, *Alma,* 1:18–23.

28. Arboleda, *Diccionario,* p. 123; Aníbal Galindo, *Recuerdos históricos: 1840 a 1895* (Bogotá: Imprenta de "La Luz," 1900), p. 5.

29. Castillo, *Núñez,* pp. 38–40.

30. Samper, *Alma,* 1:63–66.

31. *El Autonomista,* 27 August 1899.

32. Andrés Soriano Lleras, *Lorenzo María Lleras,* Biblioteca Eduardo Santos,

14 (Bogotá: Editorial Sucre, 1958), pp. 41ff.; Pérez, *Felipe Pérez*, pp. 6–8; Rivadeneira, *Santiago Pérez*, p. 3.
33. Samper, *Alma*, 1:187–88.
34. Parra, *Memorias*, pp. 39–40.
35. Peter J. Sullivan to William H. Seward, #61, 1 April 1868, in *Diplomatic Despatches*.
36. José María Quijano Wallis, *Memorias autobiográficas histórico-políticas y de carácter social* (Grottaferrata, Italy: Tipografía italo-orientale, 1919), p. 97.
37. Luis María Mora, *Croniquillas de mi ciudad* (Bogotá: Editorial A B C, 1936), pp. 21–23.
38. Fortunato Pereira Gamba, *La vida en los Andes colombianos* (Quito: Imprenta de "El Progreso," 1919), p. 11.
39. José Ramón Vergara, *Escrutinio histórico: Rafael Núñez* (Bogotá: Editorial A B C, 1939), pp. 49–50.
40. Rodríguez Piñeres, *Olimpo*, pp. 197, 229–34.
41. Ricardo Becerra, "The Republic of Colombia," *Harper's Magazine* 79 (November 1889):928.
42. Rodríguez Piñeres, *Olimpo*, p. 204.
43. Ibid.; Rivas, *Trabajadores*, pp. 145, 285.
44. Joaquín Tamayo, *Núñez* (Bogotá: Editorial Cromos, 1939), pp. 118–20. According to reminiscences dictated by Soledad Román shortly before her death, she knew Núñez as a girl and turned down his offer of marriage in 1857. He looked her up upon his return to Colombia in 1874 and, finding that she was still unmarried, renewed his attentions. See Daniel Lemaitre, *Soledad Román de Núñez: Recuerdos* (Cartagena: Mogollón, 1927), pp. 52–55.
45. Julio H. Palacio, "El segundo matrimonio de Núñez," *Revista Colombiana* 7 (15 November 1936):325.
46. Vergara, *Escrutinio*, pp. 489–91.
47. Palacio, "Matrimonio," p. 325.
48. Núñez to Miguel Camacho Roldán, 3 October 1886 (Ms. #99, BL-AA).
49. *Diario de Cundinamarca*, 7 August 1874.
50. José Joaquín García (pseud. Arturo), *Crónicas de Bucaramanga* (Bogotá: Imprenta y Librería de Medardo Rivas, 1896), p. 166.
51. *Boletín de la Sociedad Patriótica*, 6 October 1872, 16 March 1873.
52. Frank Robinson Safford, "Commerce and Enterprise in Central Colombia 1821–1870" (Ph.D. dissertation, Columbia University, 1965), p. 216.
53. Luis Ospina Vásquez, *Industria y protección en Colombia, 1810–1930* (Medellín: E.S.F., 1955), pp. 270ff.
54. *El Bien Público*, 2 August 1870; *El Mensajero*, 11 August, 18 August 1867.
55. Parra, *Memorias*, pp. 39–76.
56. Ibid., pp. 135–36, 416–17.
57. Rivas, *Trabajadores*, pp. 135–36; Salvador Camacho Roldán to Rafael Uribe Uribe, 25 November 1891 (AUU, ACH).
58. *El Bien Público*, 29 November 1870.
59. *La Reforma*, 5 February 1882; Antonio José Iregui, *Ensayo biográfico: Salvador Camacho Roldán* (Bogotá, 1919), p. 54.
60. Camacho Roldán to Uribe Uribe, 21 November 1884 (AUU, ACH).
61. Camacho Roldán to Uribe Uribe, 25 November 1891 (ibid.).

62. *El Liberal,* 4 January 1869; *Boletín Industrial,* 8 November 1872; Nicolás Pereira Gamba to Buenaventura Correoso, 26 January 1870 (AC).
63. Arboleda, *Diccionario,* p. 348.
64. Carlos Martínez Silva, "Miguel Samper," in Rafael M. Mesa Ortiz, *Colombianos ilustres (Estudios y biografías),* 5 vols. (Bogotá: Imprenta de "La República," 1916–1929), 5:115–18; *Diario de Cundinamarca,* 21 January 1874; Rivas, *Trabajadores,* p. 142.
65. *El Bien Público,* 29 November 1870.
66. Felipe Pérez to Aquileo Parra, 21 February 1879 (CAP).
67. José Benito Gaitán to Parra, 30 December 1881 (ibid.).
68. Gustavo Humberto Rodríguez R., *Ezequiel Rojas y la primera república liberal* (Miraflores, Boyacá: Publicación del Club Social Miraflores, 1970), pp. 20–21.
69. Rivadeneira, *Santiago Pérez,* p. 30.
70. José María Restrepo Sáenz and Raimundo Rivas, *Genealogías de Santa Fe de Bogotá* (Bogotá: Librería Colombiana, 1928?), pp. 195–97; Arboleda, *Diccionario,* p. 241.
71. Restrepo Sáenz, *Rivas,* pp. 124–25, 135–36.
72. Arboleda, *Diccionario,* p. 334.
73. For 1879, the men in question were drawn from the ranks of the supreme director and alternates, principal members of the National Council, and the members of the Supreme Junta of Public Instruction; for 1883, from the directory and Council. All together, these officials numbered twenty-four, nineteen of whom could be identified with a single state by virtue of birth or residence: Cundinamarca—José Caicedo Rojas, Miguel Antonio Caro, Antonio B. Cuervo, José Manuel Marroquín, Rafael Pombo, José Ignacio Trujillo, Carlos M. Urdaneta; Cauca—Sergio Arboleda, Ricardo Carrasquilla, Carlos Holguín, Jorge Holguín; Santander—José Vicente Concha, Carlos Martínez Silva; Tolima—Manuel Casabianca, José María Samper; Antioquia—Wenceslao Pizano, Vicente Restrepo; Bolívar—Lázaro María Pérez; Boyacá—José Joaquín Ortiz.
74. Arboleda, *Diccionario,* pp. 13–14, 24.
75. José María Uricoechea, "Noticias genealógicas," *Boletín de Historia y Antigüedades* 49 (September 1962):479–90.
76. Camilo Pardo Umaña, *Haciendas de la sabana: Su historia, sus leyendas y tradiciones* (Bogotá: Editorial Kelly, 1946), pp. 55–57, 118, 136, 141.
77. Eduardo Zuleta, "Los Caicedo," *Boletín de Historia y Antigüedades* 19 (June 1932):336–40; G. A. R., "Los Caicedo de Saldaña," *Boletín Histórico del Valle,* 2d ser., August 1932, pp. 78–79; Charles Stuart Cochrane, *Journal of a Residence and Travels in Colombia, during the Years 1823 and 1824* (London: Henry Colburn, 1825), 2:312–13.
78. Abraham Moreno, "Pedro Justo Berrío," in *Corona fúnebre del doctor Pedro J. Berrío* (Medellín: Imprenta del Estado, 1875), pp. 2–4.
79. Robert Henry Davis, "Acosta, Caro, and Lleras. Three Essayists and Their Views of New Granada's National Problems, 1832–1853" (Ph.D. dissertation, Vanderbilt University, 1969), pp. 296–99.
80. Luis Martínez Delgado, *Apuntes histórico-biográficos* (Bogotá: Editorial A B C, 1940), pp. 217–18.
81. See *Revista de Colombia,* 7 November 1873.

82. *Anales de la Universidad* 1 (September 1868):73–77. A few Conservatives did serve on the faculty. See Rodríguez Piñeres, *Hechos*, p. 197, and Daniel Restrepo, *El Colegio de San Bartolomé*, vol. 1, *El Colegio a través de nuestra historia* (Bogotá: Sociedad Editorial, 1928), p. 67.

83. Joaquín Ospina, *Diccionario biográfico y bibliográfico de Colombia* (Bogotá: Editorial de Cromos, 1927–39), vol. 1; Arboleda, *Diccionario*, p. 19; José María Cordovez Moure, *Reminiscencias: Santa Fe y Bogotá*, Biblioteca Popular de Cultura Colombiana, 1 (Bogotá: Editorial Kelly, 1943):57–59.

84. Arboleda, *Diccionario*, pp. 14–16, 207–09.

85. *El Taller*, 18 October 1888; Victor E. Caro, "La muerte del General Cuervo," *Boletín de Historia y Antigüedades* 19 (August 1932):497–506. When he died in 1893, Cuervo left debts totalling $11,450 and assets which included $38,768.85 in cash and sums owed to him, a quinta in Madrid near Bogotá, and 100 *fanegadas* of first-class land near the town of Funza. *Correo Nacional*, 3 March 1893. One *fanegada* equals 6,400 square meters.

86. William Scruggs to State Department, #148, 6 April 1884, in *Diplomatic Despatches*.

87. José L. Camacho, "Carlos Tanco," *Colombia Ilustrada* 1 (20 July 1889):101–03, 106.

88. This appears to be the hypothesis of Charles Bergquist, who links the Liberal party with the expansion of export agriculture in the 1840s and implies that most Conservatives had economic interests and views that differed from those of the Liberals. See his *Coffee and Conflict in Colombia, 1886–1910* (Durham, N.C.: Duke University Press, 1978), pp. 7–8. The problem seems to lie partly in the fact that Bergquist identifies the Liberal party with the tenets of classical economic liberalism, which were in fact shared, with some modifications, by both Liberals and Conservatives during much of the nineteenth century. See chapter 4.

89. Isaacs's biographers have not offered an explanation for the change, which occurred in the late 1860s, though one of them indicates that Isaacs's espousal of Liberalism was caused by a newly awakened hostility to the Catholic Church. See Donald McGrady, *Jorge Isaacs* (New York: Twayne Publishers, Inc., 1972), pp.17–18.

Chapter 4

1. José María Samper, *Historia de un alma*, 2 vols., Biblioteca Popular de Cultura Colombiana (Bogotá: Editorial Kelly, 1946–1948), 1:177–80, 2:173–76, 324–31.

2. Aquileo Parra, *Memorias* (Bogotá: Imprenta de "La Luz," 1912), pp. 612–13; Florentino Vezga, "Noticia biográfica," *Honores del Gobierno de la Unión al finado Presidente Doctor Francisco J. Zaldúa* (Bogotá: Imprenta del "Diario de Cundinamarca," 1884), p. 26.

3. For a detailed analysis of nineteenth-century Colombian attitudes toward the Hispanic heritage, see Jaime Jaramillo Uribe, *El pensamiento colombiano en el siglo XIX* (Bogotá: Editorial Temis, 1964), pp. 3–100.

4. David Bushnell, *The Santander Regime in Gran Colombia* (Newark, Del.: University of Delaware Press, 1954), pp. 192–93.

5. Jaramillo Uribe, *Pensamiento*, pp. 150–53.

6. Charles A. Hale, *Mexican Liberalism in the Age of Mora, 1821–1853* (New Haven: Yale University Press, 1968), p. 173n.
7. Luis Augusto Cuervo, *Epistolario del doctor Rufino Cuervo*, 3 vols., Biblioteca de Historia Nacional (Bogotá, 1918–20), 1:106-07.
8. José Manuel Restrepo, *Historia de la Nueva Granada*, 1 (Bogotá: Editorial Cromos, 1952):348–49.
9. Gustavo Humberto Rodríguez R., *Ezequiel Rojas y la primera república liberal* (Miraflores, Boyacá: Publicación del Club Social Miraflores, 1970), p. 69.
10. Ibid., pp. 119–22. On Rojas, see also Jaramillo Uribe, *Pensamiento*, pp. 158–66.
11. Rodríguez R., *Rojas*, pp. 69–70; Bushnell, *Santander*, p. 191.
12. Hale, *Mexican Liberalism*, p. 250.
13. *El Heraldo* (Bogotá), 15 August 1889.
14. Jaramillo Uribe, *Pensamiento*, pp. 35–36, 174–76; Robert Louis Gilmore, "Federalism in Colombia, 1810–1858" (Ph.D. dissertation, University of California, Berkeley, 1949), pp. 192–94; Aníbal Galindo, *Recuerdos históricos: 1840 a 1895* (Bogotá: Imprenta de "La Luz," 1900), p. 31.
15. Samper, *Alma*, 1:154–56.
16. *Una sesión solemne de la Escuela Republicana de Bogotá* (n.d., no imprint), pp. 4–12.
17. Cf. Gilmore, "Federalism," p. 201.
18. *El Liberal*, 28 June 1870.
19. *Diario Oficial*, 10 December 1867 (advertisement).
20. Jaramillo Uribe, *Pensamiento*, p. 315.
21. *El Tiempo*, 6 December 1859.
22. *El Liberal*, 1 July, 12 July 1870.
23. Jaramillo Uribe, *Pensamiento*, p. 443.
24. Rafael Núñez, *La reforma política en Colombia*, 2 (Bogotá: Editorial A B C, 1945):418.
25. Salvador Camacho Roldán, *Escritos varios* (Bogotá: Librería Colombiana, 1892), 1:204–44.
26. Rafael Núñez, *La reforma política en Colombia. Colección de artículos publicados . . . de 1881 a 1884* (Bogotá: Imprenta de "La Luz," 1885), pp. 393–406.
27. Carlos Arturo Torres, *Idola fori*, Biblioteca Aldeana de Colombia (Bogotá: Editorial Minerva, 1935), p. 156.
28. Cf. Jaramillo Uribe, *Pensamiento*, pp. 443–44.
29. Rafael Rocha Gutiérrez, *La verdadera y la falsa democracia: Doctrina constitucional y proyecto de constitución política para la república de Colombia* (Paris: Garnier Hermanos, Libreros-Editores, 1887), pp. 120–21.
30. "Correspondencia del doctor Manuel Murillo Toro," *Revista del Archivo Nacional* 4 (January–February 1942):85–86.
31. Núñez, *Reforma*, 1 (Bogotá: Imprenta Nacional, 1944):20.
32. Medardo Rivas, *Los trabajadores de tierra caliente*, Biblioteca Popular de Cultura Colombiana (Bogotá: Prensas de la Universidad Nacional, 1946), p. 233.
33. Camacho Roldán, *Escritos*, 3:421.
34. Quoted in *Centenario de Murillo Toro: Homenaje de la Junta Nacional* (Bogotá: Aguila Negra Editorial, 1916), pp. 196–97.

35. Luis Eduardo Nieto Arteta, *Economía y cultura en Colombia,* 2d ed. (Bogotá: Ediciones Tercer Mundo, 1962), p. 37.

36. Manuel Ancízar, *Peregrinación de Alpha,* Biblioteca Popular de Cultura Colombiana (Bogotá: Editorial A B C, 1942), p. 303.

37. [Manuel Murillo Toro], *Informe del secretario de hacienda de la Nueva Granada al Congreso Constitucional de 1850* (Bogotá: Imprenta del Neo-Granadino, 1850), p. 2.

38. Eduardo Rodríguez Piñeres, ed., *Selección de escritos y discursos de Santiago Pérez,* Biblioteca de Historia Nacional (Bogotá: Talleres Editoriales de Librería Voluntad, 1950), p. 189.

39. Justo Arosemena, *El Estado Federal de Panamá,* Biblioteca de Autores Panameños (Panama: Editora Panameña, S. A., 1965).

40. For statements of the benefits conferred by federalism, see *Gaceta Mercantil,* 12 January 1848; Cerbeleón Pinzón, *Catecismo republicano para instrucción popular,* 2d ed. (Bogotá: Imprenta de "El Mosaico," 1865), pp. 46–47; and President Murillo's inaugural address on 1 April 1872, in *Diario Oficial,* 1 April 1872.

41. Federal-state relations are discussed in chapter 5.

42. [Eustorgio Salgar], *Mensaje del Presidente de la Unión al Congreso Nacional, 1872* (Bogotá: Imprenta de Medardo Rivas, 1 February 1872).

43. *El Mensajero,* 21 November 1866.

44. *El Liberal,* 20 May 1870.

45. Ricardo Becerra, *El liberalismo en Colombia i sus detractores de por acá* (Bogotá: Imprenta de Gaitán, 1877), p. 36.

46. Antonio José Rivadeneira Vargas, *Don Santiago Pérez: Biografía de un carácter* (Bogotá: Editorial "El Voto Nacional," 1966), pp. 14–18; José Restrepo Posada, *Arquidiócesis de Bogotá: Datos biográficos de sus prelados,* vol. 3, *1868–1891,* Biblioteca de Historia Eclesiástica "Fernando Caycedo y Florez" (Bogotá: Editorial Lumen Christi, 1966), p. 111.

47. *Revista de Colombia,* 22 March 1873.

48. Carlos Martínez Silva, "Miguel Samper," in Rafael M. Mesa Ortiz, *Colombianos ilustres (Estudios y biografías),* 5 vols. (Bogotá: Imprenta de "La República," 1916–29), 1:135.

49. *El Autonomista,* 27 August 1899. See also Gustavo Arboleda, ed., *César Conto: Su vida, su memoria* (Cali, 1935), pp. 262–63, and Camilo Antonio Echeverri, *Obras completas,* comp. Rafael Montoya y Montoya (Medellín: Editorial Montoya, 1961), pp. 55–57.

50. Camacho Roldán, *Escritos,* 2:73.

51. *Diario de Cundinamarca,* 26 March 1874.

52. *La Opinión,* 18 May 1864; José Restrepo Posada, *Arquidiócesis de Bogotá: Datos biográficos de sus prelados,* vol. 2, *1823–1868,* Biblioteca de Historia Eclesiástica "Fernando Caycedo y Flores" (Bogotá: Editorial Lumen Christi, 1963), pp. 467–69; Juan Pablo Restrepo, *La Iglesia y el Estado en Colombia* (London: Emiliano Isaza, 1885), pp. 594–95.

53. Restrepo Posada, *Arquidiócesis,* 2:471–73. Archbishop Herrán returned to Bogotá on 1 September 1864. Murillo also lifted the sentence of banishment against Bishop Domingo Antonio Riaño of Antioquia, but his efforts to return to his see

were frustrated by a Liberal official in Tolima, who took advantage of a technicality to order his exile once again. Gonzalo Uribe V., *Los arzobispos y obispos colombianos desde el tiempo de la colonia hasta nuestros días* (Bogotá: Imprenta de la Sociedad, 1918), pp. 658–62.

54. *El Liberal,* 28 March 1871.

55. *El Neo-Granadino,* 3 March 1849.

56. [Eustorgio Salgar], *Mensaje del Presidente de la Unión al Congreso Nacional de 1871* (Bogotá: Imprenta de Medardo Rivas, 1 February 1871).

57. [Aquileo Parra], *Memoria del Secretario de Hacienda i Fomento dirijida al Presidente de la República para el Congreso de 1873* (Bogotá: Imprenta de Gaitán, 1873), pp. 68–70. See also *El Liberal,* 31 May 1870, and Aníbal Galindo, *Estudios económicos i fiscales* (Bogotá: Imprenta a cargo de H. Andrade, 1880), p. 250.

58. Miguel Samper, "Libertad y orden," *Escritos político-económicos,* 4 vols. (Bogotá: Editorial de Cromos, 1925–27), 2:47–48. This essay, written in 1895–96, was a reply to the British sociologist Benjamin Kidd, who in a work called *Social Evolution* (1894) discussed the failure of the Spanish American republics to achieve political stability and economic growth and attributed this failure to the racial origin of the inhabitants. See Jaramillo Uribe, *Pensamiento,* pp. 60–62.

59. Samper, "La miseria en Bogotá," *Escritos,* 1:40ff., and "Libertad y orden," *Escritos,* 2:10.

60. Samper, "La miseria en Bogotá," ibid., 1:132.

61. For an amusing but scathing description of the revolutionary cycle in Colombia, see ibid., pp. 40–59.

62. Ibid., p. 63.

63. Samper, "Libertad y orden," ibid., 2:226.

64. Samper, "La miseria en Bogotá," ibid., 1:125.

65. Ibid., pp. 59ff.; Samper, "Banco Nacional," ibid., 3:11–96; Samper, *La protección: Análisis económico y político de la República* (Bogotá, 1880).

66. Samper, "Libertad y orden," *Escritos,* 2:228–29.

67. *La Gaceta Mercantil,* 2 October 1847.

68. [Manuel Murillo Toro], *Informe del Secretario del despacho de hacienda de la Nueva Granada a las cámaras lejislativas de 1852* (Bogotá: Imprenta del Neo-Granadino, 1852), pp. 2–3.

69. Marco A. Estrada, *Historia documentada de los primeros cuatro años de vida del Estado de Santander,* vol. 1, *Años de 1857 y 1858* (Maracaibo: Tipografía de "Los Ecos del Zulia," 1896), pp. 184–92; David Church Johnson, "Social and Economic Change in Nineteenth Century Santander, Colombia" (Ph.D. dissertation, University of California, Berkeley, 1975), pp. 103–05.

70. Estrada, *Santander,* pp. 96, 192–95; Johnson, "Santander," pp. 105ff. Revenue from the property tax was to be supplemented temporarily by continuation of the state's *aguardiente* monopoly for one year beginning 1 January 1858. The tax proved unpopular and difficult to collect and contributed to the Conservative uprising of 1859.

71. [Manuel Murillo Toro], *Informe del Jefe Superior del Estado de Santander a la Asamblea Leijislativa, 1858* (Bucaramanga: Imprenta de Zapata Hermanos, 1858), pp. 28–31. This document is also printed in Estrada, *Santander,* pp. 263–307.

72. *Informe del Jefe de Santander,* 33–34.

73. *El Neo-Granadino*, 15 October 1853, reprinted in Gerardo Molina, *Las ideas liberales en Colombia, 1850–1914*, 2d ed. (Bogotá: Tercer Mundo, 1971), pp. 319–33.

74. In 1851 Murillo sponsored a bill limiting purchases of public lands by any individual to 1,000 *fanegadas* and requiring cultivation of such lands by the purchaser (*Gaceta Oficial*, 26 April 1851). The bill was passed by both houses of Congress but rejected by President López.

75. *El Tiempo*, 6 December 1859.

76. *Diario Oficial*, 1 April, 30 April 1872.

77. Ibid., 19 April 1872.

78. [Manuel Murillo Toro], *Mensaje del Presidente de los E.U. de C. al Congreso de 1874* (Bogotá: Imprenta de Medardo Rivas, 1 February 1874). A company for the manufacture of sulphuric acid began operations in January 1874 but soon ran into difficulties, apparently because there were no purchasers for its products besides the federal government. It suspended operations in August 1875. See Luis Ospina Vásquez, *Industria y protección en Colombia, 1810–1930* (Medellín: E. S. F., 1955), pp. 267–69.

79. Núñez, "Sociología," *Reforma* (1885), pp. 393–94. On Núñez's ideas, see also Jaramillo Uribe, *Pensamiento*, pp. 288–307.

80. Núñez, *Ensayos de crítica social* (Rouen: Imprimerie de E. Gagniard, 1874), pp. ix–x.

81. Núñez, "Sociología," *Reforma* (1885), p. 397.

82. Núñez, *Crítica*, pp. 139–40, 167–69.

83. Ibid., pp. 403–04.

84. Ibid., p. 4.

85. Núñez, "El positivismo," *Reforma*, 7 (Bogotá: Editorial Iqueima, 1950):191–93.

86. Núñez, *Crítica*, pp. 63, 202–03, 392–400.

87. Núñez, "Fomento de la industria," *Reforma* (1885), pp. 629–30; Núñez, "Para verdades, el tiempo," *Reforma*, 4 (Bogotá: Editorial A B C, 1946):110–11, 113.

88. Núñez, "Fomento a la industria," *Reforma* (1885), pp. 623–24, 631–32.

89. Jaramillo Uribe, *Pensamiento*, pp. 289, 294–96.

90. Ibid., pp. 295–96.

91. Núñez, "La última obra de M. de Leveleye," *Reforma*, 5 (Bogotá: Editorial A B C, 1946):110–11. See also "La causa de las causas," ibid., 6 (Bogotá: Editorial Iqueima, 1950):53.

92. *La América*, 30 March 1874.

93. *Correo de Antioquia*, 16 April 1875.

94. *La Patria*, 12 July 1867.

95. *La Ilustración*, 8 February, 27 May 1873.

96. *La Prensa*, 18 June 1867.

97. The incident in question occurred in August 1873 after the death of Ezequiel Rojas, who was buried in the cemetery of Bogotá, which devout Catholics still considered sacred ground despite the fact that it had been secularized. An anonymous article soon appeared in *El Tradicionista* censuring the archbishop of Bogotá, Vicente Arbeláez, for failing to declare that the cemetery had been

profaned. It should be noted, however, that the council took place at a time when the Colombian clergy was seriously divided over the program of secular primary education begun by the Salgar administration in 1870. Only one of the eight bishops suffragan to the archbishop attended the council, and its decisions never received the required papal approval. See Restrepo Posada, *Arquidiócesis*, 3:167–227. The controversy over the public schools is described in chapter 6.

98. *La Sociedad*, 1 November 1873.

99. [Sergio Arboleda], *Colección de artículos tomados de "Los Principios" cuya lectura recomienda la redacción a sus amigos políticos* (Cali: Imprenta de Hurtado, 1870), p. 79.

100. *Diario Oficial*, 1 April 1872.

101. [Manuel Murillo Toro], *Mensaje del Presidente de la Unión al Congreso* (Bogotá, 4 April 1872). According to the president's figures, the foreign debt had a par value of $33,362,750; 37.5 units of the customs revenue had been assigned for payment of interest and amortization. In 1872 a convention was negotiated with the representatives of the foreign creditors which provided for the emission of $10 million in new bonds, for which the old documents were to be exchanged and which were to pay an annual interest rate of 4.5 percent for the first five years and 4.75 percent thereafter. President Murillo reported that he was "very happy" about this agreement. "It singularly clarifies the fiscal situation and allows us to obtain capital in Europe for the construction of railroads." See Murillo to Buenaventura Correoso, 16 August 1872 (AC).

102. *Diario Oficial*, 10 June 1872.

103. *El Bien Público*, 26 April 1872. See also ibid., 23 April 1872.

104. *Diario Oficial*, 3 May 1872.

105. *El Bien Público*, 7 May 1872.

106. *El Tradicionista*, 7 May 1872; *El Heraldo*, 7 June 1872.

107. *El Tradicionista*, 30 April 1872.

108. *El Heraldo*, 3 May 1872. See also ibid., 26 April, 17 May 1872.

109. *El Tradicionista*, 23 April 1872. See also ibid., 30 April 1872.

110. *El Bien Público*, 4 June 1872.

111. Ibid., 11 June, 14 June 1872.

112. Medardo Rivas, *Carácter social de la lei sobre crédito público* (Bogotá: Imprenta de Medardo Rivas, 1872), p. 6.

113. *El Tradicionista*, 13 June 1872.

114. *Mensaje del Presidente 1874*.

Chapter 5

1. Leslie Lipson, *The Democratic Civilization* (New York: Oxford University Press, 1964), p. 317.

2. Karen L. Remmer, "The Timing, Pace and Sequence of Political Change in Chile," *Hispanic American Historical Review*, 57 (May 1977):207n. According to Remmer, party as presented here "could be something short of a mass-based organization, but it would be more than a faction, interest group, or formless opinion aggregate."

3. *La Unión*, 21 June 1881.

4. [Carlos Martín], *Memoria del secretario de lo interior y relaciones esteriores de los Estados Unidos de Colombia al Congreso Federal de 1868* (Bogotá: Imprenta de la Nación, 1868), pp. lv–lvii.
5. *Diario Oficial*, 27 April 1871.
6. Ibid., 18 May, 19 May 1871.
7. Ibid., 22 May 1871.
8. Aquileo Parra, *Memorias* (Bogotá: Imprenta de "La Luz," 1912), pp. 571–79; Enrique Pérez, *Vida de Felipe Pérez* (Bogotá: Imprenta de "La Luz," 1911), pp. 176–77.
9. *La América*, 14 May, 4 June 1873; *Diario de Cundinamarca*, 13 June, 15 August 1873.
10. Manuel Briceño, *La revolución (1876–1877): Recuerdos para la historia*, Biblioteca de Historial Nacional, 2d ed. (Bogotá: Imprenta Nacional, 1947), p. 61.
11. Ernest Dichman to William Evarts, #228, 12 November 1880, in *Diplomatic Despatches*.
12. These figures are based on figures in the federal budget and in annual acts of Congress fixing the size of the army. See *Constitución i leyes de los Estados Unidos de Colombia espedidas en los años de 1863 a 1875*, 2 vols. (Bogotá: Imprenta de Medardo Rivas, 1875), passim.
13. U.S., "Papers Relating to the Foreign Relations of the United States," *Executive Documents of the House of Representatives for the First Session of the Forty-Seventh Congress, 1881–1882* (Washington: Government Printing Office, 1882), 1:345; William L. Scruggs to Hamilton Fish, #27, 7 January 1874, and enc. A and B, in *Diplomatic Despatches*.
14. William Scruggs to Secretary of State, #98, 18 April 1875, in *Diplomatic Despatches*.
15. U.S., "Papers," 1882, p. 346.
16. William L. Scruggs, *The Colombian and Venezuelan Republics, with Notes on Other Parts of Central and South America* (Boston: Little, Brown and Company, 1905), p. 150; Gabriel Jiménez Molinares, *Linajes cartageneros*, 2 vols. (Cartagena: Imprenta Departamental, 1950–58), 2:116–19.
17. U.S., "Papers," 1882, p. 347.
18. Murillo to Correoso, 4 August 1872, and Correoso to Murillo, 22 August [1872] (AC).
19. José María Cordovez Moure, *Reminiscencias: Recuerdos autobiográficos* (Bogotá: Librería Americana, 1922), pp. 329–30.
20. *Star and Herald*, 11 March 1865.
21. Ernest Dichman to William Evarts, unnumbered, 20 August 1878, in *Diplomatic Despatches*.
22. Allan Burton to William Seward, #142, 3 January 1865, in *Diplomatic Despatches*.
23. Carlos Martínez Silva, "Revista del mes," *Repertorio Colombiano* 2 (June 1879):469.
24. *El Heraldo*, 11 August 1871. See also *El Tradicionista*, 6 August 1872.
25. *La Opinión*, 25 January 1865.
26. Ibid.; ibid., 21 July 1863.
27. Ibid., 7 September 1864, 25 January 1865.
28. *El Liberal*, 3 June, 26 July 1870.

29. Antonio Nieto M. to Aquileo Parra, 16 May 1876 (Ms. #1, BL-AA).
30. Cf. *Diario de Cundinamarca,* 14 June, 4 July 1879; *La Reforma,* 24 June, 12 July 1879.
31. José María Samper to Antonio B. Cuervo, 11 January 1881 (Ms.#31, BL-AA).
32. Malcolm Deas, "Algunas notas sobre la historia del caciquismo en Colombia," *Revista de Occidente,* 2d ser., 43 (October–December 1973):132.
33. *La Alianza,* 14 June 1867.
34. Contemporaries were far less consistent in applying the Radical label than modern writers would suggest, and the name *Gólgota* was used at least as often as Radical long after the 1850s. For the sake of clarity, however, Radical will be used in this chapter wherever possible.
35. Mosquera's defense of the contract can be found in *Diario Oficial,* 1 June, 5 June 1866. For the arguments of those who opposed the loan, see *A la nación: Manifiesto de los senadores i representantes que votaron en contra del contrato de empréstito de $7,500,000* (Bogotá: Imprenta de Gaitán, 1866). Other documents describing the events of 1866–1867 are in *Causa contra el Presidente de los Estados Unidos de Colombia, ciudadano gran jeneral Tomás Cipriano de Mosquera i otros altos funcionarios federales* (Bogotá: Imprenta Oficial, 1867).
36. Eustorgio Salgar, Colombian minister to the United States, purchased the warship *Rayo* (formerly the *R. R. Cuyler*) after the signing of the secret treaty between Peru and Colombia on 28 August 1866. The *Rayo* was detained in New York at the request of Spanish officials but was released when Salgar gave assurances that it was the property of the Colombian government. However, on 27 March 1867 Secretary of the Treasury Froilán Largacha stated that the *Rayo* was the personal property of President Mosquera. Upon arriving at Cartagena, the *Rayo* was seized by a Spanish man-of-war as a Chilean or Peruvian privateer (*Star and Herald,* 25 May 1867).
37. *Diario Oficial,* 3 July 1867.
38. Santos Acosta was the second *designado.* The first *designado,* Santos Gutiérrez, was not in Colombia at the time of Mosquera's deposition.
39. *Causa,* p. 813; Pablo E. Cárdenas Acosta, "La restauración constitucional de 1867," *Boletín de Historia y Antigüedades* 44 (President 1957):594–96. Mosquera took advantage of an amnesty law passed in November 1867 which permitted him to spend three years in exile instead of two years in prison. As his period of exile drew to a close, he expressed fear that "the circle of traitors of May 23" might prevent his return to Colombia or even plot to assassinate him. See Mosquera to Correoso, 13 September, 13 October 1870 (AC). On 20 December 1870, however, he reported that President Salgar had assured him that he would encounter no difficulty in returning to Colombia (Mosquera to Correoso, 20 December 1870, AC).
40. R[afael] Rocha Gutiérrez, *La verdadera y la falsa democracia: Doctrina constitucional y proyecto de constitución política para la república de Colombia* (Paris: Garnier Hermanos, Libreros-Editores, 1887), p. 19.
41. A[belardo] A[ldana], *La protesta* (Bogotá, 14 September 1867).
42. Indalecio Liévano Aguirre, *El proceso de Mosquera ante el Senado* (Bogotá: Editorial Revista Colombiana, 1966), pp. 61ff.
43. Miguel Urrutia and Mario Arrubla, eds., *Compendio de estadísticas his-*

tóricas de Colombia (Bogotá: Dirección de Divulgación Cultural, Universidad Nacional de Colombia, 1970), p. 310.

44. Mosquera to Correoso, 14 September 1868 (AC). Mosquera's reference to the return of Panama to native rule was probably occasioned by the recent death of Vicente Olarte Galindo, a Santandereano who had become president of Panama on 1 October 1866. His sudden death on 3 March 1868, supposedly of yellow fever, gave rise to the rumor that he had been poisoned. See *Star and Herald*, 5 March, 7 March, 12 March 1868; Núñez, *Reforma* [1885], pp. 750–51.

45. Mosquera to Correoso, 30 October 1871 (AC).

46. Mosquera to Correoso, 31 July 1871 (ibid.).

47. Burton, #72, 8 March 1863, in *Diplomatic Despatches*.

48. *Cinco documentos relativos al triunfo obtenido por la revolución que en el Estado Soberano de Antioquia derrocó al gobierno del Señor Pascual Bravo y sustituyó el provisorio a cuya cabeza se puso el Señor Pedro Justo Berrío* (1864); Salvador Camacho Roldán, *Escritos varios*, 3 vols. (Bogotá: Librería Colombiana, 1892–95), 3:508–21; *El Tiempo*, 24 February 1864.

49. Estanislao Gómez Barrientos, *Páginas de historia: 25 años a través del Estado de Antioquia* (Medellín: Tip. de San Antonio, 1918), 1:26; Joaquín Emilio Jaramillo, *Vida de Pedro Justo Berrío* (Medellín: Imprenta Oficial, 1927), pp. 71–77.

50. *Reconocimiento del nuevo gobierno de Antioquia* (Imprenta de la Nación).

51. Eduardo Rodríguez Piñeres, "Páginas olvidadas en 'El Olimpo Radical': La liga de 1869," *Boletín de Historia y Antigüedades* 38 (April–June 1951):254.

52. *El Correo de Antioquia*, 3 March 1875. See also *Corona fúnebre del doctor Pedro J. Berrío* (Medellín: Imprenta del Estado, 1875).

53. Gómez Barrientos, *25 años*, 1:70.

54. Jaramillo, *Berrío*, pp. 104ff.

55. *El Heraldo*, 5 April, 26 April 1872.

56. Ibid., 1 May 1874.

57. Ibid., 8 May 1874.

58. Ibid., 22 May 1874.

59. "Diario de Quijano Otero," *Boletín de Historia y Antigüedades* 19 (1932):369.

60. [Pedro Justo Berrío], *Mensaje del Presidente a la legislatura del Estado Soberano de Antioquia* (Medellín: Imprenta del Estado, 1873), p. iv.

61. The conflict between Ignacio Gutiérrez Vergara and the state legislature and its denouement can be traced in *Manifiesto del Ministerio del Gobierno Nacional sobre los acontecimientos del 9 i 10 de octubre* (Bogotá: Medardo Rivas, 1868), and Carlos Holguín, *Cartas políticas publicadas en "El Correo Nacional"* (Bogotá: Biblioteca Popular de Cultura Colombiana, 1951).

62. Holguín, *Cartas*, pp. 115–17.

63. Rodríguez Piñeres, "Páginas," pp. 260–62. The text of the agreement was not published until August 26.

64. Mosquera to Correoso, 12 February 1870 (AC).

65. Rodríguez Piñeres, "Paginas," pp. 266–67.

66. *Star and Herald*, 5 January 1869.

67. Holguín, *Cartas*, pp. 117–18.

68. Besides Mosquera, the only President who failed to complete his term was

Francisco Javier Zaldúa, who died in office and was succeeded by *designado* José Eusebio Otálora.

69. *El Patriota,* 14 October 1873.
70. *El Estandarte,* 30 November 1882.
71. *Diario de Cundinamarca,* 27 March 1873.
72. Ibid.; Miguel Cané, *Notas de viaje sobre Venezuela y Colombia* (Bogotá: Imprenta de "La Luz," 1907), pp. 150–53.
73. Camacho Roldán, *Escritos,* 3:546–52.
74. For example, a newspaper supporting the gubernatorial candidacy of Eustorgio Salgar in Cundinamarca in 1873 charged that many Liberals had indicated their willingness to back the rival candidacy of Octavio Salazar because the latter's supporters had "gotten up early" and claimed that he would be the only candidate. After Salgar had agreed to run, the newspaper asserted, there had been many defections from the Salazar ranks. See *El Patriota,* 8 July 1873.
75. Parra, *Memorias,* pp. 542–43.
76. Eustorgio Salgar to Correoso, 1 April 1871 (AC). According to an editorial in *El Liberal* (7 February 1871), Murillo's name had been proposed only after Camacho Roldán had declined to run. Parra also indicates that Camacho Roldán withdrew from the race (*Memorias,* p. 595).
77. Murillo to Correoso, 4 August 1872 (AC).
78. Murillo to Correoso, 8 October 1872 (ibid.). Carlos Martín was named minister to the United States in 1872 and did not return to Colombia until 1874.
79. *Diario de Cundinamarca,* 9 January 1873.
80. Cf. *La Palestra,* 21 October 1872.
81. *Diario de Cundinamarca,* 4 November 1872.
82. *La América,* 20 November, 25 December, 1872.
83. Parra, *Memorias,* pp. 665–66. See also Eduardo Rodríguez Piñeres, "La gran derrota de Rafael Núñez: La revolución de 1875," *Revista de América* (September 1947), pp. 328–29.
84. S. A. Hurlburt to President Ulysses S. Grant, 14 July 1870, in *Diplomatic Despatches.*
85. According to Medardo Rivas (*Revista de Colombia,* 21 February 1873), Carlos Martín had been his first choice for the presidency, but he later concluded that his candidacy might sow dissension in the Liberal party; the latter statement may have been an allusion to Martín's prominent role in the conspiracy that led to the deposition of Mosquera in 1867. However, Santiago Pérez had also fought Mosquera. See also *La América,* 30 March 1874, and Cordovez Moure, *Recuerdos,* pp. 329–30.
86. *El Tradicionista,* 2 January 1873.
87. *Diario de Cundinamarca,* 24 January 1873.
88. *La Unión Liberal* (Cartagena), 10 May 1866.
89. *El Patriota,* 17 June 1873.
90. Ibid., 8 July 1873.
91. *La Paz,* 19 June 1868.
92. *Diario de Cundinamarca,* 15 March 1873.
93. *El Bien Público,* 21 February 1871.
94. *El Patriota,* 23 September 1873.
95. Ibid., 11 November 1873.

96. *La Opinión*, 7 July 1863.
97. *Diario de Cundinamarca*, 19 June 1873.
98. *El Tradicionista*, 4 March 1873.
99. *El Patriota*, 9 September, 11 November 1873.
100. Murillo named Santo Domingo Vila secretary of the treasury, but the appointment was rejected by the Senate. See *El Deber*, 6 May 1881; Parra, *Memorias*, pp. 598, 613.
101. Juan H. Jiménez to Luis María Cuervo, 28 April 1856 (Ms. #66, BL-AA).
102. In 1873 in both Cauca and Bolívar magistrates to the state superior courts were also popularly elected.
103. Title III, Articles 13 and 14, of the state constitution, printed in *Recopilación de leyes del Estado Soberano de Boyacá* (Tunja: Imprenta de Torres Hermanos i Cia., 1873).
104. Title 3, Articles 8 and 9, of the state constitution, printed in *Constitución i leyes de la convención de Cundinamarca espedidas en sus sesiones del presente año* (Bogotá: Imprenta de Gaitán, 1870).
105. Title IV, Article 15, of the state constitution, printed in *Constitución, leyes i decretos expedidos por la Asamblea Constituyente del Estado Soberano de Antioquia, en los años de 1864 i 1865* (Medellín: Imprenta de Isidoro Isaza, 1865); Title 3, Article 10, of the state constitution, printed in *Constitución, leyes y decretos expedidos por la Asamblea Constituyente del Tolima en sus sesiones de 1870* (Bogotá: Foción Mantilla, editor, 1871).
106. *Recopilación Boyacá*, pp. 1–4.
107. *Gaceta de Bolívar* (Cartagena), 13 November 1870.
108. *Recopilación Boyacá*, pp. 1–4.
109. *Gaceta del Magdalena* (Santa Marta), 27 January 1873.
110. The official record of the imaginary meeting to which Macías referred appeared ibid., 13 May 1872.
111. *Diario de Cundinamarca*, 6 August 1873.
112. *Recopilación de leyes del Estado Soberano del Cauca: Código Administrativo* (Popayán: Imprenta del Estado, 1879), pp. 14–15.
113. *El Boyacense* (Tunja), 20 November 1873.
114. Chapter 7, Articles 40–44, of Electoral Code 39 in *Constitución Antioquia*.
115. *Recopilación Boyacá*, pp. 1–4.
116. Ibid., pp. 4–12.
117. *Diario de Cundinamarca*, 29 July 1873.
118. Thomas M. Dawson, #55, 23 August 1883, and #64, 11 September 1883, in *Despatches Barranquilla*.
119. Camacho Roldán, *Escritos*, 3:739.
120. Nepomuceno J. Navarro, *Flores del campo. Colección de producciones literarias* (Socorro: Imprenta del Estado, 1871), pp. 23ff. The author was himself a Liberal politician.
121. Ernst Röthlisberger, *El Dorado: Estampas de viaje y cultura de la Colombia suramericana*, Archivo de la Economía Nacional (Bogotá: Banco de la República, 1963), pp. 118–20.
122. *Correo Mercantil*, 8 September 1883.
123. The figures given here were compiled and made available to the author by Professor David Bushnell, Department of History, University of Florida.

124. *Recopilación Boyacá*, pp. 4–12.
125. *El Patriota*, 18 November 1873.

Chapter 6

1. *Estrella de Panamá*, 24 December 1874.
2. *El Progreso* (Panama), 24 January 1875.
3. *Diario de Cundinamarca*, 3 March 1875.
4. James Park, "Rafael Núñez and the Politics of Colombian Regionalism, 1875–1885" (Ph.D. dissertation, University of Kansas, 1975), p. 120.
5. Mosquera to Conto, 2 December 1874 (Ms. #113, BL-AA).
6. Mosquera to Conto, 13 January 1875 (ibid.).
7. Murillo, who had been on a diplomatic assignment in Caracas, returned to Colombia in late March 1875, presumably to work on behalf of Parra. See *El Elector Nacional* (Barranquilla), 5 April, 3 June 1875.
8. Ibid., 26 June 1876.
9. On the 1873 elections in Boyacá, see the manifesto of nine Trujillista members of the state assembly in *La América*, 31 October 1873, and a statement by José Eusebio Otálora, ibid., 27 November 1873.
10. Murillo to Parra, 22 January 1872 (CAP).
11. *Diario Oficial*, 30 April 1872. To justify federal action, Murillo cited Article 17, clause 6, of the Rionegro constitution, which gave to the federal government jurisdiction over inter-oceanic routes of communications.
12. Scruggs to Hamilton Fish, #45, 10 July 1874, in *Diplomatic Despatches*.
13. *Diario de Cundinamarca*, 2 June 1873.
14. Ibid., 30 June 1874.
15. Ibid., 18 August 1880; [Aquileo Parra], *Memoria del secretario de hacienda i fomento dirijida al Presidente de la República para el Congreso de 1873* (Bogotá: Imprenta de Gaitán, 1873), pp. 88–89.
16. Aquileo Parra, *Memorias* (Bogotá: Imprenta de "La Luz," 1912), pp. 638–48. For a discussion of the attempts to open a road from Vélez to the Carare River, see David Church Johnson, "Social and Economic Change in Nineteenth Century Santander, Colombia" (Ph.D. dissertation, University of California, Berkeley, 1975), pp. 283–89.
17. The newspaper was *El Ferrocarril del Norte* of Duitama.
18. Salvador Camacho Roldán, *Escritos varios*, 3 vols. (Bogotá: Librería Colombiana, 1892–1895), 3:31–90.
19. *El Telégrafo* (Palmira), 13 May 1875; see also ibid., 25 March 1875.
20. *El Correo de Colombia* (Bogotá), 3 February 1875.
21. James H. Neal, "The Pacific Age Comes to Colombia: The Construction of the Cali-Buenaventura Route, 1854–1882" (Ph.D. dissertation, Vanderbilt University, 1971), p. 191. On 6 July 1872 the Colombian government signed a contract with David R. Smith and Frank Modica for construction of a railroad between Buenaventura and the Cauca Valley. The contract was cancelled in 1874 when the promoters failed to carry out its provisions. A similar contract signed on 17 December 1874 with Charles S. Brown was rescinded for the same reason (ibid., pp. 171–81).
22. Park, "Regionalism," p. 67.

23. Public works legislation between 1864 and 1874 is discussed ibid., pp. 80–87.
24. See ibid., pp. 66–67, and Tables C (p. 70) and I (p. 253).
25. Ibid., pp. 79–80; Neal, "Cauca," pp. 130–31.
26. Park, "Regionalism," pp. 80–81; Theodore E. Nichols, "The Caribbean Gateway to Colombia: Cartagena, Santa Marta, and Barranquilla and Their Connections with the Interior" (Ph.D. dissertation, University of California, Berkeley, 1951), pp. 149ff.
27. "Diario de Quijano Otero," *Boletín de Historia y Antigüedades* 19 (1932):400.
28. *Diario de Cundinamarca*, 25 January 1875.
29. *La Luz* (Bogotá), 15 November 1881, reprinted in Rafael Núñez, *La reforma política en Colombia*, 1 (Bogotá: Imprenta Nacional, 1944):part 1, 81.
30. José Ramón Vergara, *Escrutinio histórico: Rafael Núñez* (Bogotá: Editorial A B C, 1939), p. 176.
31. Parra, *Memorias*, pp. 685–88.
32. Núñez to Parra, 3 January 1877, and 6 September 1877 (CAP).
33. Núñez to Miguel Camacho Roldán, 3 October 1866, and Núñez to Luis Carlos Rico, 29 May 1876 (Ms. #99, BL-AA).
34. The Parristas, with their home states if known, were Parra himself (Santander), Sergio Camargo (Boyacá), Gil Colunje (Panama), César Conto (Cauca), Felipe Pérez (Boyacá), Antonio María Pradilla (Santander), Medardo Rivas (Cundinamarca), Januario Salgar (unknown), and Felipe Zapata (Santander). The Nuñistas were Manuel Amador Fierro (Bolívar), Salvador Camacho Roldán (Cundinamarca), Narciso González Lineros (Santander), and Eustorgio Salgar (Cundinamarca/Santander). The preferences of two other cabinet members, Francisco Agudelo and José M. Caro, could not be determined.
35. *La Unión Colombiana*, 24 March 1875, and *El Correo de Colombia*, 10 March 1875.
36. *El Correo de Colombia*, 12 May 1875.
37. Antonio Pérez Aguirre, *25 años de historia colombiana, 1853 a 1878: Del centralismo a la federación*, Biblioteca Eduardo Santos (Bogotá: Editorial Sucre, 1959), p. 363.
38. Mosquera to Conto, 28 October 1874, and 12 December 1874 (Ms.#113, BL-AA).
39. *El Correo de Colombia*, 20 January, 3 February 1875.
40. Gustavo Otero Muñoz, *Un hombre y una época: La vida azarosa de Rafael Núñez*, Biblioteca de Historia Nacional (Bogotá: Editorial A B C, 1951), pp. 58–63; Park, "Regionalism," pp. 136–37.
41. The balloting in Congress was a confusing affair, complicated by the appearance of rival delegations from Cundinamarca and Panama, as well as an additional representative from Magdalena, the state government of which was controlled by Parristas. Before the vote by the individual senators and representatives took place on 22 February, the pro-Parra delegation from Cundinamarca was admitted as was the additional Magdalena representative. The senators from both Panamanian delegations were rejected, but the Chamber delegation with a Nuñista majority was admitted. The proceedings were further enlivened by a boycott of Congress by the Conservative members, who persuaded the divided Cauca delega-

tion to join them briefly in order to prevent a quorum. According to José María Quijano Wallis, who was a member of that delegation, the Caucanos decided to return when they realized that the boycott was futile since Parra, who was first *designado,* would assume the presidency if no successor to Pérez could be chosen. In addition, the Parristas made certain promises to the Caucanos, including a pledge to send federal troops to the state in the event of a revolution there. Parra received the votes of the delegations from Santander, Boyacá, Cundinamarca, and Magdalena, as well as two votes from Panama and four from Cauca. Núñez received the votes of Bolívar as well as eight from Cauca and three from Panama. The Conservative members from Antioquia and Tolima voted for Calvo. This account has been pieced together from reports in the *Diario de Cundinamarca* (29 January, 14 February, 15 February, 26 February, and 16–21 March 1876) and *El Tradicionista* (15 February, 18 February, 22 February 1876) as well as from José María Quijano Wallis, *Memorias autobiográficas histórico-políticas y de carácter social* (Grottaferrata, Italy: Tipografía italo-orientale, 1919), pp. 248–58.

42. The revolution of 1876–77 is described from the Conservative point of view in Manuel Briceño, *La revolución (1876–1877): Recuerdos para la historia,* Biblioteca de Historia Nacional, 2d ed. (Bogotá: Imprenta Nacional, 1947), and from the Liberal point of view in Constancio Franco V., *Apuntamientos para la historia: La guerra de 1876 i 1877* (Bogotá: Imprenta de La Epoca, 1877). A modern account appears in Park, "Regionalism," pp. 148–85.

43. For the federal government's efforts on behalf of primary education and the Conservative-clerical reaction, see Enrique Cortés, *Escritos varios,* 2 vols. (Paris: Imprenta Sudamericana, 1896), 1:79–185; Ramón Zapata, *Dámaso Zapata o la reforma educacionista en Colombia* (Bogotá: El Gráfico Editores Ltda., 1960); Jane Meyer Loy, "Modernization and Educational Reform in Colombia, 1863–1886" (Ph.D. dissertation, University of Wisconsin, 1969) and idem, "Primary Education during the Colombian Federation: The School Reform of 1870," *Hispanic American Historical Review* 51 (1971):275–94.

44. Archbishop Arbeláez to José Telésforo Paúl, bishop of Panama, 17 June 1876 (Ms.#97, BL-AA); José Restrepo Posada, *Arquidiócesis de Bogotá: Datos biográficos de sus prelados,* vol. 3, *1868–1891,* Biblioteca de Historia Eclesiástica "Fernando Caycedo y Florez" (Bogotá: Editorial Lumen Christi, 1966), pp. 109–310, passim.

45. Quijano Wallis, *Memorias,* pp. 213–19. See also the reports (29 April and 10 May 1876) of Dámaso Zapata sent by Parra to investigate the situation in Cauca (CAP).

46. Conto to Parra, 15 March 1876 (ibid.).

47. The two Nuñistas referred to were Solón Wilches and Pablo Arosemena. For the former, see Gustavo Otero Muñoz, *Wilches y su época,* Biblioteca Santander (Bucaramanga: Imprenta del Departamento, 1936), pp. 239–43, and for the latter, see Briceño, *Revolución,* p. 181. See also "Diario de Quijano Otero," p. 587.

48. [Carlos N. Rodríguez], *Memoria del secretario de lo interior i relaciones esteriores de los Estados Unidos de Colombia al Congreso de 1877,* 2d ed. (Bogotá: Imprenta de Rafael Pérez, 1877), p. 37–38.

49. Mosquera to Parra, 1 January 1877 (CAP).

50. *Diario Oficial,* 17 May 1877.

51. Ibid., 18 May 1877.
52. Restrepo Posada, *Arquidiócesis*, 3:318–23.
53. *Diario Oficial*, 27 April 1877.
54. *Diario de Cundinamarca*, 12 June 1877.
55. Juan Pablo Restrepo, *La Iglesia y el Estado en Colombia* (London: Emiliano Isaza, 1885), pp. 612ff.; Gonzalo Uribe V., *Los arzobispos y obispos colombianos desde el tiempo de la colonia hasta nuestros días* (Bogotá: Imprenta de la Sociedad, 1918), pp. 84–91; Conto to Parra, 20 February 1877 (CAP).
56. On forced loans in 1876–77, see *Diario de Cundinamarca*, 5 June, 21 June 1877; Briceño, *Revolución*, pp. 265–69; Miguel Samper, *Escritos político-económicos*, 4 vols. (Bogotá: Editorial de Cromos, 1925–27), 2:401–13; J. D. Monsalve, *Biografía del Doctor Luis María Restrepo y datos sobre la revolución de Antioquia (1876–1877)* (Bogotá: Imprenta de Antonio María Silvestre, 1892), pp. 40–43.
57. *La Luz*, 2 May 1882.
58. Ibid., 1 August 1882, reprinted in Núñez, *Reforma*, vol. 1:part 1, 251.
59. On economic conditions in Cauca, see Trujillo to Parra, 21 April 1877, and 23 October 1877 (CAP); *La Reforma*, 16 October 1878.
60. See the series of letters from Mosquera to Parra, 7 September 1877 to 7 November 1877, dealing with conditions in Cauca in CAP. Mosquera died in 1878 at the age of eighty.
61. *El Relator*, 24 July 1877.
62. Ibid.
63. Ibid., 11 September 1877.
64. Ibid., 9 October 1877.
65. Garcés to Parra, 19 September 1877 (CAP). See also 11 September 1877 and 24 October 1877 (ibid.).
66. Vergara, *Escrutinio*, pp. 190–94.
67. *Diario Oficial*, 29 April 1878.
68. First of all, the Carare River route was abandoned on the advice of a foreign engineer, Henry F. Ross, who recommended that the railroad be built northward from Bogotá to Paturia on the Magdalena River by way of the city of Bucaramanga. On 9 June 1876 President Parra informed Congress of Ross's findings and reported that Ross believed that he could raise funds in Europe for construction of the railroad via the Paturia route (*Diario de Cundinamarca*, 13 June 1876, 18 August 1880). On 18 April 1877 a bill providing for the immediate dissolution and liquidation of the national company formed in 1875 for construction of the railroad was introduced in the Chamber of Representatives. The preamble stated that further investment of public funds in the project was unwise because of the penury of the federal treasury and because of Ross's adverse report on the Carare route. All but one of the bill's seventeen sponsors were from the coastal states, Cauca, or Tolima; the lone exception was Aníbal Galindo, who represented Cundinamarca but was a native of Tolima (*Diario Oficial*, 3 May, 14 May 1877; *Diario de Cundinamarca*, 1 May 1877). As a result of this development, Parra addressed a message to the Chamber of Representatives on 3 May 1877, in which he reiterated his support for the railroad project, "on which the hopes of future prosperity of the states of the Interior are pinned," regardless of the route chosen. The bill was amended to permit the president to negotiate new contracts for construction of the railroad along the route deemed most suitable and was

approved by narrow margins in both houses of Congress, becoming Law 42 of 18 May 1877 (*Diario Oficial,* 4 May, 18 May, 19 May, 22 May, 23 May, 25 May 1877). On 24 September 1877 the federal government signed a contract with Ross, who pledged to raise capital to build the railroad, which now became known as the Central Railroad. He later requested and received a six-month extension which expired on 24 November 1878. A request for another six-month extension was turned down by the Trujillo administration (*Diario de Cundinamarca,* 26 November 1878; *El Relator,* 6 December 1878).

69. Park, "Regionalism," p. 196.

70. J. Fred Rippy, "Dawn of the Railway Era in Colombia," *Hispanic American Historical Review* 23 (November 1943):655. The Girardot Railway was begun by the Cuban entrepreneur Francisco Javier Cisneros, who took on the assignment at the personal request of President Núñez. See Hernan Horna, "Francisco Javier Cisneros: A Pioneer in Transportation and Economic Development in Colombia" (Ph.D. dissertation, Vanderbilt University, 1970), pp. 218ff.

71. *La Reforma,* 8 May 1878.

72. Ibid.

73. *Diario Oficial,* 10 March, 27 April 1877.

74. Ricardo Becerra, *El liberalismo en Colombia i sus detractores de por acá* (Bogotá: Imprenta de Gaitán, 1877), p. 3.

75. *La Reforma,* 18 May 1878.

76. Ibid., 28 September 1878.

77. [Julián Trujillo], *Mensaje del presidente de los Estados Unidos de Colombia al Congreso de 1879* (Bogotá: Imprenta de Echeverría Hermanos, 1879), pp. 7–8.

78. Aurelio González Toledo, *El General Eliseo Payán* (Bogotá: Imprenta de "La Luz," 1887), pp. 101–02.

79. *Diario de Cundinamarca,* 9 April 1880.

80. David Bushnell, "Two Stages in Colombian Tariff Policy: The Radical Era and the Return to Protection (1861–1885)," *Inter-American Economic Affairs* 9 (Spring 1956):17–18. See also *La Defensa,* 27 May 1880, and Samper, *Escritos,* 1:195–291.

81. By 1881, there were 42 banks in Colombia, 12 of them in Cundinamarca and 11 in Antioquia (Camacho Roldán, *Escritos,* 2:338–39). A sample of Radical objections to the national bank can be found in *La Defensa,* 16 April 1880, and *Diario de Cundinamarca,* 23 June 1880.

82. For economic conditions in Colombia at this time, see Camacho Roldán, *Escritos,* 1:665–74; Luis Ospina Vásquez, *Industria y protección en Colombia, 1810–1930* (Medellín: E. S. F., 1955), p. 276; Frank Robinson Safford, "Commerce and Enterprise in Central Colombia, 1821–1870" (Ph.D. dissertation, Columbia University, 1965), pp. 282–83, 291–92; Robert Carlyle Beyer, "The Colombian Coffee Industry: Origins and Major Trends" (Ph.D. dissertation, University of Minnesota, 1947), pp. 114–15, 117; Carlos Calderón, *La cuestión monetaria en Colombia* (Madrid: Tipografía de la "Revista de Archivos," 1905), pp. 46–55.

83. *Diario Oficial,* 30 August 1884.

84. See, e.g., *La Tira* (Bogotá), 25 January, 31 January 1882, and *Diario de Cundinamarca,* 7 February 1882. See also Park, "Regionalism," p. 281.

85. *La Tira,* 31 January 1882.

86. *La Luz,* 15 November 1881.

87. Dichman to William Evarts, #201, 23 August 1880, in *Diplomatic Despatches*. In addition, as governor of Bolívar and senator from that state in the late 1870s, Núñez had worked successfully for the reopening of the Cartagena *dique*. See Park, "Regionalism," pp. 200–03.

88. *Diario Oficial*, 11 August 1884.

89. Otálora, the second *designado*, became chief executive after the death of Francisco Javier Zaldúa on 21 December 1882, in order to allow Núñez, the first *designado*, to remain eligible to succeed to the presidency in 1884, for Article 75 of the constitution forbade the election of anyone who had served as president during the preceding term. The fact that Otálora contemplated a bid for the presidency, despite the questionable constitutionality of such a step and in defiance of his understanding with Núñez, outraged the Independents, who retaliated with bitter attacks in Congress. Otálora died suddenly on 8 May 1884. On the Otálora candidacy, see Park, "Regionalism," pp. 322-26; [José Eusebio Otálora], *Informe del Presidente de la Unión a las Cámaras Legislativas en sus sesiones de 1884* (Bogotá: Imprenta de Vapor de Zalamea Hermanos, n.d.), pp. 14–18; *El Conservador*, 31 March, 5 April, 17 April, 1 May, 5 June 1883; Jacobo Sánchez to Parra, 30 July, 3 August, 6 August 1883 (CAP). Wilches and Núñez had been at odds for several years. An important element in their quarrel was a controversy between the state and federal governments over the disposition of public lands (*tierras baldías*) in Santander rich in cinchona bark. Wilches's differences with Núñez are discussed in Otero Muñoz, *Wilches*, pp. 364ff., and Park, "Regionalism," pp. 282–92. On the Wilches candidacy, see Otero Muñoz, *Wilches*, pp. 381–82.

90. Samper, *Escritos*, 3:11–96.

91. See, e.g., the editorials in *La Ley* (Bogotá), 25 April, 28 April 1876, which was edited by José María Samper, who envisioned a new party made up of Conservatives and "republican" Liberals. By 1878, however, Samper had become a Conservative.

92. For an expression of Holguín and Cuervo's thoughts on this matter, see their joint address to the Conservative convention of 1879 in Ms. #30, BL-AA.

93. *El Deber*, 2 May, 16 September, 19 October 1879; [Carlos Martínez Silva], "Revista política," *El Repertorio Colombiano* 2 (June 1879):474; *El Conservador*, 24 April 1883.

94. Núñez to Juan de Dios Restrepo, 8 July 1876 (Ms. #99, BL-AA).

95. *La Defensa*, 29 July 1880.

96. Quijano Wallis, *Memorias*, pp. 412–16; *La Unión*, 13 May 1881; Martínez Silva, "Revista política," *Repertorio Colombiano* 6 (April 1881):312–15; "Cartas del Doctor Núñez," *Boletín de Historia y Antigüedades* 34 (January–March 1947):26–27.

97. *La Unión*, 13 May 1881.

98. Cf. letters to Parra from José del Carmen Rodríguez, 26 April 1879; Nicolás Fajardo, Lope Landaeta, et. al., 27 April 1882; and Jacobo Sánchez, 22 July 1883 (CAP).

99. *La Defensa*, 26 August 1880.

100. *La Unión*, 23 August 1881.

101. Santiago Pérez, Januario Salgar, Luis A. Robles, and Temístocles Paredes were the other members. See the notification to Parra of his appointment, 1 October 1884, in CAP.

102. *La Unión*, 21 June 1881.
103. *Diario de Cundinamarca*, 6 January 1882.
104. Ibid.; ibid., 17 January 1882.
105. Martínez Silva, "Revista política," *Repertorio Colombiano* 9 (July–December 1882):88, 255.
106. *Cuadro general de los funcionarios del Partido Conservador de Colombia, elegidos por la Convención Nacional* (Ms.#30, BL-AA); *El Deber*, 2 May 1879.
107. *El Deber*, 20 May, 27 May 1879.
108. Ibid., 15 October 1878. The program was drafted by José María Samper, the founder of *El Deber*, and was endorsed by Antonio B. Cuervo, Carlos Holguín, Carlos Martínez Silva, and many other prominent Conservatives.
109. Park, "Regionalism," pp. 331–32.
110. Martínez Silva, "Revista política," *Repertorio Colombiano* 11 (March–August 1884):163–64, 245.
111. The Independent appointees were Felipe Angulo and José María Campo Serrano; the Conservatives were Mariano Tanco and Vicente Restrepo. Justo Arosemena, a respected Liberal not strongly identified with either faction, was named secretary of public instruction, but he refused the appointment. See *La Actualidad*, 14 August 1884; Park, "Regionalism," p. 357; Octavio Méndez Pereira, *Justo Arosemena* (Panama: Imprenta Nacional, 1919), pp. 501–02.
112. Vergara, *Escrutinio*, p. 209. Dolores Gallegos apparently obtained a divorce from Núñez in 1871. See Rafael Serrano Camargo, *El Regenerador. Vida, genio y estampa de Rafael Núñez* (Bogotá: Ediciones Lerner, 1973), pp. 310–11, and Eduardo Lemaitre, *Núñez y su leyenda negra* (Bogotá: Ediciones Tercer Mundo, 1977), pp. 85–86.
113. Cf. Joaquín Tamayo, *Núñez* (Bogotá: Editorial Cromos, 1939), pp. 195–98.
114. Indalecio Liévano Aguirre, *Rafael Núñez*, 3rd. ed. (Bogotá: Editorial Librería Siglo XX, 1946), pp. 207–09; Park, "Regionalism," pp. 345–46.
115. Tamayo, *Núñez*, pp. 122–24.
116. Ibid., p. 195; Liévano Aguirre, *Núñez*, p. 133; Vergara, *Escrutinio*, pp. 180–81.
117. Daniel Lemaitre, *Soledad Román de Núñez: Recuerdos* (Cartagena: Mogollón, 1927), p. 17.
118. Núñez to Parra, 25 October 1876 (CAP); *Diario de Cundinamarca*, 4 February 1881.
119. Luis A. Múnera, *Núñez y el radicalismo* (Cartagena, 1944), pp. 199–200; Liévano Aguirre, *Núñez*, p. 206.
120. Enrique Pérez, *Vida de Felipe Pérez* (Bogotá: Imprenta de "La Luz," 1911), pp. 203ff.
121. On the situation in Santander, see Foción Soto, *Memorias sobre el movimiento de resistencia a la dictadura de Rafael Núñez, 1884–1885*, 2 vols. (Bogotá: Arboleda & Valencia, 1913); Otero Muñoz, *Wilches*, pp. 387ff.; José Joaquín García (pseud. Arturo), *Crónicas de Bucaramanga* (Bogotá: Imprenta y Librería de Medardo Rivas, 1896), pp. 217–21.
122. Vergara, *Escrutinio*, pp. 281–89. Santos Acosta, who had replaced Eustorgio Salgar in the cabinet on 20 August 1884, resigned on 24 December in protest of the president's apparent approval of the dissolution of the Santander convention.
123. Quijano Wallis, *Memorias*, pp. 465–66; Soto, *Memorias*, 1:203–04.

124. Luciano Restrepo to Parra, 24 December 1884 (CAP).
125. Gabriel González Gaitán to Parra, 24 December 1884 (ibid.).
126. Vergara, *Escrutinio*, pp. 293–94.
127. Ibid., p. 295. See also Julio H. Palacio, *La guerra de 85* (Bogotá: Editorial Cromos, 1936), pp. 57–65.
128. *Epistolario de Rufino José Cuervo con Luis María Lleras y otros amigos y familiares*, ed. Guillermo Hernández de Alba (Bogotá: Instituto Caro y Cuervo, 1969), p. 150. Lleras, a son of Lorenzo María Lleras, was killed at the battle of La Humareda on the Magdalena River on 17 June 1885. The Liberals won a technical victory in that the Conservatives retired from the field. However, the Liberals suffered heavy casualties and failed to pursue the enemy. Moreover, one of the Liberal steamers caught fire and exploded, with the loss of most of their arms and ammunition. The Liberal forces proved unable to recover from the effects of La Humareda. On the battle, see Palacio, *Guerra*, pp. 230ff., and Pedro Sicard Briceño, *Páginas para la historia militar de Colombia: Guerra civil de 1885* (Bogotá: Imprenta del E.M.G., 1925), pp. 234–59. Lleras's kinsman, ex-President Pérez, also had a dim view of the revolution (Santiago Pérez to Parra, 28 May 1885, CAP).
129. Palacio, *Guerra*, p. 273; *Estrella de Panamá*, 9 October 1885.
130. Palacio, *Guerra*, pp. 57–58; Serrano Camargo, *Núñez*, pp. 383–84; Liévano Aguirre, *Núñez*, p. 249; Tamayo, *Núñez*, pp. 148–52.
131. Cf. Carlos Lozano y Lozano and Fernando de la Vega, *¿Quién fué Núñez?* (Cartagena: Editorial "El Mercurio," 1939), pp. 17ff.
132. Park, "Regionalism," pp. 349–50 and Tables H (p. 252) and I (p. 253).
133. See, e.g., *Epistolario Cuervo*, pp. 84, 137.

Chapter 7

1. Carlos Martínez Silva, "Revista política," *Repertorio Colombiano* 12 (September 1886):168–69.
2. *La Nación* (Bogotá), 13 November 1885.
3. For Caro's views on constitutional subjects, see Miguel Antonio Caro, *Estudios constitucionales*, Biblioteca Popular de Cultura Colombiana (Bogotá: Editorial Iqueima, 1951).
4. José María Samper, *Derecho público interno de Colombia*, 2 vols. (Bogotá: Imprenta de "La Luz," 1886), 1:333. Samper died in 1888.
5. Martínez Silva, "Revista política," September 1886, pp. 170ff.
6. For an English translation, see William Marion Gibson, *The Constitutions of Colombia* (Durham, N.C.: Duke University Press, 1948), pp. 314–49.
7. Tulio Enrique Tascón, "La constituyente de 1886," *El Tiempo*, Literary Supplement, 16 April 1950, p. 1.
8. On the concordat, see J. Lloyd Mecham, *Church and State in Latin America*, rev. ed. (Chapel Hill, N.C.: University of North Carolina Press, 1966), pp. 126–31.
9. Jorge Franco Holguín, *Evolución de las instituciones financieras en Colombia* (Mexico City: Centro de Estudios Monetarios Latinoamericanos, 1966), p. 30; F[rancis] Loraine Petre, *The Republic of Colombia* (London: Edward Stanford, 1906), p. 305.
10. Petre, *Colombia*, p. 305. Silver pesos and half-pesos of a standard of .500

were also issued, as well as nickel coins in smaller denominations. Previous standards for silver coins had been .900 and .835.

11. Guillermo Torres García, *Historia de la moneda en Colombia* (Bogotá: Imprenta del Banco de la República, 1945), p. 262n.; Carlos Martínez Silva, *Obras completas del doctor Carlos Martínez Silva*, 9 vols. (Bogotá: Imprenta Nacional, 1934–38), 9:55–121.

12. Torres García, *Moneda*, pp. 254–62; Martínez Silva, *Obras*, 9:124.

13. Petre, *Colombia*, p. 305.

14. Torres García, *Moneda*, p. 265.

15. On monopolies, see Luis Ospina Vásquez, *Industria y protección en Colombia, 1810–1930* (Medellín: E. S. F., 1955), pp. 303–04; *Diario Oficial*, 12 June 1893, 25 May 1897.

16. Robert C. Beyer, "The Colombian Coffee Industry: Origins and Major Trends, 1740–1940" (Ph.D. dissertation, University of Minnesota, 1947), pp. 114–15.

17. Ibid., pp. 118–19; Dario Bustamante Roldán, "Efectos económicos del papel moneda durante la Regeneración," *Cuadernos Colombianos* 1 (1974):609–16.

18. Charles W. Bergquist, *Coffee and Conflict in Colombia, 1886–1910* (Durham, N.C.: Duke University Press, 1978), p. 54.

19. William Paul McGreevey, *An Economic History of Colombia, 1845–1930* (Cambridge: Cambridge University Press, 1971), p. 196.

20. Bergquist, *Conflict*, p. 23, 26–27. For the vicissitudes of a Cundinamarca coffee plantation, see Malcolm Deas, "A Colombian Coffee Estate: Santa Bárbara, Cundinamarca, 1870–1912," in Kenneth Duncan and Ian Rutledge, eds., *Land and Labour in Latin America* (Cambridge: Cambridge University Press, 1977), pp. 269–98.

21. Bergquist, *Conflict*, p. 29; Laureano García Ortiz, "Vida de ciencia y trabajo: Apuntes para una biografía de Nicolás Sáenz," *El Tiempo*, Lecturas Dominicales, 21 July 1968, p. 3.

22. *Correo Nacional* (Bogotá), 19 January 1891; Medardo Rivas, *Los trabajadores de tierra caliente*, Biblioteca Popular de Cultura Colombiana (Bogotá: Prensas de la Universidad Nacional, 1946), p. 276.

23. *La Crónica* (Bogotá), 22 July 1897.

24. Ospina Vásquez, *Industria*, p. 245.

25. Bustamante Roldán, "Papel moneda," pp. 634, 645.

26. Ibid., p. 656.

27. *El Amigo del Pueblo* (Bogotá), 3 August 1889.

28. *El Telegrama* (Bogotá), 29 April 1891.

29. *El Orden* (Bogotá), 16 May 1891.

30. *El Espectador* (Medellín), 29 April 1893.

31. See two series of articles on monetary policy written by Samper in 1890 and 1892 and reprinted in Miguel Samper, *Escritos político-económicos*, 4 vols. (Bogotá: Editorial de Cromos, 1925–27), 3:97–235.

32. Rafael Núñez, "La nueva era y la crisis metálica," *La reforma política en Colombia*, 2 (Bogotá: Editorial A B C, 1945):155–63. See also his message to Congress on 20 July 1888 in *El Taller* (Bogotá), 26 July 1888.

33. Cf. Núñez, "Anarquía monetaria," *Reforma*, 2:279–85, and "Las incóg-

nitas del papel moneda," *Reforma,* 3 (Bogotá: Editorial A B C, 1945):75–82.

34. Núñez, "El cuento de las mil y una noches," *Reforma,* 7 (Bogotá: Editorial Iqueima, 1950):115.

35. See Caro's address to Congress on 12 September 1892, reprinted in Miguel Antonio Caro, *Escritos sobre cuestiones económicas* (Bogotá: Imprenta del Banco de la República, 1943), pp. 59–68.

36. *La Nación,* 12 March 1886.

37. *Los Intereses del Cauca* (Cali), 3 September 1886. Reyes had been apolitical, though of Conservative sympathies, until his exploits during the 1885 war brought him national acclaim. Born in Boyacá about 1849, Reyes went to Cauca to join his half-brother's business firm and at the age of twenty-four headed an expedition that reached Rio de Janeiro by way of the Putumayo and Amazon rivers. He later launched an ambitious enterprise for the colonization and development of southeastern Colombia, but by 1885 he was on the verge of bankruptcy. He had decided to emigrate to Argentina when the revolution broke out. See Eduardo Lemaitre, *Reyes: El Reconstructor* (Bogotá: Editorial Iqueima, 1953).

38. Gustavo Otero Muñoz, *Un hombre y una época: La vida azarosa de Rafael Núñez,* Biblioteca de Historia Nacional (Bogotá: Talleres de Editorial A B C, 1951), pp. 250–53.

39. Ibid., p. 309.

40. *La Prensa* (Bogotá), 1 January, 8 January 1888.

41. Otero Muñoz, *Núñez,* p. 311.

42. Gustavo Arboleda, *Diccionario biográfico y genealógico del antiguo departamento del Cauca,* 2nd ed. (Bogotá: Biblioteca Horizontes, 1962), p. 340.

43. Otero Muñoz, *Núñez,* pp. 326–27.

44. *Diario Oficial,* 7 August 1888.

45. Núñez to Rico, 22 November 1888 (Ms. #99, BL-AA).

46. Rico to Núñez, 7 January 1888 (misdated; the year should be 1889) (ibid.).

47. John T. Abbott to James G. Blaine, #109, 10 August 1890, in *Diplomatic Despatches.*

48. *El Liberal* (Bogotá), 10 March 1888.

49. For a bitter attack on the Independents, see *El Relator,* 19 March 1888.

50. *El Liberal* (Bogotá), 21 February 1888.

51. For samples of attacks on Núñez by Liberal exiles, see J. M. Vargas Vila, *Los providenciales* (New York: Imprenta de M. M. Hernández, 1892), pp. 75–89, and Arturo Escobar Uribe, *El Indio Uribe (O la lucha por la libertad en el siglo XIX)* (Bogotá: Tipografía Rojas, 1952), pp. 214ff.

52. See Fernando Galvis Salazar, *Uribe Uribe,* Autores Antioqueños (Medellín: Imprenta Departamental, 1962).

53. *El Relator,* 22 October 1891; Julio Hoenigsberg, *Las fronteras de los partidos en Colombia: Historia y comentarios de la legislación escolar de la república desde 1821 hasta el 13 de junio de 1953* (Bogotá: Editorial A B C, 1953?), pp. 126–30.

54. Luis María Mora, *Croniquillas de mi ciudad* (Bogotá: Editorial A B C, 1936), p. 37.

55. *El Autonomista* (Bogotá), 23 March 1899.

56. *El Espectador,* 13 January 1888; *El Republicano* (Bogotá), 4 May 1896.

57. Dabney H. Maury to Thomas F. Bayard, #57, 19 October 1887, in *Diplomatic Despatches.*

58. Abraham C. Rodríguez to Cuervo, 18 February 1889 (Ms.#31, BL-AA).
59. J. V. Aycardi to Cuervo, 30 January 1889 (ibid.).
60. Tomás C. Varona to Cuervo, 4 January 1889 (ibid.).
61. José María Domínguez E. to Cuervo, 8 February 1889 (ibid.).
62. *La Prensa*, 28 February 1888.
63. *El Liberal*, 21 April 1888; Arboleda, *Conto*, pp. 163–64.
64. *El Espectador*, 8 May 1888.
65. Ibid., 4 July 1888.
66. *El Relator*, 16 September 1892.
67. Ibid., 12 May 1891; Circular, 14 April 1891, announcing installation of the Liberal Center (CP, ACH).
68. Parra to José María Villamizar Gallardo, Vicente Uscátegui, and Luis E. Uribe, 30 April 1891 (ibid.).
69. Circular from Liberal Center, 2 May 1891 (ibid.).
70. *La Nación*, 26 October 1888. According to Article 5 of the constitution of 1886, the existing departments could be divided into smaller units only if three conditions were met: four-fifths of the municipal councils in the region comprising the proposed new department or province had to request the change; any new department had to have a population of at least 200,000 while the remainder of the old department had to retain at least 250,000 inhabitants; and legislation to create a new department had to be approved by two successive regular sessions of Congress.
71. Ibid., 6 November 1888.
72. Ibid., 9 November, 16 November 1888.
73. Ibid., 23 November 1888.
74. From *El Meridional* of Pasto, reprinted in *El Siglo Veinte* (Bogotá), 26 September 1889.
75. *La Nación*, 19 October 1888.
76. *El Trabajo* (Medellín), 30 May 1889. Law 57 of 1887 forbade private banks to issue notes and ordered them to retire those already in circulation.
77. *La Tarde* (Medellín), 16 January 1890. The reference was probably to the unfinished Antioquia Railroad.
78. Ibid., 5 July 1889.
79. Ibid., 14 June 1889.
80. *El Telegrama*, 6 November, 13 December 1889.
81. The article was reprinted in *La Nación*, 17 December 1889, and *Revista Colombiana* 7 (15 September 1936):244–245.
82. *La Nación*, 17 December 1889; *La Tarde*, 23 December 1889.
83. *La Nación*, 15 April 1890.
84. Ibid.; see also ibid., 26 October 1888, 18 April 1890.
85. Ibid., 15 April 1890.
86. Ibid., 20 July 1890.
87. Ibid., 29 July 1890.
88. *Correo Nacional*, 22 June 1891.
89. Ibid. See also *La Prensa*, 15 July 1891.
90. *Correo Nacional*, 9 March 1891.
91. *La Prensa*, 17 March 1891.
92. Ibid., 6 March 1891.
93. Ibid., 11 March 1891.
94. *El Colombiano* (Bogotá), 4 April 1891.

95. Ibid., 23 April 1891.
96. See *La Prensa*, 21 March, 30 March 1891.
97. *La Paz* (Bogotá), 11 April 1891.
98. Ibid., 24 April 1891.
99. Núñez to Rico, 17 May 1891 (Ms.#99, BL-AA).
100. Vergara, *Escrutinio*, pp. 387–90.
101. *Correo Nacional*, 22 September 1891.
102. Abbott to Blaine, confidential, #263, 24 September 1891, in *Diplomatic Despatches*.
103. *La Paz*, 29 October 1891.
104. *El Relator*, 20 October 1891.
105. Camacho Roldán to Uribe Uribe, 18 August 1891 (AUU, ACH).
106. Liberal Center to departmental directors, 13 October 1891 (CP, ACH).
107. Parra to Rafael Aizpuru and Ramón Santodomingo Vila, 13 October 1891 (ibid.).
108. Parra to José María Villamizar Gallardo, 4 December 1891 (ibid.). See also Parra to General R. Collante, 1 December 1891, and 5 January 1892 (ibid.).
109. Parra to Cano, 18 November 1891 (ibid.).
110. Parra to the president of the Liberal Directory of Bolívar, 11 December 1891 (ibid.); *El Espectador*, 11 December 1891.
111. *Correo Nacional*, 8 December, 10 December 1891.
112. For a sampling of Liberal complaints, see *El Relator*, 19 November, 26 November, 15 December 1891.
113. Camacho Roldán to Belisario Zamorano, 19 January 1892, and to Uribe Uribe, 26 January 1892 (CP, ACH).
114. Liberal Center to departmental directors, 19 December 1891 (ibid.).
115. *El Relator*, 11 January 1892.
116. *La Unidad* (Tunja), 11 March 1892.
117. Minister Abbott reported election returns slightly different from those given above. He stated that of the 342 electoral votes for the Vélez-Ortiz ticket in Antioquia, 71 were said to have been cast by Liberals; of the 14 Velista votes in Tolima, 12 were said to have been cast by Liberals. Abbott to Blaine, #323, 9 March 1892, in *Diplomatic Despatches*.
118. *El Relator*, 31 March 1892.
119. Ibid., 19 April 1892.
120. Camacho Roldán to Liberal Directory of Bolívar, 1 March 1892 (CP, ACH).
121. *El Espectador*, 30 April 1892.
122. Ibid., 4 June 1892.
123. Ibid., 11 June, 18 June 1892.
124. Parra to Carlos Enciso, 26 September 1891 (CP, ACH). See also Parra to J. del C. Rodríguez, 25 September 1891 (ibid.).
125. Camacho Roldán to Uribe Uribe, 26 January 1892 (AUU, ACH).
126. Camacho Roldán to Uribe Uribe, 10 May 1892 (ibid.).
127. Camacho Roldán to the president of the National Liberal Convention, 11 September 1892 (CP, ACH).
128. Liberal Center to Santander Directory, 4 March 1892 (ibid.). See also letter to Cundinamarca Directory, 1 March 1892 (ibid.).
129. Camacho Roldán to Uribe Uribe, 11 August 1892 (AUU, ACH).

130. Ibid.
131. Eduardo Rodríguez Piñeres, *Diez años de política liberal, 1892–1902* (Bogotá: Librería Colombiana, 1945), pp. 9–10.
132. Ibid., pp. 10–11.
133. *El Relator*, 27 February 1893.
134. *La Crónica*, 6 November 1898.
135. *El Relator*, 6 March 1893.
136. *El Espectador*, 22 March 1893.
137. *El Relator*, 6 March 1893.
138. Pérez to Belisario Zamorano et al., 18 February 1893 (AP, ACH).
139. Ibid.
140. *El Relator*, 27 February 1893.
141. Ibid., 16 May 1893.
142. Ibid., 26 June 1893.
143. Ibid., 11 July 1893.
144. The four articles appeared on 14 December, 21 December, 28 December 1892, and 4 January 1893.
145. Details of the riots can be found in *Correo Nacional*, 1 February 1893, and *Diario Oficial*, 2 February, 3 February 1893.
146. *Correo Nacional*, 17 January 1893.
147. [Luis María Holguín], *Informe que presenta el subsecretario encargado del Ministerio de Gobierno de Colombia al Congreso Constitucional de 1894* (Bogotá: Imprenta Oficial, 1894), p. v. This may have been a mutual aid society formed in 1889 by the merger of a group of the same name with the *Sociedad de Socorros Mutuos*. See *El Taller*, 8 January 1889.
148. *Correo Nacional*, 1 February 1893.
149. Ibid., 18 January 1893.
150. Núñez, "La causa de las causas," *Reforma*, 6 (Bogotá: Editorial Iqueima, 1950):52–56.
151. Abbott to W. Q. Gresham, confidential, #498, 25 April 1893, in *Diplomatic Despatches*.
152. *Memoria Gobierno 1894*, pp. vi–x.
153. Ibid.
154. Ibid. See also *El Rayo X* (Bogotá), 6 February, 13 February 1899; Escobar, *Uribe*, pp. 27–29.
155. Rodríguez Piñeres, *Diez años*, pp. 26–27. See also Bergquist, *Conflict*, pp. 48–49; *Correo Nacional*, 24 January, 30 January, 7 February, 29 April–2 May 1895.
156. *Correo Nacional*, 4 October 1895. See also *La Crónica*, 9 December 1898.
157. McKinney to Gresham, #92, 20 January 1895, in *Diplomatic Despatches*. McKinney succeeded Abbott in July 1893.

Chapter 8

1. José Ramón Vergara, *Escrutinio histórico: Rafael Núñez* (Bogotá: Editorial A B C, 1939), pp. 457–63; Gustavo Otero Muñoz, *Un hombre y una época: La vida azarosa de Rafael Núñez*, Biblioteca de Historia Nacional (Bogotá: Talleres de Editorial A B C, 1951), pp. 396–406.
2. Luis Martínez Delgado, *Historia de un cambio de gobierno: Estudio*

crítico-histórico de la caída del gobierno del Doctor Manuel Antonio Sanclemente (Bogotá: Editorial Santafe, 1958), pp. 15–25.

3. Guillermo Torres García, *Miguel Antonio Caro: Su personalidad política* (Madrid: Ediciones Guadarrama, S. L., 1956), pp. 225–26.

4. Marco Fidel Suárez, *Sueños de Luciano Pulgar*, 2d ed., 12 vols. (Bogotá: Librería Voluntad, S.A., 1940–1943), 12:438–52.

5. Article 127 of the constitution forbade the immediate reelection of the president if he had actually wielded power during the eighteen months preceding the new election.

6. Charles W. Bergquist, *Coffee and Conflict in Colombia, 1886–1910* (Durham, N.C.: Duke University Press, 1978), p. 58.

7. Torres García, *Caro*, pp. 151–56.

8. Bergquist, *Conflict*, pp. 63n., 177.

9. Ibid., pp. 51, 59.

10. Ibid., pp. 70–71.

11. Robert Carlyle Beyer, "The Colombian Coffee Industry: Origins and Major Trends, 1740–1940" (Ph.D. dissertation, University of Minnesota, 1947), pp. 130–31.

12. *La Crónica*, 22 July 1897.

13. Charles Burdett Hart to John Hay, #286, 25 August 1897, in *Diplomatic Despatches;* Bergquist, *Conflict*, p. 104.

14. Eduardo Rodríguez Piñeres, *Diez años de política liberal, 1892–1902* (Bogotá: Librería Colombiana, 1945), p. 37; Lucas Caballero, *Memorias de la guerra de los mil días* (Bogotá: "Aguila Negra" Editorial, 1939), pp. 21–22.

15. *El Espectador,* 14 March, 25 March 1896.

16. Ibid., 14 March 1896; *El Republicano,* 12 March 1896.

17. *El Espectador,* 8 April 1896.

18. Ibid., 29 April 1896.

19. *El Espectador,* 11 April 1896.

20. Ibid., 21 April 1896.

21. *El Republicano,* 25 April 1896.

22. Ibid., 28 April, 29 April 1896.

23. Ibid., 4 May 1896. 24. Ibid.

25. *El Espectador,* 7 May, 20 May 1896.

26. Rodríguez Piñeres, *Diez años,* pp. 34–36.

27. Torres García, *Caro,* pp. 163, 183–89; *La Crónica,* 16 March, 6 June 1897; *El Progreso* (Bogotá), 20 May, 24 June, 30 July, 1 August 1897; Bergquist, *Conflict,* pp. 59ff. See also the "Revistas políticas" for February, March, May, July, and August 1897 in Carlos Martínez Silva, *Obras completas del doctor Carlos Martínez Silva,* 9 vols. (Bogotá: Imprenta Nacional, 1934–38), 2:130, 138–39, 179, 189, 219–24.

28. *El Espectador,* 24 April 1897.

29. Communication to departmental directors, 11 April 1897 (AP, ACH).

30. Communication to departmental directors, 15 May 1897 (ibid.).

31. *Convención Nacional Eleccionaria del Partido Liberal* (Bogotá: Papelería de Samper Matiz, 1897), pp. 3–5, 33.

32. Letter to Parra from José C. Borda (copy), 30 March 1897 (AP, ACH).

33. Communication to Liberals from Parra, 30 September 1897 (ibid.). Parra

attributed the fact that the convention had been able to meet in complete freedom to Caro's interest in an *evolución*. Rodríguez Piñeres, *Diez años,* pp. 42–44, 49–50, gives a slightly different account of these events.

34. *Convención Liberal,* pp. 21–22.
35. Diego Mendoza to Pedro A. Lara, 20 June 1898 (AP, ACH).
36. Parra to Juan Evangelista Manrique, 3 March [1900?] (ibid.).
37. *Convención Liberal,* pp. 25–28.
38. *El Espectador,* 3 October 1897.
39. *El Progreso,* 15 October 1897.
40. Ibid., 4 November 1897.
41. *El Nacionalista* (Bogotá), 8 December 1897; Martínez Silva, "Revista política," 26 December 1897, *Obras,* 2:255–59.
42. *La Crónica,* 30 November 1897.
43. Ibid.; *El Mago* (Bogotá), 4 December 1897; *Diario de Colombia,* 29 November 1897.
44. *La Crónica,* 3 December 1897.
45. *El Mago,* 27 December 1897.
46. Ibid., 12 December 1897.
47. *La Crónica,* 19 December 1897.
48. Martínez Silva, "Revista política," 28 November 1897, *Obras,* 2:249–50.
49. *La Crónica,* 7 December 1897.
50. Ibid., 8 December, 10 December 1897.
51. *El Espectador,* 10 December 1897.
52. *La Crónica,* 12 June 1898.
53. Parra to Jacobo Sánchez, 14 April 1898, and Parra to Julio A. Vengoechea, 6 May 1898 (AP, ACH).
54. *El Nacionalista,* 22 January 1898; Martínez Silva, "Revista política," 28 January 1898, *Obras,* 2:267–68.
55. *El Nacionalista,* 6 July 1898. According to returns printed in *El Espectador,* 2 February 1898, 2,242 electors were chosen in December, 399 of whom were Liberals. Both sets of figures indicate that the number of electors who voted in the electoral assemblies was considerably smaller than the 3,800 who Martínez Silva said should have been present ("Revista política," 10 July 1898, *Obras,* 2:318–19).
56. *La Crónica,* 20 February 1898. For Caro's alarm over the manifesto of 15 February, see Parra to Francisco García Rico, 18 March 1898, and Francisco García Rico to Parra, 19 March 1898 (AP, ACH).
57. *Extracto del informe sobre las relaciones del Director del Partido Liberal con el Dr. Rafael Uribe U.,* 15 September 1898 (ibid.). The Parra papers also contain a document in Uribe Uribe's handwriting which states the conditions under which he, Robles, and Soto were to carry out their assignment abroad.
58. Ibid.
59. Uribe Uribe to Alfaro, 2 November 1897 (AUU, ACH).
60. For a report by Uribe Uribe to President Reina Barrios discussing the political situation in Colombia, see *Exposición sobre la situación política de Colombia,* 8 December 1897 (ibid.).
61. For an embittered account of Estrada Cabrera's dealings with the Colombians, see Belisario Porras, *Memorias de las campañas del Istmo, 1900* (Panama: Imprenta Nacional, 1922), pp. 3–16.

62. *Extracto del informe;* Diego Mendoza to Pedro A. Lara, 20 June 1898 (AP, ACH).
63. Mendoza to Lara, 20 June 1898 (AP, ACH).
64. *Extracto del Informe.*
65. *Informe de las relaciones que el Director del Partido Liberal ha mantenido con el Dr. Rafael Uribe Uribe,* August 1898 (AP, ACH). See also a confidential circular from the General Directorate, 12 September 1898, which contains a letter written in Panama by Carlos A. Mendoza criticizing Uribe Uribe's Barranquilla speech (AUU, ACH). For an excerpt from the published version of the speech, which Mendoza said differed from the one actually delivered in Barranquilla, see Fernando Galvis Salazar, *Uribe Uribe,* Autores Antioqueños (Medellín: Imprenta Departamental, 1962), pp. 92–93.
66. *El Autonomista,* 20 September 1898.
67. *El Espectador,* 12 October 1898. In 1896 Congress had enacted a press law very much like the decree of 1888 which placed offenses committed by subversive publications primarily under the jurisdiction of the departmental governors and the minister of government.
68. Ibid.
69. *El Autonomista,* 28 September, 2 October 1898.
70. Communication to the departmental directors from Parra, 3 October 1898 (AP, ACH).
71. Communication (confidential) to the departmental directors from Parra, 4 October 1898 (ibid.).
72. Letter to Hermógenes Wilson, Domnino Castro, R. Santodomingo Navas, et al., 13 October 1898 (ibid.).
73. Letter (very confidential) to Carlos J. Delgado, 13 October 1898 (ibid.). The signature on this letter is missing.
74. *El Autonomista,* 7 October 1898.
75. Ibid., 6 October 1898.
76. Ibid., 2 November 1898.
77. *La Crónica,* 9 October 1898.
78. *El Espectador,* 7 December 1898.
79. *El Autonomista,* 23 November, 3 December, 7 December 1898.
80. Andrés Santos to Uribe Uribe, 22 October 1898 (AUU, ACH).
81. Vicente Parra R. to Parra, 10 November 1898 (AP, ACH).
82. Pablo Arosemena to Parra, 21 December 1898 (ibid.).
83. Max Grillo to Uribe Uribe, undated (AUU, ACH).
84. Bergquist, *Conflict,* pp. 90ff.
85. Julio A. Gómez to Uribe Uribe, 5 September 1898 (AUU, ACH).
86. Rafael Gómez Picón, ed., *Rafael Uribe Uribe en la intimidad: Su correspondencia privada* (Bogotá: Tipo-Prensa, n.d.), p. 89. The account of Uribe Uribe's reception in Cundinamarca in 1899 appears on p. 99.
87. Uribe Uribe to the Directory, 25 June 1897 (AP, ACH).
88. Justo Villamizar to Parra, 4 October 1898 (AUU, ACH). Villamizar was a supporter of Uribe Uribe, to whom he sent a copy of his letter to Parra.
89. Vicente Parra R. to Parra, 10 November 1898 (AP, ACH).
90. *El Autonomista,* 5 November 1898.
91. Martínez Silva, "Revista política," 10 December 1898, *Obras,* 2:386–88; Martínez Delgado, *Cambio de gobierno,* pp. 96–101.

92. *El Autonomista*, 18 December 1898.
93. Communication from the General Directorate, 20 December 1898 (AP, ACH).
94. Communication to the departmental directors from the General Directorate, 18 November 1898 (ibid.).
95. Paulo Villar to Parra, 4 December 1898 (ibid.). Parra's letter of 18 November 1898 and the replies he received were published in *Documentos relativos a la separación del Dr. Aquileo Parra de la Dirección Nacional del Partido Liberal* (Bogotá: Imprenta de La Crónica, 1899).
96. *Documentos*, p. 18.
97. *El Rayo X*, 16 February 1899.
98. *Documentos*, pp. 25–27, 31; *El Autonomista*, 12 March 1899.
99. *El Rayo X*, 11 March, 3 April 1899.
100. *El Autonomista*, 26 March 1899.
101. Ibid., 18 June, 24 June 1899.
102. *El Rayo X*, 14 April 1899.
103. Ibid., 3 May 1899.
104. Manrique to Pablo Arosemena, 24 September 1899 (AM, ACH).
105. Ibid.
106. Fernando Galvis Salazar, *Uribe Uribe*, p. 105n.
107. *La Crónica*, 30 July 1899.
108. *El Autonomista*, 30 July 1899.
109. Ibid., 19 August 1899.
110. Ibid., 27 July 1899.
111. Parra to Manrique, 14 September 1899 (AM, ACH).
112. Manrique to Parra, 14 September 1899 (ibid.).
113. *La Crónica*, 20 September, 3 October 1899.
114. Joaquín Tamayo, *La revolución de 1899*, 2d ed. (Bogotá: Editorial Cromos, 1940), p. 48.
115. The early events of the war are described ibid., pp. 55ff. See also Galvis Salazar, *Uribe Uribe*, pp. 124–25. There appears to be no satisfactory explanation as to why Villar not only failed to postpone the starting date of the revolution but moved it up instead. It is possible, of course, that since the 20 October date was public knowledge, he may have acted earlier in order to retain an element of surprise. One contemporary attributed Gómez Pinzón's action to the sudden evacuation of Socorro by the government garrison. See J. M. Vesga y Avila, *La guerra de tres años: Primera parte* (Bogotá: J. M. Vesga Villamizar, 1914), pp. 20–22.
116. Rough minutes of the meeting can be found in AM, ACH. See also *La Crónica*, 17 October 1899, and Caballero, *Memorias*, p. 26.
117. Vargas Santos to Directory, 19 October 1899 (AM, ACH).
118. Tamayo, *Revolución*, p. 40; Bergquist, *Conflict*, p. 103.
119. Eusebio A. Morales, "The Political and Economic Situation of Colombia," *The North American Review* 175 (September 1902):360.
120. Bergquist, *Conflict*, p. 36.
121. *La Crónica*, 12 July 1899; Tamayo, *Revolución*, p. 41; F[rancis] Loraine Petre, *The Republic of Colombia* (London: Edward Stanford, 1906), p. 303; Beyer, "Coffee," p. 130.
122. *La Crónica*, 11 August 1899.

123. J. de J. Sánchez to Uribe Uribe, 28 August, 9 September 1898 (AUU, ACH).
124. Hart to Hay, #332, 12 February 1900, in *Diplomatic Despatches.*
125. Thomas Royden Favell, "The Antecedents of Panama's Separation from Colombia: A Study in Colombian Politics" (Ph.D. dissertation, Fletcher School of Law and Diplomacy, 1950), pp. 165–66.
126. H. A. Gudger, #97, 11 November 1899, in *Despatches, Consuls, Panama.*
127. Vesga, *Guerra,* p. 31; Bergquist, *Conflict,* pp. 113–14; [Carlos Adolfo Urueta], *Historia de la guerra: Documentos militares y políticos relativos a las campañas del General Rafael Uribe Uribe,* 2d ed. (Bogotá: Imprenta de Vapor, 1904), pp. xxxvff.
128. Vesga, *Guerra,* pp. 37–40; 215–17; Bergquist, *Conflict,* pp. 124ff.
129. Winfield J. Burggraaff, "Venezuelan Regionalism and the Rise of Táchira," *The Americas* 25 (October 1968):168–72. See also Domingo Alberto Rangel, *Los andinos en el poder: Balance de una hegemonía, 1899–1945* (Caracas, 1964), p. 64.
130. Porras, *Memorias,* pp. v–viii; Antoine Rougier, *Les Récentes Guerres Civiles de la Colombie et du Vénézuéla* (Paris: A. Pedone, 1904), pp. 3–4.
131. Manrique to Soto, 18 June 1899 (AM, ACH).
132. Hart to Hay, #276, 31 July 1899, in *Diplomatic Despatches.*
133. Rougier, *Guerres,* pp. 46–47. Among other services Castro allowed the Colombian Liberals to import arms by way of Maracaibo. The story of Venezuelan efforts on behalf of Colombian Liberals and of the ensuing tensions between Venezuela and the Colombian government can be gleaned from ibid., pp. 46–57; Porras, *Memorias,* p. viii; [Urueta], *Documentos,* pp. 204–19; *Invasiones de Colombia a Venezuela en 1901, 1902 y 1903* (Caracas: Imprenta Bolívar, 1903); and Mariano Picón-Salas, *Los días de Cipriano Castro* (Caracas: Primer festival del libro popular venezolano, 1958), pp. 95–105.
134. Gómez Picón, ed., *Intimidad,* pp. 100, 104.
135. Parra to Manrique, 19 December 1899 (AM, ACH). See also Parra to Manrique, 11 December [1899?] (AP, ACH).
136. A few prominent Liberals in Bogotá remained aloof from the conflict. These included José Camacho Carrizosa and Carlos Arturo Torres, who founded *El Nuevo Tiempo* in May 1902 to work for peace. See Rodríguez Piñeres, *Diez años,* p. 201, and Caballero, *Memorias,* p. 339. The newspaper, founded with the approval of the government, attacked war as being contrary to Liberal principles and harmful to the nation and especially the poor. See, e. g., "Por la doctrina," *El Nuevo Tiempo,* 12 June 1902, and "Por los miserables," ibid., 19 June 1902.
137. The members of the Cundinamarca directory were selected from candidates chosen at meetings attended by three different groups of Liberals. One of these groups was made up of artisans, while the other two consisted of businessmen and of military men and young people. See *El Rayo X,* 24 April, 26 April 1899.

Conclusion

1. General surveys of the war can be found in Charles W. Bergquist, *Coffee and Conflict in Colombia, 1886–1910* (Durham, N.C.: Duke University Press, 1978), chapters 6 and 7, and Joaquín Tamayo, *La revolución de 1899,* 2d ed. (Bogotá: Editorial Cromos, 1940).

2. Jorge Holguín, *Desde cerca (Asuntos colombianos)* (Paris: Librairie Générale et Internationale, 1908), p. 149.

3. The revolution in Panama is described in Belisario Porras, *Memorias de las campañas del Istmo, 1900* (Panama: Imprenta Nacional, 1922); Lucas Caballero, *Memorias de la guerra de los mil días* (Bogotá: "Aguila Negra" Editorial, 1939); Víctor M. Salazar, *Memorias de la guerra (1899–1902)* (Bogotá: Editorial A B C, 1943); and Alejandro Pérez-Venero, Jr., "The Thousand Days' War: A Prelude to Panamanian Independence" (M.A. thesis, Mississippi State University, 1967).

4. By the terms of an extension granted in 1893, the deadline for the opening of an Isthmian canal by the company was 31 October 1904. See Thomas Royden Favell, "The Antecedents of Panama's Separation from Colombia: A Study in Colombian Politics" (Ph.D. dissertation, Fletcher School of Law and Diplomacy, 1950), pp. 145–46, 166–67.

5. F[rancis] Loraine Petre, *The Republic of Colombia* (London: Edward Stanford, 1906), p. 306.

6. Bergquist, *Conflict*, p. 145. See also Petre, *Colombia*, pp. 302–03.

7. Bergquist, *Conflict*, pp. 188–89; Eduardo Lemaitre, *Reyes*, 2d ed. (Bogotá: Editorial Iqueima, 1953), pp. 218–19.

8. The events leading to the deposition of Sanclemente can be traced in Luis Martínez Delgado, *Historia de un cambio de gobierno: Estudio crítico-histórico de la caída del gobierno del Dr. Manuel Antonio Sanclemente* (Bogotá: Editorial Santafe, 1958). On the efforts of disappointed Conservatives to restore him to power, see Emilio Robledo, *La vida del General Pedro Nel Ospina*, Autores Antioqueños (Medellín: Imprenta Departamental, 1959), pp. 197–220, and [Eduardo Espinosa], *Colombia: La legitimidad y el gobierno de facto* (New York, 1902). Sanclemente died on 19 March 1902.

9. Bergquist, *Conflict*, p. 186; Tamayo, *Revolución*, pp. 234–41; Antoine Rougier, *Les Récentes Guerres Civiles de la Colombie et du Vénézuéla* (Paris: A. Pedone, 1904), pp. 28ff.

10. Caballero, *Memorias*, pp. 347–54; Pérez-Venero, "War," pp. 130–33. Víctor Salazar, governor and military chief of Panama, contended in his memoirs that Herrera's military position was hopeless when he agreed to negotiate on the *Wisconsin* (*Memorias*, pp. 285–98).

11. Reyes narrowly defeated Conservative Joaquín F. Vélez, who was considered the administration's choice. See Lemaitre, *Reyes*, pp. 226–31.

12. Ibid., pp. 235–38; *El Comercio* (Bogotá), 16 July, 17 August 1904; L. E. Nieto Caballero, "El General Rafael Reyes," *Boletín de Historia y Antigüedades* 40 (April–June 1953):295, 300.

13. *El Porvenir* (Bogotá), 8 January 1904.

14. *El Espectador*, 21 July 1904.

15. *El Porvenir*, 18 March 1904.

16. Ibid., 27 April 1904.

17. Ibid., 16 May, 26 May 1904.

18. Ibid., 30 March 1904. See also [Carlos Adolfo Urueta, ed.], *Historia de la guerra: Documentos militares y políticos relativos a las campañas del General Rafael Uribe Uribe*, 2d ed. (Bogotá: Imprenta de Vapor, 1904), pp. 467–68.

19. *El Porvenir*, 7 February 1903.

20. Ibid., 8 January 1904.

21. Ibid., 15 January, 19 January 1904.

22. Reduction of the president's term to four years and the abolition of the vice presidency were achieved by 1910. A major Liberal goal of the prewar period—the retirement of Colombia's paper currency, together with the right to make contracts in currency other than the paper peso—was undertaken by Congress in 1903.

23. William L. Scruggs to Secretary of State, #75, 7 December 1874, in *Diplomatic Despatches.*

Bibliography

I. Bibliographical Aids and Other Reference Books

Anuario Bibliográfico Colombiano, 1951–. Bogotá: Instituto Caro y Cuervo, 1958–.
Arango Mejía, Gabriel. *Genealogías de Antioquia y Caldas*. 2 vols. Medellín: Imprenta Departamental, 1942.
Arboleda, Gustavo. *Diccionario biográfico y genealógico del antiguo departamento del Cauca*. 2d ed. Bogotá: Biblioteca Horizontes, 1962.
Biblioteca Nacional. *Catálogo de todos los periódicos que existen desde su fundación hasta el año de 1935, inclusive*. Bogotá: Editorial "El Gráfico," 1936.
–––––––. *Catálogo del "Fondo Anselmo Pineda."* 2 vols. Bogotá: Editorial "El Gráfico," 1935.
Esguerra O[rtiz], Joaquín. *Diccionario jeográfico de los Estados Unidos de Colombia*. Bogotá: J. B. Gaitán, 1879.
Florén Lozano, Luis. *Obras de referencia y generales de la bibliografía colombiana*. Medellín: Editorial Universidad de Antioquia, 1960.
Giraldo Jaramillo, Gabriel. *Bibliografía colombiana de viajes*. Bogotá: Editorial A B C, 1957.
–––––––. *Bibliografía de bibliografías colombianas*. 2d ed. Bogotá: Instituto Caro y Cuervo, 1960.
Jones, Tom B.; Warburton, Elizabeth Anne; and Kingsley, Anne. *A Bibliography on South American Economic Affairs: Articles in Nineteenth-Century Periodicals*. Minneapolis: University of Minnesota Press, 1955.
Ortega Ricaurte, Daniel. *Indice general del "Boletín de Historia y Antigüedades,"* vols. 1–38, 1902–52. Bogotá: Academia Colombiana de Historia, 1953.
Ortega Ricaurte, Enrique. *Bibliografía académica, 1902–1952*. Bogotá: Editorial Minerva, 1953.
Ortega Torres, José J. *Indice del "Papel Periódico Ilustrado" y de "Colombia Ilustrada."* Bogotá: Instituto Caro y Cuervo, 1961.
Ospina, Joaquín. *Diccionario biográfico y bibliográfico de Colombia*. 3 vols. Bogotá: Editorial de Cromos, 1927–39.
Restrepo Sáenz, José María, and Rivas, Raimundo. *Genealogías de Santa Fe de Bogotá*. Bogotá: Librería Colombiana [1928?].
Romero, Mario Germán; Hernández de Alba, Guillermo; and Ortiz, Sergio Elias. *Papeletas bibliográficas para el estudio de la historia en Colombia*. Bogotá: Biblioteca Luis-Angel Arango, Banco de la República, 1961.

II. Newspapers

In gathering material for this study, the single most useful source proved to be Colombia's nineteenth-century newspapers. In the period from 1863 to 1899 Liberal newspapers published in Bogotá usually appeared at least once a week and were made up of four pages, which included the following: (a) one or more editorials on current issues, ordinarily by the editor, unless signed with the name, pseudonym, or initials of another contributor; (b) informative or polemical articles on political and economic questions; (c) public documents, such as laws and presidential messages; (d) party documents, such as *adhesiones* and circulars from Liberal organizations; (e) foreign news from Latin America, the United States, and Europe, often written by a Colombian Liberal resident or traveling abroad; (f) news from other parts of Colombia, usually provided by regular correspondents; (g) letters to the editor; (h) *remitidos,* or articles printed for a fee; (i) serialized works of fiction, mainly translations of European novels; (j) advertisements for patent medicines and other products of foreign origin and for local business firms, schools, hotels, stores, etc. The most influential Liberal newspapers in the period under consideration were the *Diario de Cundinamarca* and *El Relator,* both of Bogotá.

The National Library of Colombia in Bogotá has fairly complete files of newspapers, particularly those published in the capital. The Library's holdings are catalogued by title in Biblioteca Nacional, *Catálogo de todos los periódicos que existen desde su fundación hasta el año de 1935, inclusive,* 2 vols. (Bogotá: Editorial "El Gráfico," 1936).

In the list below, the year or years given for each newspaper indicate the period for which the newspaper was consulted.

La Actualidad (Bogotá). 1883–84.
La Alianza (Bogotá). 1866–68.
La América (Bogotá). 1873–74.
Anales de la Convención (Rionegro). 1863.
El Autonomista (Bogotá). 1898–99.
La Autoridad (Bogotá). 1873.
El Aviso (Bogotá). 1848.
La Bandera Nacional (Bogotá). 1837–38.
El Bien Público (Bogotá). 1870–72.
El Boletín Industrial (Bogotá). 1866, 1868, 1869–76.
El Ciudadano (Medellín). 1875.
Colombia Cristiana (Bogotá). 1892.
Colombia Ilustrada (Bogotá). 1889–92.
El Comercio (Bogotá). 1901–4.
El Conservador (Bogotá). 1881–83.
El Correo de Antioquia (Medellín). 1875.
El Correo de Colombia (Bogotá). 1874–75.
El Correo Nacional (Bogotá). 1890–95.
La Crónica (Bogotá). 1897–99.
El Debate (Bogotá). 1896.
El Deber (Bogotá). 1878–81.
La Defensa (Bogotá). 1880.
Diario de Colombia (Bogotá). 1897.
Diario de Cundinamarca (Bogotá). 1869–84.
Diario Oficial (Bogotá). 1867–84, passim.
El Elector Nacional (Barranquilla). 1875.
El Escudo Nacional (Cartagena). 1875.

El Espectador (Medellín). 1887–88, 1891–93, 1896–99, 1904.
El Estandarte (Bogotá). 1882–83.
El Ferrocarril del Norte (Duitama, Boyacá). 1872–73.
La Gaceta Mercantil (Santa Marta). 1847–48.
El Heraldo (Medellín). 1872–74.
El Heraldo (Bogotá). 1889–91.
La Ilustración (Bogotá). 1873.
La Ley (Bogotá). 1876.
El Liberal (Bogotá). 1868–71.
El Liberal (Bogotá). 1884.
El Liberal (Bogotá). 1888.
El Mago (Bogotá). 1897.
El Mensajero (Bogotá). 1866–67.
La Nación (Bogotá). 1885–90.
El Nacional (Bogotá). 1848.
El Neo-Granadino (Bogotá). 1848–49.
El Nuevo Tiempo (Bogotá). 1902–4.
El Occidente (Chiquinquirá, Boyacá). 1872.
La Opinión (Bogotá). 1863–65.
La Opinión Liberal (Bogotá). 1876.
El Orden (Bogotá). 1891.
La Palestra (Mompós, Bolívar). 1871–73.
Papel Periódico Ilustrado (Bogotá). 1881–88.
La Patria (Bogotá). 1867.
El Patriota (Bogotá). 1873.
La Paz (Bogotá). 1868–69.
La Paz (Bogotá). 1891.
El Porvenir (Bogotá). 1902–4.
La Prensa (Bogotá). 1867.
La Prensa (Bogotá). 1891.
El Progreso (Panama). 1874–75.
El Rayo X (Bogotá). 1897–99.
La Reforma (Bogotá). 1878–84.
El Relator (Bogotá). 1877–79, 1881–82, 1888, 1889–93, 1903.
La República (Bogotá). 1867–69.
El Republicano (Bogotá). 1867–68.
El Republicano (Bogotá). 1896.
Revista de Colombia (Bogotá). 1868–72, 1873–74.
El Siglo Veinte (Bogotá). 1889–90.
La Sociedad (Medellín). 1872–75.
Star and Herald (Panama), including *Estrella de Panamá*. 1862–90, passim.
El Sufragio (Popayán). 1873.
El Taller (Bogotá). 1888–90.
La Tarde (Medellín). 1889–90.
El Telégrafo (Palmira). 1875.
El Telegrama (Bogotá). 1889–91.
El Tiempo (Bogotá). 1855–61, 1864–66.

El Tío Juan (Bogotá). 1898.
El Tolerante (Bogotá). 1872–74.
El Trabajo (Medellín). 1889.
El Tradicionista (Bogotá). 1871–76.
El Tren (Bogotá). 1891.
La Unión (Bogotá). 1881.
La Unión Colombiana (Bogotá). 1875.
La Voz Nacional (Bogotá). 1884–85.

III. Manuscripts

Conto, César. Twenty-one items, mainly letters to Conto, 1874–77. Ms. #113, Biblioteca Luis-Angel Arango, Bogotá.
Correoso, Buenaventura. Correspondence, 1868–83 (in poor physical condition). In the possession of Lt. Col. Dick DeWayne Grube, U.S.A.
Cuervo, Antonio B. Documents and correspondence, 1854–98. Ms. #30, 31, Biblioteca Luis-Angel Arango, Bogotá.
Manrique, Juan Evangelista. Correspondence, 1897–99. Academia Colombiana de Historia, Bogotá.
Núñez, Rafael. Fifty-two items, mainly letters from Núñez to Luis Carlos Rico. Ms. #99, Biblioteca Luis-Angel Arango, Bogotá.
Parra, Aquileo. Correspondence, 1870s and 1880s. In the possession of Horacio Rodríguez Plata, Bogotá.
———. Documents related to the revolution of 1876–77. Ms. #1, Biblioteca Luis-Angel Arango, Bogotá.
———. Correspondence and documents related to tenure as member of Liberal Center (1891–92) and as party director (1897–99). Academia Colombiana de Historia, Bogotá.
Paúl, José Telésforo. Letters, 1875–88. Ms. #97, Biblioteca Luis-Angel Arango, Bogotá.
Pérez, Santiago. "Programa analítico de economía política por el Doctor Santiago Pérez. Año de 1880." Ms. #166, Biblioteca Luis-Angel Arango, Bogotá.
Uribe Uribe, Rafael. Thirty-one boxes of documents and correspondence. Academia Colombiana de Historia, Bogotá.

U.S. consular and diplomatic dispatches on microfilm:

Despatches from United States Consuls in Barranquilla, 1883–1906. Microcopy #T-512. Washington, D.C.: National Archives, National Archives and Records Service, General Services Administration, 1961.
Despatches from United States Consuls in Cartagena, Colombia, 1822–1905. Microcopy #T-192. Washington, D.C.: National Archives, National Archives and Records Service, General Services Administration, 1959–68. Rolls 5–13 (1851–1905).
Despatches from United States Consuls in Panama, 1823–1906. Microcopy #M-139. Washington, D.C.: National Archives, National Archives and Records Service, General Services Administration, 1949. Rolls 17 (1884–85) and 23 (1895–1900).

Despatches from United States Ministers to Colombia, 1820–1906. Microcopy #T-33. Washington, D.C.: National Archives, National Archives and Records Service, General Services Administration, 1959–62. Rolls 12–56 (1849–1900).

IV. Constitutions, Statutes, and Decrees of Colombia and the United States of Colombia

Codificación nacional de las leyes de Colombia desde el año de 1821 hecha bajo la dirección del Consejo de Estado. 34 vols. Bogotá: Imprenta Nacional, 1924–55.
Constitución i leyes de la convención de Cundinamarca espedidas en sus sesiones del presente año. Bogotá: Imprenta de Gaitán, 1870.
Constitución i leyes de los Estados Unidos de Colombia espedidas en los años de 1863 a 1875. 2 vols. Bogotá: Imprenta de Medardo Rivas, 1875.
Constitución i leyes del Estado Soberano de Bolívar espedidas por la convención constituyente en sus sesiones de 1865. Cartagena: Imprenta de Ruiz e Hijo, 1866.
Constitución i leyes espedidas por la asamblea constituyente del Estado de Santander en sus sesiones de 1857 i 1858. Bucaramanga: Imprenta de Zapata Hermanos, 1858.
Constitución, leyes i decretos expedidos por la asamblea constituyente del Estado Soberano de Antioquia, en los años de 1864 i 1865. Medellín: Imprenta de Isidoro Isaza, 1865.
Constitución, leyes i decretos expedidos por la asamblea constituyente del Tolima en sus sesiones de 1870. Bogotá: Foción Mantilla, 1871.
Constitución política del Estado Soberano del Cauca espedida el 16 de setiembre de 1863. Bogotá: Imprenta de la Nación, 1865.
Decretos legislativos expedidos durante la guerra de 1899 a 1902. Compiled and arranged by Manuel José Guzmán. Bogotá: Imprenta de Vapor, 1902.
Gibson, William Marion. *The Constitutions of Colombia.* Durham, N.C.: Duke University Press, 1948.
Leyes y decretos del Estado Soberano de Antioquia expedidos por la legislatura en sus sesiones de 1871. Medellín: Imprenta del Estado, 1871.
Leyes y decretos expedidos por la asamblea legislativa del Estado Soberano del Tolima, en sus sesiones de 1871. Bogotá: Imprenta de Foción Mantilla, 1872.
Recopilación de leyes del Estado de Boyacá. Tunja: Imprenta de Torres Hermanos i Cia., 1873.
Recopilación de leyes del Estado Soberano del Cauca: Código administrativo. Popayán: Imprenta del Estado, 1879.

V. Other Primary Sources

A la nación: Manifiesto de los senadores y representantes que votaron en contra del contrato de empréstito de $7,500,000. Bogotá: Imprenta de Gaitán, 1866.
Ancízar, Manuel. *Peregrinación de Alpha.* Biblioteca Popular de Cultura Colombiana. Bogotá: Editorial A B C, 1942.
André, Edouard. "América equinoccial (Colombia-Ecuador)," *América pintoresca: Descripción de viajes al Nuevo Continente.* Barcelona: Montaner y Simón, 1884.

[Arboleda, Sergio.] *Colección de artículos tomados de "Los Principios" cuya lectura recomienda la redacción a sus amigos políticos.* Cali: Imprenta de Hurtado, 1870.

Arosemena, Justo. *El Estado Federal de Panamá.* Biblioteca de Autores Panameños. Panama: Editora Panameña, S.A., 1965.

———. *Estudios constitucionales sobre los gobiernos de la América Latina.* 2 vols. 2d ed. revised. Paris: Librería Española i Americana de E. Denne, 1878.

Arosemena, Pablo. *Escritos.* 2 vols. Panama: Imprenta Nacional, 1930.

Arrieta, Diójenes A. *Historia del Congreso colombiano de 1878, complementada con semblanzas de los senadores i representantes.* Bogotá: Imprenta i Estereotipia de M. Rivas, 1878.

Aubert, Georges. *Les Nouvelles Amériques: Notes Sociales et Economiques.* Paris: Ernest Flammarion [1901].

Barona Pizarro, José María. *Bosquejo histórico de la última revolución (1876 a 1877).* Panama: Tipografía de M. R. de la Torre e Hijos, 1877.

Becerra, Ricardo. *El liberalismo en Colombia i sus detractores de por acá.* Bogotá: Imprenta de Gaitán, 1877.

———. "The Republic of Colombia," *Harper's Magazine* 79 (November 1889):920–28.

[Berrío, Pedro Justo.] *Mensaje del presidente a la legislatura del Estado Soberano de Antioquia.* Medellín: Imprenta del Estado, 1873.

Biblioteca de Historia Nacional. *Correspondencia y otros documentos del General Tomás Herrera.* Panama: Tipografía y Casa Editorial "La Moderna," 1928.

Bidwell, Charles Toll. *The Isthmus of Panama.* London: Chapman & Hall, 1865.

Briceño, Manuel. *La revolución (1876–1877): Recuerdos para la historia.* 2d ed. Biblioteca de Historia Nacional. Bogotá: Imprenta Nacional, 1947.

Brisson, Jorge. *Viajes por Colombia en los años de 1891 a 1897.* Bogotá: Imprenta Nacional, 1899.

Caballero, Lucas. *Memorias de la guerra de los mil días.* Bogotá: "Aguila Negra" Editorial, 1939.

Caldas, Francisco José de. *Semanario del Nuevo Reino de Granada.* 3 vols. Biblioteca Popular de Cultura Colombiana. Bogotá: Editorial Minerva, S.A., 1942; Editorial Kelly, 1942.

Calderón, Carlos. *La cuestión monetaria en Colombia.* Madrid: Tipografía de la "Revista de Archivos," 1905.

———. *Verdaderas causas de los sucesos de Boyacá.* Tunja: Imprenta á cargo de José María Duarte, 1882.

Camacho Roldán, Salvador. *Escritos varios.* 3 vols. Bogotá: Librería Colombiana, 1892–95.

[———.] *Memoria que el secretario de hacienda i fomento presenta al Presidente de la República sobre el curso que han tenido los negocios fiscales de Colombia en el año ecónomico de 1869 a 1870.* Bogotá: Imprenta de Gaitán, 1871.

———. *Memorias.* Bogotá: Librería Colombiana, 1923.

———. *Notas de viaje: Colombia y Estados Unidos de América.* 4th ed. Paris: Garnier Hermanos, 1898.

Cané, Miguel. *Notas de viaje sobre Venezuela y Colombia.* Bogotá: Imprenta de "La Luz," 1907.

Caracristi, C. F. Z. "Business Opportunities in Colombia," *Engineering Magazine* 9 (August 1895):883–907.
Caro, Miguel Antonio. *Escritos sobre cuestiones económicas*. Bogotá: Imprenta del Banco de la República, 1943.
——. *Estudios constitucionales*. Biblioteca Popular de Cultura Colombiana. Bogotá: Editorial Iqueima, 1951.
"Cartas del doctor Núñez," *Boletín de Historia y Antigüedades* 34 (January–March 1947):19–33.
Causa contra el Presidente de los Estados Unidos de Colombia, ciudadano gran jeneral Tomás Cipriano de Mosquera i otros altos funcionarios federales. Bogotá: Imprenta de la Nación, 1867.
Censo de la población del Estado Soberano de Santander en el año de 1870. Socorro: Imprenta del Estado, n.d.
Convención Nacional Eleccionaria del Partido Liberal, 1897. Bogotá: Papelería de Samper Matiz, 1897.
Cordovez Moure, José María. *Reminiscencias: Recuerdos autobiográficos*. Bogotá: Librería Americana, 1922.
Corona fúnebre del doctor Pedro J. Berrío. Medellín: Imprenta del Estado, 1875.
"Correspondencia del doctor Manuel Murillo Toro," *Revista del Archivo Nacional* 4 (January–February 1942):73–94.
Cortés, Enrique. *Escritos varios*. 2 vols. Paris: Imprenta Sudamericana, 1896.
Crevaux, Le Docteur [Jules Nicholas] and E. Lejanne, "Voyage d'Exploration a Travers la Nouvelle-Grenade et la Vénézuéla," *Le Tour du Monde* 43 (1882):225–320.
Cuadro del censo de población del Estado Soberano de Antioquia, formado con arreglo a la lei de 29 de abril de 1864. Medellín: Imprenta de Isidoro Isaza, 1865.
Cuervo, Angel. *Cómo se evapora un ejército*. Biblioteca de Autores Colombianos. Bogotá: Editorial Cromos, 1953.
Cuervo, Luis Augusto. *Epistolario del doctor Rufino Cuervo*. 3 vols. Biblioteca de Historia Nacional. Bogotá, 1918–20.
Curtis, William E. "An Extraordinary Republic," *The Cosmopolitan* 7 (September 1889):443–48.
[Delgado, Evaristo.] *Informe del ministro de gobierno de Colombia al congreso constitucional de 1892*. Bogotá: Imprenta de Antonio María Silvestre, 1892.
"Diario de Quijano Otero," *Boletín de Historia y Antigüedades* 18 (June–August 1930): 494–527, 600–607, 650–88; 19 (February–August 1932): 69–80, 151–59, 215–40, 293–320, 365–400, 585–98.
Documentos relativos a la separación del Dr. Aquileo Parra de la dirección nacional del Partido Liberal. Bogotá: Imprenta de La Crónica, 1899.
Durán, Justo L. *La revolución del 99: Documentos importantes para la historia*. Cúcuta: Talleres Tipográficos de "El Día," 1920.
Echeverri, Camilo Antonio. *Obras completas*. Compiled by Rafael Montoya y Montoya. Medellín: Editorial Montoya, 1961.
Epistolario de Rufino José Cuervo con Luis María Lleras y otros amigos y familiares. Edited by Guillermo Hernández de Alba. Bogotá: Instituto Caro y Cuervo, 1969.
[Escobar, Avelino?] *Reseña histórica de los principales acontecimientos políticos de*

la ciudad de Cali, desde el año de 1848 hasta el de 1855, inclusive. Bogotá: Imprenta de Echeverría Hermanos, 1856.

Esguerra, Nicolás. *Coexistencia de los dos grandes partidos en el gobierno.* Bogotá: Imprenta de "La Luz," 1898.

d'Espagnat, Pierre. "Souvenirs de la Nouvelle-Grenade," *Revue de Deux Mondes* 162 (November–December 1900): 425–56, 844–77.

[Espinosa,] Eduardo. *Colombia: La legitimidad y el gobierno de facto.* New York, 1902.

Etienne, C. P. *Nouvelle-Grenade: Aperçu Général sur la Colombie et Récits de Voyages en Amérique.* Geneva: Imprimerie Maurice Richter, 1887.

Florez Alvarez, Leonidas. *Campaña en Santander (1899–1900).* [Bogotá?]: Imprenta del Estado Mayor General, 1938.

Franco V., Constancio. *Apuntamientos para la historia. La guerra de 1876 i 1877.* 2 vols. Bogotá: Imprenta de La Epoca, 1877.

Gabriac, [Alexis], Comte de. *Promenade á travers L'Amérique du Sud: Nouvelle-Grenade, Equateur, Pérou, Brésil.* Paris: Michel Lévy Frères, 1868.

Galindo, Aníbal. *Estudios económicos i fiscales.* Bogotá: Imprenta a cargo de H. Andrade, 1880.

———. *Recuerdos históricos: 1840 a 1895.* Bogotá: Imprenta de "La Luz," 1900.

Garcés, Modesto. *En defensa de mi honra y de la causa liberal.* Cartagena: Imprenta de D. de la Espriella, 1896.

[García G., Hermes.] *Estigma liberal.* Maracaibo: Imprenta Americana, 1902.

García y García, José Antonio, ed. *Relaciones de los virreyes del Nuevo Reino de Granada, ahora Estados Unidos de Venezuela, Estados Unidos de Colombia y Ecuador.* New York: Imprenta de Hallet y Brun, 1869.

Gómez Picón, Rafael, ed. *Rafael Uribe Uribe en la intimidad: Su correspondencia privada.* Bogotá: Tipo-Prensa, n.d.

Great Britain. Foreign Office. *Report on the Agricultural Condition of Colombia.* Diplomatic and Consular Reports on Trade and Finance, annual series, no. 446. London, 1888.

———. *Report on the Coffee Trade of Colombia.* Diplomatic and Consular Reports, miscellaneous series, no. 598. London, 1903.

Grillo, Max. *Emociones de la guerra: Apuntes tomados durante la campaña del Norte en la guerra civil de tres años.* 3d ed. Bogotá: Casa Editorial Santafe, 1934.

La guerra en el Tolima, 1899–1903. Bogotá: Imprenta de Vapor, 1904.

[Gutiérrez, Santos.] *Mensaje del Presidente de los E.U. de C. al Congreso de 1870.* Bogotá: Imprenta de Medardo Rivas, 1870.

Helguera, J. Leon and Davis, Robert H., eds. *Archivo epistolar del general Mosquera: Correspondencia con el general Ramón Espina, 1835–1866.* Biblioteca de Historia Nacional. Bogotá: Editorial Kelly, 1966.

Herrera Olarte, José. *La administración Trujillo.* Bogotá: Imprenta de Gaitán, 1880.

Hettner, Alfred. *La cordillera de Bogotá: Resultados de viajes y estudios.* Translated by Ernesto Guhl. Bogotá: Banco de la República, 1956.

Holguín, Carlos. *Cartas políticas publicadas en "El Correo Nacional."* Biblioteca Popular de Cultura Colombiana. Bogotá, 1951.

[Holguín, Luis María.] *Informe que presenta el subsecretario encargado del minis-*

terio de gobierno de Colombia al Congreso Constitucional de 1894. Bogotá: Imprenta Oficial, 1894.
Holguín y Caro, Margarita. *Los Caros en Colombia: Su fe, su patriotismo y amor.* 2d ed. Bogotá: Instituto Caro y Cuervo, 1953.
Holton, Isaac. *New Granada: Twenty Months in the Andes.* New York: Harper & Brothers, 1857.
Homenaje del gobierno de la Union al finado Presidente Doctor Francisco J. Zaldúa. Bogotá: Imprenta del "Diario de Cundinamarca," 1884.
Honores fúnebres al Doctor Manuel Murillo T. Bogotá: Imprenta de Zalamea Hermanos, 1881.
Invasiones de Colombia a Venezuela en 1901, 1902 y 1903. Caracas: Imprenta Bolívar, 1903.
Isaacs, Jorge. *La revolución radical en Antioquia.* Bogotá: Imprenta de Gaitán, 1880.
Kastos, Emiro. [Juan de Dios Restrepo.] *Colección de artículos escogidos.* Bogotá: Imprenta de Pizano i Pérez, 1859.
Lamus G., Ramón. *Sinceridades: Recuento histórico de la guerra de 1899 a 1902 en el departamento de Santander y porvenir del partido liberal.* Bogotá: Imprenta Eléctrica, 1911.
Lemaitre, Daniel. *Soledad Román de Núñez: Recuerdos.* Cartagena: Mogollón, 1927.
Le Moyne, A. *Viajes y estancias en América del Sur, la Nueva Granada, Santiago de Cuba, Jamaica y el Istmo de Panamá.* Biblioteca Popular de Cultura Colombiana. Bogotá: Ministerio de Educación de Colombia, 1945.
Manifiesto del gobierno nacional sobre los acontecimientos del 9 i 10 de octubre. Bogotá: Imprenta de Medardo Rivas, 1868.
Manifiestos y protestas del Presidente de Colombia Sr. Sanclemente y otros documentos relativos al crimen de alta traición consumado en Bogotá el 31 de julio, de 1900. New York: Imprenta de Eduardo Espinosa, 1900.
Marroquín, José Manuel. *Don José Manuel Marroquín íntimo.* Bogotá: Arboleda & Valencia, 1915.
[Martín, Carlos.] *Memoria del secretario de lo interior y relaciones esteriores de los Estados Unidos de Colombia al Congreso Federal de 1868.* Bogotá: Imprenta de la Nación, 1868.
Martínez Silva, Carlos. *Obras completas del doctor Carlos Martínez Silva.* Edited by Luis Martínez Delgado. 9 vols. Bogotá: Imprenta Nacional, 1934–38.
[Mercado, Ramón.] *Memorias sobre los acontecimientos del sur de la Nueva Granada durante la administración del 7 de marzo de 1849.* Bogotá: Imprenta Imparcial, 1853.
Millican, Albert. *Travels and Adventures of an Orchid Hunter.* London: Cassell & Company, 1911.
Mollien, G. *Travels in the Republic of Colombia, in the Years 1822 and 1823.* Translated from the French. London: Printed for C. Knight, Pall-Mall East, 1824.
Mora, Luis María. *Croniquillas de mi ciudad.* Bogotá: Editorial A B C, 1936.
Morales, Eusebio A. "The Political and Economic Situation of Colombia," *North American Review* 175 (September 1902):347–60.

[Murillo Toro, Manuel.] *Informe del jefe superior del Estado de Santander a la asamblea lejislativa, 1858.* Bucaramanga: Imprenta de Zapata Hermanos, 1858.

―――. *Informe del secretario de estado del despacho de hacienda de la Nueva Granada a las cámaras lejislativas de 1872.* Bogotá: Imprenta del Neo-Granadino, 1852.

―――. *Informe del secretario de estado del despacho de hacienda de la Nueva Granada al Congreso Constitucional de 1851.* Bogotá: Imprenta del Neo-Granadino, 1851.

―――. *Informe del secretario de hacienda de la Nueva Granada al Congreso Constitucional de 1850.* Bogotá: Imprenta del Neo-Granadino, 1850.

―――. *Mensaje del Presidente de la Unión al Congreso de 1873.* Bogotá: Imprenta de Medardo Rivas, 1873.

―――. *Mensaje del Presidente de la Unión al Congreso Nacional, 1872.* Bogotá: Imprenta de Medardo Rivas, 1872.

―――. *Mensaje del Presidente de los E.U. de C. al Congreso de 1874.* Bogotá: Imprenta de Medardo Rivas, 1874.

Narváez, Enrique. *Los Mochuelos.* Biblioteca Aldeana de Colombia. Bogotá: Editorial Minerva, S.A., 1936.

Navarro, Nepomuceno J. *Flores del campo: Colección de producciones literarias.* Socorro: Imprenta del Estado, 1871.

Nieto, Máximo A. *Recuerdos de la Regeneración.* Bogotá: Casa Editorial Marconi, 1924.

Noriega, Manuel Antonio. *Recuerdos históricos de mis campañas en Colombia y en el Istmo.* Biblioteca de Autores Nacionales. Panama: Tipografía y Casa Editorial "La Moderna," n.d.

Núñez, Rafael. *Ensayos de crítica social.* Rouen: Imprimerie de E. Gagniard, 1874.

―――. *La reforma política en Colombia.* 7 vols. Biblioteca Popular de Cultura Colombiana. Vol. 1, Bogotá: Imprenta Nacional, 1944; vols. 2–5, Bogotá: Editorial A B C, 1945–46; vols. 6–7, Bogotá: Editorial Iqueima, 1950.

Ortiz, Juan Francisco. *Reminiscencias.* Biblioteca Popular de Cultura Colombiana. Bogotá, 1946.

Ortiz, Venancio. *Historia de la revolución del 17 de abril de 1854.* Bogotá: Imprenta de Francisco Torres Amaya, 1855.

[Otálora, José E.] *Informe del Presidente de la Unión a las cámaras legislativas en sus sesiones de 1884.* Bogotá: Imprenta de Vapor de Zalamea Hermanos, n.d.

Palacio, Julio H. *Historia de mi vida.* Bogotá: Librería Colombiana, 1942.

[Parra, Aquileo.] *Memoria del secretario de hacienda i fomento dirijida al Presidente de la República para el Congreso de 1873.* Bogotá: Imprenta de Gaitán, 1873.

―――. *Memorias.* Bogotá: Imprenta de "La Luz," 1912.

Pereira Gamba, F[ortunato]. *La vida en los Andes colombianos.* Quito: Imprenta de "El Progreso," 1919.

Pérez, Felipe. *Anales de la revolución, escritos según sus propios documentos.* Bogotá: Imprenta del Estado de Cundinamarca, 1862.

[Pérez, Santiago.] *Mensaje del Presidente de la Unión al Congreso de 1875.* Bogotá: Imprenta de Medardo Rivas, 1875.

Pérez Sarmiento, José Manuel. *Reminiscencias liberales, 1897–1937.* Bogotá: Editorial "El Gráfico," n.d.

Pinzón, Cerbeleón. *Catecismo republicano para instrucción popular.* 2d ed. Bogotá: Imprenta de "El Mosaico," 1865.
Porras, Belisario. *Memorias de las campañas del Istmo, 1900.* Panama: Imprenta Nacional, 1922.
Posada Gutiérrez, Joaquín. *Memorias histórico-políticas.* 4 vols. Biblioteca de Historia Nacional. Bogotá: Imprenta Nacional, 1929.
Quijano Wallis, José María. *Memorias autobiográficas histórico-políticas y de carácter social.* Grottaferrata, Italy: Tipografia italo-orientale, 1919.
Quinzada, Ignacio. "Apuntamientos para la historia de Panamá (1868–1922)," *Lotería,* 2d ser., 10 (May 1965): 60–96.
Rivas, Medardo. *Carácter social de la lei sobre crédito público.* Bogotá: Imprenta de Medardo Rivas, 1872.
Rocha Gutiérrez, R[afael]. *La verdadera y la falsa democracia: Doctrina constitucional y proyecto de constitución política para la república de Colombia.* Paris: Garnier Hermanos, Libreros-Editores, 1887.
[Rodríguez, Carlos N.] *Memoria del secretario de lo interior i relaciones esteriores de los Estados Unidos de Colombia al Congreso de 1877.* 2d ed. Bogotá: Imprenta de Rafael Pérez, 1877.
Rodríguez Piñeres, Eduardo, ed. *Selección de escritos y discursos de Santiago Pérez.* Biblioteca de Historia Nacional. Bogotá: Talleres Editoriales de Librería Voluntad, 1950.
Rojas, Ezequiel. *Obras.* Compiled, with a biography, by Angel M. Galán. 2 vols. Bogotá: Imprenta Especial, 1881–82.
Rosas, Avelino. *Notas políticas, o sea diez años de Regeneración.* Trinidad, 1895.
Röthlisberger, Ernst. *El Dorado: Estampas de viaje y cultura de la Colombia suramericana.* Translated by Antonio de Zubiaurre. Archivo de la Economía Nacional. Bogotá: Banco de la República, 1963.
Saffray, Charles. *Viaje a Nueva Granada.* Biblioteca Popular de Cultura Colombiana. Bogotá: Ministerio de Educación, 1948.
Salazar, Víctor M. *Memorias de la guerra (1899–1902).* Bogota: Editorial A B C, 1943.
[Salgar, Eustorgio.] *Mensaje del Presidente de la Unión al Congreso Nacional de 1871.* Bogotá: Imprenta de Medardo Rivas, 1871.
———. *Mensaje del Presidente de la Unión al Congreso Nacional, 1872.* Bogotá: Imprenta de Medardo Rivas, 1872.
Samper, José María. *Ensayo sobre las revoluciones políticas y la condición social de las repúblicas colombianas (hispano-americanas).* Paris: Imprenta de E. Thunot y Cia., 1861.
———. *Historia de un alma.* 2 vols. Biblioteca Popular de Cultura Colombiana. Bogotá: Editorial Kelly, 1946–48.
———. *Los partidos políticos en Colombia.* Bogotá: Imprenta de Echeverría Hermanos, 1873.
Samper, Miguel. *Escritos político-económicos.* 4 vols. Bogotá: Editorial de Cromos, 1925–27.
Schenck, Fr[iedrich] von. *Viajes por Antioquia en el año de 1880.* Archivo de Economía Nacional. Bogotá: Imprenta del Banco de la República, 1953.
Silvestre, Eduardo. *Efemerides de la guerra de 1899.* Bogotá: Tipografía Augusta, 1928.

Silvestre, Francisco. *Descripción del Reyno de Santa Fe.* Biblioteca Popular de Cultura Colombiana. Bogotá: Ministerio de Educación Nacional, 1950.
Soto, Foción. *Memorias sobre el movimiento de resistencia a la dictadura de Rafael Núñez, 1884–1885.* 2 vols. Bogotá: Arboleda & Valencia, 1913.
[Torrente, Bernardo.] "Fastos de Bogotá," *Boletín de Historia y Antigüedades* 16 (March to December 1927): 190–92, 241–56, 308–20, 377–84, 437–48, 484–96, 553–60, 639–40, 690–704, 756–65; 17 (June 1928–January 1929): 53–62, 232–37, 359–89.
Torres, Carlos Arturo. *Idola fori.* Biblioteca Aldeana de Colombia. Bogotá: Editorial Minerva, S.A., 1935.
Triana, Miguel. *Por el sur de Colombia: Excursión pintoresca y científica al Putumayo.* Biblioteca Popular de Cultura Colombiana. Bogotá: Ministerio de Educación, 1950.
[Trujillo, Julián.] *Mensaje del presidente de los Estados Unidos de Colombia al Congreso de 1879.* Bogotá: Imprenta de Echeverría Hermanos, 1879.
Uribe Uribe, Rafael. *Discursos parlamentarios: Congreso nacional de 1896.* Bogotá: Imprenta y Librería de Medardo Rivas, 1897.
[Urueta, Carlos Adolfo, ed.] *Historia de la guerra: Documentos militares y políticos relativos a las campañas del General Rafael Uribe Uribe.* 2d ed. Bogotá: Imprenta de Vapor, 1904.
Vargas, Pedro Fermín de. *Pensamientos políticos y memoria sobre la población del Nuevo Reino de Granada.* Biblioteca Popular de Cultura Colombiana. Bogotá: Ministerio de Educación, 1944.
Vargas Santos, Gabriel. *La razón de mi dicho: Relación documentada para la historia de la revolución colombiana de 1899 a 1902.* Bogotá: Casa Editorial de Forero Franco & Cia., 1904.
Vargas Valdés, José Joaquín. *A mi paso por la tierra: Asuntos políticos, filosóficos, etc.* Bogotá: Tip. "COLON," 1938.
Vargas Vila, J. M. *Los providenciales.* New York: Imprenta de M. M. Hernández, 1892.
Vesga y Avila, J[osé] M[aría]. *La guerra de tres años: Primera parte.* Bogotá: J. M. Vesga Villamizar, 1914.
Villegas, Luis Eduardo, comp. *Manuel Uribe A.: Corona fúnebre.* Medellín: Imprenta Oficial, 1905.

VI. Secondary Sources: Dissertations and Theses

Bergquist, Charles Wylie. "Coffee and Conflict in Colombia, 1886-1904: Origins and Outcome of the War of the Thousand Days." Ph.D. dissertation, Stanford University, 1973.
Beyer, Robert Carlyle. "The Colombian Coffee Industry: Origins and Major Trends." Ph.D. dissertation, University of Minnesota, 1947.
Burnett, Ben G. "The Recent Colombian Party System: Its Organization and Procedure." Ph.D. dissertation, University of California, Los Angeles, 1955.
Davis, Robert Henry. "Acosta, Caro, and Lleras. Three Essayists and Their Views of New Granada's National Problems, 1832–1853." Ph.D. dissertation, Vanderbilt University, 1969.
Dix, Robert H. "Colombia: A Two-Party System in Crisis." Ph.D. dissertation, Harvard University, 1962.

Favell, Thomas Royden. "The Antecedents of Panama's Separation from Colombia: A Study in Colombian Politics." Ph.D. dissertation, Fletcher School of Law and Diplomacy, 1950.
Gilmore, Robert Louis. "Federalism in Colombia, 1810–1858." Ph.D. dissertation, University of California, Berkeley, 1949.
Harrison, John Parker. "The Colombian Tobacco Industry from Government Monopoly to Free Trade, 1778–1876." Ph.D. dissertation, University of California, Berkeley, 1951.
Helguera, Joseph Leon, "The First Mosquera Administration in New Granada, 1845–1849." Ph.D. dissertation, University of North Carolina, 1958.
Horna, Hernan. "Francisco Javier Cisneros: A Pioneer in Transportation and Economic Development in Colombia." Ph.D. dissertation, Vanderbilt University, 1970.
Johnson, David Church. "Social and Economic Change in Nineteenth Century Santander, Colombia." Ph.D. dissertation, University of California, Berkeley, 1975.
Loy, Jane Meyer. "Modernization and Educational Reform in Colombia, 1863–1886." Ph.D. dissertation, University of Wisconsin, 1969.
McGreevey, William Paul. "The Economic Development of Colombia." Ph.D. dissertation, Massachusetts Institute of Technology, 1965.
Neal, James H. "The Pacific Age Comes to Colombia: The Construction of the Cali-Buenaventura Route, 1854–1882." Ph.D. dissertation, Vanderbilt University, 1971.
Nichols, Theodore E. "The Caribbean Gateway to Colombia: Cartagena, Santa Marta, and Barranquilla and Their Connections with the Interior, 1820–1940." Ph.D. dissertation, University of California, Berkeley, 1951.
Park, James William. "Rafael Núñez and the Politics of Colombian Regionalism, 1875–1885." Ph.D. dissertation, University of Kansas, 1975.
Pérez-Venero, Jr., Alejandro. "The Thousand Days' War: A Prelude to Panamanian Independence." Master's thesis, Mississippi State University, 1967.
Safford, Frank Robinson. "Commerce and Enterprise in Central Colombia, 1821–1870." Ph.D. dissertation, Columbia University, 1965.
Sharp, William Frederick. "Forsaken but for Gold: An Economic Study of Slavery and Mining in the Colombian Chocó, 1680–1810." Ph.D. dissertation, University of North Carolina, 1970.
Weinert, Richard S. "Political Modernization in Colombia." Ph.D. dissertation, Columbia University, 1967.

VII. Secondary Sources: Articles

Aguilera, Miguel. "Discurso del académico correspondiente Dr. Miguel Aguilera en la sesión pública que conmemoró el primer centenario del nacimiento del historiador José María Quijano Otero," *Boletín de Historia y Antigüedades* 24 (January 1937):5–17.
Aizpurúa, Armando. "José Leonardo Calancha, escritor, periodista, poeta, estadista, orador, político y revolucionario," *Lotería* 12 (October 1967):65–79.
———. "María de los Dolores Gallegos y sus tragedias," *Lotería* 10 (May 1965):21–27.

Alba C., Manuel María. "Cronología de los gobernantes de Panamá, 1510–1932," *Boletín de la Academia Panameña de Historia* 3 (January–July 1932):1–182.

Arboleda, Gustavo. "La reclamación de Cerruti," *Boletín Histórico del Valle*, no. 6 (April 1933), pp. 244–64.

Bergquist, Charles W. "The Political Economy of the Colombian Presidential Election of 1897," *Hispanic American Historical Review* 56 (February 1976):1–30.

Burggraaff, Winfield J. "Venezuelan Regionalism and the Rise of Táchira," *The Americas* 25 (October 1968):160–73.

Bushnell, David. "Two Stages in Colombian Tariff Policy: The Radical Era and the Return to Protection (1861–1885)," *Inter-American Economic Affairs* 9 (Spring 1956):3–23.

———. "Voter Participation in the Colombian Election of 1856," *Hispanic American Historical Review* 51 (May 1971):237–49.

Bustamante Roldán, Darío. "Efectos económicos del papel moneda durante la Regeneración," *Cuadernos Colombianos* 1 (1974):559–660.

Cárdenas Acosta, Pablo E., "La restauración constitucional de 1867," *Boletín de Historia y Antigüedades* 44 (April–December 1957): 165–205, 393–439, 573–618.

Caro, Víctor E., "La muerte del general Cuervo," *Boletín de Historia y Antigüedades* 19 (August 1932):497–506.

Deas, M[alcolm]. "Algunas notas sobre la historia del caciquismo en Colombia," *Revista de Occidente*, 2d ser., 43 (October–December 1973):118–40.

Gilmore, Robert. "Nueva Granada's Socialist Mirage," *Hispanic American Historical Review* 36 (May 1956):190–210.

Gómez Parra, Aurelio. "Biografía del General Doctor Lucas Caballero," *Estudio* 25 (October 1956):107–30.

Harrison, John P. "The Evolution of the Colombian Tobacco Trade to 1875," *Hispanic American Historical Review* 32 (May 1952):163–74.

Huck, Eugene R. "Economic Experimentation in a Newly Independent Nation: Colombia under Francisco de Paula Santander, 1821–1840," *The Americas* 29 (July 1972):17–29.

Loy, Jane Meyer. "Primary Education during the Colombian Federation: The School Reform of 1870," *Hispanic American Historical Review* 51 (May 1971):275–94.

Lozano y Lozano, Carlos. "El golpe de cuartel del 17 abril de 1854," *Boletín de Historia y Antigüedades* 31 (November–December 1944):1074–96.

Lozano y Lozano, Fabio. "Estampa de Florentino González," *Boletín de Historia y Antigüedades* 35 (November–December 1948):662–73.

Nichols, Theodore E. "The Rise of Barranquilla," *Hispanic American Historical Review* 34 (May 1954):158–74.

Nieto Caballero, Luis Eduardo. "El general Rafael Reyes," *Boletín de Historia y Antigüedades* 40 (1953):265–311.

Nordlinger, Eric A. "Political Development: Time Sequences and Rates of Change," *World Politics* 20 (April 1968):494–520.

Osorio Lizarazo, J. A. "Biografía de un caudillo: Benjamín Herrera," *Revista de América* 10 (April 1947):36–63.

———. "Una vida ejemplar de la república: Manuel Murillo Toro," *Revista de América* 10 (May 1947):230–56.

Otero D'Costa, Enrique. "Sergio Camargo," *Boletín de Historia y Antigüedades* 20 (March 1933):125–31.
Palacio, Julio H. "Doctor Antonio Roldán," *Estudio* 2 (April–May 1933):257–62.
———. "El segundo matrimonio de Núñez," *Revista Colombiana* 7 (15 November 1936):321–33.
Payne, James L. "The Oligarchy Muddle," *World Politics* 20 (April 1968):439–53.
Peeler, John A. "Colombian Parties and Political Development: A Reassessment," *Journal of Interamerican Studies and World Affairs* 18 (May 1976):203–24.
Pinzón Quijano, Joaquín. "Eustorgio Salgar," *Estudio* 1 (November 1931):193–97.
Porras Troconis, G. "Rafael Núñez y la regeneración," *Revista de Indias* 9 (April–June 1949):209–45.
Remmer, Karen L. "The Timing, Pace and Sequence of Political Change in Chile," *Hispanic American Historical Review* 57 (May 1977):205–30.
Restrepo Posada, José, and Sanz de Santamaría, Bernardo. "Genealogía de la familia Posada," *Boletín de Historia y Antigüedades* 55 (1968):221–36.
Restrepo Sáenz, José María. "Gobernantes de Cundinamarca," *Boletín de Historia y Antigüedades* 35 (September–October 1948):473–505.
Rippy, J. Fred. "Dawn of the Railway Era in Colombia," *Hispanic American Historical Review* 23 (November 1943):650–63.
Rodríguez Piñeres, Eduardo. "La gran derrota de Rafael Núñez: La revolución de 1875," *Revista de América,* September 1947, pp. 327–46.
———. "Páginas olvidadas en 'El Olimpo Radical': La liga de 1869," *Boletín de Historia y Antigüedades* 38 (April–June 1951):252–73.
———. "Proceso del 7 de marzo," *Boletín de Historia y Antigüedades* 36 (July–September, 1949):412–44.
Safford, Frank. "Significación de los antioqueños en el desarrollo económico colombiano: Un examen crítico de las tesis de Everett Hagen," *Anuario Colombiano de Historia Social y de la Cultura* 2 (1965):49–69.
———. "Social Aspects of Politics in Nineteenth-Century Spanish America: New Granada, 1825–1850," *Journal of Social History,* Spring 1972, pp. 344–70.
Sarmiento H., Juan. "Gobernantes de Santander," *Revista Santandereana,* nos. 2–5 (June 1914–January 1915), pp. 68–73, 96–107, 138–45, 189–96.
Shaw, Carey, Jr. "Church and State in Colombia as Observed by American Diplomats, 1834–1906," *Hispanic American Historical Review* 21 (November 1941):577–613.
Tascón, Tulio Enrique. "La constituyente de 1886," *El Tiempo,* 16 April 1950, Literary Supplement, p. 1.
Uricoechea, José María. "Noticias genealógicas," *Boletín de Historia y Antigüedades* 49 (September 1962):479–90.
Vargas, Marco Tulio. "Gobernadores de Cartagena, 1533–1947," *Boletín de Historia y Antigüedades* 24 (January–March 1947):66–79.
Zuleta, Eduardo. "Los Caicedo," *Boletín de Historia y Antigüedades* 19 (June 1932): 336–40.

VIII. Secondary Sources: Books and Pamphlets

Alarcón, José C. *Compendio de historia del departamento del Magdalena desde 1525 hasta 1895.* [Santa Marta?], 1898.

Arboleda, Gustavo, ed. *César Conto: Su vida, su memoria.* Cali, 1935.
———. *Historia contemporánea de Colombia.* 6 vols. Vol. 1, Cali: Editorial América, 1933; vol. 2, Bogotá: Librería Colombiana de Camacho Roldán & Tamayo, 1919; vol. 3, Popayán: Imprenta del Departamento, 1919; vols. 4–6, Cali, 1933–35.
Bergquist, Charles W. *Coffee and Conflict in Colombia, 1886–1910.* Durham, N.C.: Duke University Press, 1978.
Bushnell, David. *The Santander Regime in Gran Colombia.* Newark, Del.: University of Delaware Press, 1954.
Calderón, Clímaco and Britton, Edward E. *Colombia: 1893.* New York, 1893.
Castillo, Nicolás del. *El primer Núñez.* 2d ed. Bogotá: Ediciones Tercer Mundo, 1972.
Caudillos liberales. Bogotá: Ediciones "Antena," 1936.
Centenario de Murillo Toro: Homenaje de la Junta Nacional. Bogotá: Aguila Negra Editorial, 1916.
Colmenares, Germán. *Partidos políticos y clases sociales.* Bogotá: Ediciones Universidad de los Andes, 1968.
Cordovez Moure, José María. *Reminiscencias: Santa Fe y Bogotá.* 10 vols. Biblioteca Popular de Cultura Colombiana. Vols. 1–2, Bogotá: Editorial Kelly, 1943–44; vols. 3–7, Bogotá: El Instituto Gráfico, 1942–44; vols. 8–9, Bogotá: Editorial Kelly, 1944–45; vol. 10, Bogotá: Imprenta Nacional, 1946.
[Corrales, Manuel Ezequiel.] *Efemerides y anales del Estado de Bolívar.* 4 vols. Bogotá, 1889–1902.
Correa, Ramón. *La convención de Rionegro.* Bogotá: Imprenta Nacional, 1937.
Crist, Raymond E. *The Cauca Valley, Colombia: Land Tenure and Land Use.* Baltimore: Privately printed, 1952.
Cuervo, Rufino J., and Angel. *Vida de Rufino Cuervo y noticias de su época.* 2 vols. Paris: A. Roger y F. Chernovez, 1892.
Dix, Robert H. *Colombia: The Political Dimensions of Change.* New Haven: Yale University Press, 1967.
Duncan, Kenneth, and Rutledge, Ian, eds. *Land and Labour in Latin America.* Cambridge, Eng.: Cambridge University Press, 1977.
Dunning, William Archibald. *A History of Political Theories: From Rousseau to Spencer.* New York: The Macmillan Company, 1920.
Duque Betancur, Francisco. *Historia del departamento de Antioquia.* Medellín: Imprenta Departamental, 1967.
Duque Gómez, Luis; Friede, Juan; and Jaramillo Uribe, Jaime. *Historia de Pereira.* Pereira: Club Rotario de Pereira, 1963.
Duverger, Maurice. *Political Parties: Their Organization and Activity in the Modern State.* Translated by Barbara and Robert North. London: Methuen & Co., 1954.
Eder, Phanor James. *El fundador Santiago M. Eder (Recuerdos de su vida y anotaciones para la historia económica del Valle del Cauca).* Edited by Luis Carlos Velasco Madriñán. Bogotá: Antares, 1959.
Escobar Uribe, Arturo. *El indio Uribe (O la lucha por la libertad en el siglo XIX).* Bogotá: Tipografía Rojas, 1952.
Estrada, Marco A. *Historia documentada de los primeros cuatro años de vida del Estado de Santander.* Vol. 1, *Años de 1857 y 1858.* Maracaibo: Tipografía de "Los Ecos del Zulia," 1896.

Estrada, Monsalve, Joaquín. *Núñez: El político y el hombre*. Bogotá: Editorial Minerva, 1946.

Fals Borda, Orlando. *El hombre y la tierra en Boyacá: Bases sociológicas e históricas para una reforma agraria*. Bogotá: Ediciones Documentos Colombianos, 1957.

Franco Holguín, Jorge. *Evolución de las instituciones financieras en Colombia*. Mexico City: Centro de Estudios Monetarios Latinoamericanos, 1966.

Galvis Salazar, Fernando. *Uribe Uribe*. Autores Antioqueños. Medellín: Imprenta Departamental, 1962.

García, José Joaquín (pseud. Arturo). *Crónicas de Bucaramanga*. Bogotá: Imprenta y Librería de Medardo Rivas, 1896.

Gómez Barrientos, Estanislao. *Del Dr. Pedro Justo Berrío y del escenario en que hubo de actuar*. Medellín: Imprenta Oficial, 1928.

———. *Don Mariano Ospina y su época*. 2 vols. Medellín: Imprenta Editorial, 1913–15.

———. *Páginas de historia: 25 años a través del Estado de Antioquia*. 2 vols. Vol. 1, Medellín: Tipografía San Antonio, 1918; vol. 2, Medellín: Imprenta Oficial, 1927.

González Toledo, Aureliano. *El General Eliseo Payán*. Bogotá: Imprenta de "La Luz," 1887.

Gutiérrez, José Fulgencio. *Santander y sus municipios*. Bucaramanga: Imprenta del Estado, 1940.

Gutiérrez Ponce, Ignacio. *Vida de don Ignacio Gutiérrez Vergara y episodios históricos de su tiempo (1806–1877)*. London: Imprenta de Bradbury, Agnew & Cia., 1900.

Hagen, Everett E. *On the Theory of Social Change: How Economic Growth Begins*. Homewood, Ill.: The Dorsey Press, 1962.

Hale, Charles A. *Mexican Liberalism in the Age of Mora, 1821–1853*. New Haven: Yale University Press, 1968.

Hallowell, John H. *Main Currents in Modern Political Thought*. New York: Henry Holt and Company, 1950.

Henao Mejía, Gabriel. *Juan de Dios Aranzazu*. Biblioteca de Autores Colombianos. Bogotá: Ministerio de Educación Nacional, 1953.

Hoenigsberg, Julio. *Las fronteras de los partidos en Colombia: Historia y comentarios de la legislación escolar de la República desde 1821 hasta el 13 de junio de 1953*. Bogotá: Editorial A B C [1953?].

Holguín, Jorge. *Desde cerca (Asuntos colombianos)*. Paris: Librairie Générale et Internationale, 1908.

Holguín Arboleda, Julio. *Mucho en serio y algo en broma*. Bogotá: Editorial Pio X., 1959.

Iregui, Antonio José. *Ensayo biográfico: Salvador Camacho Roldán*. Bogotá, 1919.

Jaramillo, Joaquín Emilio. *Vida de Pedro Justo Berrío*. Medellín: Imprenta Oficial, 1927.

Jaramillo Sierra, Bernardo. *Pepe Sierra: El método de un campesino millonario*. Medellín: Tip. Bedout, 1947.

Jaramillo Uribe, Jaime. *El pensamiento colombiano en el siglo XIX*. Bogotá: Editorial Temis, 1964.

Jiménez Molinares, Gabriel. *Linajes cartageneros*. 2 vols. Cartagena: Imprenta Departamental, 1950–58.

Latorre Mendoza, Luis. *Historia e historias de Medellín.* Medellín: Imprenta Oficial, 1934.
Latorre Rueda, Mario. *Elecciones y partidos políticos en Colombia.* Bogotá: Universidad de Los Andes, Departamento de Ciencia Política, 1974.
Lemaitre, Eduardo. *Núñez y su leyenda negra.* Bogotá: Ediciones Tercer Mundo, 1977.
―――. *Reyes: El Reconstructor.* 2d ed. Bogotá: Editorial Iqueima, 1953.
Liévano Aguirre, Indalecio. *El proceso de Mosquera ante el Senado.* Bogotá: Editorial Revista Colombiana, 1966.
―――. *Rafael Núñez.* 3d ed. Bogotá: Ediciones Librería Siglo XX, 1946.
Lipson, Leslie. *The Democratic Civilization.* New York: Oxford University Press, 1964.
[Lozano Torrijos, Fabio]. *Centenario de Murillo Toro.* Supplement to vol. 1. Bogotá: Aguila Negra Editorial, 1916.
Lozano y Lozano, Carlos, and Vega, Fernando de la. *¿Quién fué Núñez?* Cartagena: Editorial "El Mercurio," 1939.
Llano Teodomiro. *Biografía del señor Gabriel Echeverri E.* Bogotá: Casa Editorial de Medardo Rivas & Cia., 1890.
Martínez Delgado, Luis. *A propósito del Dr. Carlos Martínez Silva.* Bogotá: Editorial Minerva, 1926.
―――. *Apuntes histórico-biográficos.* Bogotá: Editorial A B C, 1940.
―――. *Historia de un cambio de gobierno: Estudio crítico-histórico de la caída del gobierno del Dr. Manuel Antonio Sanclemente.* Bogotá: Editorial Santafe, 1958.
McGrady, Donald. *Jorge Isaacs.* New York: Twayne Publishers, 1972.
McGreevey, William Paul. *An Economic History of Colombia, 1845–1930.* Cambridge: Cambridge University Press, 1971.
Mecham, J. Lloyd. *Church and State in Latin America.* Rev. ed. Chapel Hill: University of North Carolina Press, 1966.
Méndez Pereira, Octavio. *Justo Arosemena.* Panama: Imprenta Nacional, 1919.
Mesa Ortiz, Rafael M. *Colombianos ilustres (Estudios y biografías).* 5 vols. Bogotá: Imprenta de "La República," 1916–29.
Molina, Gerardo. *Las ideas liberales en Colombia, 1849–1914.* 2d ed. Bogotá: Ediciones Tercer Mundo, 1971.
Monsalve, J. D. *Biografía del doctor Luis María Restrepo y datos sobre la revolución de Antioquia (1876–1877).* Bogotá: Imprenta de Antonio María Silvestre, 1892.
Múnera, Luis A. *Núñez y el radicalismo.* Cartagena, 1944.
Nieto Arteta, Luis Eduardo. *Economía y cultura en la historia de Colombia.* 2d ed. Bogotá: Ediciones Tercer Mundo, 1962.
Nieto Caballero, Luis Eduardo. *Le Cours Forcé et Son Histoire en Colombie.* Paris: Imprimerie P. Landais, 1911.
―――. *Murillo, escritor.* Bogotá: Casa Editorial de Arboleda & Valencia, 1916.
Ocampo López, Javier. *El positivismo y el movimiento de "La Regeneración" en Colombia.* Mexico City: Centro de Estudios Latinoamericanos, Facultad de Filosofía y Letras, Universidad Nacional Autónoma, 1968.
Ortega [Díaz], Alfredo. *Ferrocarriles colombianos.* 2 vols. Biblioteca de Historia Nacional. Bogotá: Imprenta Nacional, 1920–32.
Ospina Londoño, Jorge. *Pascual Bravo: Los partidos políticos en Colombia.* Medellín: Imprenta Universidad, 1938.

Ospina Vásquez, Luis. *Industria y protección en Colombia, 1810–1930.* Medellín: E. S. F., 1955.
Otero Muñoz, Gustavo. *Un hombre y una época: La vida azarosa de Rafael Núñez.* Biblioteca de Historia Nacional. Bogotá: Talleres de Editorial A B C, 1951.
———. *Wilches y su época.* Biblioteca Santander. Bucaramanga: Imprenta del Departamento, 1936.
Palacio, Julio H. *La guerra del 85.* Bogotá: Editorial Cromos, 1936.
Pardo Umaña, Camilo. *Haciendas de la sabana: Su historia, sus leyendas y tradiciones.* Bogotá: Editorial Kelly, 1946.
Parsons, James J. *Antioqueño Colonization in Western Colombia.* Ibero-Americana. Berkeley: University of California Press, 1949.
Los partidos políticos en Colombia. Bogotá: Aguila Negra Editorial, 1922.
Payne, James L. *Patterns of Conflict in Colombia.* New Haven: Yale University Press, 1968.
Paz, Felipe S. and Solano, Armando. *Convención de Ibagué, 1922.* Bogotá: Editorial de Cromos, n.d.
Pereira, Ricardo S. *Les États-Unis de Colombie: Précis d'Histoire et de Geographie Physique, Politique et Commerciale.* Paris: C. Marpon et E. Flammarion, 1883.
Pérez, Enrique. *Vida de Felipe Pérez.* Bogotá: Imprenta de "La Luz," 1911.
Pérez, Felipe. *Jeografía física i política de los Estados Unidos de Colombia.* 2 vols. Bogotá: Imprenta de la Nación, 1862–63.
Pérez Aguirre, Antonio. *Los radicales y la Regeneración.* Bogotá: Editorial Cromos, 1941.
———. *25 años de historia colombiana, 1853 a 1878: Del centralismo a la federación.* Biblioteca Eduardo Santos. Bogotá: Editorial Sucre, 1959.
Petre, F[rancis] Loraine. *The Republic of Colombia.* London: Edward Stanford, 1906.
Picón-Salas, Mariano. *Los días de Cipriano Castro.* Caracas: Primer Festival del Libro Popular Venezolano, 1958.
Puentes, Milton. *Historia del partido liberal colombiano.* 2d ed. Bogotá: Editorial Prag, 1961.
Raffo, Tullio. *Palmira histórica.* Biblioteca de Autores Caucanos. Cali: Departamento del Valle del Cauca, 1956.
Rangel, Domingo Alberto. *Los andinos en el poder: Balance de una hegemonía, 1899–1945.* Caracas, 1954.
Reclus, Eliseo. *Colombia.* Translated and annotated by F. J. Vergara y Velasco. Bogotá: Papelería de Samper Matiz, 1893.
Restrepo, Daniel. *El Colegio de San Bartolomé.* vol. 1, *El colegio a través de nuestra historia.* Bogotá: Sociedad Editorial, 1928.
Restrepo, José Manuel. *Historia de la Nueva Granada.* 2 vols. Vol. 1, Bogotá: Editorial Cromos, 1952; vol. 2, Bogotá: Editorial El Catolicismo, 1963.
Restrepo, Juan Pablo. *La iglesia y el estado en Colombia.* London: Publicado por Emiliano Isaza, 1885.
Restrepo Euse, Alvaro. *Historia de Antioquia desde la conquista hasta el año 1900.* Medellín: Imprenta Oficial, 1903.
Restrepo Posada, José. *Arquidiócesis de Bogotá: Datos biográficos de sus prelados.* Vol.2, *1823–1868;* vol. 3, *1868–1891.* Biblioteca de Historia Eclesiástica "Fernando Caycedo y Florez." Bogotá: Editorial Lumen Christi, 1963, 1966.

Restrepo Sáenz, José María. *Documentos sobre la familia Rivas*. Bogotá: Editorial Minerva, S.A., 1930.

Rivadeneira Vargas, Antonio José. *Don Santiago Pérez: Biografía de un carácter*. Bogotá: Editorial "El Voto Nacional," 1966.

Rivas, Medardo. *Los trabajadores de tierra caliente*. Biblioteca Popular de Cultura Colombiana. Bogotá: Prensas de la Universidad Nacional, 1946.

Rivas Groot, J[osé] M[aría]. *Asuntos económicos y fiscales*. Archivo de la Economía Nacional. Bogotá: Banco de la República, 1952.

Robledo, Emilio. *La vida del general Pedro Nel Ospina*. Autores Antioqueños. Medellín: Imprenta Departamental, 1959.

Rodríguez Piñeres, Eduardo. *Diez años de política liberal, 1892–1902*. Bogotá: Librería Colombiana, 1945.

———. *Hechos y comentarios: Nova et vetera*. Biblioteca Eduardo Santos. Bogotá: Editorial Sucre, 1956.

———. *El Olimpo Radical: Ensayos conocidos e inéditos sobre su época, 1864–1884*. Bogotá: Talleres Editoriales de Librería Voluntad, 1950.

Rodríguez Piñeres, Eduardo, et al. *Don Santiago Pérez y su tiempo*. Bogotá: Ediciones Revista de América, 1952.

Rodríguez Plata, Horacio. *La antigua provincia del Socorro y la independencia*. Biblioteca de Historia Nacional. Bogotá: Publicaciones Editoriales Bogotá: 1963.

———. *La inmigración alemana al Estado Soberano de Santander en el siglo XIX: Repercusiones socio-económicas de un proceso de transculturación*. Bogotá: Editorial Kelly, 1968.

———. *José María Obando, íntimo (Archivo-epistolario-comentarios)*. Biblioteca Eduardo Santos. Bogotá: Editorial Sucre, 1958.

Rodríguez R., Gustavo Humberto. *Ezequiel Rojas y la primera república liberal*. Miraflores, Boyacá: Publicación del Club Social Miraflores, 1970.

Roll, Eric. *A History of Economic Thought*. Rev. and enlarged. New York: Prentice-Hall, Inc., 1942.

Rougier, Antoine. *Les Récentes Guerres Civiles de la Colombie et du Vénézuéla*. Paris: A. Pedone, 1904.

Ruggiero, Guido de. *The History of European Liberalism*. Translated by R. G. Collingwood. Boston: Beacon Press, 1959.

Sabine, George S. *A History of Political Theory*. Rev. ed. New York: Henry Holt and Company, 1950.

Safford, Frank. *Aspectos del siglo XIX en Colombia*. Medellín: Ediciones Hombre Nuevo, 1977.

———. *The Ideal of the Practical: Colombia's Struggle to Form a Technical Elite*. Austin, Texas: University of Texas Press, 1976.

Samper, José María. *Derecho público interno de Colombia*. 2 vols. Bogotá: Imprenta de "La Luz," 1886.

Scruggs, William L. *The Colombian and Venezuelan Republics, with Notes on Other Parts of Central and South America*. Boston: Little, Brown & Co., 1905.

Serrano Camargo, Rafael. *El Regenerador: Vida, genio y estampa de Rafael Núñez*. Bogotá: Ediciones Lerner, 1973.

Sicard Briceño, Pedro. *Páginas para la historia militar de Colombia: Guerra civil de 1885*. Bogotá: Imprenta del E. M. G., 1925.

Sierra, Luis F. *El tabaco en la economía colombiana del siglo XIX*. Bogotá: Dirección de Divulgación Cultural, Universidad Nacional de Colombia, 1971.
Sinisterra, Manuel. *El 24 de diciembre en Cali*. Cali: Imp. de M. Sinisterra, 1919.
Soltau, Roger Henry. *French Political Thought in the Nineteenth Century*. New York: Russell & Russell, 1959.
Soriano Lleras, Andrés. *Lorenzo María Lleras*. Biblioteca Eduardo Santos. Bogotá: Editorial Sucre, 1958.
Susto, Juan Antonio, and Eliet, Simón. *La vida y la obra del Dr. Gil Colunje*. Panama: Imprenta Nacional, 1931.
Tamayo, Joaquín. *Don José María Plata y su época*. Bogotá: Editorial Cromos, 1933.
———. *Don Tomás Cipriano de Mosquera*. Bogotá: Editorial Cromos, 1936.
———. *Nuestro siglo XIX*. Vol. l, *La Gran Colombia*. Bogotá: Editorial Cromos, 1941.
———. *Núñez*. Bogotá: Editorial Cromos, 1939.
———. *La revolución de 1899*. 2d ed. Bogotá: Editorial Cromos, 1940.
Tirado Mejía, Alvaro. *Introducción a la historia económica de Colombia*. 3d ed. Medellín: La Carreta, 1974.
Torres García, Guillermo. *Historia de la moneda en Colombia*. Bogotá: Imprenta del Banco de la República, 1945.
———. *Miguel Antonio Caro: Su personalidad política*. Madrid: Ediciones Guadarrama, S.L., 1956.
Ungar Bleier, Elizabeth, and Martínez, Angela Gómez de. *Aspectos de la campaña presidencial de 1974: Estrategias y resultados*. Bogotá: Ediciones Tercer Mundo, 1977.
Uribe V[illegas], Gonzalo. *Los arzobispos y obispos colombianos desde el tiempo de la colonia hasta nuestros días*. Bogotá: Imprenta de la Sociedad, 1918.
Urrutia, Miguel. *The Development of the Colombian Labor Movement*. New Haven: Yale University Press, 1969.
Urrutia, Miguel, and Arrubla, Mario, eds. *Compendio de estadísticas históricas de Colombia*. Bogotá: Dirección de Divulgación Cultural, Universidad Nacional de Colombia, 1970.
Vega, José de la. *La federación en Colombia (1810–1912)*. Biblioteca de Autores Colombianos. Bogotá: Editorial A B C, 1952.
Velasco Madriñán, Luis Carlos. *Jorge Isaacs: El caballero de las lágrimas*. Cali: Editorial América, 1942.
Vergara, José Ramón. *Escrutinio histórico: Rafael Núñez*. Bogotá: Editorial A B C, 1939.
Vergara V., J. M., and Gaitán, J. B. *Almanaque de Bogotá i guía de forasteros para 1867*. Bogotá: Imprenta de Gaitán, 1867.
Vergara y Velasco, F. J. *Nueva geografía de Colombia*. Bogotá: Imprenta de Vapor, 1901.
Zamora, Manuel M. *Guía de la República de Colombia*. Bogotá: Imprenta Eléctrica, 1907.
Zapata, Ramón. *Dámaso Zapata o la reforma educacionista en Colombia*. Bogotá: El Gráfico Editores, 1960.
———. *De los hombres que hicieron historia: Felipe Zapata (El Vidente)*. Bogotá: Editorial Kelly, 1971.

Index

Abello, Manuel, 21, 52
Acosta, Santos, 45, 46, 49, 125, 126, 156, 157, 223 (n. 122)
Adhesiones, 102
Aldana, Daniel, 46–47, 89–90, 125, 127, 139
Ancízar, Manuel, 54, 64, 66, 141
Angulo, Felipe, 125, 131, 223 (n. 111)
Antioquia, 38–39, 41–42; population of, 38; traits of population of, 38–39; Conservative strength in, 39; role in Conservative party, 56, 190; Conservative revolution in, 94–95; and 1869 *liga*, 96–97; coffee cultivation in, 137; and departmental division, 146–47
Arbeláez, Archbishop Vicente, 118, 210 (n. 97)
Arboleda, Sergio, 56, 57, 80, 82
Arosemena, Justo, 17, 20, 67, 223 (n. 111)
Arosemena, Pablo, 20, 45, 173–74, 219 (n. 47)
Artisans, 5, 10, 23, 28–31, 36, 183, 201 (n. 80)

Barranquilla, 16, 47
Barriga, Julio, 52
Becerra, Ricardo, 122, 127
Bentham, Jeremy, 61–62, 63–64, 82
Bergquist, Charles W., 158–59, 161–62, 174, 180, 206 (n. 88)
Bermúdez, Bishop Carlos, 118
Berrío, Pedro Justo, 57, 94–96
Blacks and mulattoes, 16, 18, 20–21, 22, 23–24, 41
Bogotá, 26–30, 98; location of, 14; savannah of, 26, 28; population of, 27; 1893 riots in, 156; election of 1896 in, 164; election of 1897 in, 168
Bolívar, 16–21, 91, 93. *See also* Caribbean Coast
Bolívar, Simón, 1, 3
Boyacá, 33–34, 200–01 (n. 67)

Caballero, Lucas, 179, 187
Caicedo Jurado, Domingo, 57
Cali, 22, 23, 101
Camacho Carrizosa, José, 55, 234 (n. 136)
Camacho, José L., 30
Camacho Roldán, Salvador, 107, 111, 125, 137, 165, 167, 215 (n. 76); business interests of, 53; on politics, 53; kinship ties of, 55; and sociology, 64; on tax reform, 66; on church-state relations, 69; on presidential nominations, 98; on Northern Railroad, 113; as member of Liberal Center, 144, 150, 151, 152–53, 154; death of, 188
Camargo, Sergio, 45, 120, 130, 144, 177
Canal, Leonardo, 96, 130
Cano, Fidel, 142
Caribbean Coast, 16–21, 45; grievances against interior in, 17, 110, 114; weakness of major parties in, 18; politics in, 88, 93; and election of 1875, 110–11
Caro, José Eusebio, 6, 57
Caro, Miguel Antonio, 56, 57, 58, 63, 80, 139; and constitution of 1886, 134; and election of 1891, 148–52; as vice president, 156–57, 162; and Conservative dissension, 160–61; and election of 1897, 164, 165–66, 169
Cartagena, 16
Castro, Cipriano, 178, 181–82, 234 (n. 133)
Catholic Church: church-state relations, 1, 7, 9–10, 11–12, 69–70, 118–19, 122, 135; Liberal attitudes toward, 1–2, 2–3, 68–69, 145, 166–67; Conservative attitudes toward, 78–80; and public education, 118. *See also* Religion
Cauca, 21–25, 56, 93, 118; population of, 21; regions of, 21–22; dispute over *ejidos* in, 22–23; land seizures in, 120, 123; depressed conditions in, 120
Cinchona bark, 36, 123, 129
Coffee: in Tolima and Cundinamarca, 26, 137; in Santander, 36–37, 137; growth in exports of, 136–37; Liberals as growers of, 137; fall in prices of, 162, 180
Colombia: economic conditions in, 8, 123, 136–38, 162–63, 179–80; geography of, 14; population of, 14; foreign population of, 17; names of, 193 (n. 1)
Colombian Guard, 86, 87–88, 107, 117, 130
Colunje, Gil, 45, 66
Comte, Auguste, 64, 65
Concha, José Vicente, 57, 63
Conservative party: early history of, 6; leaders, regional origins of, 56; leaders, socioeconomic origins of, 56–57; strategies in opposition of, 94; and election of 1875, 117; and cooperation with Independents, 124–25, 127; organization of, 127; faction-

ical Conservatives in, 173; and War of the Thousand Days, 180; role in Liberal party, 190
Santander, Francisco de Paula, 2–3, 5, 9, 34
Santo Domingo Vila, Ramón, 103, 117, 125, 216 (n. 100)
Sapismo, 89–90
Sarmiento, Siervo, 177
Say, Jean Baptiste, 62, 78
Slavery, abolition of, 7, 8
Sociedades democráticas. *See* Democratic societies
Socorro, 35, 37
Soto, Foción, 130, 168, 169, 170, 172, 181
Spencer, Herbert, 64–65
Suárez, Marco Fidel, 160, 161

Tamayo, Joaquín, 180
Tanco, Carlos, 58
Tanco, Mariano, 58, 223 (n. 111)
Tariff policy, 7, 29, 112, 123
Taxes, 7–8, 10, 66, 73, 162, 176, 209 (n. 70)
Tobacco, 7, 8, 22, 26
Tolima, 26, 31–33, 96, 180, 181
Torre Narváez, Eustacio de la, 137, 167
Torres, Carlos Arturo, 64–65, 163, 187, 234 (n. 136)
Tracy, Antoine Louis Claude Destutt de, 61, 63–64
Trujillo, Julián, 101, 111, 112, 121–23, 125, 141
"Truth in the debt" campaign, 74–75, 80–83

Urdaneta, Carlos M., 56, 58, 130
Uribe Uribe, Rafael, 153, 163, 187; family background of, 142; elected to Congress, 164; and arms-procuring mission, 169–71; opposes Parra, 169–75; and War of the Thousand Days, 177, 178, 179, 182, 186, 188
Uscátegui, Vicente, 45, 52

Valenzuela, Teodoro, 45, 46, 49, 69, 127, 144
Vargas, Marceliano, 178
Vargas Santos, Gabriel, 178–79
Vargas Vega, Antonio, 49, 55, 64
Vélez, Joaquín F., 21, 58, 235 (n. 11)
Vélez, Marceliano, 147, 148–52, 156, 167, 181
Vezga, Florentino, 45, 54, 115
Villamizar Gallardo, José María, 45, 176–77
Villar, Luis Eduardo, 137, 176
Villar, Paulo Emilio, 176, 177–78, 179, 233 (n. 115)
Voting qualifications, 68, 104, 148, 152, 192 (n. 4), 197 (n. 4)

War of the Thousand Days. *See* Revolutions
Wilches, Solón, 117, 124, 129, 139, 219 (n. 47), 222 (n. 89)

Zaldúa, Francisco J., 45, 46, 125, 222 (n. 89)
Zapata, Felipe, 45, 100, 101, 141–42
Zurriagueros, 23

to lead party, 126; as member of Liberal Center, 144, 151, 153, 154; named Liberal party director, 166; and election of 1897, 167–69; and dispute with Uribe Uribe, 169–75; resigns as party director, 176–77; death of, 188

Payán, Eliseo, 47, 49, 123, 125, 134, 139–40, 143

Pereira Gamba, Nicolás, 53, 55

Pérez, Felipe, 33, 48, 49, 54, 55, 86, 121

Pérez, Lázaro María, 58, 82

Pérez, Santiago, 55, 67, 125, 126; family background of, 48; education of, 49; religious beliefs of, 69, 117; and election of 1873, 100–01; and election of 1875, 110–17; as Liberal party head, 154–56; exile of, 157; elected to Congress, 164; death of, 188

Political parties: modern views of, in Colombia, ix, xiii; evolution of, xi; as national institutions in Colombia, xi, 15; definitions of, 84, 211 (n. 2). *See also* Conservative party, Liberal party

Popayán, 22

Press, 54, 98, 135, 140, 143, 145, 153, 176, 232 (n. 67)

Public order, 13, 85–87

Quijano Otero, José María, 57, 95–96

Quijano Wallis, José María, 50, 119, 122, 130

Quina. See Cinchona bark

Quintero Calderón, Guillermo, 160, 167

Radicals, 10, 131–32, 196 (n. 47), 213 (n. 34); opposition to Mosquera by, 2, 91–93; regional origins of, 45–46, 202 (n. 5); opposition to Independents by, 121, 123–24; and significance of name after 1886, 141, 145

Railroads, 15, 22, 70, 112, 121, 217 (n. 21); Sabanilla (Bolívar) Railroad, 16, 114; Panama Railroad, 16, 114, 197 (n. 7); Girardot Railroad, 122, 221 (n. 70). *See also* Northern Railroad

Rayo, 213 (n. 36)

Regeneration, 135, 138–39, 145, 149, 160

Religion, 18, 27, 48–49, 116–17. *See also* Catholic Church

Resguardos, division of, 7, 8, 37, 194 (n. 27)

Restrepo, Luciano, 41, 45, 130

Revolutions, 40, 50; 1859–62, 1, 49–50; 1839–42, 4, 48; 1851, 9; 1876–77, 50, 117–21; 1885, 130–31, 224 (n. 128); 1895, 157; War of the Thousand Days (1899–1902), 177–82, 185–87, 233 (n. 115)

Reyes, Rafael, 139, 147, 161, 164–65, 167, 169, 187, 226 (n. 37), 235 (n. 11)

Rico, Luis Carlos, 125, 140, 149

Rionegro, 1

Rionegro convention, 1–2, 11–13

Rivas, Medardo, 45, 47, 54, 55, 66, 69, 83, 177, 179, 188

Robinson & Fleming contract, 91, 92–93

Robles, Luis A., 45, 47, 144, 153, 163, 169, 170, 172, 188

Rocha Gutiérrez, Rafael, 45, 65

Rodríguez, Carlos Nicolás (father), 45, 118–19

Rodríguez, Carlos Nicolás (son), 173

Rodríguez Piñeres, Eduardo, 45, 51, 154

Rojas, Ezequiel, 54–55, 61–62, 63, 210 (n. 97)

Rojas Garrido, José María, 47, 96, 100, 101, 111, 141

Roldán, Antonio, 112, 149, 165

Román (de Núñez), Soledad, 51, 128–29, 131, 204 (n. 44)

Rudas, Juan Manuel, 168, 171–72, 175, 179

Rueda, Venancio, 103, 177

Ruiz, José María, 175, 177, 178

Sáenz Pinzón, Nicolás, 137

Safford, Frank, 38, 42

Salgar, Eustorgio, 45, 46, 67–68, 69, 71, 86, 99, 125, 126, 128, 141, 213 (n. 36)

Samper, José María, 52; and university reform, 4–5; family background of, 47–48; education of, 48–49; becomes a Conservative, 59; intellectual development of, 60; defines socialism, 62–63; and constitution of 1886, 134

Samper, Miguel, 124, 139; on Bogotá, 27–28; family background of, 47–48; education of, 49; business interests of, 53–54; religious beliefs of, 69; intellectual development of, 72–73; on Colombian federalism, 85; as presidential candidate, 167–68, 169

Sanclemente, Manuel A., 56, 167, 169, 171, 175, 186, 235 (n. 8)

Santa Marta, 16

Santander, 34–38; legislative innovation in, 10, 73–74; Liberal strength in, 34–35; population of, 35; economy of, 35–37; characteristics of population in, 37–38; Radical strength in, 46; political tranquility in, 89; crisis of 1884 in, 129–30; distrust of Histor-

Liberal party: factionalism in, 2, 90–94, 174–75; early history of, 2–11; heterogeneity of membership of, 23, 31, 39; leaders, regional origins of, 44–45; leaders, racial background of, 46–47; leaders, socioeconomic origins of, 47–48; compared with Conservative party, 56, 58, 59, 65, 83; organization of, 84, 98, 101, 126, 144, 153, 183, 187; finances of, 104, 153, 154–55; strategies in opposition of, 133; 1892 convention, 154; 1897 convention, 165–67, 230–31 (n. 33). *See also Draconianos, Gólgotas,* Independents, Radicals
Liévano Aguirre, Indalecio, x, 92–93
Lleras, Lorenzo María, 49, 224 (n. 128)
Lleras, Luis María, 130–31, 224 (n. 128)
López, José Hilario, 5–9, 62, 66

Madiedo, Manuel María, 79
Magdalena, 16–21, 111. *See also* Caribbean Coast
Manrique, Juan Evangelista, 55, 167, 170–71, 177, 178, 179, 181, 187
Marroquín, José Manuel, 56, 167, 171, 186
Martín, Carlos, 85–86, 99, 100, 101, 143, 215 (n. 85)
Martínez, Rito Antonio, 57
Martínez Silva, Carlos, 57, 88, 128, 134, 136, 148, 150, 159–60, 169, 181
Medellín, 164, 168
Melo, José María, 10
Mendoza Pérez, Diego, 55, 142, 157, 163, 167, 187
Mercado, Ramón, 23, 96
Mill, John Stuart, 64, 77
Monopolies, 7, 114, 136
Moreno, Abraham, 147, 160
Mosquera, Tomás Cipriano de: and revolution of 1859–62, 1, 11; and Catholic Church, 1, 11, 117, 119; and opponents within Liberal party, 1–2, 91–93; and election of 1848, 5–6, 198 (n. 17); as president (1845–49), 7; as candidate in 1856, 11, 18, 93; at Rionegro convention, 11–12, 13; family background of, 22, 47; as president (1866–67), 70, 85, 91–93, 94, 213 (n. 36); and 1869 *liga,* 96–97; and election of 1875, 111; and Cauca land seizures, 120; exile of, 213 (n. 39); death of, 220 (n. 60)
Murillo Toro, Manuel, 65, 66, 70, 87, 103; as secretary of finance, 8, 73; as president of Santander, 10, 73–74; on amendment of Rionegro constitution, 13; early life of, 48, 50; personal finances of, 51, 52; intellectual development of, 60, 63–64, 73–75; and "truth in the debt," 74, 80–83; and Antioquia Conservatives, 94–95; comments on candidates, 99–100; and election of 1875, 111; and Northern Railroad, 112–13; death of, 126. *See also* Election campaigns: 1856

National bank, 123, 135–36
National Election Committee, 163
Nationalists (Nationalist Conservatives), 159, 161, 164–66, 167, 176
National party, 139, 141, 148, 159, 167, 184
Northern Railroad, 112–14, 121–22, 190, 220–21 (n. 68)
Núñez, Rafael, 66, 134, 139, 156; family background of, 47, 48; marriages of, 50, 51, 128–29, 204 (n. 44); personal finances of, 51–52; intellectual development of, 64, 75–78; and election of 1873, 100, 101; and election of 1875, 110–11, 115–17; as leader of Independents, 121, 124–25, 140; as president (1880–82), 123–24; as president (1884–86), 124, 127–31; appeals to Conservatives, 130–31; addresses Council of Delegates, 133–34; elected president, 1886, 134; retires to Cartagena, 140; and departmental division, 147; and election of 1891, 148–52; death of, 159

Obaldía, José de, 21, 50
Obando, José María, 4, 9–10, 50, 195 (n. 41)
Ortiz, José Joaquín, 150, 151
Ospina Rodríguez, Mariano, 1, 4, 6, 11
Otálora, José Eusebio, 112, 124, 222 (n. 89)

Palmira, 22, 23, 24
Panama (state and department), 114, 134; population of, 16; economy of, 16; separatist sentiments in, 17, 181; politics in, 20–21, 88, 214 (n. 44); role of Colombian Guard in, 88; and War of the Thousand Days, 181, 185, 186–87, 235 (n. 10). *See also* Caribbean Coast
Panama (city), 20–21, 196 (n. 54)
Paper money, 135–36, 139, 185, 197 (n. 9), 236 (n. 22)
Parra, Aquileo, 55, 71, 125, 129, 143, 163, 165–66, 182; family background of, 48; education of, 49; business interests of, 52–53; and election of 1875, 110–17; as president (1876–78), 117, 119; and reluctance

Index

alism in, 148–50, 159–62. *See also* Historical Conservatives, Nationalists
Constitutions: 1853, 9–10, 197 (n. 4); 1863, 11–13, 129, 189; 1886, 134–35, 227 (n. 70)
Conto, César, 45, 48, 49, 118, 119, 120–21, 141, 143
Correoso, Buenaventura, 21, 87–88
Costa. *See* Caribbean Coast
Cuervo, Antonio B., 57, 58, 124, 127, 130, 156, 206 (n. 85)
Cuervo, Rufino, 2, 6, 57, 61
Cundinamarca, 26–33, 56, 180; population of, 26; economy of, 26, 137; *sapista* machine in, 89–90; politics in, 89, 96

Delgado, Carlos J., 172, 175, 176
Democratic societies, 6, 9, 10, 101, 120–21, 126
Departmental division, 145–48, 227 (n. 70)
Diario de Cundinamarca, 54, 100
Draconianos, 9–10, 91, 92

Echeverri, Camilo A., 47, 117
Echeverri, Gabriel, 41, 47
Economic development: in Colombia, 8, 15; Liberal views on, 70–71; Conservative views on, 80
Education: reform of university, 4, 60; of Liberal leaders, 48–49; offered by Liberals, 54–55, 142; offered by Conservatives, 57; debate over textbooks in university, 63; Liberal attitudes toward, 68; conflict over public primary, 118
El Autonomista, 171, 172, 175, 176, 178
Election campaigns: 1848, 5–6, 15–16, 18–20, 23–25, 31–33, 34, 35, 39, 198 (n. 17); 1852, 9, 195 (n. 41); 1856, 11, 15–16, 18–20, 23–25, 31–33, 34, 35, 39, 198 (n. 17); 1869, 96–97; 1873, 100–01; 1875, 110–17, 218–19 (n. 41); 1891, 148–52, 228 (n. 117); 1892, 152–53; 1896, 163–64; 1897, 164–65, 167–69, 231 (n. 55); 1904, 187–88
Elections, 97–109
El Espectador, 142, 157
El Liberal, 143
El Relator, 54, 142, 153, 154, 157
El Republicano, 163
Escuela Republicana, 8, 9, 62
Esguerra, Nicolás, 45, 50, 52, 98, 143, 165, 167, 187, 188

Federalism, 84–85; early support for, 3, 4; Conservative support of, 10; realized in mid-1850s, 10; in 1863 constitution, 12; Liberal defense of, 67. *See also* Public order
Fernández, Aristides, 161, 186
Figueredo, Cenón, 175, 179
Forced loans, 119–20, 122–23

Gaitán, José Benito, 54, 177
Galindo, Aníbal, 48, 62, 74
Gallegos (de Núñez), Dolores, 50, 128, 223 (n. 112)
Garcés, Modesto, 49, 121, 154, 157
Godo, 65
Gólgotas, 9–10, 91, 92, 196 (n. 47), 213 (n. 34)
Gómez Pinzón, Juan Francisco, 179, 233 (n. 115)
Gómez, Ramón, 89, 90, 111
González, Florentino, 7, 45
González Gaitán, Gabriel, 45, 130
González Lineros, Narciso, 52
Grillo, Maximiliano, 171, 174
Gutiérrez, Santos, 49, 89
Gutiérrez Vergara, Ignacio, 56, 96

Herrán, Archbishop Antonio, 11, 70, 208 (n. 53)
Herrán, Pedro A., 4, 97
Herrera, Benjamín, 185, 186–87, 188, 235 (n. 10)
Herrera, Bernardo, 45, 55
Historical Conservatives, 159–60, 164–65, 167, 181, 186
Holguín, Carlos, 56, 58, 82–83, 156; as architect of 1869 *liga*, 96–97; supports Conservative cooperation with Independents, 124, 127, 131; as *designado*, 140; proposes departmental division, 145; reelected as *designado*, 148
Holguín, Jorge, 58, 137, 148, 185

Independents: program of, 121–23; and disintegration of movement, 124–25, 131; receive Conservative support, 124–25; eclipse of, 139–41; support Caro, 149; linked with Nationalists, 159
Indians, 7, 33, 41, 46–47, 87
Indigo, 26
Isaacs, Jorge, 59, 206 (n. 89)

La Crónica, 173, 178, 179, 180
"Law of the Horses," 144, 152, 176, 179
Liberal Center, 144–45, 150–54